BILLIONS OF
ENTREPRENEURS

Also by Tarun Khanna

*Winning in Emerging Markets: A Road Map for Strategy and Execution,
with Krishna G. Palepu*

BILLIONS OF
ENTREPRENEURS

HOW CHINA AND INDIA
ARE RESHAPING THEIR
FUTURES—AND YOURS

TARUN KHANNA

Harvard Business Review Press
Boston, Massachusetts

Library of Congress Cataloging-in-Publication Data
Khanna, Tarun.
  Billions of entrepreneurs: how China and India are reshaping their
futures and yours / Tarun Khanna.
     p. cm.
  Includes bibliographical references and index.
  ISBN 978-1-4221-5728-2 (pbk.)
  1. China—Commerce. 2. India—Commerce. 3. China—Economic policy.
4. India—Economic policy. 5. China—Foreign economic relations.
6. India—Foreign economic relations. I. Title.
  HF3836.5.K593 2011
   330.951—dc22   2010043561

Dedicated to Rishi, Simran, and Ruhi.

CONTENTS

PREFACE

The barrage of news of China and India is, by now, commonplace in all forms of media, and even in popular discourse. My metric for the latter is the frequent conversations I have in car services to and from various airports all over the world. Chauffeurs in Brazil, Canada, the United Kingdom—and, indeed, China and India—have, in just the past few months of my travels, had strong views about the happenings in these two large nations. If I revert to the more systematic benchmark used in this book's introduction earlier— the fraction of major articles on the front page of the *New York Times*, to use one bellwether publication—that metric is higher than it has ever been in the past quarter century; indeed, by a rough and ready analysis it is higher than it has ever been in the past century (other than the brief years corresponding to the birth of modern Chinese and Indian nation states).

So it is useful to take stock of the thesis I laid out in *Billions of Entrepreneurs*, first published in 2008, and the antecedent argument in a coauthored article in *Foreign Policy* magazine in 2003. The thesis, to my mind, remains rock-solid. It was, simply, that the strength of China was a strong, indeed entrepreneurial, government; and the strength of India was an increasingly and justifiably confident private sector.

Each country had corresponding Achilles' heels, though. The Chinese indigenous private sector remained emasculated; despite some successes, these were too few successful enterprises for an economy of China's size, and the line between public and private was increasingly blurred. Meanwhile, the Indian state struggled to get its house in order, even though it now recognized the need for change. Indians will recall the cartoonist R. K. Laxman's creation, *The Common Man*, a silent and ubiquitous testimonial to the absurdity of everyday life in India, often featuring the antics of the country's political classes. Laxman serves, to my mind, a purpose as cathartic as that of the American cartoonist Scott Adams, creator of the *Dilbert* comic strip that parodies the futility of corporate life.

The muscle of China's government is most evident in the overflowing coffers of its sovereign wealth funds, for example those of the China Investment Corporation (CIC), whose lucre is being dispensed liberally around the world as China buys access to scarce raw materials, among other things, with nary a concern for price. As of 2010, tens of billions of dollars had been invested just in the United States, not to mention in Chinese holdings of U.S. treasury bills.

The sinews of India's private sector can be seen dramatically in the grassroots entrepreneurial efforts that have landed numerous entities on the *Forbes* Global 2000 list. In 2003, there were twenty firms on this list; today there are thirty. These have been created without conventional state-led activism—indeed, often in the face of a state characterized if not by intransigence, then at least by benign neglect.

Also in a category similar to the private sector—to the extent it remains driven by private, nonstate initiative—is the strength of civil society. Here India leads China handily. While Western nongovernment organizations continue to be active in China, they must tread warily for fear of antagonizing the state and having their activities constrained. And the oxymoron popular in China, GONGO (government-owned nongovernment organization), says it all. You can only be an NGO if you are not one! Indian civil society, with its rambunctious chaos, could not be more different than that of China.

Of course, there have been changes in both countries in the past few years. For example, in the wake of a dramatic financial slowdown in the developed world, the confidence of the Chinese has risen, and they have been less solicitous of Western investment than before. This has not gone down too well with the captains of Western industry, who claim that life is not as easy as it used to be for foreign investors in China. Notwithstanding this, perhaps some good will result if China genuinely supports indigenous private enterprise (as opposed to foreign private enterprise). Meanwhile, the appointment of a leading Indian entrepreneur to a cabinet-level position in the highest echelons of India's government has given India-watchers hope that change in the sclerotic state is nigh. But these changes are noteworthy because they are somewhat exceptional, not because they are yet the norm.

In the first edition of *Billions of Entrepreneurs*, I commented on the potential for symbiosis between China and India. There are plenty of skeptics of this view, and they are usually focused on trade statistics. As it turns out, bilateral trade has skyrocketed. China's exports to India in 2009 were $30 billion, and India's to China were just over half that, making each country a significant partner for the other. This, however, overstates the symbiosis, since India mostly exports raw materials, and is not nearly as important to China as vice versa. So indeed it is a work-in-progress, particularly given continued border tensions. But I aver that it is a mistake to read progress toward this view, or lack thereof, in annual changes in trade statistics. Rather, so-called game-changing events are likelier to herald substantive shifts. Consider the recent attempt to revitalize Nalanda University, center of Buddhist learning in the fourth to seventh centuries, by a global group of mentors, chaired by Professor Amartya Sen. It is worth restating the obvious, that the symbiosis that I spoke of then has been in evidence for most of the past two thousand years.

Since the writing of *Billions of Entrepreneurs*, so-called South-South trade has multiplied as well. I spent a week in Brazil last month, which included launching the Portuguese edition of this book, and encountered growing interest in China (as Brazil is a source of much raw material for China—iron ore, soybeans, and the like) and in India (these two countries face a number of common challenges having to do with health, education, and urbanization, among others). And this is just an example of the South-South interaction playing out daily.

As I remind my students, it is now almost commonplace to imagine that one could build a billion-dollar corporation from scratch without having to visit the erstwhile temples of high finance—New York or London—whereas, in my student days at Harvard, one could not make this claim. Entrepreneurship has truly gone global, and China and India are leading this charge, each in their own way, each with verve and enthusiasm, in a process that by and large ought to be celebrated.

—Tarun Khanna
Harvard Business School
Boston, Massachusetts
August 2010

Chapter One

Reimagining China *and* India

The educations of most Americans, even graduates of prestigious Ivy League schools, barely acknowledge China and India. In his 2001 commencement speech, Yale University's president, Richard C. Levin, lamented, "The Mayor of Shanghai asked me why . . . every schoolchild in China can identify the author and date of our Declaration of Independence and so few of ours can identify when the Qing Dynasty fell, when the Long March occurred, and when the Communists took power."[1]

How could the 2001 graduating class of this prestigious Ivy League school not know more about China? After all, the Yale-China connection has proved resilient over several decades. Yung Wing, a member of the Class of 1854 at Yale College and the first Chinese to receive an American degree, returned home and established educational missions that sent 100 Chinese boys to preparatory schools and colleges throughout New England. These missions were built on the foundation of a fortune made in India. Elihu Yale, one of Yale's earliest benefactors, was for some twenty years a member of the British East India Company and had served as the second governor of a settlement in Madras (present-day Chennai in southern India) in 1687. In 1718, Cotton Mather, who represented a small institution of learning, the Collegiate School of Connecticut, approached Yale. Mather needed money for a new building in New Haven. Yale obliged by sending him a carton of goods that the school subsequently sold for 560 pounds sterling, a huge sum in those days, and named the new building after its benefactor.[2] Thus, Yankee-India trade facilitated Yale, and Yale facilitated US-China bonhomie. So why did Yale's students seemingly pay so little attention to China and India?

Years ago in Bangalore, when it was better known as a summer residence for the British in colonial India than as the outsourcing capital of the world, my father and mother regularly invoked the names of "Yale," "Princeton," and "Harvard." The American comic book heroes Superman and Batman ruled my childhood imagination. As a teenager, I learned that Wall Street opened doors with money, Hollywood captured dreams on celluloid, and the Americanism, "upward mobility," had nothing to do with pulley systems. I applied to the American Ivy Leagues as a backup to the hyper-competitive Indian Institutes of Technology (IIT). So, even though I passed the difficult entrance exam to the IIT and was accepted to IIT Madras, I chose Princeton University because it could fulfill my wanderlust.

When I arrived in Princeton in September 1984, I was a curiosity; very few undergraduate students came from India back then, and none of my first-year roommates—talented, ambitious individuals who went on to achieve considerable success—could locate my home country on a world map. One thought it was "right by Arabia," a remark that made me retire to my bunk bed in tears.

Now, having lived more than half my life in the United States and presently raising my two children as Indian Americans in a western suburb of Boston, I remain puzzled by Americans' geographical naiveté. My colleagues and friends, who constitute a rather well-traveled and well-informed group of people, still know very little about India. How can this particular demographic maintain a worldview that excludes 2.4 billion of the Earth's population?

Today's economic projections suggest that in less than a generation China and India will become the largest and third largest world economies, respectively, in terms of purchasing power parity, and together they will account for nearly 40 percent of world trade, a position they occupied a century ago and more than their collective 15 percent today. Demographic projections based on current populations—1.3 billion in China and 1.1 billion in India—suggest that within that same period the weight of the world economy will shift from today's developed nations onto the two emerging countries. Billions of entrepreneurs will ultimately power this transition, and not just Chinese and Indian entrepreneurs who take companies public, but also politicians who lead anew and idealists who force us to imagine better futures. The world's future is irrefutably tied to that of China and India. Yet the United States is woefully uninformed about the past and present of both countries.

For these reasons, I was privately relieved to hear President Levin admonish the 2001 graduating class about its self-centeredness. His remarks struck me as emblematic of an awakening in American education to the significance of the East, which in turn reflects an awakening in American society.

The annual May Day event in 2005 at the Shady Hill School in Cambridge featured both the performance of an elaborate Chinese lion dance (wushi in Chinese) by the fifth grade and a concert, given by about fifty faculty and staff, of a vibrant North Indian dance, sung to bhangra rock by a Sikh singer Daler Mehndi. The singer now has global appeal, and his albums are available in record stores in nearby Harvard Square. What's more, the entire fifth-grade curriculum at the progressive then ninety-year-old private school is now centered on China. For the coming years, at least, the school's immersion method of teaching will allow impressionable ten-year-old minds to absorb information about the Opium Wars, the Silk Road, and calligraphic art as they learn math, literature, science, and geography.

This cultural awareness extends to the public school system. Students at nearby Martin Luther King Jr. elementary school study Mandarin for thirty minutes daily beginning in kindergarten and continuing through eighth grade and write to pen pals in China every year beginning in fourth grade. The school is one of hundreds in the United States named for the 1960s civil rights hero Martin Luther King Jr., a visionary African American who schooled himself in the non-violence theories Mahatma Gandhi developed in India. Teachers are also educating themselves about China. For example, Deborah Linder, a tenth-grade history teacher at Newton South High School in Newton, Massachusetts, spent her February vacation in 2004 on a two-week trip through southern China, a trip organized specifically for teachers by a non-profit organization called Primary Source, with the aid of Harvard's Asia center.

My student Andy Klump's transition from complete unawareness of Asia to immersion in China amidst skepticism from his peers, limited support from Harvard Business School for his China aspirations, and nothing in his working-class upbringing to predispose him to his odyssey, is another hopeful harbinger to this awakening to the riches of the East. In fact, his experience likens that of the early American ships that headed to Canton, China, in the 1770s. The destination was seen as uncertain, a journey reserved for the adventurous, especially at a time when American tracers had to compete against the more established British.

Klump's fascination with China was triggered by summer travel through Asia. It was enough to cause him to eschew lucrative high-tech job offers, and instead systematically search for an elusive sales position on the mainland. After daily Mandarin classes and months of late-night phone calls to China, Klump was fortunate to find a summer internship at Intel's software lab in Shanghai. That summer, as he sought to help disseminate Intel's technology in the region, Klump's daily routine consisted of an hour-long bus commute (costing 30 cents) during which he spoke to anyone with whom he could strike up a conversation to supplement his biweekly Mandarin lessons.

A fellow traveler once said, "You're famous because you are the only *laowai* [slang for foreigner] who has ever come here and said *ni hao* [hello] to everyone."

Work in the lab was rigorous, requiring continual interface with the government. The Shanghai government was not the slow bureaucracy he associated with federal jobs. In China, the government demanded performance and held to aggressive timelines. His boss said, "The head members of the local branch of the Communist Party set the deadline and they are reviewing the finished product. You won't feel so good saying no to a Communist Party member."

Back in Boston, Klump creatively pitched himself to Dell for work in China, at a time when Dell's 5 percent market share in the personal computer market was dwarfed by the local giant's, Legend, later renamed Lenovo. Klump was hired as the first foreigner working directly in sales in all of greater China, with the same quota as his Chinese colleagues.

His classmates' reactions? "You have got to be joking! You are graduating from Harvard Business School and accepting a job that pays less than my 24-year-old sister earns. No one in their right mind would make such a decision." Even more appalling to his classmates, Klump, who spoke Chinese with the fluency of an eight-year-old, had spoken to his direct manager in China for a total of twenty minutes, was the only *laowai* in the one hundred–person Beijing office and the three hundred–person China sales force, and had signed on in the midst of the SARS debacle when it was unclear whether an epidemic would unfold on the mainland or not.[3]

In China Klump soon learned that his manager's version of leadership was to emphasize the importance of hitting his quarterly quota of half a million dollars in sales—to be done in only ten weeks because the holidays cut short that particular quarter—and to convince him that "there is no such thing as strategy. You need to erase that word from your brain. Strategy only exists for the folks who run this company. You are here to execute. Now pick up the phone and execute." Klump's first execution in rudimentary Mandarin resulted in the phone being slammed down on him, and in his mentor's tough-love assurance that failure to reach $50,000 in sales by weekend would diminish his career prospects.

After hitting just 21 percent of his first quarterly quota, Klump comfortably exceeded his next quaterly quotas. Who would have predicted this? Klump strode up the ranks of the all-Chinese sales force. He had a four-million-dollar quota for all of China with eight salespeople reporting to him, and learned the art of persuading them to do his bidding. A number of his clients offered him lucrative positions. After three years Klump had taught himself to communicate with customers, to work with and motivate mainstream Chinese employees even as a *laowai*, and to appreciate the role of government as a customer, regulator, and even as entrepreneur.

Klump, Deborah, the Shady Hill School, and the Martin Luther King Jr. School are at the forefront of those who are preparing for a new global reality. Overall, however, the West's understanding about the East remains pretty dismal.

A powerful sign that Americans tenaciously hold onto a worldview that excludes a large portion of the Earth's population is the media's minimal coverage of China and India. For most of the past 150 years, less than 2 percent of the major stories in any given year in the *New York Times* have been on China or India.[4] Interest today, by this measure, has risen to 4 percent, nearly as high as it has ever been in the past century. What coverage there is today is largely culinary (lo mein, chicken curry), literary (Jhumpa Lahiri, Yu Hua), cinematic (Bruce Lee, Jackie Chan, Bollywood), or tourist oriented (Great Wall, Taj Mahal). Alarmism is also popular; for example, certain television pundits regularly blame American unemployment on outsourcing to China and India, even though objective data suggest that the effect of outsourcing on Western workers is insignificant.[5] Such cultural stereotyping and scaremongering reveal the West's minimal understanding of the East.

Consider Harold Isaacs's 1956 book, *Scratches on Our Minds: American Views on China and India*.[6] A journalist for *Newsweek* magazine, Isaacs covered the Chinese revolution and World War II–related events in the China-Burma-India theater. To illuminate the "Vagueness about Asia," which he deemed the "natural condition even of the educated American," Isaacs asked 181 Americans—leading academics, businessmen, diplomats, journalists, and missionaries—open-ended questions about their impressions of China and India. Two-thirds of respondents had positive images of the Chinese, describing them as intelligent, attractive, and decent. These impressions were largely based on popular novels like Pearl S. Buck's *The Good Earth* that portrayed Chinese characters favorably. American views of India were influenced by Rudyard Kipling's poem *Gunga Din*, whose main character, the water bearer whom Kipling portrays as admirable but native and therefore a lower form of life, was the Indian best known to Americans after Mohandas Gandhi. Feeding this negative imagery was Katherine Mayo's best-selling and scathing critique of Hinduism, *Mother India*, which ensured that antipathy toward Indians was at a level deeper than that prompted by policy differences. In 1982 the prominent American scholar John King Fairbank characterized Indians as "timorous cowering creatures, too delicate to fight like the Chinese . . . and they never smile at anyone," whereas the Chinese "are vigorous and smiling, the greatest contrast to the lassitude and repression of the Indians."[7]

Americans' ideas about India are even more striking given that the United States had long-standing commercial and cultural links with India. By some estimates, between 1795 and 1805 the United States traded more with India than with all continental European nations put together. Despite these links, Americans interpreted the art and curios they bought from India as the work of heathens, so that India was ensconced in the American mind as the once-great civilization in terminal decline.

I chose to write a comparative book because I believe that we can better understand China's choices when juxtaposed against India's, and vice versa. There are historical similarities—they each underwent their first significant unifications in approximately 200 B.C.E., under the Mauryas in India and the Han dynasty in China. The British humiliated India for two centuries, and China endured its own century of humiliation. Both countries were scarred deeply. Both countries underwent radical political shifts at roughly the same time: China became a modern state in 1949, when Mao Zedong took power. This was just two years after Jawaharlal Nehru assumed leadership of independent India in 1947. Mao and Nehru were the architects of visionary plans for their respective new countries; two enormously influential leaders whose very different choices had very different consequences, despite many similarities in size, proximity, and antiquity. These surface similarities, yet starkly different paths, make the past five decades represent a kind of petri dish for social scientists, where we can learn something profound about how societies develop.

Mine is an attempt to illuminate contemporary vagueness about what's happening in China and India. I argue that despite the flux and largely positive economic changes in each of the two countries in the last decades, the "iron frames" that gird these changes are radically different. China features a top-down model of development, with an omniscient Communist Party articulating a central direction and circumscribing all but marginal dissent. Local Party officials have increasing economic autonomy, which they have used to amazing effect, but only within a context of more severely constrained political centralization. The Party political line simply must be toed. India exhibits greater heterogeneity and pluralism, manifesting itself to the outsider as chaos, but also enabling productive ferment on the ground. An inefficient market, but a market nonetheless, results from competition at multiple levels in providing services, competing for talent, political horse-trading, as the media jostles for attention in undisciplined fashion. While China courts foreign capital and has only recently and reluctantly acknowledged the private sector, its internal opacity and lack of private property rights emasculate its internal markets in comparison to the parts of India where competition is allowed to run amuck. On the other hand, its unconstrained fiat allows it to override coalitions that might block material progress in a way that India just cannot. The pros and cons of the two countries' approaches differ.

In this book, I uncover China and India—Hangzhou and Hyderabad, Qingdao and Bangalore, Dalian and Chennai—to show the radical underlying differences between China and India. Westerners might be able to reimagine these two vibrant contemporaries and interpret their current events in the context of their respective rich, ancient, and varied histories. I hope to answer, among other things, many questions that naturally occur to a curious modern observer of these countries, such as these:

Why can China build cities overnight while Indians have trouble building roads?

Why does China prohibit free elections while Indians, in free and fair elections, vote in officials with criminal records?

Why do the Chinese like their brethren who settle overseas while Indians apparently do not?

Why are many Chinese so unhealthy, but healthier than Indians?

Why are there so few world-class indigenous private companies from mainland China despite the creation of a juggernaut of an economy?

Why has China out-muscled India in their common backyard?

Why was China "Indianized" in the past while India shunned China?

Why do the Chinese welcome Indians to China but Indians do not reciprocate?

The different paths taken by the two countries have another profound implication, only now becoming manifest: China and India together could have a stronger impact on each other and the world than either country could alone. What China is good at, India is not, and vice versa. The countries are inverted mirror images of each other. This complementarity creates grounds for an economic cooperation that has already begun, as native entrepreneurs tap into each other's backyards in a reprise of their long-term historical cooperation rather than their recent four decades of hostility. This mutualism is there for the world to benefit from, not only for native Chinese and Indians.

Given India's official ascendance to the nuclear club and China's massive deployment of resources to build a navy, security analysts and political scientists rightly emphasize the wariness with which the Himalayan giants glance at each other. But these analysts and academics wrongly ignore the potential of mutually beneficial economic ties, especially when each country is more squarely focused on feeding its poor than on building military muscle.

Certainly, the pundits' favorite issue, of who "wins," China or India, misses the point. I say this despite having co-authored "Can India Overtake China?" some years ago, an article that triggered this present intellectual odyssey.[8] I have come to realize that the real issue is that the differences between the two have created a jointness in new riches to be enjoyed by the countries and by those anywhere in the world who care to profit from their advent.

More than a century ago, Rudyard Kipling famously wrote,

> *Take up the White Man's burden*
> *Send forth the best ye breed*
> *Go bind your sons to exile*
> *To serve your captives' need*[9]

There remains controversy about whether Kipling intended this to be racist or altruistic; nonetheless, "the white man's burden" rationalized Britain's right and need to govern the "heathens" of India. Perhaps because India was the jewel in Britain's empire, India fell out of America's orbit.

But this image of the hapless Easterner, as well as the milder image of irrelevance that Isaacs reaffirmed, are outdated and counterproductive. Nor is the other extreme, hysteria, warranted or sensible. Journalist Lou Dobbs' program on CNN excoriates outsourcing to China and India as taking away jobs from Americans even though objective data suggest that the effect of outsourcing on Western employment is still tiny. You know that hysteria is in the air when editorial cartoonists get into the act—locally, Harvard Business School students jokingly suggested, in an April Fools issue of the student-run daily, *The Harbus*, that the search for the new Dean of the school be outsourced to India.[10]

Nowhere is this going to touch a nerve more than in white-collar professions, historically much more immune to outsourcing, and nowhere more so than in health care, an intensely personal and therefore political issue. In April 2005 the award-winning television news show *60 Minutes* broadcast a story on medical tourism that showcased India-based Apollo hospitals as a hot destination for Western patients seeking top-quality health care at a tenth of the cost of what they would pay in the United States or the United Kingdom. Soon after the show aired, the Western clientele in the Apollo Group's Delhi hospital nearly doubled. Mirroring this U.S. publicity was the British press's extensive coverage of fourteen-year-old Elliot Knott from Dorset who decided to fly to India in August 2005 for surgery on his back, thus avoiding a nine-month waiting list in his home country, facilitated by a British-Indian-owned company in the business of medical tourism.[11]

I don't believe that this is the last we'll hear of medical innovations in China or India. Diabetes, for instance, is a modern scourge, with close to 200 million sufferers worldwide. By 2030, when this number will be closer to 300 million, fully a third will live in China or India. While pure science-based cures will most likely be found in U.S. laboratories, many service innovations—such as treatment regimens, or insulin delivery mechanisms—will likely come from the need to treat the tens of millions of indigent sufferers in China and India. These in turn will benefit the poor and health-rationed in the U.S., perhaps as much as the pure science-based and probably prohibitively expensive treatments.

Gushing praise for Indian doctors from American and British medical tourists denied care in their homelands, and the possibility that the cure for chronic diseases is increasingly being searched for in China and India, hardly sound like a continuing burden on the White Man. Perhaps it foretells a reversal of this burden. Another passage from Kipling seems more appropriate.

> At the end of the fight is a tombstone white
> With the names of the late deceased
> And the epitaph dear
> A fool lies here
> Who tries to hustle the East

Far better to be wise and informed about changes the world over than to be the "fool . . . who tries to hustle the East."

But the best metaphor is not of burdens, real, imagined, or reversed, but of journeys of hope. There is renewed hope in China and India as they experience success in dealing with the world and put aside their mutual hostilities toward one another in favor of collaborations. There is hope too in the pioneering Western entrepreneurs who prefer to share in China and India's recent gains rather than attempt to derail, with misguided protectionism, the emergence of these two giants on the world stage.

Listening at Nathu La: A Happy Mutualism

On July 6, 2006, high in the Himalayas, on the border of China and India, a historical event went largely unnoticed by the West. Nathu La—which means "listening ear pass" and was once part of the Silk Road—was opened for the first time in forty years. After a small ceremony presided over by Indian, Chinese, and Tibetan officials, a barbed-wire fence, previously guarded by army personnel, was taken down, and about two hundred Indian and Tibetan traders walked the few steps through the narrow Himalayan pass and across the border between the two countries. Their steps marked the first year of official Sino-Indian friendship made possible by the bilateral trade agreements signed by China and India in the 1990s.

Historically, the *closing* of the border is the anomaly. The pass had been sealed since 1962 by India as a consequence of the months-long Sino-Indian border war, a high-altitude battle that originated in disputes over each country's territorial borders. In the late 1800s, the pass supported the traffic of over 1,000 mules. The Dalai Lama trekked its 14,000-foot terrain. Prior to contesting one another's border demarcations, China and India had maintained good relations. Since the early 1900s, India's captains of industry, Marwari traders from what is now the Indian state of Rajasthan, had sizeable businesses in China.

Although the 2006 reopening of Nathu La is chiefly symbolic—the twenty-odd items allowed for export by truck include molasses, shoes, blankets, and coffee on the Indian side and goat skins, raw silk, yak tails, and borax on the Chinese side—it is indicative of the ongoing trade taking place on a higher scale. Symbolic too are Indian Prime Minister Atal Behari Vajpayee's visit to Beijing in 2005 and the reciprocal visit to New Delhi of the Chinese Premier Wen Jiabao in 2006. As necessary as such political rapprochement may be, economic gains from trade and investment provide an even more important foundation for mutual amity. Twenty-first-century communication technology enables companies from both sides to trade money, manufacturing, marketing, intellectual capital, talent, inventory, and personnel.

The American Heartland Hears Nasik and Nanchang

One company that is already hearing rumblings from the East is John Deere, the world's leading tractor manufacturer. Its pedigree as one of the oldest industrial companies in the United States, its origins dating back to 1837 Illinois, and its blue-chip brand name are no longer sufficient for it to maintain its lead. Small tractors produced by the upstart Indian firm Mahindra & Mahindra (M&M) have made significant inroads into parts of the United States. M&M's rise marks the coming of age of indigenous entrepreneurs from India. As a manufacturing company M&M is a significant departure from the Indian software firms that have achieved success in past decade.

Moreover, M&M owns 80 percent of a joint venture with China's Nanchang city government. Named Mahindra (China) Tractor, the Chinese-Indian joint venture in turn owns assets purchased from Jiangling Tractor, located halfway between Shanghai and Guangzhou. Through its joint venture M&M developed an under-forty-horsepower tractor, tailor-made for the U.S. market. The design and engineering were done in India, and the prototype was built in China. When I spoke with Anand Mahindra, CEO of M&M, at the company headquarters in Mumbai, he sang the praises of the tractor venture: "We are breaking the myth that it is hard to make money in China, or that cultural assimilation is difficult. The local disco in Nanchang now plays [Indian] music . . . and the forty year-old ex-chairman of the company sang songs from Indian Raj Kapoor movies at our first banquet. The management compatibility is a challenge, but we've ensured that the handful of Indian expatriates—there are only 15 Indians and 385 Chinese employees—all report to Chinese bosses; they are none the worse for it."[12]

This union is all the more remarkable given the differences between the two companies. M&M is an entirely private entity, led by the third-generation scion of one of India's prominent entrepreneurial families, whereas its Chinese partner is part of the government. Indeed, the government is the entrepreneur in China; in India, entrepreneurs have stayed as far apart from the state as feasible. The joint venture's location in China rather than India is also telling: China welcomes foreign direct investment, while India remains deaf to outsiders, favoring its indigenous offspring. Private versus public, suspicious of outsiders versus tolerant—the economic models followed by the two countries could not be more different.

John Deere is clearly concerned about M&M. In an unusually pointed advertisement paid for by either the company or one of its dealers, I could not tell, the U.S. company promised a $1,500 rebate to any American farmer who traded in an M&M tractor for a John Deere. M&M's U.S. operations tracked down the targeted customers and located only a handful who responded to the ad. Further, of the M&M tractor owners whom M&M contacted, a full 97 percent were not interested in John Deere's rebate and expressed satisfaction with their M&M tractors.

In India, M&M's popularity stems from producing low-powered tractors (under seventy horsepower) suited for the country's fragmented landholdings. It has a 30 percent share of the Indian market (with one other competitor holding 23 percent). M&M realized that there is an underserved market in the United States to which its low-powered tractor is well suited: hobby farming. Increasingly, in parts of the southern and southwestern United States, baby boomers are retiring from stressful urban lives in California to places like Flagstaff, Arizona, where for the price of a luxury condo in San Francisco they can buy fifteen acres of land, ideally suited to tilling by a small tractor.

Because many of M&M's customers in the United States are women, the company responded tongue-in-cheek to the John Deere tractor ad with one of its own that featured a blonde, pony-tailed American woman driving a tractor. The caption read: "Deere John, I have found someone new." Baby boomers will recall a popular television sitcom called *Dear John* that began with a note to the star from his ex-girlfriend describing why she had left him. This, in turn, originated in the phenomenon of women penning goodbye letters to male companions long-gone in wartime theaters.

M&M's market share for under-seventy-horsepower tractors in the United States grew to 6 percent, and in core markets in southern states, its share reached 20 percent. Those percentages are remarkable given that the world's major tractor manufacturers—including New Holland, Agco, and the Japanese firm Kubota—compete aggressively in this space. In 2005 M&M's U.S. tractor division managed sales of a hundred million dollars, which represents aggressive growth at a time of industry stagnation. By 2007, I serendipitously found Mahindra USA commercials being aired during prime time hours on television stations as far north and east as rural Pennsylvania.

M&M's range of tractors also suits China. With the breakup of China's communes in the 1980s, the number of individuals who farm for their own benefit has mushroomed. Seven hundred thousand power tillers once plowed the land, inefficiently. Tractor companies emerged to service these farmers, at one point as many as 400, though lately this has come down to twenty-five, still very fragmented. Concern with energy utilization prompted the Chinese government to heavily subsidize conversion from power tillers to tractors, and M&M leaped into the fray, noting that the small landholdings in China were exactly like those in India. In less than a year sensible business processes allowed output in Nanchang to triple, despite a halving of the workforce.

Shenzhen Listens to Bangalore

Sun Yafang, chairwoman of Huawei Technologies, has good reason to be confident. Established in 1988, Huawei has grown from a small maker of telephone switches into a leading producer of equipment that telephone carriers worldwide use to run their networks. With global operations that include laboratories in Silicon Valley, Dallas, Stockholm, Bangalore, Moscow, and of course, China, Huawei is now China's leading high-tech firm and a thorn in the side of telecommunication giant Cisco Systems. As *The Economist* put it, "The rise of domestic firms such as Huawei is a disaster for the multinationals."[13] In meetings with the peripatetic Sun in Boston, Shenzhen, and London I have heard Sun forecast that Huawei will see its sales grow from four billion dollars in 2005 to ten billion dollars in 2010. Moreover, she believes the firm's growth will be powered by its increasing dominance in seventy countries, including those that U.S. firms have ignored.

During a visit to Huawei's Shenzhen facilities, I saw a disciplined and talented workforce, self-confident in its technical prowess, presiding over state-of-the-art, heavily robotics-driven, and sparkling clear factories. Employees I spoke with mentioned their eagerness to learn from leading Western companies about the softer skills the company needs to succeed in world commerce, such as communicating with customers and regulators in the West, or managing employees who are not familiar with the inner workings of a Chinese company.

Huawei is the example that belies the myth that indigenous Chinese firms can master only simple technologies. Sun emphasizes that the firm's success has nothing to do with China's low labor costs and everything to do with the low cost of its skilled engineers and research and development personnel. As the young lady sent by Huawei to greet me at Shenzhen airport commented, "I am a college graduate from Hubei province, I came here because of Huawei's reputation. I just applied on the web for the job."

I asked her why she had not sought a job closer to home. Why had she been willing to travel to Shenzhen?

"Why?" Her look told me she thought the answer totally obvious. "Because it is one of China's best companies."

Further, Huawei has taken its quest for talent to India, opening software laboratories in Bangalore. Jack Lu, now presiding over human resources for Huawei, headed the office in Bangalore for three years after its inception in 1999. One of the early challenges, he told me, was overcoming each country's stereotypes of the other. Indian media had in the past portrayed the Chinese as opportunists set on stealing India's security secrets. When the Huawei office opened, Indian businesses feared the firm was after the secrets to their successful telecommunications infrastructure.

For their part Chinese newspapers only published Indian stories about floods, railway accidents, and other disasters. According to Jack Lu, "This made our situation difficult. On one occasion a major newspaper published a story that said that Huawei personnel would be deported from India because of security risks. This was untrue, and the event passed, but it put a lot of social pressure on our Indian engineers from their family and friends, who encouraged them to leave."[14] He shook his head.

Huawei has persisted, recognizing the value of tapping into Indian employees' software skills. Generating high-end employment for Indian engineers rather than using the Indian outpost only to outsource its software development gives the company a better footing in India. Huawei's Indian laboratories have earned the highest possible level of certification for software producers, measured using a global standard for software-writing capability developed by Carnegie Mellon University. In time previously held stereotypes and the mistrust they engendered were replaced by a more realistic coexistence. Entrepreneurial Indians now cater to the culinary needs of Huawei's Chinese employees, and it is as common to find apartment blocks in Bangalore populated largely by Chinese as it is to see Indian faces in Huawei's Shenzhen facilities.

Huawei goes beyond staying in step with its Western competitors. On a trip to Johannesburg early in 2007 at a mobile phone event, I found Huawei phones prominently strewn around the conference site. They were very simple phones yet provided all the functionality that most users, including me, would consider necessary. Huawei hoped that by virtue of its engineering simplicity the low-cost phone would tap into lower-income consumer segments in Africa. But more interesting than the product's engineering design was Huawei's presence at the conference as the most aggressive marketer. By providing free samples to attendees, Huawei dared its Western competitors to follow suit. Such sure-footedness and competitive aggression have become Huawei's standard.

The Western media has entirely missed the stories of China-India mutualism and its importance to consumers in the West. These are significant rumblings from the east it has failed to hear. Instead, it has fixated on Huawei's unlikely origins, citing the fact that it was founded by Ren Zhengfei, who retired as a colonel of the People's Liberation Army in 1984. A Cisco lawsuit alleging intellectual property fraud, subsequently settled out of court, and an employee lawsuit regarding compensation added to the world's suspicion. That Huawei is incredibly opaque has not helped; American CEOs are equally amazed by their technical mastery as they are by the company being "shrouded in mystery."[15] As it turns out, it is no mystery why most Chinese firms are generally shrouded in mystery, given the lack of pressure from an underdeveloped financial system to reveal any kind of information, a theme to which I will return.

Recognizing the origins of China's competitive enterprises is integral to understanding their stories, not a reason to dismiss them. It is a mistake for Western companies not to track the investments of Chinese and Indian companies and learn to compete with them. That Huawei is not dependent on its sales in developed countries but in fact profits by its sales in developing countries not under the commercial eye of the West—for example, Nigeria, Zimbabwe, Pakistan, Kazakhstan, and Turkmenistan—is even more reason to pay attention.

A New Dance

Anand Mahindra's shepherding of the Nasik-Nanchang collaboration and Sun Yafang's persistence in tapping into markets for talent in southern India are examples of a new relationship, a new dance, which is cropping up in many places between China and India. Perhaps because the exchanges are still relatively new and the metaphorical passages between the countries have only recently opened, it is difficult to find the precise term to characterize this new relationship. It is as mutable as the partnership between two dancers, with a leader and follower alternating roles and both straining to hear music that is by turns tentative and vigorous.

For want of a better term, I call this dance mutualism. However, I need to qualify the feel-good quality the term usually connotes by pointing out that the mutualism currently existing between China and India contains mutual cooperation, but also some mutual tension. China and India are learning that acting in their own best interests can mean working together, and any good feeling that might result between them would be more of a fringe benefit than the main goal. In using the term mutualism I mean to point to the very real possibility that China and India will in time learn to capitalize on each other's strengths and compensate for each other's weaknesses.

Not all companies looking across borders are as large as M&M and Huawei. Huayi Stone Limited operates on a relatively small scale but is perhaps more significant because it represents the collaboration emerging between China and India at the grassroots level. Established in 1994 by a farmer who invested forty thousand yuan (five thousand dollars) of his own resources. Today, Huayi Stone owes its fortune to links to India. The company sells granite blocks in Fujian Province, an area famous for stone carvings. Before 2000 the company bought stones from other parts of China and sold them to stone-processing factories in Fujian. The company could barely make ends meet. Zhang Ming, the deputy manager of Huayi Stone's international department, recalls that when he joined the company as a young college graduate, it could not afford even a fax machine.

Then the firm began to experiment with stone imports from India, which happens to be one of the largest granite-producing countries in the world. In 2002 the Chinese company imported stone from India worth twenty million yuan, with profits of 15 percent or more. Imports increased rapidly, and by 2006 Indian imports had tripled, accounting for the largest share of what Huayi imported worldwide. The company's trade with India has become hugely profitable. Zhang visits India several times annually, frequenting parts off the beaten path, in the poorest mountain regions of the southern states of Tamil Nadu, Karnataka, and Andhra Pradesh. Huayi Stone's capital stock now touches a hundred million yuan, and it has thirty employees. Zhang also points out that 90 percent of foreign stone dealers in India are Chinese.

Even the state-owned petroleum sectors in both countries are becoming aware of ways they can benefit from one another. China's National Petroleum Corporation and India's Oil and Natural Gas Commission have joint investments in oil field exploration in Khartoum, Sudan, and Damascus, Syria—areas that are politically unappealing to many of the developed world's oil giants. Like Huawei Technologies, forced in its early years to seek trade in countries ignored by the West, the Chinese and Indian oil majors must duck and weave to find their own competitive passages through the ones already paved by powerful Western incumbent oil firms. Yet because the Chinese and Indian economies have contributed the greatest growth to energy consumption in recent years (though far from the greatest stock of energy consumption, that distinction belonging to the U.S.), any joint venture between the two nations has the potential to affect world energy markets. In a sense, all world commodity markets have begun to bear the force of the simultaneous advent of Chinese and Indian demand, be it in steel, or wheat, or shipping. To the extent that China and India were to learn to act in tandem, as their oil firms have done on a couple of occasions, the effect on world markets would be magnified.

Ignoring Huawei, M&M, or even Huayi is every bit as preposterous as it was to ignore Finland's Nokia and Korea's LG Group two decades ago, when these companies were beginning to grow. The latter companies have proven more attuned to the advent of China and India than have most in my American backyard, perhaps because they can better recognize the path they themselves followed. In brainstorms in Seoul with some of Korea's most prominent *chaebols*—the Korean term for family-controlled business groups—I witness their struggle to understand how they might well be stuck between some of the developed world's companies and newly resurgent Chinese or Indian companies. For example, LG's and Samsung's white goods divisions must sell against not only top-end machines made by Whirlpool in the West, but also against cleverly designed machines manufactured by much lower-cost companies like Haier, headquartered in Qingdao in China's Shandong Province.

In the last five years, when Nokia's worldwide sales shot up by one-third to forty billion dollars, the United States accounted for only 8 percent of total sales, about half its previous level, while sales to Asia doubled, accounting for 16 percent. Nokia has had major investments in China for years and has now redoubled its efforts in India, the latter eclipsing China as the world's fastest-growing cell phone market.

LG's exports have gone up sevenfold in the past decade, reaching thirty-eight billion dollars. Their story is similar to Nokia's: exports to the United States are declining while exports to Asia, especially China and India, are rising rapidly. It is hard to walk around any major Indian metropolis and not see the LG logo staring you in the face. Like some other Korean *chaebols*, LG has entrenched itself in China and India, far ahead of its American and

Japanese rivals. LG's success is reverberating in boardrooms throughout Asia. For instance, Singapore's Temasek, the government-owned multibillion-dollar investment holding company, has ceased to look purely at China and is aggressively investing in India as well.

Benefits from China and India do not have to be realized purely by corporate entities. Consider the billionaire Andronico Luksic, the Croatian-origin head of Chile's prominent Luksic Group. I last met Luksic in a café in New York's Four Seasons during the festive Christmas season in 2006. Luksic is a large, garrulous man, generous in his hospitality and opinion, and not one to suffer fools easily. Yes, he climbed the Seven Summits, the highest peak of each continent including Mount Everest most recently . . . just because. One of his friends, a quieter man, Indian-born software entrepreneur, Rajesh Hukku, joined us. Hukku built a multibillion-dollar company around the world's leading banking software product, and splits time between New York and Bangalore.

The Luksic Group in Chile has learned to leverage China and India. Banco de Chile, one of that country's leading banks and a prominent part of the group, gave Hukku's firm the contract to lead the transformation of the bank. Hukku beat out firms prominent in the Western consulting world, giving him a beachhead from which to launch into the lucrative Latin American market. (The other finalist was another Indian software company.)

"Oye," said Luksic leaning across a short, round table toward me, repeating this expression frequently, "the Indian solution was world-class, my board was horrified at the thought, but there you have it. We have not been disappointed yet, although the work is still in progress."[16]

Scores of Indian software engineers have descended on Santiago in a Chilean-Indian dance of sorts intended to propel the bank into the next century. Meanwhile, Banco de Chile has opened offices in Beijing to serve Chilean and other Latin American clients doing business. This includes business related to the copper mines of Antofagasta Holdings, the group's mining company, of great interest to resource-guzzling China.

"I am in love with China," Luksic told me. "I bought an apartment in the center of Beijing. My friends asked me, 'Why are you buying something which you can't own, at best you can just get a long-term lease?' But you can't own something freehold in central London either, you just get a lease from Duke of Westminster. I trust the Communist Party as much as I trust the Duke of Westminster."

Luksic and his family are investing in China in a broader sense as well. "Building relations with China will pay off. I knocked on the doors of Tsinghua University and they agreed to do business with me." Tsinghua is one of China's leading universities, often loosely called the MIT of China. I asked why he had done this. "My father always told me, 'Just ask, you never know what you will get.'" Luksic now finances an exchange program for twenty students annually so that young Chileans and Chinese can get to know each other. When the Chinese president Hu Jintao arrived in Santiago to address the Asia Pacific Economic Cooperation Summit in November 2004, Luksic was one of his hosts.

Luksic's son joined us, a graduate of Babson College, where Luksic is also a trustee. "I encouraged him to go to Rajesh's offices in Bangalore. Something amazing is going on in that city too, as in Beijing, I'm not sure what. He should see, it will distinguish him from others in his age group. We are well diversified. One son has asked to go to India, one to China, and one to the U.S."

Amid the frenetic activity of Chile, Finland, Korea, Singapore, and other locations, U.S. corporations have not been asleep. Some are very farsighted indeed. My favorite example of a company that perhaps has done the most to leverage both China and India is General Electric, the focus of the final chapter of the book. Of course as the stories related in this chapter make clear, the symbiosis and mutualism of China and India profits not only the Chinese and Indians but also the world.

Why Is This Happy Mutualism Plausible?

A skeptic might say that these are but whispers in the wind, not the telltale signs of a coming thunderous gale. The skeptic might point out that China's trade with India even after a few years of steep growth, is still less than twenty billion dollars (compared with ten times that amount between China and the United States or the European Union). This skepticism might be reasonable, but it is entirely misplaced.

Optimism is possible for two reasons. First, there are very few shocks to the world system, even in not-so-recent historical memory, that compare with the simultaneous entrances of China and India into the global economy. Extrapolating from short-horizon statistics is at the very least shortsighted. To the skeptic, one might offer the other statistical extreme. The Princeton economist Angus Maddison has shown that in the 1800s as much as 50 percent of world GDP was accounted for by China and India.[17] Their individual and collective falls from grace make up a story of two centuries.

Second, from a conceptual viewpoint the potential for mutualism is high. Proximate countries naturally find it convenient to trade. Until recently Chinese and Indian trade has been stifled by political hostility. Both countries have now put the feeding of hundreds of millions of hungry people ahead of relatively petty border disputes, and both have too much to lose by not working in concert with each other. This does not imply a love fest, but merely a credible cessation of mutual hostility and suspicion.

Early in the twentieth century Tenshin Okura, a founder of the Japan Art Institute and friend of the Indian poet and Nobelist, Rabindranath Tagore, began his book *The Ideals of the East* with the line, "Asia is one."[18] Today, reflecting on Okura's statement, I am led to say "Yes, but not quite": not quite, because two major countries entering the world economy in the last few decades are following radically different paths, but yes, because traversing these different paths enables the combination of the two economies—a large part of Asia—to punch above their already-substantial collective weight.

Judicious entrepreneurs worldwide are recognizing that the advent of the planet's two most populous countries on the world stage is not just a story of selling separately to 1.3 billion Chinese and 1.1 billion Indians. That would be too simpleminded. The story is much richer, more complex, and tremendously exciting. The story is about the myriad ways to celebrate the talent, ideas, and aspirations of 2.4 billion people.

To do this requires a renewal of hope in these countries. Two decades ago, a scholar described underdevelopment as a "state of mind."[19] He was referring to the importance of would-be entrepreneurs—though he did not use that term—imagining anew, rather than evincing skepticism and cynicism. In China and India, such reimagining is now under way. The dead hand of India's caste system has been swept aside in some measure, and the power of a moribund government contained. China is very far from the "immobile empire" that French scholar Alain Peyrefitte once described it as when he detailed the "dialogue of the deaf" between the Emperor Qianlong and an emissary of King George III in 1792.[20]

But the celebration of China and India also requires a jettisoning of old debilitating images harbored for centuries by Westerners. An open mind and a willingness to see new, productive imagery is needed, a mind-set that does not assume that outsiders have the answers but instead begins with respectful listening.

L'Invitation au Voyage[21]

Smart, innovative Chinese and Indian business leaders are learning to make profitable use of one another's resources and as a result have reaped huge financial gains from, for example, tractors, telephone carriers, and granite. Increasingly, business relationships between individuals in each country are no longer barbed, and entrepreneurs on both sides of the border are cultivating ways to capitalize on the new openness. Westerners too should be attuned to the rumblings of change emanating from the two most populous countries on the world economic stage or risk being overwhelmed by their thunder. This book chronicles the journeys of billions of entrepreneurs in China and India seeking prosperity, both for themselves and for the benefit of society. It puts forward a "big tent" view of entrepreneurship, not just individuals taking companies public, as it were, but creative entrepreneurship in the social and political sphere, unfolding in numerous ways in cities that are not on the tips-of-the-tongues of every businessperson, but off the beaten paths of the two countries. My thesis is that entrepreneurship in developing countries occurs in far more encompassing and far-reaching ways than in more developed settings—for the simple reason that there is *so* much more that needs to be done. It is done so very differently too, in response to the different nuances and rhythms of the societies in question. So the subjects in this book are the usual business-school types of entrepreneurs, who start successful companies and reap Croesus-like riches. There are also political entrepreneurs figuring out ways to make good things happen within some difficult constraints, and social entrepreneurs applying their creativity to solve the seemingly intractable problems that are rampant everywhere in China and India.

I have had, and continue to have, the privilege and immense good fortune to interact with dozens of intriguing people daily through my research, my work with companies, foundations, and their boards, and with entrepreneurs, politicians, and activists in the developing world.[22] Most importantly I relish hitting the pavement in any city I visit. I have enjoy recording all conversations, even those with taxi drivers, shopkeepers, restaurateurs, museum officials, and people engaged in the humdrum routines of life. I have listened to the rhythms of people talking about politics in Beijing and Delhi, heard the fear of being sanctioned by authorities in Zhengzhou, been deafened by the raucous indiscipline of Jaipur's camel-festooned streets, delighted in the vitality of a classroom at Tsinghua, and sat in the myriad boardroom meetings where uninformed but intelligent individuals insist "we *must* be in China and India," only to hear other individuals—in Cape Town, Sao Paulo, Seoul, and Sydney—express dread, mystery, and optimism about China and India. These motley experiences inform this book. Examples from these encounters appear throughout the book. A decade of research on business and entrepreneurship in emerging markets in other parts of the world—Latin America, the Middle East, and other parts of eastern and Southeast Asia—has enhanced my ability to discern interesting patterns in the data. To appeal to a broad audience, I draw equally from history and current scholarship in economics and political science. I make no pretence at being comprehensive; rather, I choose those vignettes, which I can complement with solid social science research—my own and that of colleagues—to communicate similarities and, more importantly, differences between China and India.

I had to be especially cognizant, as I am Indian-born, that I would not be biased in India's direction in any comparison with China. As a scholar, I would be mortified if this were analytically true in any sense. But as will be clear, my position in this book is that it is very difficult to unambiguously rank one of the two countries' systems as above that of the other. By my rough count, half the chapters in the book end up showing China doing a better job than India, and this was not by design.

As I write, the Chinese are capitalizing on India's opportunities, and Indians on China's, and this between two countries that have glared at each other across icy Himalayan passes, weapons systems at the ready, for the last four decades. Recognizing the availability of opportunity in China and India and the complementarity of their economic systems is a surer route to prosperity than is tilting-at-windmills, Don Quixote style, at the inevitable shifting of the locus of world economic power eastward from New York and London.

This anxiety was not always so. Centuries ago, Indian trade was central to the American economy, and financed some of the young nation's emergent romance with China. Then, not too long ago, as the West ascended economically, China and India became quaintly irrelevant. They aroused little curiosity in the Western world, even contempt. America was especially oblivious to India. Britain knew much less about China than about its Indian colony.

In the late 1940s, when both countries entered the world economy, they did so in vastly different ways. This recognition is a centerpiece of the book. Part I, "Foundations," chronicles the very different choices made by the nascent modern nation-states, choices based on deeply held beliefs about appropriate societal norms. In the first three chapters of the book, I describe some very different attitudes to simple societal mores. Who should know what kinds of things, when, and why? How should private interest be reconciled with public interest when they are in conflict? Each model has very different pros and cons. There are traces of the old ways in each country's choices, but one can see significant attempts at change.

Part II, *Enterprises*, chronicles, in a spectrum of locations and settings, and through my experiences with individual businesses, organizations, and entrepreneurs, some of the consequences of those choices being realized today. There are areas where China and India excel; these pockets of excellence are generally quite different in the two countries, and areas where each country is, at best, a massive work-in-progress.

Part III, *Future*, views the savvy companies and individuals, local as well as elsewhere from the developed and developing worlds, who are learning to leverage the skills of both China and India. The China and India of yore traded magnanimously with each other, sharing ideas and wealth; the China and India of my children's generation will likely do so again. Hope and a wary confidence are again pervasive. For the first time since the rise of the West, entrepreneurs in Asia can ignore New York and London almost entirely, and still build companies worth billions. The economic center of gravity is moving toward the East.

Part I opens with Chapter 2. "Statecraft: The Art, Science, and Illusion of Governing 2.4 Billion People," documents the efficiency of the Chinese state, and the dysfunction of India's. Today's governments build respectively on the legacy bequeathed by Mao's Communist Party (the Chinese now say he was 70 percent right and only 30 percent wrong), and that bequeathed by Nehru's passion for socialism and democracy. China governs by orderly hierarchy and India tries to govern by debate that respects the individual. The "try" is an important qualifier since there is still far too much dysfunction in India's government where accountability and probity are not widely embraced norms. There is, of course, rampant corruption in both countries, but the corrupt in China are demanding a piece of something new that is being created—the government *is* the entrepreneur—whereas India's corrupt are content to help themselves without any real contribution. The good news in India comes not from the government, but from civil society and the private sector, who are increasingly embracing some of the government's tasks. The government is at least allowing them to do so, but that it is not reforming itself, at least not yet. What better evidence than to note that entrepreneurs and the Communist Party are locked in an increasingly tight embrace, of the sort that would have been ideologically unfathomable even a few years ago, whereas in India, it is still the rare entrepreneur who has aspired to explicitly be part of the state. Smart people do join the Party in China, usually for non-ideological reasons, because it remains a route to economic well-being; talent scarcely ever contemplates public service in India.

While the government is more efficient in China, the foundations for a market economy are much more robust in India. Chapter 3, "Bias and Noise: Information Accessibility in China and India," compares *Caijing* and *Tehelka*, upstart media outlets in Beijing and New Delhi, to contrast China's policies of information control, which often do not allow outsiders or the Chinese masses access to "inconvenient" information, with India's information transparency, where a raucous press provides noisy, unbiased information that forces insiders and outsiders to piece together individual approximations of the truth. Although recent changes in China have made getting economic information much easier, any political discourse is unwelcome, making outsiders question the extent to which economic information is influenced by politics.

Chapter 4, "Fiat and Fairness: Why China Can Build Cities Overnight and India Cannot," considers attitudes to private property. China uses its fiat authority to err on the side of serving public interest, even if it means violating individual private property. India errs on the side of private property rights, sometimes to the detriment of society. Liberal economists and policy experts laud India as the rare developing country to achieve the distinction of transparency and private property rights. But the costs of failed collective action are also truly massive.

Free-flowing information and the sanctity of property rights form the bedrock of organized exchange. Illustrating how exchange does or does not occur in financial markets is the goal of Chapter 5, "Manna and Miasma: Meanderings Through Chinese and Indian Financial Firmaments." In China, where capital is allocated by fiat, domestic savings are channeled through government-owned banks to recapitalize distressed state-owned enterprises. The banks themselves are bankrupt, the stock market is riddled with inefficiencies, and capital does not find its way to where it is most needed. The indigenous private enterprise that does exist in China—and the numbers of would-be entrepreneurs are large—is constrained from attaining anything near its full potential. State-owned enterprises, while their numbers have shrunk, continue to account for half of all of China's assets, and virtually all of its massive non-performing loans. Indian equity markets, in contrast, rely on the existence of thousands of publicly traded but privately owned indigenous firms and on an industry of independent purveyors of reasonably reliable information that allow individual savers to choose where to invest. New banks are forcing the old deadwood to pick up its game. Competition is the norm, rather than the top down decision making and intervention seen in China's capital markets.

Thus India is geared to support indigenous private enterprise. China is much less so. After 1978, China used its fiat authority to assure foreign private enterprise an open door, partly to compensate for this. To some extent, the massive response of foreign enterprise has alleviated the pressure on China to build the soft infrastructure needed. Thus China's pro-foreign investor, anti-indigenous entrepreneur stance is as a mirror opposite of India's anti-foreign investor, pro-indigenous investor stance; both, in turn, are reflections of societal choices regarding information and private rights, and the role of the state.

The foundations I chronicle in Part I shape the reality of daily life in China and India today. In Part II, *"Enterprise,"* I consider different kinds of organized economic and social activities of both countries.

I start with two pairs of entrepreneurs. The first are the locals, Chinese in China and Indians in India, building successful enterprises in very different ways. The second are the foreigners in each country, lured by the storied riches to be had, sobered by the reality, but ultimately en route to building something of lasting value.

Chapter 6, "Infosys and TCL: Unshackling Indigenous Enterprise," compares the rise of one of China's leading companies, a mass manufacturer of consumer electronics, TCL Corporation, with the rise of Infosys, one of India's leading software companies, and a pioneer of off-shoring. Both are triumphant stories of entrepreneurship. In China entrepreneurship occurs in the shadow of the efficient state. The incentives of Party members are broadly aligned with the promotion of economic activity, evaluated as they are, through promotions and recognition, for enhancing local economic activity. In India entrepreneurs thrive primarily, or even exclusively, in the interstices inadvertently left untouched by the socialist state. Entrepreneurs wisely keep the state at arms length; thankfully, in the past decade or so, the Indian state has at least begun to see the wisdom of letting this happen. While both TCL and Infosys have tried to "go global," TCL, and many other Chinese companies, have faltered, betraying a misunderstanding of how markets work and inexperience on the global stage. Infosys, and other Indian companies, proceed differently, working within the market and with a fuller understanding of the rules of international commerce.

Chapter 7, "Microsoft and Metro: Views from the World's Corner Offices," tells the stories of Microsoft in China and the German firm, Metro Cash & Carry, in India to illustrate what it takes for multinationals to succeed in both countries. China's government extends a welcome mat to foreign investors—on its own terms. Well-managed technology behemoth Microsoft learns to its chagrin that raw economic logic does not rule the day in China if it runs afoul of the Party's mandate and desires. Working within the Chinese Communist Party's own entrepreneurial framework is the surest way forward. In India, the German wholesaler Metro Cash & Carry runs into its own brick wall. Despite bringing the sorely needed expertise of linking rural hinterlands to urban markets and thus bringing jobs and development where these are most needed, Metro is made to run the gauntlet by small traders whose livelihoods are threatened by its format. They use the democratic political process to end-run the hapless Germans. The public interest of feeding the hungry millions is sacrificed on the altar of the private rights of small urban traders, as inefficient as the latter might be.

The mirror-image quality of China and India emerges again: one favors multinationals over indigenous private companies, the other advantages its locals and shuns foreigners. Indigenous entrepreneurs have many more choices in India than in China. These include good choices that promote the formation of productive enterprise, and bad ones, such as lobbying the government to make life difficult for foreigners, and thus protecting defunct and parasitic enterprises. Multinationals have greater choices in China. Provinces vie for their investment. Infrastructure is widely available—often better than in the so-called developed West—and the relatively limited capabilities of local enterprises is a blessing in disguise for them, though they will never admit this. Investors' options are also different. Portfolio investments are possible in India, given the large number of publicly traded and reasonably transparent firms on the Indian exchange; it is infeasible or inadvisable in China for the most part. In China, an outside financial investor would either invest directly in a physical facility or indirectly through an investment in one of the Western multinationals that are actively involved in China.

Attitudes of the Chinese to their diaspora of fifty million and of the Indians to theirs of twenty million reflect the same choices within the countries, as discussed in Chapter 8, "Diaspora Dividends: Paragons and Pariahs from the Overseas Chinese and Indians." Because China's domestic financial markets were left undeveloped, it actively organized and relied on Chinese emigrants to provide capital. The wooing of the overseas Chinese paid many dividends. In contrast, India has until recently shunned its diaspora, surely one of the most self-defeating policies adopted by the Indian state. Although, in the past decade, overseas Indians have begun to have voice in India, the central characteristic remains: China opts for citizenship emanating for *jus sanguinis*—right of blood; India for citizenship from *jus soli*—right of soil.

The foundational choices made by China and India also affect life outside the economic mainstream of the major metropolises. Chapters 9 and 10 explore this in two theaters: rural economies and health care.

Both countries sport large rural populations. Today rural China is the source of much unrest as its development lags that of the coast. Rural India is even more deprived, combining the economic deprivation of China's villages with poorer physical infrastructure and poorer education. "Village Engineering and Reengineering: In Search of Rural Fortunes" reports my visits to villages in China's Henan Province and in India's Gujarat State. Henan is among China's poorest, Gujarat among India's richest; yet villagers in Henan seemed better off than those in Gujarat. As in the urban sector, enterprise in rural China is driven by state-led action, whereas enterprise in rural India is driven either by the private sector, which is motivated by profit, or by civil society, which is driven by individual initiative. While the authoritarian structure of China is apparent in its on-again, off-again policies toward rural China, India's villages remain mired in casteism, a centuries-old institution impervious to change. Indeed, the only institution capable of effecting economic change in rural India is private enterprise, impervious as it is to caste, responding more to lucre and self-interest.

If there is one domain where both countries have faltered badly and inexcusably it is in health care, as shown in Chapter 10, "Barefoot Doctors and Medical Tourism: Futile Attempts to Confront the Grim Reaper." China's is the steeper fall from grace. It attained near universal primary health care in 1978 but now has glaring inequities. Its embrace of the private sector, sans other safeguards, did not work in a state-dominated society. India's is a more uniformly dismal story, with some exceptions. Unsurprisingly, the exceptions are almost all in the private sector. Resourceful entrepreneurs have made the best hospitals as good as the best of the West; medical tourism is beginning to bring good technology at affordable prices to those in the world willing to travel, and telemedicine is reaching out to some fraction of the disenfranchised. Yet it is too little too late for most Indians.

Part III, "Future," explores the implications for the world of the likely evolution of the Chinese and Indian models in four settings: China and the world, India and the world, Chinese and Indian mutual relations, and the view from the developed world. Again, the choices China and India have made in the past will script their futures. Both countries will engage with the world in much the same way that they engage with their own citizens. That is, just as China's actions within its borders are state-led, so will the expansion of Chinese influence be state-led. India, as within its own boundaries, will rely on decentralized initiatives to make its mark. The Chinese and Indians, as suggested earlier in Chapter 1, will learn to leverage each other's strengths. This calculated cooperation, or mutualism, is already abundantly evident and is available for all to tap into, including the West.

Chapter 11, "Old and New Roads to Mandalay: Hard Power on the World's Oil Fields," shows how China is expanding its hard power. In parts of Southeast Asia where India has traditionally exported culture and commerce—for example, Burma (Myanmar)—the expansion of Chinese influence through investment and force is at the expense of India's influence. But China, in its rush to secure the energy and other raw materials needed for its economic development, has not hesitated to extend itself to regimes that the free world labels unsavory. In India, where entrepreneurship is almost inconsistent with the sclerotic bureaucracy, the government remains chronically incapable of matching China's display of hard power. This is most dramatically seen in how China is outmuscling India in its search for oil. This search is the modern version of the rush for last century's natural resources of the Irrawady delta in Burma. Instead, India oozes what political scientist Joseph Nye calls soft power. In India's noisy political economy, creativity and the arts thrive. Entrepreneurs run amuck. The expansion of influence—whether by India's film industry, international expansion by individual companies, or the soaring presence of yoga in the West—amounts to influencing the world through soft power, as argued in Chapter 12, "Film Stars and Gurus: Soft Power on the World Screen."

Chapter 13, "Buddha and Software: Old Links and New," examines connections forged between China and India over the last two thousand years. When politicians from both countries reference Buddhism and visit Buddhist shrines during state visits, they are attempting to symbolically bind the two nations. Symbolism has, in the last few years, become reality as bilateral trade shot from zero to twenty billion dollars annually, thus sowing the seeds of mutually advantageous commerce. Despite conciliatory political gestures from both countries—for example, conducting coordinated military exercises and adopting compatible positions on agriculture and intellectual property following World Trade Organization talks—their commercial links are likely the more resilient.

Finally, Chapter 14, "Corporate Bridges: Linking China, India, and the West," describes the corporate success story of General Electric in linking China and India in corporate symbiosis. Just as China and India are learning to leverage each other, so is GE in China leveraging GE in India and vice versa. This corporate symbiosis builds on a foundation of GE's handsome contributions to both China and India, by contributing to the policy reform debate, and by hiring white-collar professionals in cutting-edge research positions. GE has earned honorary corporate citizenship in both countries. By embracing China and India as partners, GE provides one blueprint for the West's re-engagement with China and India.

PART I

FOUNDATIONS

Chapter Two

Statecraft

*The Art, Science, and Illusion of Governing
2.4 Billion People*

During my family's annual visits with my parents in New Delhi, the moment would invariably come when my father would sigh deeply, turn to me, and begin a conversation about his dreaded "court *kacheri.*" *Kacheri* means "court" in Hindi, and the term "court *kacheri*" means "hassles of the court." India's high courts, the highest judicial bodies in individual states, are in a perpetual state of crisis. So paranoid are most Indian citizens about court *kacheri* that they will go to any lengths to avoid formal litigation, even when they clearly are on the right side of the law.

Not my father. An honest man, he believes that justice is possible, even in India's high courts. When accused of an absurd crime, he did not resort to bribery or ask that his case be dismissed by a higher authority, although social connections made either option possible. He chose to let due process play out.

In December 1997 he was being driven down an exit ramp near the gates of a factory in Faridabad, a town near New Delhi. An overloaded three-wheeler came alongside his car. Bigger than a motorbike but smaller than a compact car, the typical three-wheeler is overloaded with industrial goods or food, and carries as many as six passengers crammed together. In my father's case the three-wheeler tried to pass his car and toppled over in the process. One of its passengers sustained multiple fractures. At no time did the three-wheeler come in contact with my father's car.

The injured party lodged a case against my father and the government of India lodged another. The former case was dismissed in two months, with insurance paying the injured person forty thousand rupees (roughly a thousand dollars). The government reasoned its case as follows: because my father, the car owner, was in the "superior vehicle"' and the other party's vehicle was more "vulnerable," and since my father was not hurt and the other individual was, the car owner was per se at fault. This bizarre reasoning was only the beginning of a Kafkaesque odyssey through the system: twenty court hearings spaced four to six months apart, each entailing hours of inconsequential waiting.

I accompanied my father to one of these hearings, which was held in a courtroom on the second floor of a dilapidated building. Plaintiffs and defendants for a series of cases waited outside, often for hours on end, as there was no schedule for when a particular case might be heard. There are no seats or toilet facilities available. When our time was announced, we had to scuffle around looking for our lawyer, and hope he was within earshot. Otherwise we would have been listed as "failed to appear" in court. In my father's case, twelve of the twenty total court appearances were listed, as "the witness has not shown up, so the hearing is adjourned to another date." Lengthy discussion ensued about when this date might be. Ultimately, testimony was recorded from a police officer, a hospital official, and a car mechanic to certify that the car was fault-free. Testimony was also taken from one person who was in the overloaded three-wheeler. It took eight years to resolve my father's court *kacheri* in a summary acquittal.

My father's situation represents a common occurrence in the high courts; hundreds of equally absurd cases are heard daily. India's Supreme Court, the highest judicial body in the country, can be credited for adjudicating fairly and even at times curbing the excesses of the Indian legislature. But the state as a whole has not made the judiciary efficient.

Whenever I am in New Delhi, I visit Parliament House, seat of the legislature. "Look at the Sansad Bhavan," I say to my daughter and son, and point to a spectacular, red sandstone, circular building dating back to the 1920s, once created as a testament to British Imperial power. It became a landmark of India's independence when Nehru gave his "Tryst with Destiny" speech there at midnight on August 15, 1947, when the British formally handed over power to the Indian people.

"Like the Fourth of July?" my American-born daughter asks. "Are there fireworks?"

"No fireworks," I say. "But plenty of fiery talk."

Indians are fierce in their commitment to democracy, but they do not always know what to do with their commitment. Indian democracy is still too dysfunctional to deliver the promise of Nehru-era idealists.

In the Sansad Bhavan, on either side of the Central Hall from which Nehru spoke, there are two additional halls. One houses India's Upper House of Parliament: the Rajya Sabha, whose 250 members are elected by India's individual state legislative assemblies. The other houses the Lower House of Parliament, or Lok Sabha, comprising 552 directly elected representatives.[1] The real action is in the Lok Sabha. Although bills are proposed, debated, decided on, and vetoed in both houses, only the Lok Sabha can determine budget priorities.

Unfortunately, this venue meant for effective democracy is often the scene of chaos. For example, on August 25, 2006, an opposition member of the Lok Sabha accused the cabinet minister for railways, Lalu Prasad Yadav, of exploiting for political gain some tragic events involving underprivileged members of society. Yadav's brother-in-law, also a member of the Lower House, lunged at the accuser. The two, along with their supporters, were physically restrained. The "watch and ward" staff arrived in force and cordoned off the well of the Lok Sabha. Unable to maintain decorum, the speaker of the Lower House adjourned the proceedings.[2]

Such shenanigans are not rare. At particularly low points, Members of Parliament (MPs) have been known to hurl their *chappals* (footwear) at their opponents to express disagreement. Catcalls, sit-outs, sit-ins, and walkouts are common. This abuse of parliamentary procedures halts meaningful debate, paralyzing India's legislature in farcical soap operas. Although economic and financial reforms have been instituted, no comprehensive effort has been made to improve the efficiency of the government meant to deliver those reforms. In pursuit of power, India's democratically elected leaders have wasted the country's resources. Even more alarming, this chaos reflects the criminalization of politics. By some estimates, in the 2004 general elections nearly a quarter of India's elected Members of Parliament had criminal records.[3] Here lies the most telling symptom of the limits of Indian democracy: in free and fair elections—indeed, the Election Commission of India is repeatedly and appropriately lauded as "clean"—the electorate routinely puts unsavory individuals in office, thus reinforcing the norm of nonaccountability.

Contrast Sansad Bhavan's chaos with the consensus and order evident in Beijing's Great Hall of the People, the building housing China's highest legislative body, the National People's Congress (NPC). In this ten thousand–seat auditorium, which was built in just ten months by volunteers in 1958–1959, harmony prevails. Among the reasons the NPC meets in the Great Hall are to amend the Chinese Constitution, enact basic laws of the state, and elect leading personnel of the highest state organs of China. Instead of sandal throwing, here one sees the orderly assembly of NPC deputies, all dressed (including women) in dark suits. Most major policy decisions in China are passed here with virtual unanimity. Unlike India, where opposition parties routinely veto legislation, even bills they would have passed were they in power, members of the NPC voice no dissent. But with its dearth of audible dissent and abundance of orchestrated support for its agenda, the NPC, unlike India's Lok Sabha, cannot engage in meaningful debate.

In China what you see is not what you get. Behind the order in this Great Hall of the People, debate and discussion, even rumblings of dissent, do occur, but only within the Chinese Communist Party (CCP), sequestered from public airing. Competition and factionalism within the party in fact propel a meritocracy in which the best and brightest percolate to the top. Competing with the party as an institution is what is not tolerated. By not airing its dirty laundry in public, the CCP has successfully steered China from communism to a socialist market economy over the last thirty years. In return for a monopoly on power, the CCP promises, and largely delivers, material well-being.

As the average Chinese has become wealthier, the CCP has embraced a wider array of members, including private entrepreneurs. This in an amazing ideological sleight of hand for an entity nominally dedicated to communism. Remaining open are the questions of whether the CCP can continue to accommodate both its steadily expanding membership and the concomitant diversity of demands and aspirations, and whether it can countenance the protests of those left behind in a society with enormous inequalities.

Learning from Others

In October 2006 I visited the Shanghai Party Institute, also called the Shanghai Administration Institute, in southwestern Shanghai, because I was interested in seeing how Party personnel were formally trained. I wanted to learn about the general intellectual atmosphere and thinking within the Party. Founded in June 1949 with the goal of training mid- and senior-level civil servants, the Shanghai Party Institute is second only to the school in Beijing in the CCP's hierarchy of training institutions.

The campus ambience resembles a well-funded academic institution or think tank in the West. There is a bustle of activity, with well-appointed lecture halls, and warrens of cubicles and small conference rooms. In addition to catering to the training needs of party officials, the school functions as a regular tertiary educational institution for local students. Ten thousand students passed through the campus each year between 2003 and 2006, and dormitory capacity was stretched to its limit. Some of the students were there because the government mandated certain kinds of training for officials moving up the hierarchy. Others wanted to attend refresher courses; study specific topics, like China's membership in the World Trade Organization; or attend short programs devised in response to student demands.

For example, a program on environmental protection was staffed in a 2 + x formula, by one faculty member from the school, one Party member from outside the school, and the + x denoting representation from the environmental function in the city that had expressed interest in the program, and that would finance the students going through it.

I got the impression that the CCP trainers were proponents of the study of ideas, even those they opposed. The principles of a free-market economy and the tenets of the U.S. Constitution and Bill of Rights were offered as ideas that, although markedly different from Chinese thinking, were nevertheless useful. Even I, an academic from the Western bastion of capitalism, was invited to lecture on any subject. These exemplify a new Party openness. John Thornton, former chairman of the blue-chip investment bank Goldman Sachs, has been lecturing to CCP members in Beijing for several years on equity markets and interest rates. The Shanghai Party Institute has sent delegations to Harvard's Kennedy School of Government to absorb new pedagogical ideas such as a research program where high-potential individuals are put in groups to brainstorm initiatives for tackling problems.

I asked Professor Lu, a high-ranking academic and an adviser to both the Shanghai government and to Beijing, a gentleman who describes his job as providing input to the Party's human resources strategy, what he thought were the origins of the party's commitment to a training program that exposes students to a spectrum of ideas. In response Professor Lu cited the importance of the open-door policy, "learning from others," that Deng Xiaoping's China embraced. Indeed, when Deng visited Singapore in 1978 he witnessed the country's remarkable transformation from nothing to a prosperous economy. Deng met Lee Kuan Yew, the person most associated with the rise of Singapore, who assured him that if Singapore could get ahead as "the descendants of illiterate, landless peasants," China certainly could do equally well as "the progeny of the scholars, mandarins, and literati."[4] The following June, China appointed Dr. Goh Keng Swee, the former finance and defense minister of Singapore, to oversee the development of the first four special economic zones on the mainland, thereby borrowing Singapore's foreign investment model.

Professor Lu quickly pointed out another important factor motivating China to expose students to a spectrum of ideas: shame. Why had their society, once dominant on the world stage, fallen behind?

Informing Debate

Whereas the agents of change in China, schools like the Shanghai Party Institute, are government controlled, their counterparts in the India are more likely to come from civil society or the private sector.

For instance, Parliamentary Research Service (PRS) is an independent nonprofit research initiative founded by C. V. Madhukar.[5] Before launching PRS Madhukar spent ten months at Harvard's Kennedy School of Government and a year at the World Bank. He told me about the origins of PRS:

> I noticed that election debates in the United States usually raise a number of critical issues. On a flight back to India in October 2002, I watched a short clip of a debate for an upcoming state election in India. The debate was devoid of any meaningful references to either performance or policy. The contrast was striking. That was a disturbing flight, and potentially life changing for me. I wanted to find a way of "framing the debate" in elections. From that initial thought, the idea gradually evolved into Parliamentary Research Service.[6]

PRS ambitiously aims to change the nature of the conversation between India's leaders and the population they claim to lead. This dialogue relies on informed and intelligent public discussion. Nobel Prize winner Amartya Sen argues, in his *The Argumentative Indian*, that this is the essence of democracy. Per Sen, the Greeks had no monopoly on the idea of democracy. Discourse was a part of Buddhist *Sangha* (associations) and the court of the Mughal emperor, Akbar. *Rahi akal* (the way of reason) was a part of the latter's kingdom.[7]

Madhukar speaks passionately about the limitations of the existing conversation between citizens and their elected representatives. Often the interaction consists of constituents merely presenting an MP with lists of requests, casting the politician as the *annadata*, "the provider of food and other life necessities," and therefore omnipotent over citizens. Madhukar explained the relationship to me:

> It is not about any candidate's legislative record, or whether he has performed his other functions responsibly in Parliament. It does not also seem to matter that the candidate has a criminal record. It's about what this person has done for you, for your caste, for your street, for your neighborhood. Has he gotten you a phone connection? Your drain cleaned? Got you train tickets? Got someone in your family a job? Politics is very personal and local.
>
> It is not uncommon for someone to walk into the local MP's house and say, "My wife is sick and I need some money to take her to the hospital" or "My daughter is getting married and I need some money for the wedding." The MP, in many cases, takes money out of his pocket and gives for the sick wife or the daughter's wedding. This is the feudal mind-set. The politician becomes this all-powerful person who can get things done, and reinforces the patronage system. The average Indian thinks, "So long as he is able to address my immediate concerns, I should vote for him rather than someone who does not pay attention to the constituency after the elections are over."

Abstract issues like the nature of governance are exactly that—abstract.

Moreover, the educated and well-off opt out of the conversation altogether and are less likely to vote. This cynicism stems from a distaste of politics. When I reminded Madhukar that 25 percent of the Members of Parliament have criminal records, he said, "Let me tell you, if you present that figure, even the average educated person will disbelieve you. They think the numbers are higher than just 25 percent. Such is the lack of trust and confidence of the average educated Indian towards politicians." Others suggest caution at quantifying this number, because it might well include people who have cases lodged against them that are in interminable litigation. Nonetheless, few dispute the pervasiveness of a nexus between the very wealthy classes and politicians. Madhukar asks how one could expect otherwise:

> Election spending limits are still governed by archaic laws in India. Everyone knows you must spend a lot of money to win elections, and it is not legal to spend that much money. So you must be able to mobilize resources from people who can give you unaccounted-for cash, and that's where the problem begins. In fact, a committee back in 1993 examined the nexus between politicians and criminals and found enormous pressure mounted by political leaders to go slow when criminals are being investigated or prosecuted.

The average constituency of an MP is about two million residents, nearly three times that of a member of the U.S. House of Representatives. Yet the spending limit for an Indian MP election is a paltry Rs. 2.4 million (roughly $55,000). Even the Supreme Court called the election spending limit an "eyewash" and said that the law establishing it "has ceased to be even a fig leaf to hide the reality."[8]

PRS sees its primary role as giving politicians access to the reliable information needed for meaningful debate. Madhukar explains the monumental task he faces: "Our small team of analysts is trying to fulfill a similar role as the federally funded, nearly five hundred–person Congressional Research Service fulfills by providing inputs to members of the U.S. Congress. We provide facts and analysis to MPs and other stakeholders to make the debates in Parliament better informed. We do not make any recommendations but see our role as an explanatory one."

In the second quarter of 2006, for example, PRS produced five-page briefings on three bills due for debate in Parliament. The topics ranged from the prevention of communal violence to the forest rights of the disadvantaged "scheduled tribes of India" to the maintenance of India's diversity of seeds and crops. "In some sense, we are like the personal staff members of the U.S. Congress," Madhukar told me. "Not all Members of Parliament can be experts in all subjects."

PRS has been proactive. It anticipates issues that Parliament will likely discuss, tracks its success by measuring the use of its services by Members of Parliament, and predicts the kinds of requests that have begun to come its way from various political parties. Encouragingly for its nonpartisan image, requests come from across the political spectrum. Some briefs the team has written lately are on topics like suicides among farmers in rural India, terrorism in India in the past decade, and the Indo-U.S. nuclear deal. Madhukar gave me other examples:

> Recently, when a bill discussing financial derivatives came up in Parliament, we had a Member of Parliament call us at 10 p.m. the night before the debate for help understanding what derivatives were. Or take the case when the government hiked the prices of petrol—a major political party called PRS late on a Sunday evening and asked for background on fuel price hikes in the past decade, their origins and effects, before they decided their public stance on the issue. It is these moments that make us feel that we are adding value to the nature of the debate; and fortunately for us, more and more MPs from across party lines are calling us for inputs.

Perhaps the ultimate accolade for Madhukar was a speaking request from neighboring Pakistan, surely a bid to raise the quality of analogous conversation there.

PRS faces many challenges, the primary one being the time needed to change behavior. A sea change is required for politicians to reject the presumption that they are masters of the universe and embrace debate that is grounded in specialized information. Likewise, MPs need to start considering themselves accountable, rather than casting every vote as a show of hands, which is not documented in parliamentary records. To help effect these changes, PRS must be viable for the long haul. Grants from the Ford Foundation launched PRS, but it needs a workable funding model for the future, with various stakeholders paying enough for the organization's services to allow it to continue investing in relevant research without compromising its independence and integrity. Among the issues confronting PRS are whether to specialize in certain topics and whether to restrict itself to Parliament or to expand its horizons to include the state assemblies.

Pathways of History

Mao Zedong, standing in Tiananmen Square before the Heavenly Gate on October 1, 1949, announced that the "Chinese people have stood up"—*zhong guo ren zan qi lai le*. Less than two years earlier, Jawaharlal Nehru acted as midwife to India's birth. At the stroke of midnight on August 15, 1947, a lone unidentified enthusiast in India's Constituent Assembly blew a conch shell—a traditional call to the Gods in a Hindu temple—and Nehru proclaimed, "Long years ago we made a tryst with destiny, and now the time comes when we shall redeem our pledge, not wholly or in full measure, but very substantially." Thus a third of humanity reentered the world polity, for the first time in several centuries, on its own terms.

How did the Chinese and Indian governments get where they are today? What legacy does each country inherit and shoulder as it opens up to the twenty-first century? Although this book focuses on the first years of the new millennium, its questions require a look back at the story of how each country entered the modern era and the consequent choices initiated by the clarion calls of Mao and Nehru. The trajectories China and India followed in the second half of the twentieth century to reach their respective and very different goals are a study in differences, the very differences each country must now understand about the other if both are to deepen their relationship for future dialogues.

China: The Promise and Perils of Hierarchical Governance

Traditionally, the Chinese used ritual to achieve their ideal of harmony. Rituals ensure that people do what they are supposed to, predictably. Laws, in contrast, engendered trickery as people found ways around them—they were meant for times when ritual broke down.

Arguably, the emphasis on ritual arose with Confucius (551–479 BCE). One can speculate that this quest for stability itself was a reaction to a period of incredible turmoil at the time he was advocating his views.[9] The signature imprints of some of these rituals are discernible today. Rituals are specific to one's station in life's hierarchy, and one has no right to appeal the decision of someone in a higher position in the hierarchy.[10] But—and this was Confucius's revolutionary innovation—one's station in life is not a function of birth but a result of merit and moral fitness that can be aspired to and acquired. The scholar-bureaucrats who ran China for millennia arose from a quest for such personal fitness that, in turn, led to positions of influence. Mao's unchallenged writ in the PRC was akin to that of the so-called Son of Heaven.[11] Today's analogue is the group of people atop the CCP hierarchy, people who achieved their positions through competition and whose political will remains unchallenged.

The Legacies of Mao Zedong

We must affirm anew the discipline of the Party, namely:

(1) the individual is subordinate to the organization;
(2) the minority is subordinate to the majority;
(3) the lower level is subordinate to the higher level; and
(4) the entire membership is subordinate to the Central Committee.

Whoever violates these articles of discipline disrupts Party unity.

—Mao Zedong[12]

Chinese statecraft has always aimed for order, harmony, and hierarchy. In 1949, when Mao led the CCP to victory over the Guomindang (Chinese Nationalist Party) in a hard-fought civil war, he made it clear that China would be ruled by a single party and he would be its undisputed leader. The country's harmony and order, as well as its destiny, would be intimately linked to a hierarchy, at the apex of which ruled Mao Zedong and a close-knit group from the CCP.

Mao promptly set about reorganizing the military to bring the country under the control of his People's Liberation Army. Then he took economic, political, and administrative control by nationalizing the banks and putting himself in charge of all credit. He established state control over grain procurement, production, and sale, and exercised control over many private companies.[13] He created administrative cadres that would carry out the communist revolution according to Mao Zedong thought, a mixture of Marxism and Leninism. The CCP's membership of 2.7 million in 1947 grew to 6.1 million by 1953.[14]

Mao established a constitution in 1954. For all practical purposes the Chinese government became subordinate to the CCP, its role simply to implement party policies. The primary organs of state power were the National People's Congress, the president, and the State Council. Within the State Council a hierarchical layer of congresses, each answerable to the one above it, was established at all levels of administration. But real power was exercised by the CCP committees that shadowed each level of government. Mao held the state chairmanship; the army reported to the Military Affairs Commission, which reported to Mao; and the Party controlled public security. Putting himself at the head of the Party and the government, Mao preserved the mandate of Confucian tradition, that hierarchy is key to preserving social order and, by extension, good governance.

In the 1950s Mao unrolled his economic program called collectivization, replacing the village economy and organizing the entire rural peasantry into agricultural communes. All activities in rural China—production, schooling, education, farming, and social and cultural events—transpired within this ordered framework. As a result of collectivization the individual Chinese peasant was buried under six layers of state administration. At the top was the province, followed by the prefecture, county, commune, brigade, and production teams. Hierarchy and order were presumed to bring about harmony. The urban corollary to the commune was the work unit, or *danwei*, through which people were employed, paid, housed, educated, provided health and medical insurance—and thus controlled. Like the commune, the *danwei* was a community that achieved the goals of order, harmony, and hierarchy.

Any country hoping to engage in meaningful dialogue with China must recognize that the flip side of order, harmony, and hierarchy are rigidity, censorship, and state control. In the decade beginning in 1958, Mao presided over two massive socioeconomic and political disasters. First, the Great Leap Forward embodied Mao's belief that China ought to embark on rapid development of both agricultural and industrial sectors by using its massive supply of cheap labor. His vision was implemented with extraordinary zeal by cadres throughout the country. Tragically, this phase ended in a massive man-made famine in which nearly thirty million Chinese perished.

The second disaster was the Cultural Revolution, a political movement initiated by Mao. The People's Liberation Army and the Red Guards brutally muted opposition within the CCP's ranks. By the end of the Cultural Revolution a hundred million Chinese had been publicly denounced, exiled, "reformed," or, in the case of ten million people, killed.[15] Although Mao's death in 1976 essentially ended these brutalities, memories linger of the violence done to those who oppose government order.

Deng Xiaoping: Taking China from One Red Star to Many Expert Stars

Twice purged and rehabilitated under Mao's political experiments, Deng Xiaoping was a CCP stalwart who assumed full power in 1978. He was aware that the excesses of the Cultural Revolution had cost the party its legitimacy and that the CCP needed new thinking, new leadership, and new slogans. Deng recruited experts into the party, valued for their technical excellence rather than ideological purity. He famously intoned, "It does not matter whether the cat is black or white as long as it catches the mice." Thus a communist regime presided over the greatest capitalist makeover in history.

Like the imposition of Mao Zedong thought, promulgation of Deng Xiaoping's theory was systematic and relentless. Deng embarked on creating Party cadres and state officials who would effectively carry out his reform agenda—creating a distinctive socialist market economy. Administrative reforms focused on professionalizing state bureaucracy, imposing a rule of law, and regulating the market. Although Deng's reforms were not accompanied by the widespread violence of Mao's political and administrative restructuring, no doubt Deng did benefit from the reputation of Maoist excesses. Opposing the CCP remained unfathomable. Indeed, the CCP still controlled the state, CCP members still monopolized top ministerial positions in government, and the CCP was still in charge of the People's Liberation Army.

Administrative reforms continued parallel to policy changes. At the outset of the reforms, only a small percentage of Party leaders at every level of the hierarchy were college educated—at most 20 percent and by some estimates only 4 percent. Although China was primarily an agricultural country, just 3.6 percent of leading cadres in charge of agriculture at the provincial, prefecture, and county levels had formal training in agriculture.[16] The pressure for professionalism was intense. To qualify as a Party member, applicants had to go through a one-year probationary period to prove themselves both "red" (ideologically aligned to Deng) and "expert" (technically qualified). Under Mao, workers and peasants were the foundation of the Party, intellectuals had no place. Deng's innovation was to recategorize some intellectuals as "workers."

Edgar Snow had immortalized Mao's ascent with the epithet "Red Star over China" in his 1930s memoir describing the advent of CCP supremacy.[17] But under Deng that one Red Star no longer sufficed. A host of expert stars was ascendant.

In an August 1980 speech Deng declared that power was overcentralized and concentrated in the hands of individuals who often acted arbitrarily, following no institutionalized procedures. He abolished the bureaucratic practice of life tenure for senior positions and in 1981 proposed recruiting a younger, better-educated leadership corps from among cadres who had trained at colleges or technical secondary schools. The CCP's Central Committee and the State Council decided in 1982 that cadres at central agencies of the party and government must reach the level of a polytechnic or college education in three to five years, thus promoting an ethos for diligence and excellence.

Deng's critics claimed that his administrative reforms did not go far enough in practice. Existing CCP cadres responded creatively to subvert the reforms. For example, in "diploma mania," cadres inflated their educational backgrounds by upgrading the levels of the universities they had attended some two decades ago or by forging or simply buying diplomas.[18] But by the summer of 1985 Deng had persuaded nearly half of 470,000 veteran officials to retire, and two years later an additional 70,000 were drawing generous pensions. Deng had exchanged pension packages for new ideas and ushered in an entirely new generation of educated, high-caliber bureaucrats whose success is still felt today.

The other most important element of Deng Xiaoping's reforms was the state officials' and Party cadres' adjustment to the new socialist market economy. "Enterprise mania" resulted.[19] Some cadres and officials found their way onto company boards and payrolls. Their connections expedited the entrepreneurs' work. Other cadres participated in the enterprise fever by investing in companies formed by local businessmen. Thus a Party official might serve not only as a bureaucrat but also as a shareholder. Some state officials set up shadow companies, using the financial resources of the state-owned firms they managed.

The 1989 Tiananmen Square pro-democracy protests in Beijing, called the June 4th movement in China, were a strong reminder that the CCP's grip on power was undiminished. Growth slowed, but resumed following Deng's famous tours of southern China, re-emphasizing economic reform. Thus, over two decades the world watched in awe as the CCP transformed China economically. China's GDP per capita rose from $673 in 1978 to $5,878 in 2005.[20] Further, the number of people living in absolute poverty dropped from roughly 250 million in 1978 to an estimated 26 million in 2004.[21]

Lost in Translation: Government and Party as Entrepreneur

In 2001 President Jiang Zemin's announcement of his theory of "Three Represents" confused the Chinese and China watchers. What was implied in phrases like "advanced social productive forces," "the progressive course of China's advanced culture," and "the fundamental interests of the majority"? Why was Jiang talking in euphemisms? Did "advanced social forces" mean "businessmen"? Did the phrase "fundamental interests of the majority" mean "democracy"? The clear communication required for meaningful dialogue seemed lacking, and the meaning of Chinese communism—built on Marx, Lenin, Mao, and even Deng—seemed lost in translation.

In fact, Jiang was primarily rationalizing the recruitment of the most successful private entrepreneurs into the CCP. Despite the press hoopla around this event, however, the 2001 announcement was official recognition of the emergence over the last decade or so of a new class of entrepreneurs—often known as red capitalists—who also held Party membership. One scholar has called this the "ex-post legitimization of a long-standing fact."[22] In the late 1990s some 40 percent of surveyed entrepreneurs across several provinces were deemed CCP members. Many were *xiahai* entrepreneurs—former officials who left their posts and plunged into the sea of the private economy;

others were successful entrepreneurs who had subsequently been convinced to join the Party.[23] Gradually, hybrids of public and private sectors thus emerged, allowing the CCP to reinvent itself successfully and pragmatically. The Party had successfully broadened its membership base. By 2006 it had 71 million members.[24]

As Party members' involvement in business grew so did corruption. The Central Discipline Inspection Commission (CDIC) suggests that the probability of criminal penalties against corrupt cadres is almost negligible. According to a CDIC report published in 2006, roughly 82 percent of CCP members known to have committed acts of corruption received nothing more than a slap on the wrist. Further, of those punished, only about 18 percent were expelled from the CCP during the six-year phase covered by the report.[25]

Chinese citizens rely on a petitioning system for reporting acts of official corruption. The roots of this system go back to imperial China, when persons claiming that local officials had violated their rights could take their petitions all the way to the highest levels of government. The modern petitioner appeals to the State Ministry, the People's Supreme Court, or the National People's Congress.

I visited the Beijing Petition Office on Justice Road, just east of Changan Avenue, within walking distance of Tiananmen Square. Tall trees provide succor from summer heat, and an unusually long divider separated traffic bound in opposite directions. Tour buses mingled amidst taxis and bicycles. Police cars were ubiquitous and surveillance equipment was easy to spot, but the large red gate of the Petition Reception Office was closed. Many of the people waiting were plaintiffs, and most were there to demand compensation for being laid off from state-owned enterprises or other government entities. One person expressed the frustration of the crowd: "Who would come here if they don't have any case? We all have our grievances . . . We come here three days a week, others come the other two days. We select a representative to go inside, telling them how many of us are present. I have worked for the military for almost thirty years in the northeast but ended up with nothing. Lawyers' starting charge is five thousand yuan (six hundred dollars). How can laid-off workers come up with such money?"[26]

Ultimately, faith in the petition process is naive. Beijing responds to a very small fraction of petitions, two of every thousand. A perverse irony worsens petitioners' fates. The State Ministry has installed a grading system to rank each local government based on the number of petitions it generates: the more petitions, the worse the ranking. Thus when petitioners arrive in Beijing, instead of safely voicing their concerns, they are sometimes intercepted by local law officials from their own cities. The officers interrogate and threaten the petitioners and often send them home.

Legend has it that Bao Gong, a Song dynasty courtier was given a golden rod, which authorized him to censor the Emperor. Alas, there is no modern analogy as the CCP is beyond reproach.

Unlike economic decision making, political decision making in China is not decentralized. Party bureaucrats have some economic freedom to implement policies in their provinces, but they have no political freedom to question directives from the central decision-making offices in Beijing. The management of the tension between economic freedom and political obeisance is integral to China's ongoing development.

In fact, many Chinese are familiar with the phrases *lìchǎng* (standpoint), *guān diǎn* (viewpoint), and *fāngfǎ* (method). Translated, this essentially means that a qualified Party official must have a firm political (communist) standpoint and viewpoint along with right thinking and working methods.

India: The Promise and Perils of Pluralism

Whereas harmony through merit-based autocracy is a defining characteristic of the Chinese state, the Indian state is probably best characterized by pluralism. India's diversity is so great that a key to sustaining its democracy has been finding a way to balance the often inconsistent demands of various groups with the needs of the collective.[27] The good news is that the Indian system has worked to devolve power so that influence and prestige are distributed to more than the usual socioeconomic elites to include several disparate historically disenfranchised groups. The bad news is that this accommodation has often come at the expense of useful collective action.[28]

Democracy

"My legacy to India? Hopefully it is 400 million people capable of governing themselves."

—Jawaharlal Nehru

Nehru was deeply skeptical of authoritarianism, and India watchers were skeptical of his vision of a democratic India, asserting that the country was too poor, too big, too diverse, too illiterate, and ultimately just too complex. But in 1950 Nehru and other leaders presented their people with the Indian Constitution, enshrining in law a plural, secular, socialist, democratic India. It would have all the trappings of a "checks and balances' democracy: free elections based on universal suffrage, a parliament, a judiciary, a legislature, a civil service, and a free press.

A year later an independent body, the Election Commission, was entrusted with carrying out the largest elections ever held anywhere in the world. The odds—logistical, physical, and financial—were staggering: 176 million voters deciding from among more than seventeen thousand candidates from seventy-five political parties contesting 489 parliamentary seats and 3,375 state legislature seats. Remote villages, previously unreachable, were involved. The Indian navy provided polling stations in remote islands off the coast of India. In the course of a nine-week tour, Nehru covered twenty-five thousand miles, committing to secularism and the abolition of "untouchablility" and "landlordism"—arguably the two biggest impediments to modern development. In an election with a respectable 60 percent turnout, his Congress Party achieved a landslide victory.

Once the election was won, good governance had to be established. Nehru envisaged a federal system with central and state governments. Defense, foreign affairs, atomic energy, banking, and communication would be governed by the central government, while police, management of local governments, trade, commerce, and agriculture would be the responsibility of the state governments. The central and the state governments together would deal with criminal and civil procedures, marriage and divorce, education, economic planning, and trade unions.

Unfortunately, this attempt to strike a balance between autonomy and unity had the unintended effect of stymying governance and policy implementation. Several layers of horizontal and vertical chains of command, all intertwined by legislation and subject to electoral vagaries, made it nearly impossible to implement any policy speedily, a problem India still wrestles with. The issues of weak accountability and little transparency that modern India faces are also rooted in Nehru's nightmarish federal system.

Nehru chose to retain the "steel frame" of India, the Indian Civil Service—a group of highly educated, elite professionals organized into three categories: one serving the entire country and the other two intended to serve the central government and each state government. Members were recruited on the basis of rigorous examinations conducted by an apolitical body. In independent India the Indian Civil Service was renamed the Indian Administrative Services (IAS).

Nehru envisioned an economy controlled by the public sector. He believed that only the state could redistribute wealth equitably in favor of the majority and that India was too vast and too poor to risk everything on the "market mechanism." By Nehru's logic, for example, government-owned banks would lend to sectors like agriculture that otherwise would not attract funds. This thinking fueled the creation of a large public sector and a massive bureaucracy to implement distribution and redistribution of all resources and goods.

A Flirtation with Dictatorship

When Mrs. Indira Gandhi, Nehru's daughter, was elected prime minister of India in 1965, she inherited a country that lay under a heavy malaise. Three years earlier Nehru, unwavering in his belief in solidarity among developing nations, especially between two socialist countries, underestimated China's determination and military capabilities and moved into border territories without listening to Chinese opposition. Chinese forces struck, initiating the Sino-Indian War. China won, and India continues to feel the wounds of its defeat, despite the eventual reopening of the Nathu La, the Himalayan pass that serves as a trading border post between China and India.

The government Indira Gandhi inherited had become synonymous with corruption and inefficiency. India was still desperately poor, with most people lacking access to the basics—water, education, health care and sanitation. Indira Gandhi's solution was to dragoon the economy into a miasma of regulation. One statesman called this, tongue in cheek, the "License Raj," correctly foreseeing its deleterious effects on the economy. Middle-class citizens were so ensnared in daily bureaucratic processes over such mundane tasks as paying an electric bill or acquiring a telephone that nothing was accomplished without *baksheesh*, or bribes. The economist Raj Krishna coined the phrase, Hindu rate of growth, to describe the pathetic 3.5 percent annual growth rate from 1950 to 1980 that doomed India and Indians of the time to mediocrity.

Unlike Nehru, Indira Gandhi used her ascent to power and her clarion call for *Garibi Hatao* (Remove Poverty) as a mandate to centralize power. She argued that Nehru's steel frame, the IAS, as a remnant of the British Raj, was elitist in nature. While thus far the civil services had enjoyed considerable credibility based on their professional qualifications and apolitical past, under Mrs. Gandhi the IAS became a pawn on a political chessboard. Sanjay Gandhi, the prime minister's younger son and key adviser, presided over a notorious culture that prized loyalty to his mother and himself above all else. He was often accused of circumventing the law, sometimes quite blatantly.

The politics of Indira Gandhi reached a climax in 1975 when, responding to accusations of electoral fraud and facing a political crisis, she declared a national emergency, suspending the constitution, muting the free press and jailing opposition leaders. Under increasing pressure Mrs. Gandhi called for an election in 1977. In a vote dubbed a victory for Indian democracy, the Congress Party lost to a hastily assembled coalition called the Bharatiya Janata Party (*janata* means "people" in Hindi). Apparently, regardless of how ineffectual and chaotic democracy seemed to Indians, they were not ready to give it up.

The Janata government miscalculated its popularity when it arrested Mrs. Mrs. Gandhi for alleged crimes committed during the national emergency.

The public viewed Mrs. Gandhi as the victim and returned her to power in the 1980 elections after the Janata government collapsed from infighting. Thus began the biggest paradox of Indian democracy. A politician who had been accused of electoral fraud and had arbitrarily suspended the constitution of the country, arrested political leaders and journalists, and presided over a deeply corrupt government was reelected and leading the country again. Today parochial interests still rule and Indians still elect unsavory individuals to public office in free and fair elections.

Checked-and-Balanced into Paralysis

By 1991 decades of economic mismanagement had created a financial crisis. The fiscal deficit was at an unsustainable 8.5 percent of GDP. Foreign exchange reserves—money needed to pay for imports—had sunk to around one billion dollars, roughly equal to two weeks of imports. Under Finance Minister Manmohan Singh, the government introduced unprecedented economic reforms. Unlike China, however, India focused its reforms on the financial and industrial sectors, not the agricultural sector comprising the villages where most Indians lived. Although the 1991 reforms were incredibly significant for unleashing the Indian private sector, they did much less for improving the efficiency of basic institutions of the state.

The start of India's reform era marked the end of the dominant party system and the advent of coalition politics. Since 1989, no single party had held a majority in Parliament. In 1991, when Congress ushered in economic reforms, it was leading a coalition of several regional parties that were by nature combative, focusing on the expediency of plebiscitary politics rather than the efficiency of clearly outlined policy. The costs of an unstable economic agenda are visible in India's halting efforts at privatization.

At the end of 1992 the government owned majority equity capital in 1,180 firms categorized as government companies: 239 owned by the central government and 941 by state governments.[29] Inefficiencies were well documented in many of the firms. Unlike China, however, India could not launch privatization by executive order. It needed legislative clearance that was unlikely to come from the fractured legislature run by coalitions.

The Indian Iron and Steel Company (IISCO), a subsidiary of the Steel Authority of India Limited, had accumulated losses of nearly nine billion rupees, equal to roughly two hundred million dollars in recent years. A buyout by the private company Mukund Limited was seen as more likely to restore the viability of IISCO than having the government put in more money. Because IISCO had been nationalized by acts of Parliament, bringing in a private firm required abolition of the acts. But the fractured legislature could not do that; the left-wing parties simply would not allow it. Mukund withdrew in frustration.

Within this political context rose Arun Shourie. A Syracuse University-trained, former World Bank economist, Shourie made a name for himself in Indian journalism by exposing some of the country's biggest political scandals in the 1980s. In 2000 he was reincarnated as "disinvestment czar," a colloquialism of his real title, union minister of disinvestment. The word *disinvestment*—intended to highlight the withdrawal of government equity—was a euphemism for privatization.

Shourie did not have long to wait before his first test. When he decided to sell Bharat Aluminum, its workers threatened to fast until death.[30] Shourie was unmoved and launched the bidding process. A strike lasted two months, but the company was sold to a private entity for Rs. 4.7 billion (about $115 million). Next on Shourie's target was Maruti-Udyog, a joint venture between the government and Japan's Suzuki Motors. Suzuki was allowed to increase its share, and part of the government's share was offered to the Indian public. When Maruti-Udyog went on sale the response was overwhelming. The issue was oversubscribed tenfold.

Although Shourie considered the sale a victory for his privatization initiative, his euphoria was short lived. Despite its relative transparency, the process of privatization had never been entirely depoliticized. When Shourie put up for sale two state-run oil firms in 2002, every party immediately attacked him. Defense Minister George Fernandes, a member of Shourie's Bharatiya Janata Party (BJP), believed the sale was a threat to India's energy security already unsettled by the conflict with neighboring Pakistan.[31] Manmohan Singh, the architect of the 1991 reforms and a member of the opposition, was against the sale as well. In September 2003 the Indian courts also came into the picture and ruled that privatization of two state oil companies required a vote in Parliament. Shourie's privatization effort, for which he had won acclaim in the international press, stalled, and India's checked-and-balanced paralysis was reaffirmed.

When Shourie and the BJP were voted out of power, in a widely unanticipated electoral verdict, some colleagues at Columbia University and I decided to objectively analyze the privatization debacle. For social scientists, a surprise event like the electoral reverse is quite revealing. Stock prices often move dramatically in response to such surprises. These movements reveal how the markets, and by inference the investing public, interpret the event. In this case, the stocks of companies slated for privatization plunged more than seven percentage points in a day. The market had expected the prospects of the firms to improve once the BJP had privatized them, and when those efforts proved disappointing, the market reversed the gains those firms had been enjoying.

We also discovered that there was a way in which, apparently, privatization could be made less reversible, at least in the eyes of investors. Those state-owned firms slated for privatization and making credible progress toward that goal—such as laying off surplus employees—did not see their stock price gains reversed by nearly as much. In contrast, those for which privatization announcements were not accompanied by credible action—that is, when there was just cheap talk that served to stall and, yes, paralyze— were dismissed by investors.

As it turned out, cheap talk outstripped credible action. Most of the excitement about privatization came to naught, ensnared in the checkerboard of Indian politics.

Making the Trains Run on Time

However interesting it may be to examine whether India's infrastructure should be privately or publicly owned, perhaps more useful is to take a closer look on the ground at the damages to daily life wrought by India's political paralysis. One example is Indian Railways, originally installed by the British in 1853 and now employing more than 1.6 million people, making it the world's largest commercial or utility employer. The trains travel the length and width of India, covering a total of 39,462 miles. As a boy I often traveled a small portion of those miles in summer trips with my family from Delhi to Bombay.

The Hazrat Nizamuddin Train Station is only a few minutes' drive from my grandmother's imposing brick house in old Delhi where my schoolboy journeys began, but it took my family a half hour to navigate the narrow, snaking lanes, *galees*, congested with street hawkers, roadside barbers, and meandering cows. When we finally reached the station, which was ancient even in the 1970s, we were accosted by *coolies* (porters) dressed in unwashed red uniforms, the standard government-issue attire, and *pagrees*, cloth headdresses. I remember emerging from the car to a crush of people, baggage, and stray dogs. Families stood, sat, or milled about, patiently waiting for a train that would leave at some future, indeterminate time. My father engaged a *coolie*, who piled our suitcases impossibly high on his wiry frame and ran improbably fast through the crowd to our train, where he was appropriately compensated by my frazzled father. Before boarding the train, typically a dirty brown row of cars with cream-colored roofs, we joined the other travelers peering at a seating chart posted at the end of each compartment. Invariably one or two passengers found that their month-old reservations had not secured their privileged seats. Vociferous supplications and threats were directed toward the omnipotent conductors, who rationed out the seats to the pleading travelers, presumably not without a great deal of money changing hands.

This might remain a quaint memory but for the fact that with a few exceptions, such as the sophisticated and excellent Delhi subway system, the situation remains unchanged today. Indian railway carriages are still routinely crowded with two or three times as many passengers as they are meant to carry, making every arrival and departure a stampede of hundreds of people; a massive, surging sea of humanity jostling to find their bags in the caboose, and then solicited by dozens of coolies for the job of carrying those bags to waiting cars. More than an inconvenience for passengers, overcrowding often permits passengers without tickets to sneak aboard, leading to financial losses for Indian Railways. Moreover, railway accidents cause about three hundred deaths a year, most caused by people being run over by trains.

In Bombay Central Station, where we disembarked during my childhood summer sojourns, I remember often arriving to a city submerged in knee-deep water—a result of the summer monsoons and substandard city drainage. We children sailed paper boats on the flooded roads; motorists, who had abandoned their cars by the roadside until the water receded, went to great trouble to protect the matches they needed to dry out their carburetors once it became possible to restart their cars. This extreme flooding, a direct result of a mismanaged and thoroughly faulty government infrastructure, happened in Bombay as recently as 2005.

Government-owned utilities need not succumb to the deplorable inefficiency of Indian Railways and the Bombay sewer system. China's Maglev train is a striking case in point. *Sleek, efficient, immaculate,* and *orderly* were adjectives that immediately came to mind during my first high-speed ride from Shanghai airport to Pudong. A space-age construction based on German technology, the rail was built by the Chinese government in just three years, with exactly one accident (no injuries) in two and a half years of operation. *Maglev* is short for "magnetic levitation"—itself a metaphor for China's prowess—whereby a magnet on the bottom of the train runs over a piece of metal "track," causing electric currents to flow through the metal and produce enough force to push the magnet upward.

Maglev may be an exception, but even regular trains—that is, public services—work far better in China than in India. A train ride I took from Nanjing to Shanghai revealed the differences. The Nanjing Station resembles a modern airport, not the New Delhi–like higgledy-piggledy of human activity. The architecture of the Chinese station is not unusual—rows of platforms into which trains pulled in with overarching pedestrian bridges—but Nanjing's modern escalators are in sharp contrast to the dilapidated stairs, often crowded with beggars, that one is forced to climb in New Delhi. The government employees of the train station look worn down in New Delhi; in Nanjing, they were smartly dressed, some in maroon uniforms and some in white. Finding a seat is not a chore in Nanjing, one seat is not assigned to many people, and, although crowded, the trains move smoothly toward on-time arrivals, all unlike New Delhi. The only time when there are hundreds of people milling around the station is during Chinese New Year when all of China is on the move. In short, public services work in China.

Meaningful Dialogue Redux

Whereas order, harmony, and hierarchy have been the constant goals of the Chinese state, India has a proud tradition of pluralism, dissent, and debate. Anyone seeking to engage in dialogue with these countries must understand the fundamentally different ideologies and political antecedents of their current practices. They are deep seated and long lived.

If the CCP wants to continue to run China, it must work toward meeting the rising aspirations of an increasingly greater proportion of the people, moving beyond providing basic material goods and services. Its success has sown the seeds of its future challenges. Its hold on power is predicated on a sufficient number of people continuing to accept efficient provision of material needs, and perhaps the lure of Party membership, in exchange for letting the Party delay political freedoms further into the future.

The Indian state must embrace a culture of accountability. Heterodoxy and diversity are justly celebrated attributes of a plural India but to be truly laudable, they must foster democracy rather than slow it down. While India has had celebrated periods where constructive discourse among its diverse constituencies was the order of the day, modern India has not adequately capitalized on democracy.

Chapter Three

Bias and Noise

Information Accessibility in China and India

Not long ago, on a trip to Shenzhen, city that's home to iPod manufacturing Huawei headquarters, and gleaming new skyscrapers on the Pearl River Delta, I logged on to the Internet. I soon noticed that many Web sites I visited featured two cartoon characters dressed in blue and black uniforms. At first I took them to be the mascots for Beijing's 2008 Olympic games, *Fuwa*, a set of five dolls symbolizing friendship; but a closer look told me that the Disney-inspired characters were, in fact, police officers: a male officer named *"Jing,"* and a female officer named *"Cha."* Added together, *"Jing"* and *"Cha"* make the Chinese word for police, *"jingcha."* What are two cartoon police officers doing on the Internet? They are censors, designed to alert Chinese netizens that the government monitors their online activity.

Of course government censorship and information control in China are not new. For years China has claimed that media channels—newspapers, magazines, radio, and television—can be used to spread antigovernment ideas and propaganda that destabilize society by increasing the possibility of political dissent. The phrase, *wending yadao yiqie*, which means "stability overrides anything," is a central belief in the Chinese government and as a tool for maintaining stability, censorship has long been justified and accepted. What is new is that as China hears and is heard by the world, its information restrictions pose challenges to potentially profitable communication

India's information access policies and practices are the opposite of China's. Visitors to India find themselves puzzled by the onslaught of media and information. No subject is taboo for India's free press. Every shade of opinion is expressed, largely free of political propaganda and interference; every political crisis is reported with great passion; and Indian political leaders are perpetually criticized in magazines and newspapers, and on televisions across the country. This confrontational attitude has empowered people to use information to voice concerns, disappointments, and dissent. But media credibility is not a given. It is earned through competition and safeguarded by rules—imperfectly enforced, but rules nonetheless. Although India's information environment is transparent compared with China's, it suffers from what statisticians call white noise. The truth is hidden in a morass of irrelevant, though not intentionally inaccurate, information.

Given these starkly opposing attitudes toward disseminating and accessing information, how can China and India communicate? How can Western countries access and interpret information in China and India? The Indian system generates noisy but unbiased information; the Chinese system generates noise-free but biased information. Once again, each country's strength is the other country's weakness.

India's Tehelka.com: Exposing Corruption

In March 2001 Tarun Tejpal, a fixture in India's journalism scene, created a sensation, a *tehelka*, by exposing the biggest political scandal in the almost half century of independent India's existence. Tejpal's Web-based news magazine, Tehelka.com, released a video of the climax of a sting operation it devised: a senior politician from the ruling party was shown taking a bribe in an apparently clandestine defense deal.

Tehelka.com called the sting "Operation West End." The video both shocked and surprised the nation. The shock stemmed not from the fact that political corruption at the highest level had been made known; sadly, the common man (*aam admi*) in India accepts corruption among government officials as a fact.[1] What surprised the nation was the modus operandi of the exposé. A relatively small, non-traditional media outlet had caught a politician in the actual act of accepting the bribe. In the days that followed, Defense Minister George Fernandes resigned and Bangaru Laxman, president of the ruling Bharatiya Janata Party and the protagonist of the sting video, was expelled from his party. Ten days after Tehelka.com released the tapes, the government embarked on a three-year-long vendetta against Tehelka, raiding its offices and those of its angel investors, ostensibly for investigating income tax compliance, and thus provoking a protracted legal battle between Tejpal and the government.

Tejpal commented, with obvious emotion, in his small, unglamorous New Delhi office, "We were run into the ground. You should have seen the stuff they had in court filings. They accused us of being Dawood's people, ISI's people. They accused us of bringing down the stock market.[2] They were vicious in their assault. I had a staff of 125 reduced to 4. Every day we were selling a chair here and desk there to keep up with legal fees for the twenty lawyers fighting our cases."[3]

The two journalists who carried out the sting, Aniruddha Bahal and Mathew Samuel, became sitting ducks in the government hunt, and another Tehelka.com reporter, Kumar Badal, was jailed for six months before being released by the Supreme Court. Tejpal himself was linked to the opposition party. On trial were the Web magazine's investigative methods— Tehelka.com used prostitutes to bait the defense officials—and its primary motive for carrying out the sting operation, allegedly to bring down the government.

Six months after resigning from his post, Defense Minister Fernandes regained his title, and eventually Bangaru Laxman was accepted back into his political party, albeit with his political career emasculated. Despite Tehelka.com's bankruptcy, Tejpal has resuscitated his organization in the form of the weekly newspaper Tehelka, which boasts a rapidly growing readership, now at 75,000. Indeed, as proof of his ubiquitous presence, when I was on a recent trip to New Delhi, a street vendor thrust the latest exposé in my hands, asking for 20 cents. Tejpal also remains surprisingly upbeat for a man whose twenty-two-year stellar journalism career seemed virtually destroyed in the aftermath of the scandal. "I am very optimistic about Indian journalism. The Tehelka story is a pointer not to how democracy in India does not work but to how well it works . . . Tehelka told the story, survived its telling, and is back doing more of the same now . . . [M]oreover, we created the paper in the teeth of the same administration that had run us to the ground."

Clearly the Tehelka.com episode prompted several important, albeit largely intangible, changes. The private media's new activist role has won many supporters, particularly among the Indian middle classes for whom Tarun Tejpal reached the status of hero. It was no coincidence that soon after the Tehelka.com scandal broke, Indian Express, one of India's leading dailies, printed stills from a video it received showing a central minister accepting a cash bribe. Television channels aired the video. Although the minister protested his innocence, he was expelled from the central government. The media has gone from being a passive, often cynical observer of Indian politics to one with some clout.

China's *Caijing:* Pushing Boundaries

In Beijing I spoke with a journalist and editor at *Caijing*—the name means "finance and economy"—who agreed to an interview on the condition of anonymity. Like Tarun Tejpal, he has twenty years' experience and unique insight into the role of the media in his country. I was interested in *Caijing* because the independent publication is a sign that information is becoming more accessible in China. On the day of our meeting in 2005, I stepped from a sunny Beijing thoroughfare into the dark *Caijing* offices. My eyes adjusted to the lower ambient light. I mused that this adjustment was akin to what Chinese readers must be going through—transitioning from brightly whitewashed news to more the accurate shades of gray that newer media seek to provide. Then, as if to underscore the change in the media climate, the editor greeted me by saying, "Twenty years ago we would not have been able to meet with you."[4]

During our lengthy conversation the editor explained how Chinese investigative journalism, at least of the economic and business variety, had emerged gradually. The reforms of the 1970s left most of the media set up, subsidized by, or otherwise beholden to the state. Until the early 1980s everything ran according to the plan devised and orchestrated by the central government, a plan that obviated the need for the analyses that business newspapers could provide. But by the mid- to late 1980s many companies facing the onset of competition from the increasing presence of foreign enterprises, began to need detailed, accurate business data and analyses. At first, companies were not sure what they needed, as accustomed as they were to receiving government instruction. The government, not knowing what information to provide, initially launched publications with pedestrian, descriptive data—for example, where coal was available and how to get textiles. It took until the mid-1990s for Chinese companies and consumers to increase in their level of sophistication, and in that climate, *Caijing* was born. Indeed, their offices resemble any newsroom in the West, with dozens of reporters busy meeting editorial deadlines.

As my editor informant continued, I realized that *Caijing's* physical setting was deceptive. "Table tennis is very popular in China," he said. "We have a term called 'edge hitting' . . . [I]f you can hit the table tennis ball to the other side and get the edge of the table, the ball shoots off, and it becomes very difficult for your opponent to respond. That's what we try to do, we try to find the edges, the boundaries, of what is allowed."[5] As it turns out, "what is allowed" is not strictly defined. Although business journalists say the government imposes no limits on investigating issues in business—in fact, the authorities especially welcome the exposure of media coverage—this openness is true only in business reporting. Journalism that questions political decision making—that is, hits the ball entirely off the table—terminates the game altogether. This happened in March 2003 to the weekly newspaper *21st Century World Herald* (*21 shiji huanqiu daobao*), based in Guangdong province, when it was shut down for publishing an interview with a former Mao aide who called for free elections.[6]

Constraints on exposing or criticizing political issues extend to foreign journalists in China as well. While the CCP cannot control the content of foreign news, it can control the source, that is, the interviewee. After the protest at Tiananmen Square, the government tightened restrictions on foreign journalists and in 1990 enacted "Regulations Concerning Foreign Journalists and Permanent Offices of Foreign News Agencies." Foreigners, as the writer Simon Leys (a pseudonym) has eloquently written in his book, *Chinese Shadows*, were in the past shepherded to sanitized locations, and denied access to anything like the "real" China. To some extent, Western expatriates living in Beijing and Shanghai are even today seeing a version of China that is very distinct from life that plays out a few hours' drive away. More recently the government passed rules regarding distribution in China of news and media content by foreign media organizations like the Associated Press and Reuters. According to the new rules all foreign media agencies must deliver their information through the Xinhua News Agency, China's official press agency and monopolistic information distributor.

In a country where constraints on reporting economic matters have been relaxed but exposing political issues has become more difficult, journalists are especially challenged to develop creative rhetorical strategies and find gray areas—issues that are not explicitly allowed or disallowed. During my visit to *Caijing* my hosts reminded me that some ambiguity surrounded how and whether to cover the 2003 outbreak of severe acute respiratory syndrome (SARS) in China at a time when, as has since become clear, the central and local governments did their best to cover up and minimize the health and humanitarian fiasco. *Caijing* decided to carry SARS stories but framed these as business issues with economy-wide impact.

Caijing's existence is all the more remarkable considering the impressive degree to which the government controls information. Using a host of physical, technological, and social barriers, the government screens and cleans information from the outside world. Sensitive information from foreign countries must enter China from the top down. When I first began visiting China I found this a bit perplexing. After all, I could walk into the business lounge at the St. Regis Hotel in Beijing's tony Central Business District and apart from seeing soldiers in their immaculate, starched uniforms guarding the various embassies on the street, I could be in any Starbucks-studded Western metropolis, with full access to the *Financial Times* or the *International*

Herald Tribune. Most foreign papers and television channels like CNN are not readily available. Even Hong Kong papers like the *South China Morning Post* have subtle barriers preventing their distribution. Because the *South China Morning Post* is considered a foreign newspaper it cannot be printed on the mainland: it must be flown in every morning from Hong Kong. Then, to ensure its limited dissemination, the paper doesn't arrive until early afternoon and can only be found in hotels and select outlets, thus limiting its distribution to affluent readers. Similarly, information that can be accessed at the grassroots level across China is progressively filtered up through the editorial chain to desensitize it. Editors at *Caijing* and its ilk, struggling to find the edge of the table tennis table, receive periodic "guidance" from the authorities about this shifting boundary.

These tight controls have a virtual analogue as well. With the largest Internet-ready population in the world—111 million users at the end of 2005—China has successfully implemented sophisticated Internet-filtering systems.[7] While restricting access to content that the regime defines as sensitive, it otherwise encourages access. Negative pages about the government are filtered out, but the positive pages remain. For example, phrases like "Falun Gong" and "Cultural Revolution" lead either to pages that are inaccessible or to select pages that support the government's official interpretations. Other restricted content areas include pages having to do with human rights, Tibet, Taiwan, and Inner Mongolian independence. Laws have been introduced to imprison or even execute users attempting to breach the Internet barriers.[8] In March 2005 one of the mainland's most popular chat rooms for debate, the *Shuimu* ("water and tree") Tsinghua Web site (www.smth.org), was shut down. Howls of protest and palpable outrage ensued from its users, but to no avail. Nonstudents were to be prohibited from accessing the chat room, a blow that successfully crippled the Web site's emergent role as the virtual location for intellectual debate, social commentary, and dissemination of new technology. The previous summer a Web site on the Peking University campus, Yitahutu, had been shut down.[9]

Such control and censorship requires nothing technologically complex. Minor adjustments to products provided by mostly Western computer and communications technology giants are sufficient. The apparent willingness of some Western companies to cooperate in the state's endeavor—actions Microsoft and Yahoo have been publicly raked over the coals for—as a condition of their doing business in China has only aided state control. Laws have been introduced to punish violators with imprisonment and even death. Google, whose motto is "Do no evil," may be the Western company most morally liable.

Not only do cartoon characters Jing and Cha police the Web, but approximately 30,000 cyber police monitor Internet content and users. This might seem like a large number until one recalls that labor is cheap and that there are 100 million Internet users in China. Cell phone users—for voice communication and Internet access—now number 350 million and rising. Even these cell phones and pagers are targeted for disseminating sensitive content. In the same universities and at exactly the time when chat rooms with allegedly subversive content were shut down, I met a handful of U.S.-educated Chinese entrepreneurs who were building businesses in Beijing and Shanghai to capitalize on the popularity of the cell phone. They had developed technologies enabling cell phone users to connect with webs of people with whom they most often interacted socially or professionally, the so-called social networking function. Ironically, the same technology might ultimately be used both by the government for its own purposes, or, equally, to mobilize masses against the authorities. There is an ongoing horse race between the people's interest in unfettered communication among themselves and the Party's interest in curtailing some aspects of this communication.

China has atleast thirty-one journalists behind bars, making it the world's leading jailer of reporters for the eighth year in a row, according to the New York–based Committee to Protect Journalists.[10] The Chinese state behaves very rationally in policing behavior it deems antithetical to its interests. First, if someone is caught, punishment is purposely draconian to serve as a credible deterrent. One example is Jiao Guobiao, the author of "Crusade Against the Propaganda Department," an anti-information control pamphlet that circulated through the Web in the summer of 2004. While visiting the United States at the invitation of the National Endowment for Democracy, a nongovernmental organization funded by the U.S. Congress and charged with promoting democracy, Jiao received a letter effectively dismissing him from his position as a professor at Beijing University. Another example of China's take-no-prisoners approach is Gao Qinrong, a reporter for the state news agency Xinhua who broke a story about major corruption on an irrigation project in the Yuncheng District of Shanxi Province. Xinhua never carried the article, but the People's Daily published it on May 27, 1998, in an edition distributed only to a select group of Party leaders. Several other news agencies also reported on the scandal. Seven months later Gao was arrested on charges ranging from bribery to corruption. On April 4, 1999, the Yuncheng City People's Court tried him behind closed doors and sentenced him to twelve years in prison.[11]

Finally, it is important to understand that China's monitoring methods and acceptable standards are intermittent and arbitrary rather than pervasive, qualities sure to make Internet users uncertain and insecure. As outsiders quickly learn, many things in China are state secrets, but the reasons for that label are not always obvious. One journalist writing for the New York Times was jailed recently for speculating when Jiang Zemin would step down from his post as chairman of the CPC Central Military Commission (accurately, as it turned out), and the SARS outbreak presumably was hushed up because admitting it would have been an acknowledgment of the health system's failure.

Confronting a Tangible Problem

Finding reliable, useful financial information is a real problem that anyone wanting to work at, sell to, buy from, or invest in a Chinese or Indian company must face. I am often asked for guidance in solving this problem and have found that the answers are different for the two countries.

In China, can I believe the financial information in a company's annual report?

Not really, I say. The annual report does not serve the purpose it does in market economies, that is, to communicate reliable information. Several of the companies with which one might interact may not even be legal entities in their own rights: almost surely they will have a blurred responsibility to traditional business constituents and to government.

What about analysts' reports on Chinese companies?

Two issues are at stake. First, most of the domestic assets of Chinese companies are not publicly listed. Those that are listed locally are not necessarily the companies' best assets but are the results of the government's attempt to leverage domestic savings toward salvaging bankrupt state-owned enterprises. Assets listed overseas—and on which reliable foreign analyses presumably exist—are not all the assets of the corporations in question. For example, the Bank of China's overseas operations are listed in Hong Kong but represent only a small part of the bank's operations on the mainland. Second, Chinese financial analysts are not independent but state owned or state controlled, as are the companies on which they issue reports.[12]

How about relying on credible business media?

Caijing and a few other media outlets like it have made some progress, but for the most part credible business media are still scarce. One reason is that Xinhua, China's official news agency, is directly controlled by the Central Committee of the CCP. Newspapers that carry a Xinhua story are allowed to rewrite or shorten but not add to or otherwise revise the text. Since Xinhua is the only agency with correspondents based overseas, every other media outlet depends on it for international news. The government control of Xinhua is far from subtle. Typically a working group from the party's propaganda department meets every week to draw up detailed guidelines for what issues Xinhua should cover and how those issues should be presented. Xinhua officials then pass the guidelines along to lower levels.

Market information—information gathered by impartial, objective observers in return for monetary compensation—is also scarce in China. One recourse is to turn to what economists awkwardly call non-market information.[13] Inconveniently, there is no compendium of what passes as reliable non-market information. In China the primary source of this type of information is *guanxi*, a term referring loosely to relationships. Legions of academics have published studies documenting the value of *guanxi* in China. These are valuable precisely because they are the primary conduits of reliable information in a society where impartial sources of information are non-existent. As an example, observers of Zhongnanhai, the government compound in Beijing around Tiananmen, are busy figuring out who's in and who's out of the Party hierarchy, presumably with a view to discussing the future embodiments of state power. The very reliance of *guanxi* makes it unlikely, in the short run, that credible, impartial, objective purveyors of market information will emerge. Why invest in building such an organization if everyone relies on relationships?

Is it easier to find reliable information about a company in India?

Yes. First, as a result of a legal system derived from the common-law tradition, annual reports provide the basic rudiments of information that Western observers expect, and familiar rules govern corporate disclosure. Real-time stock market data are readily available on all publicly traded companies, a result of vigorous competition between the National Stock Exchange (NSE) and the Bombay Stock Exchange (BSE).

Private-sector intermediaries in India use business models that include information synthesized from company disclosures and intelligence that they gather from the ground. The Center for Monitoring the Indian Economy (CMIE), for example, is a privately owned clearinghouse for reliable information on publicly traded firms and some privately held firms in India. Founded in 1976, CMIE is the brainchild of the entrepreneur Narrottam Shah. Numerous credit-rating agencies work off the primary information available from companies and from CMIE to provide risk analyses for debt claimants.

Indian business magazines compete ferociously. *Business Today* and *Business World* have effectively challenged *Business India*, once the dominant publication. These three publications claim top rankings among readers and advertisers, and their fortunes ebb and flow as one would expect in a competitive environment, keeping the companies and information providers relatively honest. The libraries and archives of these business magazines and of the daily business newspaper the *Economic Times* are accessible to any person on the street, either free or for a nominal charge.

Government-affiliated organizations keep pace with these competing private entities. The Indian Statistical Institute, an eminent think tank and bastion of statistics and economics, maintains data banks and discloses companies' decisions regarding debt holdings and equity. The Planning Commission, the Reserve Bank of India, and other government-linked bodies regularly massage and report data. These reports are heavily analyzed, debated, and criticized in the independent business media and serve as additional checks on the micro information they publish.

And what about interpreting accurate country-level information in China and India?

Again, this is possible only with equally reliable data on specific industries and the economy in general. For China watchers, the limited availability of reliable statistics continues to be the biggest stumbling block. Numerous caveats accompany discussions of the levels and growth of China's GDP, in itself a veritable cottage industry. China does have governmental data banks—for example, the China Securities Regulatory Commission (CSRC) in capital markets.[14] But they do not appear to function as intended. The CSRC is responsible not only for providing information but also for the very performance of the stock market—heavily in hock to the government as it is. Such a structure inevitably engenders conflicts of interest.

Thomas Rawski, a professor of economics at the University of Pittsburgh, is a close observer of the Chinese economy and a longtime student of Chinese economic statistics. In his view, China's growth rates from 1997 to 2001 were probably less than half the official annual figure of 7.6 percent, and China's official statistics were unlike any seen previously in Asia. In Japan in the late 1950s, Taiwan in the late 1960s, Korea in the late 1970s, and China itself in the late 1980s, cumulative growth in real output exceeded 30 percent. Each expansion sparked higher energy consumption, increased employment, and raised prices. During the 1997–2001 period, however, China's energy use, employment, and prices fell. Unless the Chinese have identified a radical new way to use energy, the growth rates appear exaggerated.

Digging into these figures, Rawski cited numerous Chinese-language materials complaining of *jiabao fukua feng*, or "the wind of falsification and embellishment."[15] Was political manipulation part of this tornado of false reporting?

Yes and no. Deception is not new in China, but it has become rampant since 1998, when targeting 8 percent GDP growth became a "great political responsibility." The Chinese leadership certainly did not want to be fooled. They wanted to learn what was happening on the ground, but they had no direct control over the details of reporting. As a result, the cadres who exaggerated their performances got promoted, and those who gave honest, less-than-rosy reports were blamed for incomplete tasks. This is why the former director of China's National Bureau of Statistics (NBS), Zhang Sai, slammed "administrative interference in statistical work" in 1999 and Premier Zhu Rongji complained about rampant "falsification and exaggeration" in 2000. After 1999 NBS publicly dismissed provincial growth estimates as "cooked local figures." It substituted its own more conservative measures but did not explain how it arrived at them. *China Daily* warned of "statistical fraud," and domestic critics blamed "agencies of the national government" for "statistical illegalities."[16]

Indian companies and financial institutions are not free from fraud and error. On the contrary, India's financial scam of 1992, which I discuss at some length in a subsequent chapter, was at least as egregious as the stock market fever that gripped China in the same year. Both countries have seen their share of financial shenanigans, but their responses to the systemic problems in their financial sectors could not be more different. India celebrated information and embraced competition and market forces, whereas China left intact and arguably strengthened government control of the stock exchanges.

Historical Antecedents

How did Chinese and Indian governments reach their current positions on information access and control? What legacy does each country bring with it as it opens up to the twenty-first century, and what changes is each country already making?

In 1969 India passed the Monopolies and Restrictive Trade Practices (MRTP) Act in response to fears that economic power was becoming concentrated in a few hands, an anathema to Nehruvian India's socialist mindset. The subsequently created MRTP Commission appointed Professor R. K. Hazari to study the causes of the concentration of economic power.[17] Hazari's seminal study of leading Indian capitalists concluded that "the business group, not the individual joint stock company, is the unit of decision and, therefore, of economic power."[18] Further, the business group was held together not only by equity investments but largely by a range of familial and other control mechanisms that operated in less-than-transparent ways. The economic fates of several entities that were legally separate were in fact bound together. Hazari's findings aligned with an earlier report that concluded that the study of enterprise control is "unreal if divorced from a study of communities."[19] For example, regardless of how much of an enterprise's equity a particular individual owned, the controlling body of that enterprise would also ensure that equity was distributed among the individual's close relatives. In the India of the mid-1900s, this typically meant wives, sons, and daughters-in-law. Thus the MRTP Commission knew what data to go after.

In time the MRTP Act spawned all manner of excesses unimagined by Nehru, Hazari, and their colleagues. Beginning with Rajiv Gandhi's government in 1984, it was progressively weakened and ultimately dismantled. Nevertheless, it compiled an impressive repository of useful information on companies that was, and is, publicly accessible. These data now belong to the Planning Commission, itself an outgrowth of India's socialist past. Today's Planning Commission head is a cabinet minister, Montek Singh Ahluwalia. He is a respected economist interested in devolving economic power. This is the opposite of the economic centralization the planners used to pursue.

Like India, China has collected and disseminated information through a formidable apparatus. The Han Dynasty (206 B.C.E.–220 C.E.) had state historiographical offices to "engage in the world's most systematic continuous gathering of historical data prior to the twentieth century," points out William Alford, the Harvard Law professor and prominent scholar of Chinese intellectual property law.[20] China differs from India, however, in the restrictions it has placed on access to the collected information. Further, there are few checks and balances on those privileged few who can access data.

China's reliance on a hierarchy to filter information dates to imperial times, when the implicit bargain was that the people were loyal to the ruler, and he, as the parent of this figurative family, was responsible for their well-being, material and otherwise. A small group of people around the ruler had the "mandate of heaven" to decide what information was relevant and who could access it. Alford argues that curtailing the dissemination of printed laws in Imperial China was due as much to a feeling that there was no need for anyone other than the ruler to know the laws, for he would be trusted to use them wisely, as to illiteracy in the population.[21] The modern analogue to this, of course, is the Party hierarchy. The Party decides what information is to be revealed, to whom, and what is to be kept within the Party's system (*neibu*). Several rules and regulations and documents are thus classified.[22] For a long time it was only the hierarchy's apex, the elite of the CCP, that could turn to internal circulation papers like *Cankao Xiaoxi* (Reference News) to read sensitive translations of foreign news reports.[23] Today some of my Chinese students inform me that they circumvent these rules by persuading their work units to "officially" subscribe to internal publications.

Future Directions

Critics point to India's caste system as the ultimate hierarchy. Although this is a legitimate point of view, two caveats should be noted regarding its current applicability. First, information on economic opportunity was not always more accessible to the upper castes than to the lower castes. A trader-businessman always had greater access to economic information than did a member of the priestly class above him. Second, caste remains an issue in rural India but less so in urban areas where many lower-caste people are more affluent than their higher-caste neighbors.

Even outside India's urban areas, information is becoming more accessible. For example, fish farmers in rural Kerala can monitor the prices of fish in the nearby big city markets through simple devices that allow them to prevent being exploited by city middlemen.[24] Land records in several of India's more progressive states are increasingly accessible on the Web, so that there is greater clarity on who has property rights over these assets. Companies are pioneering ways not only to provide information to undeveloped areas but also to make outreach profitable. Hindustan Levers, Unilever's long-established Indian subsidiary, reaches the deepest parts of rural India with consumer items tailored to low-income, small-quantity consumption patterns. ITC, the descendant of British American Tobacco, has created a virtual electronic distribution center and marketplace (a so-called e-*choupal*, choupal meaning "market place") for rural inhabitants. These are entirely decentralized, private-sector efforts and represent economic empowerment of the previously disenfranchised.

One of the most positive pieces of legislation coming out of India today is the Right to Information Act, passed in 2005.[25] Whereas citizens in Western democracies have long enjoyed nearly unrestrained access to government documents and communications, Indians were restricted by the Official Secrets Act of 1923. Under the new act any citizen can request information from a "public authority." The act further requires every public authority to computerize their records for wide dissemination with a thirty-day time stipulation. The impact of such legislation on matters of accountability and transparency cannot be overstated.

In China information flows more freely today than in the early days of the People's Republic. A person need not be a Party elite to subscribe to *Cankao Xiaoxi* and access translations of news from foreign media, such as the *New York Times* and Reuters newswire. Moreover, China has made meaningful steps toward what the West would recognize as democracy; for example, China held its first village election in 1987, and by the late 1990s most villages' Party committee members were elected rather than appointed. With those steps comes some accountability for available information. The grass roots increasingly sends views up the chain of command and is not merely a passive receptacle for views coming down from the top of the hierarchy. Since technology is widely available—Internet users outnumber Party members— the urban citizenry does have access to what sensitive information manages to seep through technological and ideological firewalls. The Party is not as immune to outside criticism as it once was, nor can it closet as much information as it did in the past. After all, China's economic motor depends on access to the outside world, whereas Mao's regime was entirely inward-looking.

However, in a country where being true to the past is "roughly equivalent to truth in the west,"[26] departing from the tradition of hierarchy is done cautiously. The Guomindang government, in power between the Japanese invasions and the advent of the CCP, revealingly expressed the opinion that "democratic rights . . . must not be clearly bestowed."[27] China has learned from its modern admirers, such as Singapore's Lee Kuan Yew, by slowly opening the spigot of democracy in a controlled fashion.[28]

Most protests heard in China, at least those not deemed antithetical to the government's interests, are agitating for the fair application of existing rules rather than the institution of new rights. Harvard scholar Elizabeth Perry refers to this as "rules consciousness" as opposed to "rights consciousness," and it reflects a long tradition of seeing rights as decreed by the power structure.[29]

The continuing power of the Party hierarchy is also evident in the blacklists of individuals prohibited from visiting China.[30] Nineteen scholars have been deemed anti-China by China's Ministry of Public Security, and the list of Chinese people prevented from returning to their homeland is much longer.

I know of no such list for democratic India. In fact, the story of Jean Dreze points to India's capacity to tolerate dissent from the outside as well as the inside. Dreze, born in Belgium and educated in Britain, arrived in India in 1979 and studied for his doctorate in economics at the Indian Statistical Institute. Over the next two decades Dreze's academic publications, built on fieldwork accomplished by extensive travel by foot or bicycle, earned him a reputation as one of India's best analytical economists. His credentials were firmly established by co-authoring, with friend and Nobel Laureate Amartya Sen, *Hunger and Public Action* and *India: Development and Participation*. Dreze's work has been highly critical of India's record of governance and socioeconomic development. He has constantly highlighted gender- and caste-based inequalities and relentlessly criticized India's poor record at alleviating poverty. Despite Dreze's staunch critique of almost every administration's record, today he is known among Indian government circles as a conscience keeper of economics and democracy. In 2002, he was granted Indian citizenship. Today Dreze serves on the prominent and influential National Advisory Council and has been instrumental in drafting one of the most ambitious pieces of legislation of the recent government—the National Rural Employment Guarantee Scheme, which guarantees employment to every household for a minimum of one hundred days a year in an attempt to ensure basic subsistence to the poorest of the rural poor in about two hundred districts in India.

America's False Romance

Despite Chinese opacity and Indian transparency, U.S. media give significantly more coverage to China than to India. In the first chapter, I recounted a decades-long tally of substantial articles on the front pages of prominent U.S. newspapers. Usually, China coverage is far more pronounced than is India coverage. Intriguingly, however, when the same analysis is run on the London-based *Financial Times*, or on the *Times* of London, the difference between China and India coverage is far less.

Because I lecture internationally to companies or associations about business in China and India, I have observed how familiarity with China *or* India is often a condition of where in the world one stands. At the Pacific Pension Institute's Summer Roundtable in San Francisco in 2004, where I spoke to representatives of pension funds from around the United States and other developed triad countries, collectively representing several hundreds of billions of dollars of investable assets, the interaction was typical. Ostensibly a talk about China and India, it rapidly evolved to being more about India. The material on China was, apparently, much more familiar to the primarily American audience. When the same material was presented not long after to the Abu Dhabi Investment Authority, in the United Arab Emirates, also a repository of several hundreds of billions of dollars of investable assets, the part of the discussion that drew the most animated response was quite different. Here, because of the relatively close geographical proximity to India as well as a large Indian diaspora in the UAE, the India story was not as novel to the sheikhs as was the China story.

It is ironic that the West pays less attention to, and thus has less understanding of, the more information-rich country. This is even more surprising because, as Jay Taylor points out, the similarities between India and the United States—the only two large countries where democracy has preceded economic development—are quite striking. It is worth briefly reproducing some of the commonalities he noted in the political realm: "survival oriented rather than ideological politicians seeking to placate interest groups; a plural and divided polity that is cynical and enthusiastic simultaneously; movie-star politicians; the festival of elections; ethnic politics; popular movements that well up and die suddenly; circle of corruption and reform; noise of a press that lives on the meat of incumbents; cries of despair from intellectual ivory towers; sounds of millions of partisans shouting and mostly enjoying themselves."[31]

How did the West come to better understand the society that is more different from it? One resolution of this paradox lies in historical serendipity.

During its long relationship with Britain, India was out of the American sphere of influence. This isolation was cemented by the events of the cold war, when Indira Gandhi embraced the Soviet Union, a response at least in part to Nixon's romance with China. Only since the 1990s, with the fall of the Soviet Union, the acquisition of nuclear power status, and the emergence of an economically resurgent Indian diaspora, has India attracted some attention in the United States.

Western societies, other than America's, do not have nearly as much proximity to China. Perhaps this is why the China-centered media coverage that I mentioned above is less evident there. Perhaps this is also a reason why audiences in the Middle East are less familiar with China. The front pages of Dubai newspapers cover many Bombay events. Apart from the ubiquity of Arabic script, many of the streets in Abu Dhabi are indistinguishable from some Mumbai neighborhoods. In comparison, the Indian diaspora in the United States has only just begun to come of age.

But the paradox is a bit deeper than just this passing attempt at resolution. The paradox is that American audiences, despite their rather long historical romance with China, do not fully understand the bias in Chinese data, even after the efforts of analysts like Rawski. Guy Pfefferman of the International Finance Corporation has pointed out that one must carefully adjust the numbers coming out of China to interpret them sensibly in a comparative context. Thus China accounts for foreign direct investment quite liberally, while India does so quite conservatively, which means an apples-to-apples comparison takes some care and time.[32] Unfortunately, such analytical caution has not undergirded most comparisons between China and India in the popular discourse. Some Western consulting firms actually emphasize to their trainee consultants that one route to competitive advantage in China is learning to acquire sensible data, rather than focusing primarily on cleverly analyzing existing data.

Chapter Four

Fiat and Fairness

Why China Can Build Cities Overnight and India Cannot

Shanghai and Mumbai are the respective commercial capitals of China and India. Each city features a stretch of waterfront—the Bund in Shanghai and Marine Drive in Mumbai—as *the* defining architectural feature of the urban landscape. Old colonial buildings, remnants of a bygone era, ring each waterfront. Beyond their crescent-shaped waterfronts, however, the two cities could not be more different. A comparison of their origins and development reveals the opposing sets of priorities China and India hold regarding public and private property rights. Different priorities led to different policies that shaped the different physical environments in which billions of people now live. As with statecraft and access to information, an understanding of property rights in China and India is as crucial for Westerners as it is for the Chinese and Indians who wish to work together.

Visitors to Shanghai are immediately struck by the gleaming district of Pudong, which has emerged in just over a decade as the highlight of the city's strategy to accommodate its eighteen billion residents. Pudong was mainly farmland until 1990 when the Chinese government decided to set up a Special Economic Zone there. Today Pudong epitomizes the government's massive effort to rebrand Shanghai from the Paris of the East, as the city was once known, to its Manhattan. Pudong now boasts more skyscrapers than Manhattan, and some say that its Lujiazui financial district, host to several hundred multinationals, puts London's Canary Wharf to shame. Pudong has become a "must see" phenomenon. Its landmarks, the Jin Mao Tower,

Oriental Pearl TV, the Broadcast Tower, and Shanghai Maglev Line, among others, are modern marvels.

How did this happen? First, the idea of creating Pudong was not a matter of public debate but came from the very top of the CCP hierarchy, more specifically, from Deng Xiaoping himself. Such an "agreement" would be harder to reach in a heterogeneous society like India where leaders who represent a multitude of ethnic, religious, and socioeconomic interests, are often at odds on all public policy matters. Second, even if there had been opposition to the idea, it would have been difficult to publicize without a free press or other organs of civil society independent of the Party. Nor could the judiciary, also beholden to the Party, have adjudicated disputes fairly. But perhaps most importantly, once the decision had been made in Beijing, virtually nothing could have prevented the Chinese government from carrying out its agenda.

In contrast, the prestige of Mumbai's *nouveau riche* Cuffe Parade development has been marred by the presence of Machimaar Village, a malodorous, albeit colorful, fishing community that has shared real estate with skyscraper's upscale homes for some thirty years. During that time any city politicians or administrators daring to suggest a redevelopment plan that would clear Macchimaar Village or any other shantytowns in Mumbai have been ensnared in political turmoil. A vicious cycle of slum clearance and rebuilding has gone on for decades. If a political party legitimizes a certain slum one year, the other party outlaws it the next election cycle. As a result, slum dwellers and average *Mumbaikaars* (residents of Mumbai) alike suffer. Clearly the city can make no tangible gains under its paralytic politic system.

Pudong is a visible example of what the CCP's fiat authority can accomplish. With public infrastructure projects ongoing throughout the nation, China has shown that, at least in the early stages, a country can have economic growth without embracing individual property rights. But can the rights of the state permanently trump those of individuals? To what extent can national development be an altar on which personal freedoms are sacrificed? Are those who decry the loss of personal freedom too easily silenced? Or is it a worthwhile bargain to gain material wealth at the cost of submitting to the control of a political authority that gets things done? Mumbai's mess illustrates how private rights and public interests can collide. Is it right for a nation to invariably err on the side of individual rights, even at severe costs to the public?

But this is not all. No sensible planner could interpret Mumbai's situation as a mere result of theoretical debates about public versus private interests. Institutional inefficiency—resulting from well-intentioned constraints on the government, like the free press, judicial processes, and civil society—has checked and balanced India into paralysis. Are private rights truly protected? In India, one never knows whether the rich or the poor, the foreign or the local, the administrator or the politician will win a battle of disputed property rights.

Pudong: Why the Chinese Can Build Cities Overnight

Pudong was always just a river away from Nanjing Road, the commercial center of old Shanghai. But an old Chinese saying reflected the lack of regard most people had for this marshy farmland: "One would rather have a bed in Puxi [west of the river] than a house in Pudong." This is no longer true. Today there are five tunnels and five bridges connecting Puxi to Pudong, with many more links planned.

The city's development journey started in the mid-1930's with a proposal by Chinese American architect Lin Tongyan, but the plan stalled until Deng Xiaoping launched his famous Southern Tour in 1992, an effort to allay post-Tiananmen fears and recommit China to economic reforms. For Deng, a consummate bridge player, Shanghai was a key card in his plan to develop China.[1] In April 1990 the Chinese government designated Pudong as the "dragon head" to lead the development of all coastal cities in the larger Yangtze Delta area. Beijing's political will was matched by its generous financial commitments—grants, low-interest loans, and relocation expenses for affected factories and their workers.[2] Unusually, Beijing also let Pudong retain revenues above those usually allowed. Further, as a measure of how important it was to Beijing, Pudong received an elevated status in the government hierarchy. Asked if Pudong was part of Shanghai, the deputy director of the Pudong Academy of Development, Wang Guoxing, said that although they had hoped to be independent of the Shanghai municipal government and to deal with the central government directly, they had failed. Yet Pudong attained and still retains, a higher status than other districts of Greater Shanghai.

Zhu Rongji, then Shanghai's mayor, was told to attract foreign governments and international financial institutions able to supplement the project's funding by providing long-term, low-interest loans. To accomplish this, Zhu was given unprecedented powers and became known as the "one-chop man" for his dedication to cutting the red tape in the city's approval processes. In 1996 Lujiazui was selected as the first district in China where foreign banks could conduct business in local currency. Of course foreign banks had to commit to Lujiazui if they wanted a license.[3]

Meanwhile, state-owned development companies were admonished to think of innovative ways of financing their parts of the Pudong project. The municipal authorities created a land market by selling rights only land use to approved development companies. This served as collateral to get loans. The government gained revenues from the resulting real estate developments by charging transaction fees and real estate taxes. A host of incentives were offered to make Pudong the destination of choice for foreigners, including reduced income taxes for Sino-foreign joint ventures, tax exemptions for foreign investments in infrastructure in the first five profit-making years, and a 50 percent tax reduction for five years after that.[4] The Shanghai municipal government even granted residency permits to anyone from outside Shanghai who bought an apartment in Pudong worth at least Rmb 500,000 ($60,200).

The result? Today, Pudong's economic output nearly equals the total output of Shanghai ten years ago, and from an area of thirty square kilometers in 1990 the district burgeoned to 100 square kilometers by 2004. During the same period Pudong's GDP rose from RMB 6 billion ($1.1 billion) to RMB 140 billion ($17 billion). More than nine thousand foreign companies entered Pudong, including more than 180 Fortune 500 companies, and the Lujiazui financial district alone hosted 150 Chinese and foreign financial organizations. This success is infectious; for example, the city of Jiading, northwest of Shanghai, is trying to develop an auto specialty corridor. Despite a 26 billion RMB ($3.1 billion) price tag, the governments of Shanghai and Jaiding are intent on building a state-of-the art stadium to lure Formula One racing. Do they hope to break even with the venture? That concern seems to have been lost in the rush to acquire this Western symbol of prosperity.

What about Pudong's three hundred thousand displaced farmers? Under the Sunshine Relocation Policy they were methodically and incrementally moved to previously prepared accommodations and received some cash compensation based on the acreage they lost. Although not large sums by today's standards, they were considered significant a decade ago. Many young farmers took jobs in Pudong's new factories and moved their families out of the district. The older farmers took on miscellaneous jobs. Many of them became local officials, entrepreneurs, or salaried workers in nearby factories. Observers pointed out that most displaced farmers were better off, even if they became janitors in the offices built on what had been their land. Finally, the plan identified distressed households in need of government assistance. In the case of Pudong, where relocation methods were exemplary, it's hard to find much dissent. This is not true for other development-related moves in China that I discuss later.

Machimaar Village and Street People with Cell Phones: Why Mumbai Cannot Be Shanghai

The fishermen were here first . . . when Bombay was a dumbbell-shaped island tapering, at the center, to a narrow shining strand beyond which could be seen the finest and largest natural harbor in Asia.

—*Midnight's Children*, Salman Rushdie[5]

In the 1960s and 1970s Cuffe Parade, at the southernmost tip of Bombay, was the destination for the nouveau riche in India. Manicured apartment complexes were inhabited by the city's socially prominent while upscale bakeries, selling French bread and lemon tarts, sat between the skyscrapers. But an eyesore encroached on this luxurious landscape. The fisherfolk of Machimaar Village displayed hundreds of square feet of prawns and fish in sidewalk stalls beside the hovels they called homes, commandeering what could have been a prime beach for the glitterati.

It is somewhat embarrassing to remember the many days I walked past Machimmar Village on my way to my daily tennis games. Dressed in tennis whites, I was blissfully oblivious to the vast disparity between my life of priv- ilege and the poverty of the mothers I passed along the way carrying baskets of fish and squirming naked children. How preposterous it was that a poor village could coexist with Bombay's premier real estate and that it could be only a matter of time, at least in my mind, before one of them (read Machi- maar Village) would have to go. Yet nearly three decades later, both Cuffe Parade and Machimaar Village are unchanged. While Cuffe Parade remains one of the country's most expensive real estates, home to the rich and fa- mous, thousands of fisherfolk still make their living by casting their nets from Macchimaar Village into the waters of the Arabian Sea.

In 2007 I reenacted my boyhood stroll past the fishing village. Ramnath, a wizened sixty-year-old, claimed to have lived in the village for forty years, and had retired, sort of. His son still fished daily, his wife took the catch to the local market, and he helped out by cleaning and drying the fish. Although Ramnath's family earned just Rs. 10,000 per month (about $250), they man- aged to make ends meet. How? As part of the "informal sector" they paid no taxes, they ate what they caught, they paid no rent for their makeshift home, and they put nothing aside for a future that seemed impossibly utopian to plan for given their day-to-day existence.

"Why don't you move away?" I asked Ramnath.[6]

"Why would we? We have the best view in the city!" he replied. Indeed, they overlooked the same seashore and cityscape as some of the best-heeled citizens of Mumbai. "And," he added, tongue-firmly-in-cheek, "we have the Ambanis as our neighbors." The Ambani family is India's first family of the nouveau riche. Its founder, Dhirubhai, built a fortune in petrochemicals, and his two heirs, Mukesh and Anil, independently launched their own multibil- lion-dollar business conglomerates. During my conversation with Ramnath we were joined by a young mother named Usha, carrying a baby on her hip. "This is a great place," she told me. "I hope I can settle here. I'm moving here from a coastal village in Maharashtra where things are pretty bad. I hope I can get into the *dhandha*." *Dhandha* is Hindi for "trade" and refers to the fishing trade.

I asked, "Don't the rich people try to move you out?"

"Not anymore," replied Ramnath. "At election time people come around pretending to do things. But we can't trust anyone. If they offer us something, I'm sure they'll not follow through once election season is over, and then where would we be?"

These descendants of the Koli tribe (koli in Marathi, the local language, means both spider and fisherman; both capture their prey with nets) were exactly the way I remembered them two decades ago. Time has stood still in Machimaar Village. Indeed, the Koli have witnessed the handing of Mumbai from the Gujarat Sultans to the Portuguese, and then from the Portuguese to the British in the form of the dowry of Catherine of Braganza to Charles II, and finally from the British to independent Indians.

How is it that the Kolis have not been removed as part of some urban renewal scheme, as they surely would have been in China? Historically Indian law has protected their habitat as a matter of principle. In the 1990s the Supreme Court restricted land reclamation and the removal of fisherfolk when it implemented Coastal Regulatory Zones. Justice Jeevan Reddy of the Supreme Court, while upholding the *Monsoon Trawl Ban*, expressed the court's view of development:

> . . . public interest cannot be determined only by looking at the quantum of fish caught in a year. . . . The government is perfectly justified in saying that it is under obligation to protect the economic interest of the traditional fisherpeople and to ensure that they are not deprived of their slender means of livelihood. Whether one calls it distributive justice or development with a human face, the ultimate truth is that the object of all development is the human being. There can be no development for the sake of development. Priorities ought not be inverted nor true perspective lost in the quest for more production.[7]

The law spells it out: "the object of all development is the human being." Unlike China, where laws allowed Pudong to be built overnight, India puts a priority on "development with a human face." True, Cuffe Parade's wealthy residence associations have periodically urged the city government to demolish the shanties. Occasionally demolitions follow such entreaties, but the ramshackle homes are always rebuilt. Although the rich could force their politicians' hands and bribe their way to a fish-free nirvana, the reality is that the rich rarely vote. In contrast the residents of Machimaar Village do vote, and the politicians, the ultimate *homo economicus*, respond to those votes by protecting the property rights of the poor. Further, the symbolism of uprooting a poor fisherwoman to cater to elites enjoying Cuffe Parade's posh facilities would generate political heat in socialist India.

Machimaar Village's saga is not an isolated one. Whenever I drive from the airport toward South Mumbai, to Cuffe Parade, I pass Dharavi on the right-hand side, a 175 hectare of swampy land that is home to nearly one million people and is reportedly Asia's largest slum. The stench emanating from the open sewers is unbearable, yet the inhabitants of Dharavi manage a vibrant, informal economy that generates $500 million in goods and services annually. Schools, clinics, shops, and bakeries gainfully employ thousands of people in the Dharavi slum. Gods and politicians are everywhere; temples and mosques easily coexist, and pockets of the slum are divided among strongholds of various political parties and slumlords who lay down the law, mafia style. Like Machimaar Village, Dharavi is a landmark, a symbol, even a force of nature.

Successive governments have tried to redevelop Dharavi by converting parts of the slum into legal properties. The catch, of course, is that the slum dwellers are not recognized or given legal status and therefore have no right to the properties. Rather than fight the move in the courts, the disenfranchised often simply pick up and reestablish down the street, carrying television sets, bicycles, motorcycles, cell phones, and reconstructing their makeshift structures.

As if to underscore the enormous differences between Indian and Chinese urban reform, in 2003 the management consulting firm McKinsey and Company published *Vision Mumbai,* a report that laid out a to-do list for the "Shanghaization" of Mumbai. One of McKinsey's face-lift suggestions was amending government regulations to allow the construction of taller skyscrapers,[8] a move that undoubtedly would have entailed clearing several slums where 50 percent of Mumbai's population made their homes. No sooner was the report issued than it became a lightning rod for criticism from environmentalists, former bureaucrats, academics, and activists. The media suggested that the only redeeming feature of *Vision Mumbai* was that it was prepared gratis by a firm known for its exorbitant rates. The fiery reaction to the report demonstrated that for most Indians, changing infrastructure for the sake of national development was an abstract and unwelcome concept. The people could not embrace massive change when it conflicted with personal well-being, and no leader emerged with the political imagination needed to make the case for public interest.

These attitudes are not changing. In 2005 Vilasrao Deshmukh, the chief minister of the state of Maharashtra (of which Mumbai is the capital), embarked on a grand project to rid *"akha* Mumbai" (in Marathi, the local language, "all of Mumbai") of slums. Bulldozers demolished twenty-five hundred shanties and displaced about a million people. Then Deshmukh was put in his place. He received a phone call from Sonia Gandhi, the national president of the Congress Party and reputedly the power behind

Prime Minister Manmohan Singh, asking him to back off. He did. Another Congress Party member stated, "Mumbai can never be Shanghai," and it became politically suicidal to use the term *Shanghaization* in India.

So how *does* urban renewal happen in India? One thriving example can be found south of Delhi, where in the last two decades farmland has given way to urban development. Here, a private-sector entrepreneur has achieved—albeit much more slowly—what the state achieved in Shanghai. K. P. Singh, the head of Delhi's DLF Group, has transformed fragmented holdings of agricultural land into a modern metropolis.

DLF is arguably India's leading real estate development company, and K. P. has built DLF into a real estate and construction group with revenues of about Rs. 150 billion ($35 billion) and, in 2007 a market capitalization greater than $30 billion. He is now one of the world's wealthiest men.[9] Equally extraordinary is K. P.'s transformation of vast acres of undeveloped land into one of the most modern places in India, Gurgaon. This city bordering south Delhi is now famous for its sleek office towers, shopping malls, multiplexes with state-of-the-art projection systems, upscale homes and condominiums, and even a world-class golf course. How did K. P. accomplish this in India's paralytic political climate?

I spoke with him at his office in the DLF Building, located in the heart of Delhi's business district. In the manner of a headmaster chiding his young tutelage, he said, "A lot of you young people don't know that DLF has been around for many years. You think Gurgaon just sprung up from nowhere. Raghuvendra Singh started DLF in 1946, before partition."

I told K. P. that twenty years ago my parents moved south of Delhi to what was then the village of Gurgaon. Friends and family derided the move saying, "There's nothing there. You're moving to the sticks." Now it's a bustling community, a desirable address. K. P.'s eyes glistened. "Most of South Delhi was developed by DLF. People don't know that."

That afternoon in his office, I learned just how far back K. P.'s history with DLF stretched. In 1954, he married the eldest daughter of DLF's founder, Raghuvendra Singh. He explained how his association with the family business coincided with India's changing land policies, reminding me that in 1957 the government passed the Delhi Development Act, making land development a concern of the state. K. P. waved his hand dismissively. "The socialist way of thinking came into play in the early 1960s. You see, in the first ten years after independence the urban development policy was very good— DLF was doing well. There were major incentives to private developers, and most of South Delhi was developed then." He shook his head. "But since 1961, there was a socialist shift and a total elimination of private sectors in urban development. This was the start of a plethora of fly-by-night developers operating under state patronage. Of course state patronage is a loosely defined term. Sixty percent of Delhi is unauthorized." Throughout the 1960s DLF made few gains. When K. P. joined the company in 1971, it was ripe for change.

> In the sixties, DLF receded. We just did not want to do business under these circumstances. But then, in 1971, wanting to do something new, I joined DLF. Hungry for business, I started to lobby the government and build alliances. It has taken me thirty years. During Rajiv's [Prime Minister Rajiv Gandhi] time things started to look up. Rajiv saw the potential to business when the state got out of the business of being in business. Under him things started to change on the policy front, and I had already started to acquire land. So the timing was good.
>
> You know these three and a half thousand acres on which DLF sits? The government did not just hand it to me and say "go build." I began acquiring the land in the late 1970s. I negotiated day and night with seven hundred families who each owned four or five acres of land. Remember we are talking about a heterogeneous society. If brothers owning land were hostile to one another, we had to negotiate with them; if the daughter had a stake and lived in a village a hundred miles out of Delhi, we had to get her on board. To earn their trust, I dressed like a farmer, went to their houses evening after evening, when the farmers come home from the day's work. I had to make sure we got the records straightened.

K. P. Singh sighed, as if still recovering from the effort of those negotiations. I thought about farmers in northern India, the very people who use the tractors made by Mahindra and Mahindra. Unlike the American hobbyist who buys a brand-new vehicle, the Indian farmer typically has a tractor that is in disrepair, second- or thirdhand, polluting, and noisy. In my mind's eye I saw the farmer perched on his tractor, his skin dry and parched from spending all day in the sun, dressed in a turban and loose-fitting garments. "You see, assemblage of land remains the biggest problem in developing it," K. P. explained. "Unlike in other countries, I can't run a bull-dozer over the occupants. If one of them goes to court, I'll be in litigation for the rest of my life."

"Were you ever in court?" I asked. "And how did you convince the farmers?"

I thought of the women on the farms, the saris they wear draped over their heads as protection from the sun as they haul bricks on a construction site, work in the fields, of course carry babies on their hips, prepare meals, and care for the home. I thought of their dignity, the colored bangles on their arms, nose rings and earrings, and I wondered if it had been difficult for K. P. to convince them to give up their land. K. P. leaned back in his chair, smiling with pride, to tell me he'd acquired most of DLF land without any major litigation, and on credit. "I took a loan from one farmer and then promptly used it to buy additional land. The farmers became my bankers and I became the bank for them. It was literally all about trust. At the end of each month, my guys would deliver the interest to these farmers personally. That kind of thing doesn't happen nowadays."

This, I thought, was truly incredible. Much like contemporary U.S. businesses that consolidate so-called fragmented industries, K. P. bought out the farmers to do things with the large properties that an individual farmer could not. Today DLF continues to operate in much the same way. Brokers sometimes represent unknown buyers and sellers, and often brokers don't know one another's identities. That way K. P. can buy land at less than what it's worth. The full market value of the land is high because of government distortions that constrict effective land supply: the Urban Land (Ceiling and Regulation) Act,[10] rent control, a very high stamp duty preventing efficient property transfers, and blocks of *sarkaari zameen* (government institutions holding prime real estate) that cannot be used for anything.

DLF's story is portrayed throughout India as a massive entrepreneurial feat. But some people question India's big developers, claiming that they profit unduly from the opacity of the land market and are complicit in perpetuating such opacity. As Pratap Bhanu Mehta, a leading political scientist in India, says, "No one quite knows how the large builders acquire land from the government. No detailed public records exist. How can some builders who are supposedly bankrupt continue to live in such affluence? There is widespread suspicion of a nexus made of the mafia, the media, builders, and politicians. What is good however is that the judiciary does poke holes through this once in a while."

It is important, however, to keep efficiency and accountability conceptually distinct. The Chinese government is efficient, even if not accountable and transparent. A privately held company, as DLF was until recently, is not accountable either, at least in the sense of a public corporation, but it does get the job done. In India the DLFs must compensate for a state that resists development for fear of treading on individual property rights.

The Power of Rivers

Yet another challenge both China and India face is tapping into the power of their rivers. The Yangtze River in China and the Narmada River in India have been mythologized for centuries by poets and writers in their respective countries. The Yangtze, which originates in the Qinghai-Tibetan Plateau, also known as the Roof of the World, runs 6,380 kilometers eastward across mainland China before it pours into the East China Sea, passing through land inhabited by four hundred million people. The Narmada River, which rises on Amarkantak Hill in the state of Madhya Pradesh, passes through the Marble Rocks at Jabalpur and the valley between the Vindhya and Satpura ranges, and continues through the states of Madhya Pradesh, Maharashtra, and Gujarat. Finally, eight hundred miles later the Narmada pours into the Arabian Sea at the Bharuch District of Gujarat. Hindus, some of whom consider the Narmada even holier than the Ganges, believe the river sprang from the body of Lord Shiva and that the mere sight of its beauty will purify the soul.

Plans to engineer dams great enough to harness the natural power of these immense rivers have long histories of contention. In China the idea dates back to Sun Yat-sen, who estimated the Yangtze could power all the country's railways, electricity lines, and factories. India first considered damming the Narmada in 1901, when the British Raj established the First Irrigation Commission of India, but it was only after independence that the project gained momentum.

Despite countless studies and commissions, construction of dams in both countries was suspended for decades. By the late 1980s Chinese efforts to tame the Yangtze had to contend with a new global political economy. India's proposed Narmada Dam came under increasing attack from engineering and environmental experts as well as the public. Big dams had become unfashionable, if not completely taboo, among development professionals; and environmentalists and activists argued that the human and environmental costs, displacement, and degradation far outweighed any benefits.

Each nation responded to its dam controversy in a manner consistent with the ethos of its decision-making process: China by fiat authority and India by democratic dissent.

China's most enduring and outspoken critic of damming the Yangtze was Wangli Huang, the late professor of hydrology at Tsinghua University. By the 1950s Huang had conducted years of research on the Yangtze and determined the dangers of a building design that did not consider potential sedimentation problems. For daring to criticize the CCP, Mao sent Huang to a labor camp in 1958, and during the subsequent Cultural Revolution even the professor's children were pressured to denounce him. Still the project remained just a matter of study. In the late 1980s Dai Qing, a trained missile engineer who worked with Chinese military intelligence before becoming a journalist, published a scathing political critique called *Yangtze, Yangtze*.

Nevertheless, in 1989 two feasibility studies, one by the Chinese and the other by the Canadian International Development Agency and the World Bank, concluded that a dam more than 550 feet tall would be technically, economically, socially, and environmentally sound. The project was sanctioned by the National People's Conference in 1992, and soon after that the Fifth Plenary Session of the Seventh National People's Congress approved a resolution to proceed with the Three Gorges project with a vote of 1,767 to 177, with 664 abstaining—indicative of legislative dissent by Chinese standards, where most resolutions pass nearly unanimously. In 1994 the project officially got under way, and in 1995 the resettlement of about 1.5 million people began.

International opposition to the building project soon translated into financial hurdles. In 1996 the World Bank and the U.S. Export-Import Bank declined to provide assistance, citing environmental concerns. But in January 1997 the State Planning Commission approved the issuance of 1 billion yuan ($121 million) in corporate bonds for financing further construction. In March 1997 Chongqing was upgraded to a municipality, a move to ease resettlement and expedite the project. Over the course of the project, allegations of corruption and fraud surfaced. Many observers feared that substandard materials were being used, ultimately risking the lives of millions.

In 1999, after some high-profile construction accidents at the site, Premier Zhu Rongji, the man responsible for Shanghai's redevelopment and an advocate for higher construction standards, sounded caution. In 2000, while addressing the Ninth Plenary Session of the Three Gorges Project Construction Committee (TGPCC), which was under the State Council, Zhu urged the builders to step up environmental protection and ecological construction in the dam area and improve the resettlement of local people. Observers saw the premier's comments as a response to the increasing corruption scandals that had engulfed the project. He emphasized that builders bore a "mountain of responsibility on their heads." The premier's comments were widely reported in the press.[11]

China's official media reported in 2003 that the reservoir at Three Gorges was deep enough for the dam's turbines to begin generating hydroelectric power.[12] But that same year a report published by an international nongovernmental organization pointed out several problems. Compensation to the resettled population had fallen short, promised jobs no longer existed, police used excessive force to mute protests, and embezzlement of construction funds was continuing.[13]

The Three Gorges Dam finished ahead of schedule in 2006. Officials stated that when its twenty-six turbines become operational in 2009, the dam will have a capacity of more than eighteen thousand megawatts. However, unlike the model relocation program for the farmers of Pudong, the damming of the Yangtze will not end happily. An estimated one million people will have been relocated from their homes and more than twelve hundred towns and villages will be submerged under the rising waters of the new dam.

As for India's plans to dam the Narmada River, initial work on the project started in 1961, but controversy surrounding the sharing of water and costs between the three concerned states stalled construction for nearly twenty years. Not until the 1980s, when the sheer scale of the dam became public, did the project once again acquire notoriety. Taming the Narmada and its tributaries involved building 30 big dams, 135 medium dams, and 3,000 small dams. Today the Narmada Valley Dam controversy has split the nation in two. Some quote Nehru's famous lines describing dams as "temples of modern India"; others, digging deeper, have found that Nehru also called dams "a disease of gigantism."[14]

Unlike China, however, India can tolerate controversy. Medha Patkar came on the scene in 1985 as a student studying the fate of communities threatened with submersion. She, along with her group, *Narmada Bachao Andolan* (Movement to Save the Narmada), is effectively the Mother Teresa of dam dwellers. Arguing that building the dam violates the fundamental rights of the people who will be displaced, Patkar has succeeded in internationalizing the issue. She served on the World Commission on Dams, an independent body sponsored by the World Bank to review the performance of large dams and make recommendations for future planning of water and energy projects. Patkar's *Andolan* single-handedly changed the World Bank's perspective on large dam projects across the world.

While the World Bank waffled and Patkar agitated, the Ministry of Environments and Forests provided the project with a conditional clearance in 1987. Five years later the World Bank commissioned a study of the project to be conducted by an independent team led by Bradford Morse. The so-called Morse Report concluded that the project overstated its benefits and underestimated its environmental and human costs, and suggested that the bank take a fresh look at it. The government of India refused to accept the findings of the Morse Report. This provoked Patkar's movement to file public interest litigation in 1994.[15] In response, the courts halted work on the project in 1995.

The court did a complete turnaround in October 2000 when the majority of the judges of the Indian Supreme Court cleared the way for the construction of the Sardar Sarovar Dam, one of the biggest dams to be built on the river. Patkar responded, "The Supreme Court, thus, has betrayed the tribal and peasant communities in the country at large and specifically, those in the Narmada Valley. Judiciary in this country is clearly under various political pressures and probably cannot act with the law honestly, can't decide on merit of the case alone."[16] Supreme Court rulings in 2005 stated that raising the height of the dam above 360 feet was illegal until families that were temporarily and permanently affected by the construction were relocated.

By March 2006, however, authorities had allowed the addition of 33 feet to the height of the Sardar Sarovar Dam. In protest, Patkar went on an indefinite hunger strike outside the house of the ruling party's leader. Such fasts in India are associated with Mahatma Gandhi's fasts in protest of various aspects of British rule and have a moral aura to them. Other protesters fasting with Patkar told the press that they were there because their land stood to be submerged by the additional height of the dam and they had not been offered any compensation for it. Patkar was eventually arrested.

Two months are a long time on the Indian political scene. In June 2006 Patkar was somewhat vindicated when the state government of Madhya Pradesh issued an order to stop construction of the Maheshwar Project, another of the dams slated to be built on the Narmada. The state ministry announced that work on the dam would not continue until a comprehensive rehabilitation plan was created.

That dam was supposed to have been completed in 1995.

A Tale of Two Other Singhs: How Individual Can India's Individual Property Rights Be?

My first impression of Surat Singh, a lawyer in the Indian Supreme Court, was how different he appeared from the Boston Brahmins and legal pundits to whom I had become so accustomed. There was no tweed jacket, no bow tie, no glasses, and no tan briefcase in hand. When I contacted him on the phone, he'd described himself as a "short, arrogant guy with a loud laugh." Because he'd participated in several high-profile cases in India, and held masters of law degrees from Delhi and Oxford Universities, and a doctorate in law from Harvard, I'd asked him to guide me through the thicket of Indian property law. On his suggestion, we met in the lobby of the Park Royal Hotel in south Delhi.

Dr. Singh's most discernable accoutrement was a small hand towel that doubled as a handkerchief. He accentuated the urgency of what he had to say by periodically leaning across the coffee table and dabbing the perspiration off his nose and forehead. The only break he took was when he glanced askew at his companion, a Delhi real estate broker, looking for authentication of what he had just said. I merely took notes during this virtuoso performance, occasionally posing a question.

Dr. Singh's story began, not quite at the beginning of how property rights came into being in India, but rather at how they evolved immediately after independence when a number of constitutional articles specified the fundamental status of property rights in India. Any Indian was guaranteed by law to be able to own property.[17] There were caveats, of course. Under

Article 31, for example, no one can be deprived of their property except by law, but the law is required to set compensation or principles on which such compensation is to be paid. At this point, Dr. Singh alerted me that despite the "sacrosanct" place of property rights in the Indian Constitution, the two most important institutions of Indian democracy—the judiciary and legislature—soon found themselves at loggerheads over the status of those rights.

"You have to understand the socialist ideology and land reform background," warned Dr. Singh.[18] He explained that property rights law in independent India arose in the context of an overwhelming desire for equitable land reform in the aftermath of the exploitative *zamindari* (land tenure) system, under which the propertied few, the *zamindars*, had lorded over the masses. "There was an unavoidable tension between citizens' right to property and the government policy of fashioning an egalitarian society." At the time, Nehru's Congress Party particularly wanted the government to be able to acquire (preferably without compensation) and control private assets (read as land and some businesses) for public good. Soon after independence, several land reforms were passed. *Zamindari* was abolished, ceilings were fixed on land holdings, cultivating tenants secured permanent rights, and in some states the law regulated the share of the landlord. No sooner had these laws been enacted, however, than differences between the judiciary and the legislature on the question of property rights became apparent. Behind this tension were several prominent cases in which the legislature continued to demand powers to appropriate private property, and the judiciary continued to question the right of the legislature to do so.

At first the legislature seemed vindicated. In the First Amendment to the Indian Constitution, enacted in 1951, the judiciary permitted the government to acquire *estates*—a term broadly defined to cover almost all agricultural land and, in particular, properties owned by *zamindars* and other revenue farmers—in the public interest. Another part of the amendment (termed the Ninth Schedule) declared that none of the laws related to several agrarian reforms could become invalid on the grounds that they violated fundamental property rights embodied in the constitution. When landowners continued to petition courts on grounds that appropriation of their land violated their rights, the Supreme Court, in two well-known cases, rejected the argument and confirmed Parliament's right to amend the constitution. A minority of dissenting judges continually questioned that parliamentary right. However, Nehru's towering personality and charisma, and the idealism of the first years of independent India, contributed to the legislature's upper hand until his death in 1964.

The tussle between the judiciary and the legislature over the question of property rights eventually culminated in their being relegated to a weaker statutory right. Property rights were no longer fundamental and so were vulnerable to legislative whims. Dr. Singh emphasized one of the most severe consequences of this: "The problem was that in removing the right to property as a '*fundamental right*', no citizen has the right to approach the Supreme Court under Article 32 [which allows a redress of any violation of fundamental rights]. And with it goes the possibility of speedy adjudication."

Over the years each act of judicial activism in favor of individual property rights prompted Parliament to simply amend the constitution. One such case was *Golakhnath v. the Union of India*. Golakhnath was a well-known priest and religious personality who had owned an estate that had largely been declared "surplus" under the Punjab Security of Land Tenures Act of 1953.[19] The Golakhnath family petitioned the Supreme Court, claiming that their rights to acquire and hold property had been violated.

Eleven Supreme Court judges heard the Golakhnath case in 1966. Chief Justice Subha Rao, who had acquired a reputation of favoring individuals' right to property over the government's right to acquire it, stated that Parliament could not meddle with individuals' fundamental rights. He suggested that there was an inviolable basic structure to the constitution and that fundamental property rights were part of that sacrosanct portion, making them immune to legislative maneuvering.

"Mrs. Gandhi was furious," Dr. Singh exploded as he mimicked Indira Gandhi's rage. "She said that the Supreme Court does not really know the real situation in India. The property is concentrated in the hands of the few and the masses are suffering." Bold judicial activism ran afoul of the political establishment's then-populist policies. Even though the Golaknath judgment would not affect any previously enacted land-related amendments, it had set off alarm bells in Parliament. To make matters worse, within just a few weeks of the Golakhnath verdict, the Congress Party incurred heavy losses in the parliamentary elections.

Meanwhile Parliament had a new battleground on which to flex its muscles. Reiterating its socialist suspicion of concentrations of wealth, the legislature went after princely families who had exerted their power over the populace through the end of British rule; the so-called privy purses offered to those families in return for their recognizing the sovereignty of the Union of India; and the banks, deemed instruments through which economic power could be concentrated to the detriment of the common people. Overnight, and without compensation, estates were taken and banks nationalized. But the Supreme Court once again upheld property rights and struck down the parliamentary order. Further, the court ruled 10 to 1 that the nationalized banks had not determined compensation properly. The Parliament reacted with equal ferocity. Two amendments in 1971 authorized the Parliament to amend any part of the constitution and removed from judicial purview the right to question compensation paid to property owners.

Another case involved an individual petitioning the Supreme Court to preserve his estate (*Keshavananda Bharati v. the State of Kerala*) but also spoke to the extent of Parliament's power to amend the constitution. The verdict was split. "Six voted along what I call British lines. That is, they took the view that elected parliamentarians are the voice of the people, and this voice can move to acquire property. Six voted along what I call American lines, that is, embracing the view that the powers of government should be heavily constrained and individual right to property was paramount. The last, Justice H. R. Khanna, took a courageous stand. He said that some basic rights in the constitution are indeed above laws. But he said there is a separate issue of whether the right to property until this time thought of as part of Basic Rights, was in fact one. He decided it wasn't."

So, concluded Dr. Singh, "the operation was successful, but the patient was dead." As it stands today the right to property is not a part of the inviolable basic structure.

"But India is a land of paradoxes," he also advised. In 1978, the Supreme Court focused on the scope of Article 21, which says that "no person shall be deprived of his life or personal liberty except according to procedure established by law." It interpreted "liberty" expansively, including the right to live with human dignity. And it insisted on reasonable, just, and fair procedures, and ruled against arbitrary action, preferring instead the American "due process" clause.

Thus what Parliament took away in 1978 by deleting Article 31 (right to property) from the list of fundamental rights, it brought back through judicial interpretation under Article 21 (right to life and liberty). The net result is that the right to property can be protected as a fundamental right. "But whether it is America or India, there is no free lunch. One has to be extremely resourceful because it costs property to protect your property rights, even in democracy," warned Dr. Singh humorously. Thus property rights in India are unclear because of the very institutions meant to guarantee them. This includes not just the courts and the legislatures but also bureaucracies. The role of the latter is apparent in another Singh story—a story both incredible and true.

I ran into the second Mr. Singh in Vasant Vihar, an upscale Delhi residential area. The former CEO of British Oxygen in India, this Mr. Singh rents the upper half of his two-story house to an American journalist and his Indian wife. Unable to save much in the cash-poor, perk-rich era of his working life, the Singhs use the rental income from the house to maintain a comfortable way of life. So it came as a surprise when Mr. Singh received a letter from the court saying that his house would be seized by the court, apparently because he had not paid back a loan on which the house was listed as collateral.

"I had never put up the house for anything. We don't need any loans, thanks to the house," he assured me. After some investigating, Mr. Singh unearthed a bizarre scandal. From the records kept by the Delhi Development Authority (DDA), a government body that oversees all urban development projects in Delhi, his neighbor had acquired a copy of all legal papers pertaining to the house and used the house as collateral to take out a loan on which he neglected to repay. The notorious DDA had required copies of the papers during a pro forma change of the house's status. "How the neighbor got access to these papers, who was complicit in DDA, I don't quite know, but I suspect even the bank was involved," explained Mr. Singh.

The discovery pushed the eighty-three-year-old into high gear. "You see, first, I contacted my brother—a well-known Supreme Court lawyer—and he assured me that that the matter would be solved, because the city does maintain proper records on homes, it takes a while to unearth them, but they have them and with his contacts, we didn't need to oil any palms. Plus, I keep Xeroxes of everything. When the local court did not respond, my lawyer-brother threatened to take the matter to the high court, and that is how we got a hearing. Eventually we won the case. What I still don't get is how the bugger had the guts to forge the deed and how the bank failed to verify ownership. He still greets me in the park like nothing happened."

A series of mild and hilarious English curses, reminiscent of his British education and British bosses, followed.

From Private Ownership to Party Ownership and Back Again in China

To guide me through the thickets of Chinese property law, I turned to Katherine Wilhelm, a lawyer in the Beijing office of a New York law firm. She readily agreed to assist, saying "the whole question of what you do with property rights in a fast-changing economy is a major issue."[20]

Wilhelm began by explaining that private land ownership and transactions came to an end under Mao. In rural areas all land was acquired by the government and placed under collectives. Every peasant received a rural *hukou*, a license to live in a particular village. In cities almost all land became the property of the government. In line with its social agenda, the CCP subsequently allocated land use rights, free of charge, to the *danwei*, the state-owned work units around which urban social and economic life was organized.[21]

The constitution mandated that the *danwei* not transfer those rights. Through the 1970s housing was almost completely socialized. City rents were ridiculously low, and the *danwei* bore the lion's share of housing costs, which amounted to roughly a quarter of total labor costs for a typical state-owned enterprise.[22] Thus the *danwei* and the *hukou* system, rather than the market, allocated land and housing.

"The situation changed with the reforms in 1978," continued Wilhelm. Deng transformed moribund land around Shenzhen into an economic laboratory. This included the creation of the first market for land use rights and housing. Deng allowed rent increases, sold public housing to private individuals, allowed commercial construction by private developers, and promised to protect private property rights.[23] Yet the state did not let go of its land. To eliminate possible ambiguity, the 1982 constitution set the record straight by declaring that all urban land belonged to the state and all rural land belonged to collectives.

Further, classes of property rights were created as a way of managing the transition. According to Wilhelm, "The state's ownership rights were absolute; but agricultural collectives could have their land requisitioned by the state in the public interest."[24] Foreign investors' rights were also protected.[25] Economic realities necessitated this. For example, it became a problem when the only thing a Chinese partner was contributing to a Sino-foreign joint venture was land that ultimately belonged to the state, not the partner. A simple chronological reading of land reform laws reveals that the contributions of property made by the Chinese joint venture partners were not entirely legal; they predated the land legislation of the 1980s that allowed legal transferability of land rights. Before the 1980s, most state owned enterprises (which later became partners in joint ventures) applied to the government to use land that was not transferable and could not be leased or mortgaged

Wilhelm emphasized that today there are two issues. "One is of scope and one is of enforcement," she said. Referring to the 1982 constitutional amendment she added, "The problem of scope has gone away, as much can be privately owned. But the problem of enforcement remains." It is in the mechanisms of enforcement that one can most clearly see the Chinese government's stance on questions of individual versus collective rights.

One example is the problem of demolition and relocation that is part of any urban redevelopment effort. Wilhelm explained how relocation often plays out in China: "[R]elocation and demolition licenses are meant to be won via public auctions, but everyone knows it's largely done privately. If a developer has got a *chai qian* [demolition and relocation] license for where you live, the city government puts up signs telling you exactly that. Then someone from the local government will pay you a visit to estimate the value of your home. Sometimes these folks don't let the appraisers in, so the appraisers make estimates from standing outside the house." She laughed at the absurdity. "It's a black box, in that no one really knows how the compensation figure is determined. Some say it's the cost of replacing the home—the cost of the wood and steel, et cetera. But anyone knows that the intrinsic value of material is hardly the way to arrive at compensation—they don't take into account, for example, that the wood used in your house dates back to the Qing era. Or location. As you know, in real estate location is everything. So compensation varies significantly."

Indeed, some scholars have pointed out that the range of compensation is wide, from more than $750,000 for a high official's home, to between $10,000 and $50,000 for some affected families, and finally, to nothing for residents who did not cooperate with the redevelopment process.[26] Examples of ad hoc and inadequate compensation abound. In one resettlement project in Beijing that required the resettlement of 3,328 families, only 14 percent of the families were paid, and compensation ranged from $12,500 to $50,000 instead of the expected $67,500 for each family. Further, 86 percent of the families were assigned to apartments in remote suburbs for which they paid rent—even though one-third had owned their original houses.[27]

Wilhelm then explained the final punch in property compensation procedures: "Once you are told the amount [of compensation] you can either take it or leave it. If you take it, you get paid from designated banks, and during this stage, a significant amount of the money can 'disappear.' Sometimes they offer you alternative homes—but you may find that a few months into moving to your new home you are asked to pay rent. Now if you refuse to leave, if you become one of the nail-head families—what the Chinese call a *dingzihu*, basically a stubborn nail that needs to be hammered in—they harass you."

I asked if she could clarify who constituted "they." She elaborated: "*They* are often developers who were formerly running state-owned construction companies in the early 1990s. *They* can also be real estate firms run by the sons and daughters of former high-ranking CCP leaders; here we call them the Red Princes. The lines are not really clear. Essentially, private developers exercise eminent domain rights of the state."

In recent years scores of stories on the plight of urban Chinese residents caught the government's attention and resulted in a few resident-friendly edicts. In March 2005 the Shanghai city government improved the management of relocations by forbidding resettlement companies from stopping water or electricity supplies to force people off their property. Wilhelm acknowledged the change of heart. "It's my sense that the forced nature of these relocations has caught the government's attention and has decreased. Now officers of the law must be present when the eviction process is taking place."

I wondered whether that made the relocation process more just. "Well," Wilhelm mused, "they have added more process, but the substance of the law remains the same. In reality, you still can't petition the courts on property matters, the courts are not independent. Under Chinese law, the People's Supreme Court works as a ministerial-level organization, which makes it equal, *not* superior, to the Ministry of Construction granting these licenses. But people continue to petition the justice ministry under the age-old *xinfang* petitioning system that is outdated and ineffectual."

Why do people continue to petition and protest if the justice system offers no respite? Wilhelm had a ready response: "If a newspaper story or a journalist reports on one of these forced relocations, they can sometimes get a better deal and the government realizes that they can't afford this to be a destabilizing issue."

Wilhelm's explanation was echoed in my meeting with a Yale-educated expatriate lawyer in Beijing: "Street protests," he assured me, "are really street theater. They are not really about whether it's fair to tear down my home or not. The owner knows that he can't hold up the developer once the process is under way. The best he can do is become inconvenient and extract some money or concessions from the developer. So he does perform, and is better off as a result of doing so. But doing something extreme like standing in front of the bulldozer can only earn him the right to be carted away by state police, that's all."

Twisting Fate of the *Siheyuan*

Not long after talking with Wilhelm I found myself walking Beijing's maze of narrow footpaths, the *hutongs*, where the boxy courtyard houses known as *siheyuan* are still found. The courtyard garden served as an open-air living room where family members met to converse. In feudal times the courtyard dwellings were built according to the strict rules and hierarchies of feng shui; for example, the gate was at the southeast corner, which was the Wind corner, and the main building was on the north side, which was believed to belong to Water, the element that quenches fire. A wall or curtain over the entrance kept out evil spirits. The lord and lady of the house lived in the northern, sunny main building and their children in the side chambers. The southern row on the opposite side, those nearest to the entrance gate, was generally used as the study, the reception room, and the servants' dwelling.

In fact, Beijing's *siheyuan*, with their strict rules and forms, closed to the outside and open on the inside, are seen by some as an expression of the Chinese character. Regarded with nostalgia, the twisting fate of the *siheyuan* pointedly embodies China's changing property laws. Before 1949 the size and grandeur of a *siheyuan* denoted the social and financial status of its owner.

When Mao Zedong outlawed private property, all *siheyuan* became the property of the state. Unsurprisingly, Mao lived in a coveted courtyard house, as do many of today's Chinese Party leaders. During the Cultural Revolution most Beijing *siheyuan* were owned by the local residence bureau, which could allocate as many as a dozen families to live in one house; overcrowding and poverty then caused the houses to deteriorate.

The most recent twist occurred in 2004, when the Beijing government allowed foreigners to buy *siheyuan*. They have quickly become a trendy piece of real estate. Billionaire media mogul Rupert Murdoch plunked down $1.2 million for his property. Negotiations can involve as many as thirty families claiming ownership of the previous cramped residence and entitled to compensation for moving out. Less well known, however, is that the official government policy is to return the *siheyuan* to their original pre-1949 owners. The catch is that many of the original owners' descendants hold no property titles or papers to prove their claims.

As I walked toward the Forbidden City, its grandeur preserved as a historical anomaly, I thought about the last part of my conversation with Wilhelm. How and why has the Chinese government gotten away with trampling private property rights during the last three decades? Wilhelm sounded a prophecy and a warning: "When experiencing intense economic growth, it appears that society as a whole is benefiting, and the problems are not immediately perceptible. But property rights are the foundation on which efficient markets are built. Currently uncertain property rights are just a part of the larger 'China risk packet,' and so investors are able to justify it. But at some point the Chinese government's attempt to create a top-down market for property won't work. At some point the middle class is going to ask why they cannot pass on their property to their children, why they can't pass on the wealth that for the first time in history they are being asked to create."

Most scholars who study the link between property rights and economic growth argue that the more clearly defined are the former, the greater the possibility of the latter. But in China economic growth has occurred without formal property rights of the sort familiar to and lauded by the West. Property rights in India, too, are ill defined, overlapping, and ambiguous. Although in China these ambiguities have not prevented the state from building a dam or a city, in India the ambiguity of rights inevitably leads to an impasse. Indians never know who will win a battle of disputed property rights. They only know that the battle will play out against the setting of overburdened court systems, free and noisy press, vibrant civil society, and of course India's legislative and electoral systems that laud the right of the individual and deplore development without a human face.

Chapter Five

Manna and Miasma

Meanderings Through the Chinese and Indian
Financial Firmaments

When I was a boy my father would send me, passbook in hand, to our branch of the Punjab National Bank in Delhi's Safdarjung neighborhood. Standing guard outside the bank was a Sikh, resplendent in his flaming orange turban and holding a long-barreled rifle that looked incapable of being fired. He reminded me of the pictures in my history textbook of Sikhs standing guard outside British banks in Shanghai earlier in the century, ready to confront unfair aggression with more gallantry and chivalry than effective weaponry. I discovered that flashing a friendly smile was all I needed to do to gain a closer look at the rifle, which was my real reason for agreeing to run the errand for my father.

When I squeezed through the bank's narrow iron doors, I immediately smelled the dampness in the dimly lit, cavernous main room in which many desks, all untidy, were strewn around. Dusty files formed unstable towers in almost every corner of the room. A dozen ceiling fans groaned as their tired blades spun out warm air in the sweltering Delhi heat. Navigating the maze was difficult, so as I'd seen my father do, I shouted in the general direction of a clerk who eventually nodded pleasantly at me.

"Please update the passbook," I said. The palm-sized, resin-covered book was, allegedly, a record of all our family's banking transactions.

"Come back later. It will take several hours." He waved his hand dismissively, and busied himself with something at his desk. Several hours later I came back, only to be told again that updating my passbook would take several hours.

Often this would go on all day, which I did not mind because it meant frequent visits to the Sikh guard and his rifle. Eventually, however, my father would tell me not to go back, it was no use. This sort of experience was commonplace and presumably contributed to Indians' general reluctance to use banks. Even today most middle-class Indian homes are storehouses of gold, diamonds, and jewelry—almost $200 billion in illiquid investments that comprise half of the aggregate bank deposits in India.

Despite the many gains and reforms in India's overall financial picture since 1991, these problems persist in the core of Indian public-sector banking. Abhijit Banerjee and other economists at the Massachusetts Institute of Technology have studied the skewed incentives that exist for bankers, and conclude that Indian bankers display rational inertia, a response to ambient incentives.[1] They are characteristically risk averse. Having spent their careers lending to either the state or state approved industrial houses at state-directed rates, they have grown used to making safe bets. Managers lending to entities that are not state approved could be reprimanded if the loans ultimately go bad. These reprimands result from a rational fear emanating from the law's failure to differentiate between bad loans and bad bankers. The emergence of specialized credit-rating agencies and databases in the past decade has only slightly mitigated that fear. Further, because bankers' salaries are fixed, they have no incentive to pursue lending beyond the minimum required to appear active. Finally, high interest rates on risk-free government bonds remain the "sounder" alternative for bankers.

At the macroeconomic level the resulting collective risk aversion curtails lending to creditworthy customers. Rakesh Mohan, deputy governor of the Central Bank, created a stir when he used the term *lazy banking* in a speech at a bank economists' conference in 2002. Mohan pointed to a legitimate concern: overinvestment in government securities means less financing available for the private sector, which adversely affects entrepreneurs. Mohan also critiqued other issues with Indian banking: the inability of Indian banks to bring down lending rates in line with lower inflation rates, persistent high rates of lending that put a burden on small and medium-scale enterprises, and general risk aversion for long-term project lending.[2] Banerjee's analysis validates Mohan's claims that "[l]ending to industry is lots of trouble. Lending to firms that are not blue chip is even more trouble. So why bother?"[3]

Banking in China tells a similar story. Until recently banks in China and India were under state control, lending money based on political rather than economic criteria. Under the pretense of economic development, they consistently directed funds into unprofitable government concerns (known as public-sector units in India and state-owned enterprises in China). The waste was extraordinary. Today nonperforming loans (NPLs) totaling some $11 billion, about 3 percent of all loans, have clogged the Indian financial landscape,[4] and the situation at Chinese banks is worse. In 2005 China had $300 billion in NPLs, an estimated at 40 percent of all loans.[5]

However, a difference has emerged in the two countries' banking landscapes. Despite economic reform, China has made no significant move to separate banks from state and CCP control. Good money flows after bad. In India, although banking retains its rotten core—plagued by inefficiency, opacity, and government meddling—new private-sector banks are meeting world standards and forcing some government-owned banks to get their books in order.

A close look at Chinese capital markets suggests that several Western "truths" about corporate finance do not hold in the Middle Kingdom. Consider the presumed truth that entrepreneurs frequently tap securities markets outside their home base when the latter are not developed enough to provide the capital they need. For example, the Mexican cement company Cementos Mexicanos (Cemex) tapped the Spanish debt capital markets in the early 1990s to escape the excess cost of debt its Mexican locale caused it to pay. Earlier the Chilean phone company Compania Telefonos de Chile financed a massive telecommunications project by raising capital in New York, sparking similar capital raising by a wave of Latin American companies. Further, South African companies in the postapartheid era drew on London's markets to escape the uncertainty of South Africa and the illiquidity of the Johannesburg capital market in the mid-1990s.

The pattern in these international issuances is that they follow, rather than precede, domestic capital raising.[6] A track record at home appears to reassure distant investors that the entrepreneur is worthy and reliable. In India the software giants Infosys and Wipro listed domestically before raising capital on the NASDAQ and NYSE, respectively. By contrast, in China, companies have issued equity overseas before coming home to issue in China.[7] This unusual reversal has a simple explanation. Listing in Shanghai or Shenzhen does not signal credibility to foreign investors who know the listing process is governed by a political calculus designed to prop up companies rather than by the free competition that allows public access to the best securities.

Despite severe government intervention and control of Chinese capital markets, the country grows by leaps and bounds. If China can grow with a nonexistent domestic capital market, perhaps that "necessary" condition for economic growth is not really necessary after all; or perhaps the condition must be coated with even more generous caveats than is *de rigueur* in the caution-ridden world of academia.

Indian bourses, on the other hand, have achieved significant credibility since the reforms of 1991. Mumbai now boasts one of the most rapid evolutions of an equity market, from third-world to very near first-world status, accomplishing in a decade what one expert opined took well over fifty years for the United States to accomplish.[8] Further, despite early scandals that threatened to undermine the stock exchanges, India's general proclivity toward information dissemination and private property rights has predisposed it to allowing capital markets to develop in Mumbai.

A Tale of Two Stock Exchanges, Part 1: Tango in Mumbai

Mumbai houses two stock exchanges, the Bombay Stock Exchange (BSE) and the National Stock Exchange (NSE). But it wasn't always so. The BSE is housed in its dilapidated 130-year-old premises on Dalal Street. Historians say that a group of twenty-two stockbrokers first began trading under a banyan tree opposite Bombay's Town Hall in the mid-1850s, each investing the then-princely amount of one rupee. In 1875 this informal group was called "The Native Share and Stockbrokers Association," later to formally become the Bombay Stock Exchange (BSE). In 1956 the government of India recognized the BSE as the first stock exchange in the country under the Securities Contracts (Regulation) Act.

The BSE had always functioned as a clublike regional exchange run by powerful groups of Gujarati and Marwari businessmen.[9] Located in the commercial epicenter of India, along with its smaller affiliate exchanges in Ahmedabad and Calcutta, it monopolized trading throughout the country and operated with high commissions, little disclosure of transaction prices, serious paperwork problems, and an unreliable clearing and settlement system. Although the BSE styled itself as a self-regulating organization, it was generally considered more "self" and less "regulating." Its governing bodies were all composed of practicing brokers, and close community ties were used to exclude others to the detriment of the overall system. Unrestricted by any law against insider trading, company executives were free to buy and sell just before major announcements, and brokers, part and parcel of this manipulation, had no incentive to change.

In early 1991 a crisis engulfed India. A high fiscal deficit, overdue payments to the International Monetary Fund, and Gulf War–precipitated soaring oil prices reduced India's foreign currency assets to $1 billion, barely enough to cover two weeks of imports.[10] Manmohan Singh, the finance minister and darling of economists and policy experts everywhere, responded with a clarion call to reform. The markets rallied. It had taken years for the BSE, which handled 70 percent of trading volume in India, to get from one hundred points to one thousand, but under Singh's call to reform it rocketed past two thousand in just two years.[11]

At the center of this bull run was Harshad Mehta, christened Big Bull and the poster boy of the new can-do attitude of the Indian investor. Because Mehta believed that the market was all about perception, he would buy large amounts of a particular stock at a higher-than-market price, theorizing that his actions would further drive up the price of the security. Mehta convinced many companies that they were undervalued but by choosing to give him a stake in their company they could realize their true value. Yet a piece of the puzzle was missing. Where was Mehta getting the money to prop up the stocks?

Sucheta Dalal was the investigative journalist who eventually broke the story. Mehta and other brokers had siphoned money out of the banking system—in particular the interbank market in government securities—to the corporate stock markets. The origins and aftermath of the scandal was the focus of much subsequent analysis, including the following:

> Banks, for their part, tempted by the booming stock market of the time, overlooked prudent lending norms. They lent to unregulated brokers They ignored the guideline of handing over money only when collateral securities were in their possession. Brokers took positions in the stock market with others' money. Soon blue-chip foreign banks, including Citibank, Standard Chartered PLC and ANZ Grindlays, succumbed to the same pressures. All violated regulations of both the Securities and Exchange Board of India (SEBI), a body formed by the Government of India with loosely defined authority to regulate the securities industry in 1988, and the Reserve Bank of India.[12]

The scale of the scam came as a shock, with damages in the neighborhood of $230 million. But Mehta's Bombay mischief was one of countless examples of egregious manipulations. In the weeks following Mehta's exposure, 17 percent was shaved off the market. Ultimately the incident was feasible because of collusion among market participants, compounded by regulatory inaction, resulting in an opaque haze engulfing the markets.

Despite the severity of the scam, it was not obvious that reform would follow. On the contrary, observers warned that the stock market scandal could reverse the preceding economic reforms. Fortunately, Manmohan Singh, who understood that he had to rebuild trust in the markets, effected significant change. He immediately announced that the Reserve Bank of India and the Central Bureau of Investigation (equivalent of the Federal Reserve and the Federal Bureau of Investigation in the United States) would look into the matter. Singh urged Parliament to remain calm and acknowledged that there had been "prima facie evidence of the banking system's failure and collusion between bank officials and some outsiders."[13] While the public investigations ensued, the government set out to reform the capital markets.

Although the Ministry of Finance now backed the SEBI to reform the Bombay Stock Exchange, the SEBI was not the primary actor. The key to reforming capital markets was to create competition for the BSE. In retrospect the creation of the National Stock Exchange was an acknowledgment that regulatory reform without accompanying competition had limited efficacy. The government tapped the Industrial Development Bank of India (IDBI) to lead the project. The IDBI was owned and controlled by the government and dedicated to providing long-term finance in India.

Everyone I spoke to about the origins of the NSE said, "Talk to Ravi." Ravi Narain was one of five IDBI employees invited to create a new exchange and is now its managing director and CEO. I met him in the NSE's headquarters in Mumbai's Bandra-Kurla district in December 2004.

"I was an unusual choice," acknowledged Narain. "I was educated at Cambridge and had an MBA from Wharton. Everyone else at IDBI was typically an engineer or chartered accountant." Although Narain would not have been an unusual choice in the United States, in India at that time, when exchanges were regulated, MBAs were not held in especially high esteem. Certainly R. H. Patil, whom the IDBI picked to head the new exchange, had the more "classic" background: long and successful stints at the Reserve Bank of India and IDBI.

Patil, only three years from retirement, approached the creation of the NSE with a reformer's zeal, but Narain did so with an explorer's daring. "I saw it as a pure experiment. We were like real venture-capital-backed entrepreneurs," explained Narain. S. S. Nadkarni, then the chairman of IDBI, was enthusiastic about building an online exchange and gave Narain full rein. "Nadkarni said go do this, do it quickly and don't tell me what you are doing," Narain recalled, shaking his head in astonishment. "Nadkarni did not even ask me for a budget. We did it ourselves. From the IDBI scheme of things the cost was puny, but for us it was significant."

Despite IDBI's support, many market watchers predicted imminent collapse and questioned the viability of a technology-based exchange. "People told us, 'Exchanges are not about technology, they are about people.' We understood that," explained Narain, "but we thought that technology could help people do things they couldn't do before." As Narain recounts, the technological hurdles were not trivial. "There was no viable telecommunications infrastructure on the basis of which a state-of-the-art exchange could be launched. We obviously couldn't rely on terrestrial lines. So we set up our own satellite telecommunications company and pulled together equipment and software from vendors in the U.S., Canada, France, Israel. We had all these vendors together in a consortium, led by TCS—Tata Consulting Services."

The biggest group of soothsayers predicting demise comprised brokers at BSE, who referred to the new exchange in derogatory terms as *sarkari share bazaar* (government stock exchange) and were confident that it would pose no challenge to BSE, which boasted a market capitalization of $130 billion and listed some six thousand companies.[14] Even the intelligentsia doubted the government's ability to set up an exchange that would be professional and able to compete with the venerable BSE.

Narain was indignant at this. "In Calcutta, brokers used to earn several lakhs of rupees [each lakh is approximately $2,500] per day in addition to the legitimate brokerage because of the opacity in the system, which allowed them to charge the customer the highest price of the day for a buy transaction and the lowest price of the day for a sell transaction. For this service they would call themselves charitable nonprofit organizations for tax purposes!" Patil described the BSE as an anachronism, a democracy as existed in Britain in the fourteenth century—for the few, of the few. Narain, in contrast, "wanted a regular company that made profit and returns to owners. No single institution would have a predominantly large share. We were visualizing a utility that would provide a public service infrastructure that would pay taxes and receive no subsidies."

Trading began on November 4, 1994. In stark contrast to its older rival, the NSE provided investors across the country with simultaneous access to a single screen through a satellite-linked network of VSATs (very small aperture terminals).[15] Installation of all the equipment brokers needed—the VSATs, antennas, uninterrupted power systems, and other internal connections—was done by the NSE itself.[16] The system documented the exact time and price of each transaction, allowed investors to see orders and trades in real time, and removed the haze that engulfed the erstwhile pricing system. Never before had India's twenty-two regional exchanges used this type of technology.

Narain recalled the opening day.

We didn't know if all this fancy stuff would work on day one. The finance minister came to inaugurate it. We went live. We had built cubicles with computers for all brokers to participate. Each Gujarati gentleman came in his traditional white dhoti and with a young person in tow.[17] The latter was to help the broker operate the keyboard of the terminal! I thought to myself that if we can get the broker comfortable with using the computer, even through a helper, we will have cracked a major psychological barrier.

Within months BSE realized it would have to upgrade its technology and alter its entire modus operandi. "When volumes began to grow, BSE felt threatened," recalled Narain. One significant reason for the NSE's growing turnover was the rate of order conversion. In the BSE's "shout out" system, with brokers on the floor literally shouting buy and sell orders, only about 30 percent of the orders were actually converted into trades. The automated system, however, raised the percentage to 90. In response to the stiff competition, BSE halved the $1 million price of a seat on the exchange, but that was still almost 50 percent more than an NSE seat, which cost $215,000.[18]

The NSE rented the mezzanine floor on the top of a building in Kalaghoda,

a central location in Bombay, for the purpose of collecting the papers needed to fulfill paper-based settlement. Historically, settlement was not complete until the buyer had transferred the physical ownership certificate to the settler. This "certificate" grew into, for each traded security, an untidy bundle of papers, documenting each time the security had changed hands, tied together with shoestring, possibly yellowing at the edges and sometimes torn and frayed. These were legal documents, the bedrock of the financial system! Now the NSE became systematic. Each bundle was thoroughly examined, junk paper removed, and illegitimate trades were marked "nondelivery"—that is, the trade had not been consummated. As the trading volumes grew, the floor became strewn with paper. Into this melee one day came the municipal authorities, brandishing hammers, and starting to break down the roof, asserting that the NSE had illegally occupied the premises.

When I saw all our employees—young men and women—put wet hankies on their faces to protect themselves from the flying debris, collect the myriad pieces of paper and finish the settlement, come what may, I knew that the market knew that we were not going to run away.

In an attempt to counter its erosion in market share, the BSE started to operate the Bombay Online Trading (BOLT) system, but its connectivity was still restricted to Bombay, a far cry from its competitor's national reach. By the end of 1995 the NSE had about six hundred VSAT-using members in twenty-one Indian cities and had contracted to provide a total of 1,750 links by the end of the following year. In addition, Patil estimated that 40 percent of the exchange's business came from outside Bombay.[19] By 2003 the NSE had relegated the BSE into second position in equity, wholesale and retail debt, and derivatives markets. In equities, for example, its daily trading volume was more than twice that of the BSE.

But the heart of the difference between the two exchanges was conceptual. The state-of-the-art technology and day-to-day best practices adopted by the new exchange allowed a transparent and speedy trading system, but these were only symptoms of better decision making and organizing, which were rooted in a fundamentally different governance structure. While the BSE was organized as a brokers' association with significant barriers to new members, the NSE was incorporated as a tax-paying company owned by a large group of development financial institutions. While the BSE elected one of its broker-members to administer the exchange, the NSE was run by professionals led by with a managing director. Effectively, the NSE completely separated ownership and management and made "value maximization" a primary goal for the NSE.

Given the general state of disrepair of government-run organizations in India, how did a government-owned financial institution act as midwife to the birth of a state-of-the-art exchange? The ownership structure was legally engineered to keep a safe distance from the government, despite being owned by several quasi-governmental institutions. This aspect of the NSE's evolution is worth noting because although strictly speaking it was a *sarkari share bazaar*, practically speaking it was anything but On the other hand, when the NSE broke down barriers to the brokerage industry, brokers were no longer assured of fat-cat profits but were disciplined by fair competition. This in turn ensured a fetish for cost minimization within the NSE itself.[20] Patil mentioned to me that the cost savings for investors financed the NSE, and that subsidies were not needed.[21] Indeed, as trading volume surged over the first year, the NSE not only generated enough income but declared a dividend for its shareholders.[22]

Establishment of the NSE was the most important reason behind the pace and the depth of reform in Indian capital markets during the early 1990s The NSE had made the BSE redundant, particularly because the former's regional scope could not match the NSE's national reach. In a curious twist, with the NSE dominating current trading, some people fear the BSE will go out of business and therefore hamper competition.

Competition is a hard taskmaster. A tango ensued where the NSE led and the BSE had to follow. In 2007 the BSE sold a minority equity stake to Deutsche Borse as part of its strategy to revamp itself, following the NASDAQ's alliance with the NSE.

The Harshad Mehta scam was the last straw for the Indian government. Before that, attempts to rein in the BSE had failed. As Narain put it,

The government had tried forever to persuade BSE to reform. Fiat, coercion— nothing worked. It reached a point where even the income tax inspectors had to roll back on their inspections. There was an incident where the IT [income

tax] guys had organized a raid, BSE went on strike, and the inspection was called off. A day's shutdown was worth Rs. 2–3 billion [$40–$60 million] of trading, and therefore it was far more important to keep the trading going.[23]

So competition worked when regulation and threats did not.

The Chinese government responded to their own financial scam very differently, opting for more regulation, control, and draconian punishment. While technology, best practices, and corporate governance became the new mantra on the Indian market, in China regulation and centralization of powers triumphed over a structural reform of the markets.

A Tale of Two Stock Exchanges, Part 2: Stasis in Shanghai

The Shanghai Stock exchange, closed by Mao's Red Army in 1949, opened for business again in 1990 on the orders of his successor, Deng Xiaoping, who needed a symbolic and substantive way to show reform in post-Tiananmen China. The reopening prompted the world to ask how a stock market, capitalism's most potent symbol, could coexist with communism.

An informal market for company stocks had existed in China since the 1980s.[24] At that time companies experimented with internal employee shares and debentures. Black markets in these securities developed in various cities across the country, and speculation became rampant. To bring some order to the markets, the government created an "official" and centralized exchange in 1990. With Deng's approval, stock exchanges were established in both Shanghai and Shenzhen,[25] to be overseen by the municipal governments and the People's Bank of China (PBOC). But like India's BSE, these exchanges were essentially self-regulating organizations in which the central government played only a minor role.

Deng's high-profile calls for economic growth and investment threw the nascent markets into a frenzy in 1992. A *gu piao re* ("stock market fever") broke out. Uncontrollable share issuance rocked the markets. Officially the PBOC approved all new shares issued; in practice the local leaders greenlighted local PBOC staff to sanction share issuance. Further, as bank lending increased, also in response to Deng's new economic agenda, money supply surged. The stresses posed by the specter of mass privatization and the threat of impending inflation were compounded by a botched initial public offering (IPO) on the Shenzhen exchange, leading to one of China's most violent demonstrations. The riots were sparked when a million people who had gathered outside Shenzhen to buy five million IPO application forms were told that the forms had been sold out. Initially the government had stated that roughly 10 percent of the forms would be subject to a lottery, with the chosen owners then allowed to buy IPO shares. The people suspected mass corruption, later confirmed by a government investigation.[26]

Despite this flurry of activity, the term *stasis* still applies to the state of stock markets in China. When the dust settled, essentially nothing had changed. Whereas the story of the Indian capital markets in the 1990s has been one of a crisis-mediated shift from collusion to competition, Chinese bourses lurched from one form of government intervention to another over the same period. The guiding hand of the government had been used for very different purposes in the two countries.

After the riots the government established the State Council Securities Committee and the Chinese Securities Regulatory Commission (CSRC). Premier Zhu Rongji, apart from instituting greater control over share issuance, oversaw the creation of different share categories. Separate categories of shares were introduced, depending on the exchange they could be traded on (Hong Kong, Shanghai, or Shenzhen) and the currency in which they were denominated (yuan, Hong Kong dollars, or U.S. dollars), with foreigners allowed to participate in some kinds but not others. Further, through even more Byzantine share categorizations, about two-thirds of each traded firm's equity was locked up in state-controlled organizations, severely curbing market liquidity. Moreover, virtually no private companies were listed on the Chinese stock exchange. Listing was purely of the state, by the state, for the state.[27]

This share categorization, along with new quotas governing the issuance of all securities by the State Planning Commission, provided levers for the government to manipulate the market.[28] On July 28, 1994, the government unveiled three "market-saving" measures, explicitly to stem share price declines: banning the issuance of new shares, permitting Sino-foreign joint funds to buy stocks on the A-share market, and raising funds for state-owned securities firms. Predictably, share prices rallied. Four days later the Shenzhen Composite Index and the Shanghai Composite Index rose 31 percent and 33 percent, respectively. Although the surge continued for two months, it proved ephemeral.

By the second half of the 1990s, with the central government's grip on the market established, Chinese authorities focused on using the stock market to revive nonfunctioning and bankrupt state-owned enterprises. Little had come of their hitherto half-hearted attempts at corporatization of these defunct entities, which were experiencing distress of crisis proportions.

Ironically, just as the focus on financing of state-owned enterprises renewed, another phenomenon threatened the control of Chinese authorities. While the Indian capital markets surged ahead on the basis of the competition between the BSE and the NSE, the curious thing about China is that there was, in a sense, ready-made competition, especially for new listings, between the Shanghai exchange (SHGSE) and the Shenzhen exchange (SHZSE).

One reason for the underlying competition was that until 1993 officials in each of Shanghai and Shenzhen primarily catered to companies in their respective cities. Under Deng's reforms local officials were rewarded for spurring local growth and therefore tended to encourage listings in their local exchanges. They could benefit from stamp revenues, the tax levied on each transaction. Each stock exchange spurred its own local support services. But the transaction frenzy drove markets to unsustainable heights. On December 5, 1996, the total daily turnover of shares in China was $4.2 billion, more than three times the volume recorded at the Hong Kong Stock Exchange on a good trading day.

When the government's patience finally ran out, it came down heavily against the local authorities. Steps were taken to rein in the SHGSE and SHZSE. A new issuance quota of $1.2 billion was introduced, along with limitations on how much prices could move daily. The daily allowable increase for each stock could not exceed 10 percent, referred to as the raising limit regulation or the Zhang Ting ban.[29] Investigations were launched into banks, and the stamp tax–sharing ratio was changed from a fifty-fifty split between center and local governments to an eighty-twenty split in favor of the center. That is, Beijing decided to take a bigger piece of the tax pie.

Perhaps as a result of these regulations, a summer of scandals ensued in 1997. A highlight was the illegal diversion of $120 million in bank funds into the stock market. Although the scandal was much like the Mehta scam, China's reactions were quite different from India's. Whereas the Indian scandal provoked the creation of the NSE, the Chinese stock market scandal strengthened the regulatory powers in the CSRC. Top officials at the two exchanges were removed. The banks were constrained from operating in the treasury markets, new listing quotas were announced, and trading in the shares of several firms was suspended. The chief economist of the State Statistical Bureau in Beijing stated the rationale for the measures: "Big rises and big falls are detrimental to social stability, it's not that the government is very worried about the problem. Rather, the government wants to make the stock markets develop in a stable and healthy manner and not become distorted."[30] In fact these clumsy interventions made things worse. Panic selling resulted.

The scams of 1997 severely restricted the self-regulating status of the SHGSE and SHZSE. The exchanges also lost their authority over listings, and no new A shares could be listed on the SHZSE. This was partly done in anticipation of all new A shares moving to the SHGSE and a new NASDAQ-type exchange for smaller stocks being established as the

SHZSE. The government's grand design was to have one national exchange for established firms in Shanghai.

The second significant episode took place five years later. In May 1999 China's stock markets experienced a steep decline. Between May 12 and May 18, the Shenzhen Composite Index went from 520.3 points to 308.3 points. On June 15 the front page of the *People's Daily* carried an editorial titled "Consolidating Confidence and Regularizing Development."—*Jian Ding Xin Xin, Gui Fan Fa Zhan*. This editorial would put to shame all the euphoric documents prepared during the Internet boom. It confidently projected a surging market.

And surge the market did. Like clockwork, it rebounded massively. On June 30, the Shenzhen Composite Index recovered all the grounds it lost and reached 528.89 points. In thirty-one trading days after the publication of the *People's Daily* editorial, the market rose by as much as 70 percent. Obviously the editorial did not reflect the consensus opinion of Chinese business forecasters. An opinion piece aired by the CCP's mouthpiece would normally carry a lot of weight, but this particular episode exceeded China's own standard of politicization.[31] Editorials on page one of the *People's Daily* normally announce the most momentous political decisions by the party, not deliberations over business matters. Further, it was penned by a "special commentator" whose appearance in the *People's Daily* has long been associated with palace intrigues of the highest order in the Byzantine world of Chinese politics. For example, Mao's tongue-lashing attacks on rivals appeared as "special commentator" columns. On April 26 1989, two months before the massacre in Tiananmen Square, a front-page editorial condemned student unrest as the cause of chaos.

China's securities market saga is one of continual intervention, even though rhetoric has changed from chastising capitalist roaders to praising capital adequacy ratios. The bigger interventions, in 1994 and 1999, are telling in another regard: neither had any long-lasting effect. In 1994 the market realized that of the three market-saving measures, only one—the ban on new issues—was enforceable. Beginning in October of that year the market began to slide again. In May 1995 the Shenzhen Composite Index reached 112 points, giving up almost all the gains since July 28, 1994, when the market reached 97 points. The intervention in 1999, with all its hype, was even less enduring. Beginning in September 1999 the market began to contract again.

Mr. Chen is a middle-income retired professional typical of the millions of small investors who had lost most of their investable income since the market's peak in 2001. He lives in a shabby five-story apartment building outside Beijing's fourth ring, an hour from Tiananmen He was moved there in 1997, without cash compensation and from a more attractive Beijing location, as part of one of the city's frequent apartment exchanges. He was visibly upset when discussing the market, saying that he'd stopped watching the television channel that reports stock market news.

> From the 2001 peak, small investors wanted to leave the stock market again and again, simply realize their loss and never enter again. But the government came up with stabilization policies and speeches again and again. In September 2004, just when small investors began to wash out, Premier Wen Jiabao said that the financial market must develop to be healthy and stable. The state council came up with Circular No. 9. Small investors once again believed in the government, and stayed in the market. Now the market is much lower than last year, what are those people in the CSRC and part of the State Council doing?[32]

Chen had the impression that companies dressed up their financials in preparation to going public, only to crash and burn naive investors. "We believed in the government, but they let us down. As soon as the market goes up a little bit, responding to a new policy or a speech, CSRC lets in more IPOs or lets some already listed companies raise second round of financing." He had an apt metaphor for the process: "It's like farmers who are so hungry that they never wait for the crops to mature to cut them."

The short duration of these interventions suggests several interesting possibilities. One is that the influence of politics has waned, which might have contributed to the extraordinarily low impact of the much-hyped *People's Daily* editorial. But if the effects are so fleeting, why do it in the first place? One hypothesis is that the political intervention served to create a window of opportunity for the state-owned institutional investors to dump their holdings on hapless and ill-informed small investors.

The failure of Chinese equity markets to allocate capital is exemplified in a curious episode revealed by a pair of academic bloodhounds. Randall Morck is a professor of finance at the University of Alberta. But more importantly, he is an astute and skeptical observer of everyday economic realities. In 2001, while teaching in Xian, he noticed something startling in data on Chinese stock prices. On any given day most stock prices in China moved in tandem—that is, most of them moved either up or down. As a rough benchmark, on the New York Stock Exchange on any given day, roughly half the stock prices move up and half move down. For a financial economist steeped in U.S. market lore, it is a nightmare to see stock prices move in such lockstep with each other. It means that the movement of the stock price of a particular company isn't really telling the markets anything about what happened to the company. With no credible firm-specific information available, no market can exist. After all, a market needs reliable information to appropriately match buyers and sellers of capital. But when this information is absent, stock prices are meaningless, and investors cannot figure out whether a particular company is worth funding.

Morck shared his findings with his longtime partner and confidante Bernard Yin Yeung, a scholar of Hong Kong Chinese origin, who now presides over an impressive group of financial economists in New York City. The two have danced a prolific academic minuet over the better part of the past two decades. Their analysis was diligent and thorough. China, they found, was among the worst offenders of the several dozen countries on which they amassed data—only Vietnam and Poland were comparable.[33] There was virtually no other country where the stock price data were as comprehensively meaningless as China.

The Spectacular CICI

My earliest memories are of watching miles of pilgrims snaking their way up treacherous, poorly lit mountain paths, the snow-capped mountains of Jammu and Kashmir in the background, to pay homage to Devi Mata ("Mother Goddess"). Our family trips to Vaishno Devi were somewhat chaotically scheduled. Hindu lore has it that visits to the shrine should occur when *bulaava aata hai,* or "when God's call comes." In those days our pilgrimage was, almost by definition, an unpredictable event. The logistics entailed scrambling for train tickets (another act of God), going by overnight train from Delhi to Jammu, taking an adventurous two-hour ride in a dilapidated taxi to Katra at the foot of the mountains, and finally trekking eight miles up the mountain path leading to Vaishno Devi. We could choose to ascend by making a half-day climb up stairs hewn into the rock and mud on the mountainside—this was akin to doing a Stairmaster continually for half a day!—or by riding a mule, a deceptively seductive method that typically shook the rider's innards and left the untrained back sore for a week. Children often mounted the backs of resilient Sherpas from Nepal, whose ability to clamber up the hills mocked the hapless urban pilgrims.

On reaching the summit we stood in another interminable line outside the shrine. We would then prostrate ourselves to be allowed through the sunken roofs of the shallow grotto leading to the physical embodiment of the deity. After a minute or two of devotion, efficient priests whisked you away.

This Vaishno Devi rush has persisted day in and day out for decades.

Now devotees can access God through the Internet using a product called Anytime Blessings. Anyone with a bank account can make donations through an automatic teller machine (ATM) and ask for a *Mancrath* or *Rajbhog*—two ancient practices of making offerings to a deity through a priest who performs the necessary devotions on the buyer's behalf. By pressing just a few buttons, anyone with a conventional bank account can divert funds to the donation *hundis*—traditional pots overflowing with devotees' donated cash, jewelry, and heirlooms—to Vaishno Devi or one of the many other Indian shrines. Crass commercialism? Perhaps, but nothing stops those answering the call of Mata's *"bulaava"* to visit in the traditional way. Anytime Blessings merely greases the wheels of devotional commerce. Bullish supporters see this as a creative marrying of India's centuries-old traditions and the needs of its modern Web-savvy populace. Anytime Blessings is one of ICICI's many innovations, an example of the visionary entrepreneurship that catapulted the bank from a burdened state-run enterprise to India's leading private domestic bank.

How did this happen? In 1991, when the regulatory and economic environment moved toward the market and away from socialism, a new breed of private domestic banks emerged. Eager to compete and take risks, these new banks offered an alternative to the poorly run state-owned banks where updating a passbook took days. ICICI was one of these new players. Set up in 1955 as a development finance institution (DFI), it came under the indirect ownership of the state when the Indian government nationalized its major shareholders, mostly insurers. Its mandate was to finance large industrial concerns. This meant lending money to a government-approved list of clients at government-directed interest rates. In that era the bank raised funds by issuing bonds guaranteed by the government. But as early as 1985 ICICI became burdened by large amounts of nonperforming assets and could not rely on government-subsidized funding.

Just as the National Stock Exchange circumvented the problem of stasis in the cabal that controlled the Bombay Stock Exchange, the Indian regulator bet that the way to tackle India's rotten state-owned banking core was not to confront it directly but to introduce competition at the margin. Narayan Vaghul, a career banker and the man then in charge of ICICI, saw an opportunity to steer the bank away from state patronage and into the dangerous and unpredictable but profitable waters of the market economy. As restrictions on domestic banks were lifted, ICICI set up its commercial-banking arm in 1994.

By the time K. V. Kamath, the current CEO of ICICI, came onto the scene, Vaghul had laid a solid foundation and ICICI boasted a blue-chip corporate clientele. However, it was still primarily focused on project financing, which Kamath did not think could sufficiently fuel the institution's growth. He began implementing a massive structural transformation of the bank. Over the next two years ICICI went through a metamorphosis, from dormancy in the historically sheltered chrysalis of state ownership to full flight as one of India's premier financial enterprises. Even more importantly Kamath started financing dreams.

At the time young and highly educated professionals, who began their careers through the 1980s, could not afford to own their own homes. Companies usually provided their employees with an automobile allowance and housing, benefits that expired on retirement. The all-encompassing firms were essentially the *anna-daata*—literally "food providers"—for all. Because retail financing was unavailable and upfront lump-sum payments unaffordable for salaried professionals, an employee was likely to retire with no house, no car, and often meager insurance coverage.

Entering the retail financing space presented opportunities as well as risks for ICICI. True, an underserved market with a burgeoning middle class flush with disposable income showed promise. The retail sector was expected to grow annually at 30 percent. On the other hand, inherently difficult market realities weighed heavily on ICICI's decision. Analysts then considered a large part of the Indian consumer base "unbankable,"[34] making it difficult to imagine a business model that could lend to them profitably. Some 60 percent of Indians didn't even have bank accounts, no credit bureaus existed to track credit histories, and no agencies existed to collect bad loans. Further, several entrenched players had cornered the market for some of the lucrative services. Citibank virtually owned the credit card space, marketing the product to upper-income consumers through a vast network of direct selling agents. The Housing Development Finance Corporation (HDFC), a name very closely associated with the housing market, had a 70 percent share of the housing finance market and boasted default rates on home loans as low as 1 percent.[35] Deepak Parekh, often ranked among the Who's Who of Indian industry and the man in charge of HDFC, was a formidable opponent. Under him the company had grown 25 percent a year, with housing mortgages as the core.[36] Did ICICI have the talent base necessary and would its strength in banking to corporations and using technology in its operations help it to succeed in the retail market?

Kamath smelled opportunity and took on the risk. He knew hungry, motivated talent was lurking around; he just needed to look outside the usual places. Paying just 60 percent of the salaries other banks provided, Kamath banked on the unrewarded talent still latent in India and offered employees autonomy and incentive pay. But talent was only one ingredient in his recipe for success. Technology, according to Kamath, was essential to the transformation. Existing systems, both virtual and physical, were built to cater to hundreds of corporate clients, not to the millions of retail consumers he anticipated. So while other banks competed via elaborate networks of branches and in some cases direct selling agents, ICICI decided to develop an entirely new network. Kamath believed that he could overcome the absence of an adequate physical infrastructure by using Internet banking and ATMs. At one point ICICI was installing three ATMs a day. Kamath was clear that he wanted to own the technology. "We did not want to be hostage to any one vendor," he told me. "Massive backup systems ensured connectivity at all times."[37]

The investment paid off. ICICI had unseated HDFC by 2000 and over the next few years took the lead in five of the six retail products in which it competed. Moreover, international markets have given their vote of confidence to this strategy—foreign institutions own 71 percent of ICICI.

Banking professionals in India remind me that until the early 1990s, banking was just a means of collecting funds for the government. No one cared about profitability—growth in assets was the measure of performance, and no bank CEO knew what "return on assets" really meant. But the private sector put state-owned banks on notice. Narain of the NSE told me, "State Bank of India is the big daddy of them all and is changing quite rapidly. SBI, Punjab National Bank, Bank of Baroda, all state owned, have all done good things. They are listed so that part of the equity capital is now in private hands." One estimate suggests that the better banks in India have reached 55 percent of the efficiency of U.S. banks, with India's best banks comparable to the best worldwide.[38] Kamath was more upbeat, saying that India's best banks are as good as banks anywhere. Indeed, on a per-transaction basis, the cost structure of the best Indian banks is 10 percent that of a comparable transaction in a global bank.

Indian bankers are no longer the inefficient paper gatherers of my childhood. It is not unusual to see ICICI executives speaking about data-driven scientific progress in financial markets to economists at Harvard, MIT, or Wharton. Lalita Gupte, a retired ICICI managing director once ranked thirty-first in *Fortune*'s list of the fifty most powerful women in the world and presided over a massive team of women occupying corner office suites at ICICI.

ICICI's commitment to women—both employees and customers—is unusual anywhere but especially in India. The bank's inclusion of women in its business plan was another innovation of Narayan Vaghul, the man responsible for ICICI's first risky step from state patronage into the market economy. His vision for ICICI existed in the larger context of a socially equitable India, in which the talent of women, currently heavily underutilized, would be a central part of both urban and rural entrepreneurship. Kiran Mazumdar-Shaw of Biocon, India's leading biotechnology firm, told me that if she had not received the unwavering backing of ICICI in the first decade of her struggle, her company would not be the world-class, biotechnology shop it is today.

Mazumdar-Shaw is the poster child not only for India's emerging biotechnology industry but also for women entrepreneurs across the country.

Helping women in rural India attain a higher level of financial strength is especially important to Vaghul. When I met him in his ICICI office, he told me, "Economic independence is important for urban women, and in rural areas it's a really big deal. This is where laws of the land don't apply—for example, no monogamy and frequent desertion of women after fathering children. So how do we foster entrepreneurship in this sort of setting?"

Astonishingly, here is a bank that flourishes in data-driven scientific inquiry, has committed to encouraging women in the corner offices, and is pioneering the delivery of financial services to severely under-banked rural India. At Harvard Business School ICICI serves as a case study leading to discussions on banking possibilities and innovations. But does its idealism dovetail with economic value? Can ICICI continue its successful operations and remain true to its social mission? According to Kamath, ICICI boasts of one of the lowest cost structures of any world-class bank. This accomplishment is not merely a result of the lower cost of talent in India. Even if Kamath's audacious claim—that ICICI's cost structure is 10 percent of that of a global bank's operations in India—is part hyperbole, ICICI's lead is indisputable.[39]

As a further measure of ICICI's success, other developing countries are looking to the firm, and to India, as a model to emulate. One example is Tony Elumelu, a Nigerian banker whom I met at Harvard on one of his periodic knowledge-gathering trips. Elumelu was keen that I "introduce him to India." Although his country may be known more for its ethnic and religious bloodshed and get-rich-quick e-mail scams, as head of a holding company with investments in financial institutions, most notably the Standard Trust Bank in Lagos, Elumelu represents a nascent, and clean, private sector in Nigeria. He was planning to spend an educational week in India with some of his senior colleagues, so I set up and led some discussions for them with the Indian business community and introduced them to some well-run companies, including ICICI.

Not until my new Nigerian colleagues checked into the Taj Mahal Hotel in South Mumbai did I understand the full historical weight of the Nigeria-India connection. Elumelu and his team immediately noted similarities between Lagos and Mumbai. The Taj Mahal Hotel borrows its name from India's best-known architectural symbol, located in the northern Indian city of Agra, and stands facing the Gateway of India, a spectacular structure overlooking the Arabian Sea built to commemorate the visit of King George V and Queen Mary to Bombay in 1911. The British had also colonized Nigeria and followed a "company to colony" pattern there. In India the British East India Company's trading privileges morphed into the political supremacy of the British Crown in 1857. Similarly, in 1901, seeking to consolidate their commercial interests in the Niger, the British chartered the Royal Niger Company as the United Africa Company. This meant the company was formally placed under British protection and provided Britain with far-reaching rights to administer territories transferred by treaties with native chiefs.

So it was that in the early part of the twenty-first century that Elumelu and his team persuaded bankers at ICICI to take them to a flagship retail operation in Prabhadevi in Central Mumbai, where they took copious notes on the Indian banks' state-of-the-art electronic retail outlets and its superb customer service.

Banking in China: Of the Party, by the Party, for the Party

In 1948 Mao Zedong created a new bank, and not surprisingly called it the People's Bank of China. All banks in the country were nationalized and incorporated into the PBOC. For thirty years the PBOC was the only bank in the People's Republic of China, solely responsible for both central banking and commercial banking. By the early 1980s the functions of the PBOC were split among four new entities: the Bank of China, the Agricultural Bank of China, the Industrial and Commercial Bank of China, and the Construction Bank of China. Their collective mission was to support the economic and industrial policy of the government by making state-directed loans to state-owned companies.

Mao's move to directed lending, as opposed to hands-off lending by bankers to entrepreneurs, was so complete that Chinese banks have repeatedly made loans to any sick state-owned enterprise that asked, with no commercial criteria. The four largest state-owned banks still dominate the banking landscape, accounting for nearly 75 percent of loans and capital and presiding over nonperforming loans worth $230 billion. Several attempts to recapitalize these banks have accomplished little. Their fates are tied to bankrupt state-owned enterprises virtually impervious to reform.[40]

Another problem plaguing Chinese banks—one that has received much publicity—is corruption, petty and grand. At the same time they are making life difficult for small and medium-scale enterprises applying for loans, the state-owned banks are facing a series of scandals, revealing lax internal control and monitoring. In February 2005 several dozen people tied to the Jilin Province branch of the Construction Bank of China were charged by authorities with stealing $65 million from several branches starting in the late 1990s. Most of the amount was lost in Macau casinos or wagered on soccer games through underground bookies.

Among the many other cases of bank criminals are the Bank of China branch managers implicated in a fraud case involving deposits worth hundreds of millions of dollars in Harbin, capital of northeastern Heilongjiang Province. This at a time that the Bank of China was being dressed up to receive potential foreign investors![41]

Unfortunately many financial criminals in China "evaporate" before investigators can figure out what happened. In 2004 the Ministry of Commerce estimated that in the past twenty years four thousand corrupt officials had fled the country with a total of $50 billion, and China's Ministry of Public Security estimated that five hundred outstanding "economic crime suspects" were living overseas.[42]

Corruption arises from the unchecked autonomy granted to provincial officials. The bankers are beholden to the local party officials—in fact the banker and policy maker are often one and the same—leaving no credible way to deter bankers bent on siphoning off funds.

The eagerness of Chinese bankers to have, or at least appear to have, good assets on the books contrasts sharply with the nonchalance of their counterparts in Indian state-owned banks who would rather buy government bonds. Chinese bankers, at least in senior positions, know that their promotions up the Party hierarchy are tied to local growth. At the very least they must maintain a facade of local growth by not pulling bad loans and forcing defunct enterprises to close. In a country where information, available to Beijing about the true nature of assets in the provinces and local fiefdoms is scanty at best, bankers can be reasonably sure of promotions.

Both China and India have histories of successful private banking. As far back as the early eighteenth century, the most popular banks were known as *piaohao*, or Shanxi banks after the northern Chinese province where they were most common. The Xiyuecheng Dye Company had several branches across the country and invented a system of intracompany cash transfers to move money around these branches. Gradually others demanded this remittance service. The owner of the dye company moved from his original business to banking and set up Risenchang Piaohao. By the end of the nineteenth century thirty-two *piaohao* with 475 branches were spread across China's eighteen provinces.[43]

In the past few decades China, like India, has witnessed a banking sector dominated by sclerotic state-controlled institutions. However, the evolution of Chinese banking differs in several ways from Indian banking. First, no bank like India's ICICI has emerged in China. Wu Li, a senior researcher at China's Academy of Social Sciences, explained, "All banks are de facto state owned, or at a minimum the state controls a majority of the shares. Banking is too important to the government because of the risk involved; it's the bloodline of a country; banking is something special."[44]

I was at first heartened to hear about the new private banks, most prominently Minsheng Bank, until I spoke with bankers in Beijing and Shanghai who could not discern the qualitative difference between Minsheng and other banks. Eventually I concluded that Minsheng Bank is only symbolically private and is essentially state owned. However, this symbolic status ensures its survival, just as enduring symbols of pluralism exist in the People's Congress, with its token ethnic minority and noncommunist members.

While the issue in India has been state-owned banks' passive "underlending" to credit worthy customers, the issue in China is unproductive "overlending." Lending in China, which focuses on state-owned enterprises, discriminates against even the most efficient and productive private entrepreneurs. Sun Dawu, founder of the Dawu Farm Group, was a victim of this bias. His private, profitable business, in existence for two decades, had fixed assets of $13 million, excluding 330 acres of land, and a total debt of $3.6 million. Sun Dawu, born in Xushui County, Baoding District of Hebei Province, developed his business from a thousand chickens and fifty pigs into a large-scale enterprise, combining livestock and poultry breeding, manufacturing, and education. He created job opportunities for 1,600 employees, provided financial sponsorship to local schools, invested $200,000, and built a road that benefited six nearby villages. Despite his middle-school-level education, Sun has been invited many times by Beijing University and China Agriculture University to give talks on agriculture.

Yet even Sun Dawu's successful private enterprise (min ying qi ye) could not get bank loans. From January 2000 to May 2003, Sun financed his company's growth with funds collected from his employees, their relatives, and friends at an interest rate higher than the going bank rate. This led to Party accusations of disturbing the financial order, detention in May 2003, and arrest in July. He was sentenced to three years in jail with four years' grace period, a personal fine of $12,000, and a company fine of $36,000. As a result, his company laid off hundreds of employees, shrinking its operations by half.[45]

Sun's case immediately attracted media attention. His lawyers disputed the charges of fostering financial disorder, pointing to the general disarray of China's finances. Other lawyers collectively wrote to the People's Congress, providing pro bono services to Sun. Harvard Law School–educated Xu Zhiyong, one of China's leading lawyers, published an article titled "Why We Should Defend Sun Dawu." Liu Chuanzhi, Lenovo's founder, wrote a personal fax to Sun, encouraging him to continue his work, promising a personal loan of RMB 120,000 to his company, and expressing his belief that the case would eventually be settled fairly and justly. By the end of 2003 several Chinese banks contacted Sun, willing to extend credit.[46]

Given the sorry state of affairs in China's banks, why do millions of Chinese citizens continue to invest in the banking sector? Part of the answer is that they have few alternatives. The roulette wheel nature of the stock market, one of the world's worst performing for many years, hardly inspires confidence. A lot of money that leaves China for investments in, say, Hong Kong then reenters the mainland masquerading as foreign money. The returns legally available to Chinese-owned capital must be low enough to justify taking on the inefficiencies of moving capital in such a roundabout fashion, an issue I discuss in a subsequent chapter on multinationals. Of course another crucial piece of the puzzle is that government controls on capital prevent the Chinese from investing their money outside China, unencumbered by regulatory and legal barriers.

Some investments are not entirely voluntary. I spoke with an employee of one of the first companies to list on the Shenzhen exchange who recounted how all the employees of the financial institution, when told to invest in the initial public offering, refused. Buying the shares, she said, was generally viewed as the equivalent of a tax or, amazingly, as a contribution to a disaster relief fund. Finally the bank mobilized all party members among employees to accept bigger investment quotas, and department heads used personal funds to make up shortfalls in their quotas.

Does the average depositor fear the banks will declare bankruptcy? Apparently not. The big banks—with 116,000 branches across China accounting for 67 percent of the country's deposits and 61 percent of the loans—are solidly backed by a government flush with cash. Besides, they are too big to fail, because their failure might spark widespread unrest. "Whether they know of bankruptcy is not important," explains Liu Bing, a one-time visiting scholar at Harvard's Fairbank Center for East Asian Research, and then confidently adds, "all they know is that the government is behind all banks. As long as the government is in the business, their money and deposits are safe."[47] China's high rate of savings—money forcibly channeled into banks—means new money is cheap enough that a banker has every reason to make a double-or-nothing wager rather than declare a bad asset nonperforming. As The Economist asks, "What kind of bank makes loans of which a third will not be repaid? The communist kind."[48]

One reason for the Chinese tendency toward large savings must be the lack of a formal social security net and the fraying of the familial version of that support, at least in the urban areas. The iron rice bowl—the name given to indefinite state provisions—has cracked, and the family-based social security system is under stress, forcing people to fend for themselves. As the Nobel Prize–winning economist Franco Modigliani argued a few years before his death, the Chinese policy of one child per family ensures that fewer working people will be available to care for the elderly in the future, prompting more savings.[49] Ironically much of these hard-earned savings—deposited in bankrupt banks and thereby channeled into the party's coffers—ends up financing excessive U.S. consumption. The Chinese state is the second-biggest holder of U.S. Treasury bonds, after Japan.

How could Chinese regulators not understand how to improve the banks? Certainly the diagnosis of the problem was well within the reach of most technocrats, of which China had many, especially from Hong Kong. Pondering these questions while in Beijing, I sought out a mainland Chinese man who both had experience working with global banks and was a Party member. Everyone knew how to align the incentives of the bankers in the state-owned banks and that cleaning up the banks had to involve some pain. But at a deeper level, almost everyone was inexperienced with the market mechanism and had no idea how the government could credibly be "hands off" toward banks it wanted to subject to unfettered market forces.

The Party's handling of the corruption scandal at China's Construction Bank was a case in point. Zhang Enchain, chairman and CCP secretary of the Construction Bank of China, was said to have resigned "for personal reasons" after news reports indicated that he was under investigation for corruption. Zhang had devoted forty years to the bank, working his way up from intern to the corner office. He led the Construction Bank's transformation to a commercial stock company so successfully that China's state-run TV hailed him as one of its Economic Leaders of the Year in 2004. Yet his fall from grace was dramatic and belied the common assertion that corruption in Chinese financial circles happens only at the periphery of the system.[50] The net result was that the Commercial Bank's attempted overseas listing was stalled.

Zhang's bank had a heavyweight board, including some directors listed as independent. In a market economy the board would have been the agent that relieved the CEO of his responsibilities. Yet the Party apparently did not see fit to involve the board in its deliberations or inform the board of the CEO's impending departure. What kind of signal does this send regarding an entity that is being prepared for a public listing, where presumably the board acts to protect shareholders' interests? The Party did not seem to realize the importance of sound corporate governance procedures to a reasonably functioning market economy. It thus failed an acid test for the government's commitment to loosening its control over the nation's banks by meddling in the way senior appointments are made. Currently senior bankers are all political appointees, a procedure that cannot stand in a market economy. Several observers assert that recapitalizing bankrupt banks was all that was needed to fix the problem. This seems to me to be equivalent to merely suppressing a fever resulting from an internal infection and pronouncing the patient cured.

My experience teaching senior executives in Beijing corroborates this assessment of inexperience with market forces. Executives from Hong Kong have a much clearer understanding of markets than their mainland colleagues. The difference should not be surprising. In India, as well, public sector managers, unfamiliar with competition, were paralyzed by the deregulation that followed the 1991 financial crisis. As discussed in the next chapter on indigenous entrepreneurs, Chinese managers have an even harder time with this because China's private-sector "memory" was comprehensively erased during the Cultural Revolution (1966–1976).

The systemic changes needed to fix Chinese banking cannot be forgotten. The party's watchword is *stability*, and it will not countenance a repeat of Tiananmen, with unrest in the streets and protests against the government. Reforming the banks will mean calling in bad loans, which will mean shutting down the bankrupt state-owned enterprises. The result will be tens of thousands of job losses, releasing teeming workers into the streets to join the few hundred million rural migrants striving to enter the urban workforce. This is a recipe for disaster, one that China wants to avoid at all costs. Although the theoretical solution is clear to any economist with scratch paper and a sharp pencil, justifying the real human cost in the short and perhaps medium run is more difficult.

Learning from India, What a Shock

As early as 2001 the *China Economic Quarterly*, an English-language newsmagazine published in Beijing, had a column with the title "China Tries the India Thing."[51] The article described the dilapidated state of financial markets in China and carried an admonition that unaccustomed as it was to looking to its southern neighbor for lessons on economics, China ought to learn from the rapid strides India had made in financial markets.

In both the Chinese and Indian financial systems, banks are much more important than equity and debt markets. Banking accounts for a high percentage of GDP in both countries. In 2005 domestic bank debt was 136 percent of GDP in China and 60 percent of GDP in India, whereas stock market capitalization in China and India amounted to 35 percent and 69 percent of GDP, respectively.[52] Compared with China, India has more ICICI-like banks doing a better job of allocating credit. As appendages of the government, Chinese banks continue to have as their primary objective preserving stability rather than efficiently allocating bank debt.

Why do China and India have such fundamentally different financial systems? My colleague Yasheng Huang and I have posited one reason for China's decision to court foreign direct investment (FDI).[53] The Cultural Revolution in particular, and the communist experiment in general, decimated whatever infrastructure existed in the country to support market exchange. FDI offered a relatively quick fix, especially when sold first to overseas Chinese communities and when initially contained in experimental locations like Guangdong Province. Of course FDI is what most Westerners have heard about, as they watch their major companies building factories and distribution systems all over China. FDI in China in 2005 was $55 billion, amounting to about 5.5 percent of domestic gross fixed investment in that year and representing a disproportionate share of FDI in developing countries worldwide.[54]

In contrast postindependence India did not have its economic infrastructure decimated. Although Indians continue to debate the overall impact of British rule, the imperial power did establish infrastructure and nurtured Indian entrepreneurs whenever doing so did not challenge colonial rule. Despite periodic repression, a vibrant anticolonial entrepreneurial class was always evident. FDI was needed much less that in China, and even when needed it was often opposed by indigenous interests for reasons not in the interest of India. Given this history, India could more easily rely on portfolio flows and flows of venture capital from overseas than on FDI. Whereas only $5 billion in FDI entered India in 2004, portfolio capital flows in the same year were much higher at $9 billion. China, in contrast, does not allow its equity markets to allocate domestic savings to domestic uses. Instead, the government ensures that most funds entering the stock market are used to sustain rapidly fading state-owned enterprises.

One lesson that China should learn from India is better management of equity markets. But that lesson takes time to learn. Reforming the Chinese system requires political will, not yet in evidence, and experience with market-based allocations of capital.

China's willingness to learn from its neighbor to the south is colored by the experience of its northern neighbor, Russia. When the Chinese analyze the meltdown in Russia in the 1990s, they conclude that the premature liberalization of financial markets made capital controls porous and transformed bank officials into private oligarchs who took short positions in 1998 before the Russian financial crisis and default. Russia's sobering catastrophe prompted China to be tremendously cautious.[55]

Weak financial institutions make corporate governance an oxymoron in China, ensuring that, barring a financial crisis, its current path is one of lesser resistance than the path of fundamental reform. The first ratings of firms across several emerging markets, including China and India, published by the investment banking firm Credit Lyonnais Securities Asia (CLSA), dramatically highlighted China's failed corporate governance.[55] The criteria CLSA used to assess corporate governance were management discipline, transparency, independence, accountability, responsibility, fairness, and social responsibility. On CLSA's weighted scoring scale of 1 to 10, India scored 5.4 for corporate governance and China at 3.4. India ranked sixth in the study overall, behind Singapore, Hong Kong, and Taiwan, among others. China ranked nineteenth.

The leading Chinese economist Wu Jinglian famously referred to China's stock exchanges as no better than casinos.[57] Securities firms, using their political clout, exert very little pressure on listed firms. Share price manipulations and misuse of investors' funds are rampant among securities firms in China. In 2001 the China Securities Regulatory Commission published a list of stock trading companies that had not misappropriated funds deposited with them by their clients. This list accounted for about 73 percent of the firms in the securities industry. Thus the sobering fact is that 27 percent of Chinese securities firms engaged in fund misappropriations. Moreover, about 15 percent of accounting firms routinely refuse to issue reports certifying the annual or interim reports issued by the listed companies.

Share price manipulation is one of the favorite activities of Chinese securities firms. The infamous Yorkpoint case illustrates the problem. In 1998 four securities firms in Guangdong pooled together funds and began to accumulate shares in Yorkpoint Science and Technology. By 2000 the four firms held 85 percent of the traded shares of Yorkpoint, and they began to trade among themselves through 627 individual accounts and three company accounts, driving up share prices of Yorkpoint. They then dumped their shares on unsuspecting new investors and realized a profit of $54 million.

One area in which China rated relatively favorably compared with India is government regulation and supervision. Historically the CSRC boasts some of the most visionary and capable leaders, including Zhou Xiaochuan, its chairman during much of the 1990s; Laura Cha, an official from Hong Kong's securities exchange recruited to be vice chair of the CSRC in 2001; and Gao Xiqing, a lawyer trained at Duke University who was CSRC's vice chair from 1999 to 2003. Under enormous political pressures and constraints, the CSRC did its best to uncover wrongdoings and fraudulent cases. Between 1993 and 2001 the regulators identified 563 fraud cases involving securities markets. In 1999 and 2000 they put 285 cases on notice, exceeding the total number of cases filed in the preceding eight years.

Securities fraud cases in China are routinely treated as criminal rather than civil offenses, and punishment can be harsh and swift, most likely bereft of all the legal niceties that would hamper the Indian courts. The case of Hainan

Minyuan, an agriculture development firm, illustrates the kinds of treatment shown to those found guilty. In April 1998 the CSRC issued a finding that Hainan Minyuan fabricated its income and capital reserve fund, involving more than $120 million, and referred the case to the judicial authority. Only seven months later the First People's Court of Beijing sentenced the company's general manager and chief financial officer to three years and two years in prison, respectively.

The lesson of this regulatory vigilance is that malfeasance within China's stock exchanges did not originate from poor regulatory oversight alone; the causes are deeper and more structural. Even a country equipped with the most vigilant and dedicated regulators cannot completely make up for a poorly designed system. The biggest problem afflicting China's stock exchange is government activism.

Unlike India, where capital markets, however imperfectly, strive to serve the most efficient firms, the Chinese government chose to list only firms whose objectives aligned with the government's political goals. Favored firms, virtually all state-owned enterprises, had very little to show on their bottom lines and were often "bailed out" either by falsifying financial statements or by government-led management, to use a euphemism, of their stock prices. They thus had little reason to clean up their acts.

Indian capital markets, particularly on the equity side and on the provision of bank debt, are far ahead of China's. But the systems are sufficiently different that one can be skeptical about the claim that China can easily learn from India.

PART II

ENTERPRISE

Chapter Six

Infosys and TCL

Unshackling Indigenous Enterprise

I recently spent a day with some of the leaders of a major European steel company at Harvard. The subject of Mittal Steel's 2006 acquisition of Luxembourg-based Arcelor came up. The group exchanged views on how Lakshmi Mittal, an Indian entrepreneur, had turned the industry upside down with his $23 billion deal.

"It's not likely that we'll see more deals like that," remarked one of the visiting steel executives. "Besides, it's really a Dutch company, not Indian." The latter statement has merit. Although the founder of Mittal Steel and many of his top managers are part of the Indian diaspora, the company is headquartered in Europe and has little of its assets in India.

"What about Tata?" I asked. Tata Steel, a subsidiary of the Tata Group, one of India's largest business groups, had been engaged in protracted bidding for Corus, an Anglo-Dutch steelmaker.

"Not relevant," snapped the visiting executive. "That'll never come through."

The next morning a BBC News headline read, "India's Tata Wins Race for Corus."

The unshackling of indigenous enterprise signifies an enormous shift within China and India. The acquisitions of Arcelor and Corus by "emerging giants" are harbingers, not isolated occurrences. Underestimating their significance is a mistake that Western companies cannot afford to make.

Two examples of successful indigenous enterprises are the consumer electronics giant TCL from China's Guangdong Province and the offshore software pioneer Infosys from Bangalore. Both TCL, under chairman Li Dongsheng, and Infosys, under former CEO Narayan Murthy and his successor Nandan Nilekani, are dissimilar ambassadors of their origin countries. Li Dongsheng acquired assets from French corporations Thomson and Alcatel, saving jobs, endearing himself to France, and winning him the title of officer of the *Ordre national de la Légion d'honneur*. Whether it won his shareholders anything is much less certain. Corporate success in China commonly comes at the government's bidding, with the CCP deciding how, when, and where to project China. In 2006 at the Boao Forum—an event that draws politicians, businesspeople, and academics to discuss global economic and political issues—the government mandated the creation of fifty global champions like TCL. China scheduled the event to coincide with the World Economic Forum (WEF) at Davos, Switzerland.[1]

Indian companies, especially successful ones, rarely do the government's bidding. Rather, it might be only a slight exaggeration to say that the government bows to the suggestions of successful firms like Infosys regarding the most expedient course of action to improve the Indian business climate. As the international editor at *Newsweek*, Fareed Zakaria, stated, "I think Indian society has been a better ambassador of India than the Indian state. For too long the public sector presented an image of India that was arrogant, verbose, ideological, and closed to the world. In particular, the Indian private sector has represented the true India—pragmatic, forward-looking, diverse, open to the world."[2]

The Ascent of Infosys

Standing in the lobby of the Steigenberger Belvedere Hotel in Davos, I watched Nandan Nilekani mingle with CEOs, politicians, celebrities, and activists at a corporate soiree hosted by Infosys, the celebrated Indian software company of which he is the CEO. Focused, crisp, and engaging, Nilekani gave the impression of being supremely interested in everyone he met. The occasion was the 2006 WEF, a meeting of the world's top business and political leaders.

Nilekani had assumed the position of CEO and managing director of India's best-known software company in March 2002, taking over from Narayana Murthy, himself an icon of the Indian technology boom of the 1990s. Infosys had spearheaded what Nilekani, a "Davos man,[3]" had called India's debutante appearance. Corporate India had come of age, and Nilekani and Infosys had organized the coming-out party.

It was the first time that an Indian executive was one of the WEF's chief organizers, and India was the focus of the closing talks. Throughout the event participants enjoyed both the breathtaking beauty of the Alpine landscape and the intoxicating aroma of Indian foods prepared by a chef flown in from a celebrated London-based Indian restaurant, Benares. Buses winding their way through the snowy, pedestrian-clogged Davos streets sported Indian emblems—Tandoori chicken, *saris* and the Alps. "India Everywhere," the branding slogan for the forum, highlighted this unusual juxtaposition of cultures. And, of course, comparisons of India with China were de riguer throughout the meetings.

Earlier that year Infosys had contributed $150,000 to the India Brand Equity Foundation, a nongovernmental organization set up by the Confederation of Indian Industry, the leading Indian private-sector lobby group. The check was to finance the "India Everywhere" plan to market India. This was rapidly followed by one of the companies in the Tata Group offering to underwrite the "India Everywhere" gala dinner that closed out the annual Davos forum. Other commitments followed speedily. Even more important than the initial financial commitment was Nilekani's intellectual and emotional leadership of the India-branding campaign. By spending a few million dollars, India garnered worldwide exposure worth much more.

How did Infosys get into trying to brand a country?[4] It has been, by some measures, a quarter-century-long saga. The company was founded in 1981 by seven engineers on a shoestring budget of $1,000. The government offered them no contractual guarantees, soft loans, or equity investments. The team immediately focused on the demands of the international market, perceiving an insignificant domestic opportunity. Their decision to do business outside the country reflected in part a recognition of pre-reform India's lack of free markets and Indian companies' lack of incentives to invest in efficiency-enhancing software services given the protected environment in which they then operated. Entrepreneurship in India has since thrived, but mostly in the interstices left untouched by the state. Nehru's postindependence regulation focused on brick-and-mortar assets and neglected the intangible sectors of the economy, underdeveloped at the time, like software, media, advertising, and biotechnology.

Infosys is inseparable from the Narayan Murthy mystique. One of the seven original founders of the company, Murthy is largely credited with Infosys's tremendous ascent. His early career involved working in France for a software company for three years, donating his assets to charity, and traveling through Europe back to India. An eventful sojourn in Bulgaria convinced him that pure socialism was not the answer to mankind's problems and that redistribution of wealth, without first creating it, was a dead-end road. Yet the man whose entrepreneurial success epitomizes Indian capitalism did not abandon all the ideals of a socialist. He is famous for eschewing ostentatious living even while amassing Croesus-like riches, and taking self-deprecating actions in return for long-term success.

What underlies Infosys's success? Beyond superior software design skills, Murthy points to the firm's global delivery model: the ability to work non-stop to deliver software services to clients around the world and the ability to figure out which part of the business can be retained in India and which part must be on the client's premises. Infosys was the first to develop these skills, which are essential to competing from afar. Obviously U.S. competitors operating in India, like IBM and Electronic Data Systems, have no need for these skills because they are headquartered in their clients' backyards. But can they replicate Infosys's accomplishments? To some extent yes, Murthy says.

> But their coming here doesn't change the basic economic differences between their businesses and ours. Typically, in the application development work we'd do for an average client, about 70 percent of the work is done in India or another cost-competitive country. Our general and administrative expenses are centered in India and are about 7.5 percent of revenues today. By contrast, the US companies that are our competitors, despite a strong presence in a country like India, by and large have the majority of their workforce in the United States or in the local market. It is not easy to let go off that workforce. So the economics differ.[5]

Equally important, however, are capabilities that have less to do with software writing or global delivery models than with the idea that Infosys was the first to credibly offer a way for the West to tap into cheap Indian talent reliably, ethically, and transparently. Infosys's core entrepreneurial insight is that clean corporate governance is valuable, especially in India, traditionally considered the backwater of good corporate governance. As K. Dinesh, another Infosys cofounder, says, "Our values are to have very high integrity and high transparency. We'd rather lose business and have a good night's sleep."[6]

But there is more to Infosys's success than a strongly held belief in probity. Murthy says,

> In the early '90s, when we went to the United States to sell our services most Chief Information Officers didn't believe that an Indian company could build the large applications they needed. The CIOs were very nice to us, of course. They offered us coffee and tea, listened to what we had to say and then said, "Look, don't call us—we'll call you." We realized there was a huge gap between, on the one hand, how prospective western clients perceived Indian companies and, on the other, our own perception of our strengths.[76]

Scrupulous transparency was an essential part of what it took to reassure large corporate clients in the United States. Infosys constrained itself by listing on the NASDAQ. Importantly, when it did this in 1999, Infosys was the most cash-rich of any Indian software company and did not need capital. The listing was a means of reassuring clients that the firm would be forced to subscribe to the norms of good corporate governance demanded by U.S. public markets.[8]

Several incidents, most occurring before the public listings, reinforce this characterization of a company committed to fairness.

> *In 1992 Infosys gave a fixed price bid to a company. The fixed price was based on assumptions about the time and people it would take, etcetera. After a short while on the project Infosys realized it had vastly underestimated what the cost/time requirement would be. They had two choices: 1) to try to change the contract or 2) to honor the contract. The law would have permitted some room for Infosys to back out, but they didn't. They put more people on the project and honored the contract.*

Thus Infosys made it absolutely clear that the concerns of its customers came first.

For several years Infosys has been the top-rated firm in India and elsewhere in Asia in terms of its overall corporate governance practices, as documented by the independent Hong Kong–based Credit Lyonnais Securities Asia.[9] Infosys strives to adopt global reporting standards beyond those mandated by the Indian environment as well as the NASDAQ.

Particular events complement these published rankings. Infosys was the first in India to adopt U.S. Generally Accepted Accounting Principles (GAAP) as a means to build trust with its customers. Today it reports financials in the GAAPs of many major countries in which it does business, a feat performed by only a few corporations worldwide. It was also one of the first companies to enable shareholders to access important company information by broadcasting annual shareholders' meetings over the Web, posting press releases on the firm's Web site, adopting advance quarterly reporting, and voluntarily behaving like the U.S. issuers listed on NASDAQ rather than opting for that stock market's less stringent rules governing foreign issuers. (For example, it distributes quarterly reports to U.S. shareholders although it is not required to do so.) In 2000 Infosys was the first company worldwide to comply with new NASDAQ regulations, demonstrating an ability to file some paperwork within eight or nine days rather than the ninety days typically allowed.[10]

> *Infosys collected a lot of money through its public offering in the early 1990s. It was waiting for the government to give it clearance to invest that money in*

a subsidiary in the U.S. While it was waiting, several board members sug-
gested that the money, instead of sitting in the bank, should be invested in
Indian stocks. Infosys lost quite a bit of money in the ensuing transaction.
Then there was the question of what you tell people about what happened.
Most Indian companies would not have disclosed this, and Indian law would
not require such disclosure either. But Infosys decided to disclose the losses. The
board was ready to face the wrath of the investors, and they figured they
would be kicked out and replaced. But when the meeting came, the investors
said 'we respect what you have done. Because you have disclosed something
when you are in trouble, we can trust you.' The real indicator of good corpo-
rate governance is how you respond in difficult times.[11]

Starting in 1996 Infosys was one of the very few Indian companies that began to publish in its annual report a human resource self-assessment. Human resource management might be the major delineator between Infosys and some of its rivals. For example, rarely does a company hire, train, and deploy hundreds of programmers in an unfamiliar site and an unfamiliar country as quickly as Infosys does. Certainly the firm is faster than any non-Indian multinational operating in India and possibly faster than its leading Indian rivals. According to Murthy, Infosys is 10 percent to 15 percent more productive per employee than most other Indian software service companies. Of 250,000 people who interviewed with them in a recent quarter, they hired just over 1 percent.[12]

Accolades for Infosys are pervasive. Perhaps the only complaint is that the charisma of Murthy and his top managers is so strong that no constraint on their actions is plausible. That is a bit like complaining that the *foie gras* is not just right, not about debating whether *foie gras* is available in the first instance. But the market's demand for superior performance does not respect Murthy's charisma, only Infosys's performance.

From Merchants to CEOs: The Changing Face of Indian Business

Business historians usually anchor their study of modern Indian business in the mid-eighteenth century, the time of England's Industrial Revolution and its colonization of India.[13] Before that time Indian textiles were sold in Britain, and until 1813 the British East India Company held exclusive rights to all Indian trade. Once the Crown ended that monopoly, British citizens were granted licenses to trade, bringing scores of entrepreneurs from Great Britain to India.[14] Through the 1800s British-owned businesses dominated the Indian private sector. Indian cotton competed with Britain's for the Chinese market on the strength of lower labor costs, proximity to China and easier access to raw materials. Bombay-based merchants, most prominently from the Parsee and Gujarati communities, made enormous profits through the cotton trade. To the China cotton trade was added opium, a segment in which the Parsees had a virtual monopoly. Several Bombay merchants set up big industrial textile mills. Through the 1860s consolidation of the cotton textile industry—which were almost entirely owned, financed, managed, and run by Indians—gave rise to a new industrial elite.[15]

By the turn of the century Indian political leaders were agitating for freedom from Britain, exhorting Indians to boycott foreign products and buy only *swadeshi* (homemade) goods. This call coincided with the success of several local business families—Tata, Birla, Bajaj, Lalbhai, Wadia, and others—industrialists who had acquired a status in India akin to the Carnegies and Rockefellers in the United States. These wealthy industrialist-entrepreneurs supported Nehru's freedom movement in cash and kind. The Marwari magnate G. D. Birla, who had demolished the Scottish monopoly of jute in India, was a close ally and patron of Mahatma Gandhi. In 1954, just a few years after India won independence, Nehru declared that India wanted to create a "socialistic pattern of society." Unlike China, where Mao Zedong banned all private property rights after establishing the PRC in 1949, independent India never banned private ownership. Nehru said:

> I have no shadow of doubt that if we say "lop off the private sector" we cannot replace it. We haven't got the resource to replace it, and the result would be that our productive apparatus would suffer . . . Let the state go on building up its plants and industries as far as its resources permit. Why should we fritter away our energy in pushing out somebody who is doing it in the private sector? There is no reason except that the private sector might build up monopoly . . . [P]revent that; control that; plan for that; but where there is such a vast field to cover, it is foolish to take charge of the whole field when you are totally incapable of using that huge area yourself. Therefore you must not only permit the private sector, but I say, encourage it in its own field.[16]

Although Nehruvian socialism has been blamed for many of the ills of India's private sector, Dwijendra Tripathi, India's leading business historian, qualifies this rush to judgment. Initially Nehru supported Indian business, and nationalization of private assets was not extensive, even though many stridently favored it. Instead, Nehru helped create financial institutions that extended funds for large-scale industrial projects. Because the nascent Indian banking sector could not fill the wide gap between long-term industrial projects and financial instruments at their disposal, several hybrid policy banks were created at the national and state levels.

Gradually a love-hate relationship developed between big business and government. For example, in 1948 air transport was set aside as a government-only sector. The government decided to partner with the Tata family, who operated an airline and planned to launch an international carrier, to form Air India International. Forty-nine percent of the company was government owned, the Tatas held 20 percent, and the public owned the remainder. Four years later, however, over the Tatas' objections, air transport was nationalized. Only two airlines were permitted in India: Indian Airlines would operate domestically and Air India internationally. Decades later these airlines became synonymous with delays, bad customer service, and limited schedules. The Tatas also lost their insurance business to nationalization. Undaunted by these setbacks, however, the family ventured into oil, tea, jute, and other industries and prospered.[17]

After Nehru the hand of the state encroached more aggressively. Indira Gandhi won the general election of 1967 on a very populist stance. Soon after, she nationalized fourteen banks and mandated that all banks provide 40 percent of their net credit to heavily underserved sectors (the proportion has since dropped to 10 percent). Thus agriculture, small-scale industry, retail trade, and small businesses were deemed priority sectors, all in the service of social and developmental goals. Then in 1969 the legislature enacted the Monopolies and Restrictive Trade Practices Act—India's version of antitrust legislation. The act placed draconian barriers on existing businesses seeking to expand capacity, modernize, or enter new lines of business. Conglomerates with assets exceeding a certain threshold were not permitted to expand without getting approval from the MRTP Commission.[18] Small businesses were also subject to government interference. The result was a plethora of rules and regulations to oversee even innocuous business decisions. India's entrepreneurs responded by finding ways around the red tape. Their energies were directed to such unproductive pursuits as hoodwinking regulators and circumventing the "License Raj." To avoid scrutiny, companies were floated in the names of relatives, wives and daughters especially, and electricity and other utility bills were often in the names of fictitious individuals.

When Indira Gandhi's government unceremoniously ushered out India's multinationals in the 1970s, most famously Coca-Cola and IBM, she inadvertently created space for local entrepreneurs.[19] Reliance, India's first private-sector entry into the world's Fortune 500, began when its founder, Dhirubhai Ambani, ran a trading operation between the Gulf port of Aden and his home in western India. The firm has since become one of the world's largest petrochemical refiners as well as an infrastructure developer par excellence. Part of its entrepreneurship was to find ways around the License Raj while building more conventional capabilities, like obtaining excellent financing in an underdeveloped financial market. As a result, Reliance dramatically increased the acceptance of equity holding among lay investors in India. Another example of local entrepreneurship is Hero Honda, a joint venture between Honda and the Munjal family to make motorcycles and mopeds in India. As one of the world's largest manufacturers of motorbikes—a distinction also claimed by Chongquing Lifan Group in China—Hero Honda's manufacturing is world class and its distribution in remote Indian villages unparalleled. It remains one of the very few examples anywhere in the world of Honda sharing control with a local entrepreneur.

Despite the criticisms of several observers about the "excess" diversification of Indian business—as characterized by American economists—my colleague Krishna Palepu and I have found this diversification appropriate in an emerging market like India's.[20] In an article debated extensively in developing countries worldwide—first published in the *Harvard Business Review* in 1997—we argued that being in multiple industries was a natural response to the absence of supporting mechanisms that those of us living in the West find easily accessible.[21] Businesses relied on cash flows from their existing activities to fund new activities, often seemingly distant ones, when there was no other source of capital easily available, and that this was not *per se* bad, as one might believe it more likely in New York or London, where there are plenty of ways to raise capital. Similarly, the House of Tata, whose corporate scope has both increased dramatically over its one and a half centuries of existence, and contracted when it has left some businesses behind, could use its talent from some of its businesses to help launch newer businesses. Using scarce talent in this fashion, across settings more diverse than are typically seen in a developed market, made sense.

Thus indigenous private-sector entrepreneurship continued to thrive in India, when necessary ducking and weaving away from the state's predation or finding ways around undeveloped capital and talent markets. If it did not look exactly like Western entrepreneurship, this was natural given how private initiative often plays out in the early stages of development. As a commentary on both the adaptability of indigenous entrepreneurs and the morass of government enterprise, even in the 1960s the private sector contributed as much as 87 percent of India's GDP and was a key employment generator for the country.[22]

Finance Minister Manmohan Singh advocated a new "Manmohanomics," replacing political gaming and bribing with renewed market-based reform in 1991. He continued to chip away at the License Raj, made the rupee partially convertible on the current account, rendered the draconian Foreign Exchange Regulation Act redundant as foreign exchange became easily available, and reduced tariffs drastically. The Indian capital markets were opened to foreign institutional investors. To solve the problem of mammoth, inefficient public-sector companies, the concept of disinvestment (the government's euphemism for privatization) was contemplated for the first time, and industries previously reserved for the public sector were opened to all.

As a result of these reforms, garment and textile exporters made small fortunes. Mom-and-pop stores in urban India showcased everything from Gillette razors to Twix candy bars. Everyone had an uncle who was supplying bedspreads and linens to Macy's and a cousin who was a software engineer at Infosys. Multinationals arrived for the first time since India had ushered them out in the 1970s. Symbolically, the first McDonald's opened its doors in upscale parts of New Delhi in 1996. By 2004 fifty-eight McDonald's were scattered over mostly northern and western India. Consumer products saw a revolution. Foreign brands, extensively advertised on TV, gave consumers choices. The Maruti 800 now faced, among others, General Motors' Opel cars and Honda's Civic. For a few years Indian businesses responded defensively, with some finding they could compete if they chose to invest rather than solely lobby government for protection.

The TCL Story, Part 1: The Rise of Chinese Companies

In 2004 Li Dongsheng, chairman of TCL, was named Asia's top businessperson by *Fortune* (Infosys's Murthy and Nilekani shared that honor the previous year). His French title, *"Officer de la Legion d'Honneur,"* the country's most senior order, had a long pedigree, first established by Napoleon Bonaparte. Cited as a leader in Sino-French relations, Li had recently bought two French assets with brands of debatable value, Thomson televisions and Alcatel cell phones. The Thomson deal made TCL the world's largest television manufacturer at that time. TCL Thomson Enterprise (TTE) was a joint venture in which TCL owned 67 percent and Thomson owned the remainder. Both Thomson and TCL were believed to have contributed assets valued at more than $500 million. How did Li, a member of the CCP Central Committee who describes his most difficult assignment as tending rice paddies during the Cultural Revolution, become a celebrity entrepreneur?

His rise at TCL mirrors that of indigenous manufacturing in China and serves as an example of considerable entrepreneurial hustle on the mainland.[23] In 1982, when Li joined the company almost at its inception,[24] TCL produced a range of audio-related consumer electronics equipment—most famously, high-quality fixed-line telephones. From the outset the Huizhou city government nurtured the fledgling firm, offering a guarantee for the initial 5,000 RMB ($670) borrowed by TCL's founders. In effect, the city government served as a venture capitalist. It rarely interfered in management decisions, even though as recently as 2004 it continued to be the largest single shareholder, holding more than 25 percent of the company's equity.[25]

TCL's founding took place in the context of the newly created Town and Village Enterprises (TVEs), which served to blur the lines between private and state ownership.[26] TVE began to replace and reclassify the people's communes created by Mao. TVEs were generally involved in nonagricultural work and were divided into three major types: township enterprises, village enterprises, and private (rural) enterprises. Village enterprises were owned by all village citizens and controlled by the village committee. On paper all the citizens in a township (or village) were owners, as per central government regulations. "But because an individual citizen automatically becomes a nominal owner by his local citizenship, he thus has no rights to choose asset ownership. A nominal owner typically holds no (explicit) shares and cannot transfer, sell, or authorize for inheritance his part of the collective assets."[27]

Once the party established TVEs, a rural industrial revolution was unleashed. "TVEs gave rural communities the ability to transform control over assets into income in the absence of asset markets. This could be done without resorting to privatization. the profits of those enterprises could then be used for the benefit of the entire community. These local government units also facilitated the channeling of funds (mostly from households) in the absence of a well functioning banking system."[28] In the decade from 1984 onward, TVE output grew by 25 percent annually to reach a level of that of urban state-owned enterprises.[29]

By the early 1990s, TCL, successful as a TVE, began to develop a nationwide distribution system that soon proved to be a formidable barrier to indigenous and foreign companies that tried to compete on its turf. Around the same time TCL began to sell televisions. Rather than reflecting a premeditated strategy, the move appeared motivated by developments at a Hong Kong–based source for TVs. Significantly, television sales demonstrated that TCL's distribution network could be used to sell all manner of consumer electronics goods. Thus TCL began to push personal computers, mobile phones, white goods, and electronic components through its distribution channels.

Good management practices infused TCL. As early as 1997 the company used the World Wide Web to monitor inventory in its disparate sales channels, and it aligned the incentives of its sales organization to ensure that the right data showed up in the system. As a result, TCL's inventory management was first rate. In the fast-moving consumer electronics industry, it was rarely caught with the obsolete equipment that other companies were forced to severely discount. Compared with its competitors, TCL had much less surplus stock and therefore much less capital tied up in maintaining those stocks. It also collected money from its customers more speedily than competitors in China like Sony and Samsung. At any point in time in 2004, outstanding receivables were only 10 million RMB of 10 billion RMB ($1.2 million out of $1.2 billion) in sales, a miniscule percentage.

In 2001 fierce competition broke out among TV makers on the mainland. TCL was well positioned to survive, especially with its superior management of factory operations and its well-honed distribution networks and revenue collection mechanisms. In fact it emerged as one of the three leading TV manufacturers in China. But this competitive episode was only one of a series of pitched battles for market share. Of the more than one thousand firms assembling televisions across mainland China in the early 1990s, only a handful were left standing a decade later. TCL and Konka each had about a 17 percent share in the domestic market, with Skyworth and Changhong following closely behind with 13 percent each. A quarter-by-quarter struggle had the four companies alternating as the share leader. Margins were under enormous pressure, and TCL's return on assets was a meager 5 percent.[30]

Local banks readily advanced money to the leading TV businesses in their regions, regardless of the true state of financial health of the borrowers. Throughout China the banking system was heavily compromised by enormous bad debt on the bankers' books. Bankers preferred to extend the lines of credit to their borrowers rather than declare them defunct and call in the loans. Not that TCL was bankrupt, but the system made getting credit easy to obtain, resulting in leverage that was probably higher than was prudent. No global financier would have bankrolled a white-goods manufacturer with returns as poor as TCL's, regardless of how spotless its factory floors looked and how quickly it collected its bills.[31]

Why were so many TV manufacturers in mainland China—one in each subprovince? A surfeit of producers in almost any category is a general feature of China's indigenous enterprise and originates in a particular feature of the country's political decentralization. Each province's officials seemed happy to promote their own industrial enterprises, that being the basis on which they were evaluated, even if that led to competition with similarly promoted enterprises in the neighboring provinces. Further, interprovince barriers to the movement of goods and services were very high. As a result of too many subscale production facilities, efficiency was compromised. It took a lot more labor, raw materials, and electricity to produce a unit of anything than it might have in the absence of such protectionism and fragmentation. Much of China's growth seemed to come from plowing in more inputs, rather than from more efficient use of a given quantity of inputs over time.[32]

What accounts for TCL's emergence from this competitive morass? No one should doubt that strong management played an important role. Although Li Dongsheng kept a firm hand on the tiller of this ship, he assembled a superior team of managers and motivated them to be creative. Charls Zhao, the president of TCL Multimedia, the entity that housed the world television operations, explained that TCL differed from most Chinese enterprises, which tended to be either family owned or run in a strict "militaristic" hierarchy: "TCL has an immigrant culture. That means independent ideas can flourish here. Chairman Li makes the rules of the game but leaves each manager with the autonomy to deliver results." He added that a personality test had revealed thirty-five of TCL's forty managers as "tigers, each powerful within its own territory." Mirroring the CCP's decision to decentralize its control over enterprise, TCL used a combination of decentralized incentives and accountability mechanisms to promote its growth.

Another factor in TCL's success was its location in the relatively market-friendly southern province of Guangdong. The origins of Guangdong's hospitality toward entrepreneurs go back at least to actions taken under Mao. In building up the People's Republic of China, Chairman Mao had certain strongholds where he naturally concentrated his time, staying away from the forces of his nationalist foe, Generalissimo Chiang Kai-shek. China's northeast region, closer to the border of what was then the Soviet Union, was the focus of the Communist Party. In contrast provinces to the south were deemed unsafe nationalist strongholds. This meant that the northeast was characterized by much heavier state intervention and much less market-oriented reform than the southeast. As a result, TVEs thrived in places like Guangdong, where "antimarket ideology" was less common.[33] Guangdong Province has been home to many of China's multibillion-dollar success stories, including Huawei Technologies, Guangdong Media Group, and Guangdong Galanz Enterprise. The local government's support of TCL should be contrasted with intervention elsewhere in China, which is often more draconian.

The TCL Story, Part 2: The Global Stumble of Chinese Companies

At Beijing's Tsinghua University, I led a discussion on TCL's acquisition of Thomson with a group of senior executives. At that point, TTE, as the Sino-French venture was called, was having a tough time and had experienced a litany of management problems. Melding French and Chinese cultures within the company was probably the most problematic, especially when it came to compensation. Chinese executives were being paid considerably less than the French managers reporting to them.[34]

Class participants were senior managers from mainland Chinese companies (mostly state owned) and from companies in Hong Kong, Taiwan, and Singapore. Discussions among the managers were revealing. The class split on its evaluation of TCL's Thomson acquisition. The mainland Chinese executives were largely inclined to give Li the benefit of the doubt regarding the wisdom of the French acquisition. Given his track record of building the business in China and his steadfast membership in the Party, they argued, Li should have been given a free hand in propelling TCL to new heights. Like the majority of mainland Chinese, they believed it was important for China to own a handful of globally recognized brands. TCL was one of the very few companies that could have aspired to such recognition. Charls Zhao, the leader of the TCL TV business, had said quite frankly, "The country can't be strong without top level firms, but China has no brands besides Lenovo or Haier."[35] TCL also convinced itself that it had to acquire heft to compete with Sony and Samsung. Even though TCL was then one of the largest companies in China, with a market capitalization of $4 billion, Samsung's market capitalization was eight times larger and Sony's sixteen times.

On the other hand the executives from Hong Kong and other overseas Chinese companies were adamant that an acquisition as big as Thomson was inappropriate. In their opinion the deal was too much of a risk, and demonstrated the government's failure to check and balance Li. To support TCL's overseas operations, China's Export-Import Bank had made the company two loans, including one of RMB 6 billion ($720 million).[36] The overseas executives thought that the willingness of the local banks to support such activity meant that financial markets were not disciplining management appropriately. Those executives who disliked the deal were especially incredulous that TCL would embark on such a venture after it had tried and failed, to buy a TV company in Germany. The German acquisition was much smaller—TCL had spent $8.2 million ($8.4 million) to acquire Germany's seventh-largest TV manufacturer, Schneider. As with Thomson, the purpose of the Schneider acquisition was to acquire a known brand and known research and development, and in exchange give Schneider access to China's low-cost manufacturing. The Germans were especially unwilling to close down their factories and therefore willing to sell the company to TCL cheaply. Despite shipping unassembled TVs for assembly in Germany, however, the costs remained high enough that ultimately TCL was forced to shut down the plants.

The rift between the opposing points of view in the classroom discussion is indicative of the issues faced by Chinese companies eager to build global brands. Their enthusiasm often stems from party mandates to create companies that will be among the Fortune 500. In other words the government as entrepreneur can demand that particular companies become global, regardless of the company's ability to manage and sustain a global venture.

There have been several high-profile attempts by flagship Chinese companies to acquire overseas assets. In July 2005 Haier bid for the assets of Maytag, once the leading provider of washing machines in the West, but was stymied by a competitor, Whirlpool. Much more successful was Lenovo, China's leading manufacturer of personal computers, which successfully secured access to IBM's PC business and at the end of 2004 became the third-largest manufacturer of PCs worldwide (behind Dell and Hewlett Packard). In addition, Lenovo negotiated the rights to use IBM's ThinkPad and ThinkCentre trademarks for a five-year period. Although the reason behind the Lenovo and TCL deals was the same—access to low-cost manufacturing in China in exchange for recognized brand names in the developed world—Lenovo was better able than TCL to bridge the cultural gap. Lenovo understood the symbolic value of retaining New York, rather than Beijing, as its world headquarters for global operations. IBM in turn understood the symbolic value to the Chinese in seemingly innocuous details, such as sending a car to the airport for arriving Lenovo executives.[37]

In June 2005 the biggest buyout so far was attempted by the oil giant China National Offshore Oil Corporation (CNOOC), which offered $18 billion for the American oil company Unocal. Despite being a state-owned company, CNOOC appeared to have paid attention to some global corporate governance norms. At the time it proposed the transaction, it had several independent directors on its board, including a former Shell executive providing oil industry experience, a senior partner from the investment bank Goldman Sachs providing information on global financial markets, and a former Swiss ambassador to China providing his political antennae.[38]

Additionally, CNOOC's chairman, Fu Chengyu, presided over a top management team that included several people with degrees from leading Western universities. Fu himself was a skilled geologist with a masters degree in petroleum engineering from the University of Southern California and thirty years of experience in the oil industry in China, mostly in various positions at CNOOC.[39] Further, CNOOC was reputed to be the most internationally savvy of the three major oil companies from China because it primarily worked with foreign firms and listed roughly a third of the equity of CNOOC Limited, its offshore oil and gas exploration vehicle, in Hong Kong and New York in 2001.

Its international orientation did not protect CNOOC in the fiasco that ensued. Why was its bid for Unocal stymied? I spoke with Dan Spiegel, a partner in the firm retained by CNOOC to shepherd the transaction through Washington. As a former U.S. permanent representative to the United Nations in Geneva and a partner at one of the world's largest law firms, Akin Gump, he is an insider in this environment.[40] Especially important, he had been the head of his firm's international trade practice and had watched prior waves of foreign acquirers, the British in the 1970s and the Japanese in the 1980s.

Spiegel explained that Unocal, although nominally a U.S. company, had most of its assets in Asia and was rumored to have been for sale for a while. "In late March 2005," he continued, "CNOOC and Unocal had a deal and were ready to walk hand in hand to Washington for regulatory approval. But the independent directors, impartial outsiders on CNOOC's board, balked at the deal, presumably because it seemed too risky. The revolt of the independent directors was a critical turning point which had serious implications for the transaction."[41]

It seemed extraordinary that, in a deal of this magnitude, Fu hadn't brought the board along before making his move. Ultimately CNOOC behaved more like a state-owned enterprise, clumsy in the face of international commerce. CNOOC, like the other Chinese oil companies, answers to the State-Owned Assets Supervision and Administration Commission, which has the last word on, among other things, all management personnel decisions.

Meanwhile, a U.S. oil company, Chevron, jumped into the breach and negotiated a merger agreement with Unocal with a $500 million breakup fee; that is, if Unocal reneged and merged with another entity, that entity would have to pay Chevron the half billion dollars. CNOOC's independent directors hired another prominent law firm, Skadden Arps, as their own advisers, along with global merchant bankers Rothschild to analyze the situation. Spiegel explained, "They had legitimate concerns. Fu was bidding $18 billion, as much as CNOOC was worth, so it was a big-deal transaction. They were concerned about the difficulty of integrating the American and the Chinese company and they were concerned about political reactions in the U.S."

Chevron played the Washington community expertly. "They and their allies in Congress whipped up such a frenzy about a Chinese company buying U.S. assets. You'd think CNOOC was buying Exxon with a market capitalization of about $380 billion rather than Unocal with a market capitalization of about $18 billion. Fu was operating with one hand tied behind his back. CNOOC had zero employees in the U.S. and no political presence and no spokesperson here, and it was now bidding against a U.S. company for a U.S. company." In addition, CNOOC was a bantam compared to U.S. heavyweights like Exxon Mobil, Chevron, and ConocoPhilips, which had combined revenues just shy of $1 trillion, more than the individual GDPs of 189 countries. CNOOC's revenues were in the range of $11 billion, large in absolute terms but tiny in comparison.

Chevron ultimately bought rival Unocal for $18 billion in August 2005, prevailing over CNOOC's offer. CNOOC withdrew after Congress threatened to block a Unocal sale to a company outside the United States.[42] Spiegel was surprised that members of Congress openly raised concerns about Chinese espionage as a reason to oppose the transaction. He rationalized, 'All during 2005 the alleged undervaluation of the Chinese renminbi was in the press all day, U.S. security concerns had gone up, trade frictions were as high as ever before with China's trade surplus with the U.S. scaling new heights, and Congress had no tangible opportunity to express itself. Then here comes CNOOC and Congress pokes its finger in the Chinese eye. A perfect storm."

Good political counsel reminded Fu that the Republicans, the strongest political force in the United States at the time, were quite concerned about China. Perhaps Fu was overly influenced by Lenovo's ability to consummate the IBM transaction, even though many in the United States had objected to it. Spiegel explained, "[T]hat was then, this is now. It's not even clear that Lenovo would have gone through in this time of heightened sensitivity to things Chinese. Opponents are objecting less to China's economic rise and more to China as a military power, China as a potential spy in the U.S."

Interestingly, the stock price of CNOOC rose sharply by one-third during the twists and turns of the attempted deal.[43] Despite the deal's failure, Chinese markets may perceive some benefit for CNOOC in the context of China's economic aspirations. Perhaps they think that the growth of Chinese giants is inevitable and the CNOOC deal was a valuable learning experience. "CNOOC did not win the deal but won the course," stated the *China Entrepreneur* magazine, suggesting that Fu's reputation had not quite suffered as much as might be expected.[44]

What are the differences between Indian and Chinese cross-border deals? First, India is perceived as a U.S. ally. After years of being more aligned with the Soviet Union than with the U.S. during the cold war, this warmer viewpoint is relatively recent. Much less political opposition was directed toward Indian companies than toward Chinese companies. Second, with the exception of Tata Steel, which bought Britain's Corus Steel, Indian companies initially stayed away from high-profile acquisitions like those brokered by Lenovo, TCL, CNOOC, and Haier. Indians have proceeded cautiously, bidding on smaller, more manageable assets. Numbers like $100 million are more common than numbers like China's $18 billion. These deals naturally attract less attention, especially because they are spread far afield. The Tatas bought Tetley Tea in the United Kingdom, Daewoo's truck business in South Korea, a steel business in Southeast Asia, and small software companies all over Latin America. While the aggressive Chinese purchases are backed by the state's political mandate and unlimited capital, with reputation rather than return on capital as the driver, Indian purchases must respond to conventional shareholder pressures. When the Indians have attempted big purchases—for example, the Indian petroleum company wanted to bid for a deal in Kazakhstan—the deal collapsed in intragovernment acrimony and a spat between the CEO of the state-run company and the petroleum minister. Such a public airing of differences, which is sometimes dysfunctional but can also result in meaningful discussion about feasibility and strategy, is unimaginable in China.

Finally, unlike China, India has an explicit private-sector lobby group from its flagship global industry the software industry, working to smooth the waters for cross-border commerce. Kiran Karnik, the CEO of the National Association of Software and Service Companies based in New Delhi, is often in New York and Washington meeting with Congress and the administration to try to fashion common ground on issues like Internet security, outsourcing, and the future of competition between the United States and India.

Red Hats, Small Hats, and Foreign Hats: Private Entrepreneurship, Chinese Style

As entrepreneurs we are condemned either to being the concubines of state enterprises or the mistresses of multinationals.

—Wu Kegang, Yunnan Hong Wine[45]

One of my students said it best: "The government in China *is* the private sector." The Chinese government finances entrepreneurs to such an extent that a genuinely private company, completely devoid of government support and backing, will likely remain a small-time operation. Although Town and Village Enterprises like TCL seem to resemble Western private companies, with local governments increasingly taking a backseat role, the party apparatus is never far behind. A significant number of CCP members are involved in business, and the Party embraces business. Thus doing business *in* China as a truly private enterprise is not something to wish for, and doing business *with* China requires understanding the nuances and connotations of the term *private*, which means something quite different in the West. As Bill Kirby, a preeminent China historian at Harvard, points out, it is fallacious to believe that the "Western model would be the essential vehicle for *private* Chinese economic development."[46]

A case in point is Red Flag Linux, China's leading open-source software company, which owes its existence to technology provided by the state-run China Academy of Sciences and its initial financing to a state-connected venture capital firm. Another major investor in the company was the Ministry of Information Industry.[47] The quid pro quo is that Red Flag, even though run by alumni of major Western multinationals, on occasion must do the state's bidding. If Red Flag became a purely private company, local officials would not receive a cut of the firm's profits and would therefore have no incentive to further its interests. Being "too private" appears to open a company up to unwanted attention. At least one prominent private Chinese company, recognizable to most in the West, asked me not to write about them. Its success, and the fact that the local government did not own a large portion of it, was attracting unwarranted attention.

In addition, a company that is "too private" may find itself less eligible to receive bank loans. Until 1998 China's four commercial banks, which together control most of China's banking assets, were instructed to lend to state-owned enterprises, while smaller credit cooperatives were asked to lend to private firms. Even banks chartered to lend to private enterprises largely fail to do so. The reticence to lend to private entrepreneurs is understandable. Loans to state-owned firms are protected—the state simply bails out likely defaulters—in an attempt to forestall the distress that unemployed workers would cause to the system. No such guarantees exist for the private sector. Loans also tend to be made more through relationships than on the basis of available collateral, and banks are not entirely sure to whom they are lending.

To sidestep restrictions on private firms and get better treatment from the government authorities, many entrepreneurs have presented themselves as collectives. This strategy is variously known as wearing a red hat, a small hat, or a foreign hat.[48] These firms evade state control by staying under the radar screen as small entities or buying protection by affiliating with foreign entities. Many private entrepreneurs also decide to coinvest with state or collective firms, quite often under legal joint stock or shareholding agreements. Other private entrepreneurs distribute shares among family members and local governments, often giving high-ranking officials seats on their boards. Clearly this ambiguity in ownership, shareholding patterns, and accounting makes banks even more nervous to lend.

Even so, recent estimates suggest that as much as half of China's GDP comes from private firms—the statistics vary, mostly reflecting the ambiguous definition of *private*—and that private companies actually absorb more of the funding from the financial system, though still in the range of 10 percent to 27 percent. For the most part, however, private companies must resort to the informal market, where interest rates are much higher.[49] Only 1 percent of the companies listed on the Shanghai and Shenzhen stock exchanges are private firms.[50]

China's experiments with private enterprise continue, and its ability to learn from its experimentation is undeniably superb. As it once did with Deng's Special Economic Zones, expanding from Guangdong and Fujian to the rest of China, and with the freeing up of interest rates over a quarter century starting in Wenzhou in 1980 and spreading to other parts of China, it is now experimenting with private banks, beginning with Minsheng Bank.[51]

The West should recognize, therefore, that the rising economic activity being attributed to private enterprise in China does not mean that the government is backing off. But equally important, the government's incentives are aligned with would-be entrepreneurs. So as long as the entrepreneur wears a hat—red, small, or foreign—business can proceed.

Chapter Seven

Microsoft and Metro

Views from the World's Corner Offices

"Can I *really* make money in China and India?" is a question I am frequently asked by colleagues and friends. Just as often executives already convinced of the money to be made in Asia tell me, "We simply *must* be in China."

Yes, a company can make money in China and India, but it cannot do so overnight and may have to wait five years or more to realize profits. A lot depends on how much a foreign company is willing to respect and work *with* indigenous ways of doing business, including adapting to government regulations and the political climate. Although competition from the state in China and from local companies in India will always, to a certain extent, constrain multinationals, my own research shows that both these forms of competition are equally effective. It is unclear that multinationals do unambiguously better in China than in India, or vice versa. The most successful multinationals, those building long-term positions in either country, invariably pay more attention to contributing to local welfare than to their bottom lines. Landing on foreign soil to make a quick buck virtually never works.

The sagas of two companies, each superbly managed in its home environment, illustrates these points. Microsoft faced daunting challenges in China, as did Germany's Metro Cash & Carry in India. Much can be learned from the solutions they eventually discovered that have put each on a path to long-run success.

Microsoft in China: Changing the Code of Conduct

On April 18, 2006, President Hu Jintao arrived in the United States. His first stop was not Washington, D.C., but Redmond, Washington, home to Microsoft Corporation and its founder Bill Gates. At Microsoft's headquarters, Hu exclaimed, "Because you, Mr. Bill Gates, are a friend of China, I'm a friend of Microsoft." He then added, "Also, I am dealing with the operating system produced by Microsoft every day." Laughing, Bill Gates responded, "Thank you, it's a fantastic relationship . . . if you ever need advice on how to use Windows, I'll be glad to help."[1] It was a shining moment in the decade-long Microsoft-in-China drama that has had its share of dark days.

The story began in 1993, when Microsoft's Far East division oversaw the corporation's China strategy from its regional headquarters in Tokyo.[2] In hindsight the location outside mainland China was costly; it kept Microsoft apart from the internal information flow. Nevertheless, in 1993 the timing seemed right for formally introducing Windows to the mainland. The estimated one million PCs already bought seemed a good start, and annual purchases were growing at a healthy 22 percent.

However, the growth in PC adoption masked real problems. First, software piracy was rampant throughout Asia, and China had been singled out as the source of the largest losses. Experts estimated that more than 90 percent of software in use in China was pirated, resulting in anticipated losses of roughly $300 million annually. A survey showed that Microsoft's FoxPro database application accounted for 65 percent of database installations in China, yet Microsoft had not sold a single legal copy.[3]

Second, Microsoft had to contend with some unique features of the Chinese software landscape. The government was the biggest buyer of software. Before 1978 China had almost no privately owned businesses, certainly none of any consequence. Revenue from a state-owned enterprise accrued to the national or provincial government and to the ministry to which the enterprise reported. Often the reporting relationships appeared extremely complicated to the outsider. Certainly figuring them out from Tokyo was a problem for Microsoft's Far East division.

As if selling to the bureaucracy was not enough, the key suppliers—the software talent writing the applications needed to support the use of the operating system—worked for the same bureaucrats and government officials. Most of these suppliers were small local companies—5 to 100 employees— that spun off from software vendors, usually state-owned enterprises or universities. In a manner of speaking Microsoft was squeezed by the same entities when it hired talent as when it sold its products. A typical example of the ingenuity of local entrepreneurs in adapting products for China was their use of English-language Microsoft software—without paying the company for it, of course—for which they created overlaying "shells" that made the software accessible to Chinese users. This process involved creating new screen displays and new keystroke combinations to accommodate Chinese characters.

A local business thus hastily customized the interface to Microsoft's software. This was used by friends and family, with perhaps a few thousand users. Inconsistency across versions was widespread, and no version achieved critical mass. In the United States application software writers develop an array of programs to work with an operating system for a critical mass of users, but in China it made no sense to invest time developing such programs with no likelihood of earning a return. Piracy, of course, compounded the problem. Without applications, the operating system—the software that tells the computer how to process instructions from the user—was not useful. Although Microsoft had nothing to do with the fragmentation and variety of shells, many users turned to Microsoft for support, holding it responsible for badly written shells and adding to the company's image problems.

The technical wizards of Redmond decided that the only way to trump the local entrepreneurs was for Microsoft to create a consistent Chinese-language shell of its own. Working with its Taiwan subsidiary, Microsoft did just that when it introduced a localized version of Windows 3.1 in China.

The backlash was swift and merciless. In February 1994 China blacklisted Windows 3.1. The official reason was that the software had failed to meet local standards of character input. Microsoft ended up selling a paltry number of copies.

The following month, mortified by China's rejection of Windows, Bill Gates arrived in Beijing to convince President Jiang Zemin that blacklisting his company's software was a mistake and that it was in China's interest for Windows to become the standard operating system, as it was in the United States. "There is no Government ministry that has to get involved in every new software that comes into the marketplace," he proclaimed. "Microsoft Windows is a product that is known around the world. It is quite clear it should have Chinese support."[4] If Bill Gates thought his personal appearance would help Microsoft's cause, he was wrong. Unperturbed by assertions of Windows' supremacy, Jiang Zemin threatened to ban it entirely. It was suggested to the visitors that they ought to study Chinese culture to appreciate how to deal with the Chinese.

What had happened? Why was Microsoft cold-shouldered? Producing software shells was an important business to the small local software vendors, and they did not take kindly to the U.S. giant trampling their turf, especially since they were not only suppliers but also buyers, through the common bureaucratic connection. Despite Microsoft's economic logic, it was a mistake to push an action that was not in the interest of the government.

Much backpedaling followed to assuage feelings. Several rounds of negotiation yielded a memorandum of understanding between Microsoft and the ministry. Six local software vendors were enlisted in joint ventures. In late 1996, however, Microsoft experienced a new set of problems with its major upgrade, Windows 95. The program's Chinese map graphic lacked the character for Taiwan, implying that Taiwan was not part of China—a notoriously sore point for the mainland government. Worse, the character selection window, used to input Chinese symbols, included anticommunist slogans. Microsoft was forced to delay shipments. The source of these "features" was never determined, but one conjecture was that a disgruntled programmer, perhaps in Taiwan, had been responsible. Much of Microsoft's localization of English software to Chinese occurred in Taiwan at that time.

More embarrassments followed. A June issue of *Fortune* reported that Bill Gates told some American business students, "Although about three million computers get sold every year in China, people don't pay for the software. Someday they will, though. As long as they're going to steal it, we want them to steal ours. They'll get sort of addicted, and then we'll somehow figure out how to collect sometime in the next decade."[5] The addiction metaphor, stirring memories of opium addiction during part of what the Chinese refer to as their "century of humiliation," cost Bill Gates heavily.

On December 17, 1999, the Beijing First Intermediate People's Court handed down its judgment in a landmark case, *Microsoft Corporation (China), Ltd. v. Beijing Yadu Science and Technology Group*. Though piracy had been the scourge of all software firms, this was the first time a foreign entity had sued for copyright infringement. Microsoft claimed that its agent, the China United Intellectual Property Investigation Center, had joined the local authorities in raiding the Yadu Building and discovered more than a dozen pirated versions of its software.[6] Microsoft sued for $181,000 to cover lost profits and litigation-related costs. In the United States aggressive copyright litigation had become a rewarding norm, but in China the court dismissed Microsoft's claim on the basis of insufficient evidence.

The litigation was part of Microsoft's multipronged approach to fighting piracy in China. The firm had also tried technological fixes—requiring a hardware device be inserted at the back of the PC to make a program work, creating CD-ROM keys or passwords, or using high-quality holographic printing—all to no avail. A range of other attempts had also failed—establishing stores that could assure customers that products were authenticated, setting up hotlines to authenticate products or where people could call to get tips about avoiding illegal software, giving people incentives to share tips about piracy, and offering users incentives to buy rather than pirate. Microsoft had also vowed that it would donate any proceeds from antipiracy enforcement to China. Mobilizing international pressure made no difference, nor did mobilizing most major software firms in the West to form the Business Software Alliance in Washington, DC.

Why did all Microsoft's efforts have no effect? Without a substantial indigenous software industry, it was not in Beijing's interest to enforce antipiracy standards. After all, piracy ensured dissemination of technology; and even if Beijing were serious, it would have a tough time getting local government compliance. Piracy affected just about all branded products, not just the highly technical ones, and even had an impact on some Chinese personally. For example, He Qinglian, the author of a bestseller in China called *The Pitfalls of Modernization*, became a victim of piracy when a book called *Behind the Pitfalls of Modernization* was published bearing her name and without her knowledge.[7]

Harvard-based China legal scholar Bill Alford points to the traditional Chinese saying "To steal a book is an elegant offense" as illustrating a view of intellectual property that contrasts sharply with the Western perspective.[8] In a Chinese student-teacher relationship, copying is a form of tribute to the master. Since all work was deemed equal during the Cultural Revolution, and since many physical products do not identify their creators, it was unclear to the Chinese why the output of intellectual work should be associated with a particular individual. If British force and eventual victory in the Opium Wars—fought between 1840 and 1860 when China resisted Britain's continued attempts to sell opium to the Chinese—did not change China's perspective on intellectual property, Microsoft's attempts at force majeure were unlikely to succeed.

At the turn of the millennium Microsoft's record in China was lackluster. Legal sales were miniscule, and Microsoft's image was tarnished. Coincidently the company was beginning to have image problems at home as well. As early as 1990 Microsoft had come under the radar of the U.S. Department of Justice (DOJ) for antitrust violations. The latter had been steadily blocking mergers and filing petitions in the courts against Microsoft. In 1998 the DOJ and twenty state attorneys-general filed an antitrust suit against Microsoft, charging the company with abusing its market power to thwart competition. In April 2000 government lawyers argued that Microsoft ought to be split into two companies as a penalty for breaking antitrust laws. The Europeans had joined in the attack and were threatening to carry out their own litigation against the company.

The antitrust actions in the West did not go unnoticed in China. In 2000 a *New York Times* article stated,

> *Janet Reno [the U.S. attorney general] is not the only one worried about Bill Gates' software monopoly: China's leaders are, too. They are concerned that the country is growing overly dependent on Microsoft Corp.'s Windows operating system, which controls microcomputers running everything from banks to President Jiang Zemin's e-mail box. But the Chinese government, itself a master at monopoly, is taking its case against Microsoft not to the courtroom, but to the marketplace, albeit with a bit of administrative fiat.[9]*

The fiat in question was a declaration from the top that China would not be beholden to Microsoft's proprietary standard. Linux had emerged as a viable competitor to Microsoft worldwide. As an open-source provider, Linux made its source code available to everyone. Microsoft, China believed, went well beyond simply guarding its crown jewels. The Chinese press alleged that Microsoft had "back doors" in the Windows source code that allowed U.S. companies and the U.S. government to spy on Chinese computer users. Putting its policy into action, the Chinese government preferred and directly supported Red Flag, a Chinese Linux provider.[10]

Red Flag was set up in June 2000, the result of research conducted by the Chinese Academy of Social Sciences, which had backed other information technology ventures, including Lenovo, the company that went on to acquire IBM's PC assets. Red Flag's management team was built with top executives from places like Oracle, Novell, and Hewlett-Packard. Not only were government agencies the key buyers, but also the Chinese government had spent RMB 200 million (an estimated $24 million) on Red Flag since its creation. Help had come from the government-owned Shanghai New Margin Venture Capital Fund. In March 2001 Bloomberg News reported that CCIDNET Investment, which was a venture capital arm of China's Ministry of Information Industry, had become Red Flag's second-largest shareholder.[11]

In the same year researchers with the Gartner Group reported that the Beijing municipal government had selected six vendors out of a pool of seven bidders to provide an operating system, office automation software, and antivirus software for the government's PCs. The one non-Chinese firm, Microsoft, was the only bidder Beijing rejected. The article listed a host of reasons why Microsoft had lost the bid. These included "unique deal negotiation processes, and the criticality of building ongoing relationships with key parties, such as the Chinese government."[12]

By now the writing was on the wall. Despite more than a decade of activity in China, Microsoft had never really been welcomed. The Chinese were not discreet about painting Bill Gates as a greedy Western capitalist, an antipiracy activist committed to expanding his monopoly to China. Some serious introspection must have transpired at Microsoft's Redmond headquarters, because the company's conduct toward its biggest critic showed signs of significant change.

In 2000 CEO Steve Ballmer addressed Premier Zhu Rongji in a tone that did not carry the hubris Gates had demonstrated in 1993. "Our strategy in China really focuses on long-term investment," he said. "We would like to cooperate with local industry, partners and government organizations to build up a win-win relationship and to help China embrace the knowledge economy."[13] Microsoft's rhetoric had gone from "no government" to "with government." Well aware of the Chinese government's policy to boost local software industry, Ballmer announced that Microsoft would explore opportunities to establish joint ventures with local companies. Since the local companies were mostly state-owned enterprises, this amounted to cooperation with the government. Microsoft also pointed out that it would help further development of the Beijing Zhonguancun high-tech zone.

Ballmer's visit launched an attempt at cooperation. A joint venture was established to develop business application software with the Chinese companies Centergate Technology and Stone Group.[14] In 2002 Microsoft signed an agreement with China's State Development Planning Commission, committing to invest $750 million in China over three years "to support both China's locally owned software industry and its intellectual property."[15] Bill Gates and the head of the planning commission, Zeng Paiyan (who later became the vice president of China), jointly determined where to invest the money.

In 2003 Microsoft hired Timothy Chen as its China CEO. Following a successful stint at Motorola's profitable China subsidiary, Chen was going to project a "softer strategy" and change the "threatening letters approach" Microsoft had thus far pursued.[16] Additionally, Microsoft gave money to universities and stepped up investment in research and development. Microsoft Research Asia (MSRA), the Beijing-based lab founded by the firm in 1998, developed a reputation for churning out world-class research. By 2003 MSRA had grown to 170 researchers and was hosting more than 250 visiting scientists and students from China as well as around the world. Approximately 200 graduate students from local universities conducted research at the lab through Microsoft-sponsored internship and fellowship programs. In November 2003, in yet another attempt to convey to the Chinese that Microsoft was committed to developing China's local software industry, the firm announced the creation of the Advanced Technology Center, formed to develop products based on MSRA research.[17] Further, Microsoft partnered with five Chinese universities to establish labs in other areas of China.

Perhaps the biggest impact from Microsoft's new strategy, one that entailed courting rather than dismissing the Chinese government, was felt in 2003 when Bill Gates, meeting with President Jiang Zemin (the man who a decade earlier had banned Windows and chided Gates for a lack of knowledge of Chinese history and culture), promised to give the Chinese access to one of the "most zealously guarded industrial secrets in Corporate America: the Windows source code."[18] Admittedly, Microsoft had agreed to share the source code with several international governments in response to rising concerns about the security of Windows operating systems. But the risk that Microsoft was taking in China was especially high given the country's continued high levels of piracy.

Finally, just a few weeks before Hu Jintao's 2006 visit to Bill Gates's Redmond campus, Microsoft signed agreements with four Chinese computer manufacturers to preinstall Windows, with the idea that installation before the sale of the PC made it less vulnerable to piracy. Lenovo, China's leading PC firm, said it would spend $1.2 billion over the next year on Windows.[19]

Thus the Chinese president's declaration in 2006 that Bill Gates is China's friend reflects a complete transformation of Microsoft's code of conduct in China. In slightly more than a decade Microsoft had gone from arrogance and certainty to cooperation and caution. Its lecturing, hectoring, and litigating were replaced by copious donations, grants, and technology transfer agreements—all ways for China to demand and get its due. By adopting a softer strategy, sharing its source code, and building a laboratory to leverage China's talent, Microsoft made substantive moves intended to help China build its information technology industry, not to suppress it. These acts gave credence to Microsoft's assertion that it had undergone a genuine change in its outlook to China.

With piracy rates stuck around 90 percent after a decade of extraordinary effort, some questioned whether China was worth Microsoft's time. In *Newsweek*, Microsoft executive Kevin Johnson explained the virtue of patience by recalling "a Chinese fable in which an old woman makes a needle from an iron rod by rolling it back and forth on a rock, even though her neighbors tell her she is crazy." Patience had paid off in South Korea and Taiwan. Both those markets became profitable for Microsoft when indigenous industry took off and piracy declined. In China, with the second-largest PC market in the world but a penetration rate still under 5 percent, substantially higher profits were possible. Microsoft was investing $1 billion a year—over and above the $750 million it committed in 2002—and presumably this large sum was manageable to a company whose global net income was $15 billion (on global sales of $40 billion) in 2005.[20]

Hu Jintao's hand of friendship did not mean that the Chinese were backing away from supporting their domestic industry. In 2005 new rules cementing the mandate that governments favor local vendors were under way.[21] U.S. companies lobbied against these regulations on the grounds that they violated the conditions of China's membership in the World Trade Organization (WTO). However, government procurement was not within the scope of China's WTO protocol, and China had not signed the WTO's Agreement on Government Procurement.[22] The government also began investing heavily in technology programs, including one that provided $1.3 billion to fund domestic high-tech research in 2004.

Microsoft has said it can foresee waiting up to another fifteen to twenty-five years to earn a profit in China.[23] In the interim by investing in China and helping the CCP's agenda of building the indigenous technology industry, it is hoping that the Chinese government will cheer for Microsoft from the Beijing Olympic Pavilion.

From *Mandis* to Metro: A Bumpy Road to India's Agricultural Markets

In the summer of 2005, as I trudged through a government-run food auction yard, or *mandi*, in Bangalore, I surveyed a disastrous scene. Piles of fresh produce lay everywhere, rotting on the edges. Mangy dogs roamed freely in the large yard, and mice scampered toward cavernous back rooms where grain was stored. Everywhere deals were being made with plenty of hustling and shouting. Huddles of impecunious farmers, *kisaan*, wearing traditional *dhotis*, waited for a government agent to buy their produce. The agent, dressed in a printed short-sleeved shirt and Western trousers, a pen tucked behind his ear, held an official-looking pad and called out the terms of deals. The farmers, weary and thin, looked resigned. Their day had begun in the predawn hours, or even the previous night, patiently tolerating various modes of transportation to reach the auction yard—a combination of ramshackle public buses, bullock carts, trucks, and even tractors chugging away on narrow so-called highways. Once they sold their produce they typically found a shady corner to sleep in for a few hours before retracing their steps homeward. Every day away from their farms represented lost income.

The rotten mess of India's *mandis* is the result of well-intentioned but misguided and badly implemented government policies. Pity the *kisaan*, the farmer. His reform began in the 1950s and 1960s, when the government tried to curtail the rights of wealthy landowners who had long exploited poor tenant farmers. Land ceiling acts eliminated large holdings, and tenant farmers were then given the right to own land. Cooperative credit institutions were created to minimize the exploitation of farmers by private moneylenders. Large-scale irrigation projects were undertaken.[24]

Despite these reforms, it soon became clear that agricultural production would not be increased by land redistribution or by bringing more land under cultivation. The productivity of agriculture had to be improved to keep pace with the population. In the mid-1960s India teetered on the precipice of famine. The country responded by importing high-yield varieties of wheat and rice and providing fertilizer and water subsidies to encourage new seed adoption. The Green Revolution was under way. Wheat and rice production increased by thirty million tons in just six years after 1965, a 168 percentage higher increase than in the preceding fifteen years.

Unfortunately the Green Revolution also prompted some less productive interventions. To encourage new seed adoption the government tried to ensure stability by mandating minimum support prices. Further, the famine-induced goal of food self-sufficiency prompted the creation of buffer stocks. Later the state used those stocks to interfere in agricultural markets; a massive public distribution system was created to provide subsidized food and grains.

All states enacted versions of the Agricultural Produce Market Committee (APMC) act mandating all agricultural products to be sold only in markets regulated and run by the government.[25] Every state was divided into market areas under the jurisdiction of marketing committees established by the local governments. Private entrepreneurs were barred from wholesaling. Thus were created the *mandis*, or wholesale trading markets. Permanent ones operated at the *taluk* (district) level, and temporary ones were set up at the village level. An open-auction system was meant to operate, with farmers having the right to reject or accept bids for their produce. Commission agents, *arthiyas*, were supposed to assist the farmers and buyers. But the *kisaan* had traveled many miles. He had to repay the local moneylenders, and had no option but to take what was given. The *arthiyas* mercilessly exploited the situation. Over time the *mandi* functionaries came to replace the exploiting landowners that they had been legislatively set up to replace, and the *mandis* became local monopolies.

Into this regulatory morass that engulfed the pitiful *kisaan* stepped Professor Greipl, a distinguished, lanky academic from Germany. Professor Greipl accompanied me through the slush and rot of the *mandis* that day in 2005, impeccably dressed in a completely out-of-place charcoal gray suit. He had traveled from Düsseldorf to Bangalore and was disgusted by the waste that surrounded us in the *mandi*. There were nine thousand trucks stuck in the yard, literally jammed against each other, the same trucks on which the produce had arrived.

We noticed a row of freshly constructed stalls, each intended to hold a particular trader in one section of the *mandi*. These clean stalls looked incongruous compared with the dingy surroundings. They were empty. Apparently the property rights were in dispute. A case was pending in court against those to whom these stalls had been allocated, by others who thought that the allocation process was suspect. Thus, the one fresh part of the *mandi* remained unused.

Professor Greipl had come to India from Düsseldorf to eliminate the waste and corruption of the *mandis*. He would replace rot with freshness and corrupt deals with regular pricing, and most importantly he would help to open many new, clean stores. Professor Greipl, a reputed expert in wholesaling, is a member of the supervisory board of Metro Cash & Carry's parent company. The cash-and-carry form of wholesaling requires businesses and retailers to pick up the goods and transport them directly to their own premises after paying cash for them. Metro's brand of cash and carry catered almost exclusively to business professionals, in contrast to the American wholesalers Costco or Sam's Club whose customers were primarily individuals.[26] Metro Cash & Carry was one of its parent corporation's fastest-growing and most profitable divisions and had already propelled global acceptance of the wholesaling format in emerging markets across Eastern Europe and Southeast Asia.

In Bangalore, Metro competed with existing distributors, creating the infrastructure needed to allow a direct route from rural farmers to urban hypermarkets, where small businesses could procure what they needed. The *mandis* were cut off. Metro calculated that by getting rid of redundant distribution layers, it could reduce wastage and cut, for example, tomato prices easily and immediately by 20 percent and cauliflower prices by 10 percent.[27] Naturally, existing wholesalers, formal and informal, did not like lower prices.

The long-term benefits of the cash-and-carry system were an order of magnitude higher. Because sales were only to registered businesses, fewer transactions were hidden in the informal economy. The transparency allowed the government to collect more tax revenues. Naturally, existing buyers and sellers who had been avoiding sales taxes did not like the idea of having their revenues become more transparent.

Metro introduced standardization. It guaranteed that a fish of a particular type was indeed caught fresh as advertised and weighed exactly what the label claimed it did, no longer allowing wholesalers to surreptitiously sneak in stale or undersized fish in an attempt to make a buck. Naturally, the fish wholesalers did not value this new transparency.

Metro built state-of-the art cold-storage bays which refrigerated trucks with perishable meats and fruits backed into, thereby dramatically expanding the available repertoire of food available in the markets. But these modern, efficient bays lay idle in the Bangalore stores, waiting for economic logic to triumph. Naturally, existing wholesalers did not like the idea of customers getting more at the Metro outlet. Metro's methods also induced others to invest near its wholesale hypermarkets, where numerous entrepreneurs set up their own transport businesses to help the cash-and-carry customers cart away their goods.

Metro's customers, however, loved the improved quality and availability of goods in the stores. The Bangalore stores were Metro's trademark format—large blue boxes with bright yellow lettering; spacious parking lots; and wide, well-lit aisles. It was a stunning contrast to the grime of the *mandi* and the dilapidation of typical Bangalore retail establishments. I remembered Russell Market, which I had frequented in my teens, and went to visit my old haunt with Erik Schmit, a veteran of Metro Cash & Carry in the Czech Republic, Slovakia, and Russia. After twenty years Russell Market was the same dilapidated brick structure I remembered, housing rows of produce and livestock vendors, butchers, and fishmongers. Schmit tried to compare the price of a particular kind of fish with that in the Metro store, but it was difficult to do the comparison. In Russell Market customers are never quite sure what they are buying.

Also happy with Metro's methods were mom-and-pop stores—called *kirana* stores. They could conveniently acquire many of their goods from Metro rather than patronizing a medley of specialized wholesalers. Their on-premise storage requirements were reduced, which in turn facilitated a wider inventory in their typically small stores and tied up much less of their working capital. One small manufacturer of pickles raised his daily sales from 100 to 400 kilograms by accessing hotels, caterers, and restaurants that previously had proved elusive.

Some months before meeting with Professor Greipl and Schmit in Bangalore, I received a call from Harsh Bahadur, then the head of Metro Cash & Carry in India. Harsh is a heavily bespectacled, earnest man, with a great deal of experience in the retail sector in India. He wanted to discuss his concern about the protests outside Metro's Bangalore stores. Ostensibly the protesters objected to a foreign entity selling beef in a Hindu-majority country. Although it is true that Hinduism proscribes the consumption of beef, there is substantial beef consumption in India. It turns out that some so-called lower-caste Hindus do not respect the beef proscription, and the country has plenty of people of other faiths—Christians, Muslims, Jews, and Zorastrians, among others—who consume beef. The protests appeared to be merely a ploy to generate outrage against Metro's alleged insensitivities.

In addition to the beef protests, other complaints contributed to the media's anti-Metro drumbeat. The Swadeshi Jagran Manch (National Awareness Forum), an affiliate of the ruling political party (Bharatiya Janata Party), accused Metro of behaving like a monopolist and charging exorbitant prices. They also charged that Metro, by selling directly to retail customers, was violating its license to operate in India as a wholesaler only; Metro was only permitted to sell to registered businesses.[28] Another organization, the Bangalore Traders' Action Committee, ominously raised the specter of colonialism: "Retail trade is the bread and butter of India . . . They are undercutting us and will wipe us out. This is nothing but another version of the East India Company that has entered our country now."[29] The Confederation of Indian Industry (CII), an influential consortium of Indian businesses, urged the central government to clarify the terms of Metro's license. Sanjiv Goenka, then the president of the CII, and chairman of the large Indian RPG Group of companies, told the press, "While the company is not selling to retailers like us, it is approaching various companies and selling its products to their employees at cheaper prices in violation of foreign direct investment norms."[30]

The central government and the government of the state of Karnataka (where Bangalore is located) buckled under the sustained barrage from local industry. They admonished Metro for not doing enough to prevent sales to retail customers. In India the administration of taxes is a state matter, so the central government is restricted to issuing guidelines and recommendations.[31] The barrage continued, with new allegations suggesting that Metro was retailing liquor, in further violation of its license. Harsh Bahadur, Metro's man in Bangalore, vowed to fight.[32]

The seeds of this fight, in hindsight, were obvious. Retail trade employed 8 percent of India's population, the largest employer after agriculture. In India's democracy this amounted to many votes. The country had the highest retail outlet density per capita in the world, with more than 12 million small retailers in India, 96 percent of which were small mom-and-pop stores, each occupying less than 500 square feet. The opening of the retail sector to foreign investment had already proven highly charged. As early as 1993 some foreign retailers had been issued licenses to invest in India. But the next government revoked the licenses in 1996. Subsequent attempts to reverse this reversal followed, and Metro Cash & Carry, along with Shoprite Checkers of South Africa, was permitted to operate wholesale cash-and-carry stores. But protest dies hard, and it was exacerbated by Metro's coming to India in the middle of the main shopping season of the year, the Hindu New Year festival of Diwali, the equivalent of Christmas in the West.

To Professor Greipl, connoisseur of the cash-and-carry format, these objections sounded all too familiar. He quickly pulled out a series of analyses and charts accumulated over the years in his Düsseldorf office. He had encountered similar objections in Germany decades ago, when retailers' complaints that Metro Cash & Carry would drive them out of business had proven unfounded.

The retail sales brouhaha in India was merely a protectionist ploy on the part of homegrown retailers whose antics perpetuated India's horribly inefficient distribution system. Organized distribution—including hypermarkets and cash-and-carry wholesalers—accounted for a mere 2 percent of overall distribution compared with 75 percent in a developed market. Fragmented channels, mostly in the informal economy, proliferated in India. The protest against Metro was thus enormously costly to the country, especially because the resulting inefficiency had cascading effects.[33] Poor infrastructure meant that farmers could not get their produce to market easily, resulting in enormous waste and ultimately limiting any incentive for farmers to invest in better agricultural methods.

In India, where 70 percent of the population lives off the land in remote villages, each with an average population of about fifteen hundred people, the effect was amplified. Rural India has been crippled by policy makers' comprehensive neglect since the country became independent. Among rural households 89 percent do not have telephones and 52 percent do not have domestic power connections. The average brownout in India is three hours per day or seventeen hours daily during the monsoon. Twenty percent of rural habitations have partial or no access to safe drinking water. The average village is more than a mile away from an all-weather road. People living away from the main village do not have access to any such roads.

Symptoms of this government underinvestment are everywhere. India exports food and grains, yet large sections of Indian society still have the lowest per capita caloric consumption in the world. India wastes more grain than Australia produces and more fruits and vegetables than the United Kingdom consumes. As Professor Greipl told me, "[I]f the largest producer of fruit in the world couldn't provide more than two or three types of packaged fruit juice, you know something is seriously wrong. Fruit rots on the roadside, right next to hungry children." In Bangalore, 25 percent of the entire fresh tomato stock perishes somewhere between the farm and the retailer.[34]

To allay the concerns of the protesters, Metro had to agree to numerous restrictions that Professor Greipl considered unwarranted. The Bangalore stores, for example, mandated minimum package sizes that were not required at Metro Cash & Carry stores in other countries. At the Bangalore stores only men could shop. The protesters concluded that because women typically shopped for the home, their presence in the store violated the "no retail" condition of Metro's license. Metro also had to cancel the memberships of some three thousand vendors that, as is common in India, operated on the fringes of the formal economy and could not convincingly document that they were registered businesses. Most significantly walking through the Metro store was a curious experience. I walked through aisles stocked to the brim with hard goods ranging from the best-selling staple of any Indian house or shop, the jhadoo—a broom made of thin slivers of shaved wood used to sweep the floor—to a variety of items unimaginable to the Indian consumer, only to reach the threadbare shelves of the grains and produce section. The APMC Act of 2003 prohibited Metro from competing in the sale of these goods. That corresponded to the unavailability of more than one-third of the average Indian shopping basket.[35] Of course none of this added to the customer experience.

Among the critics of the APMC Act was Finance Minister P. Chidambaram, who in April 2005 called for stepped-up foreign direct investment in agriculture. Addressing the Agriculture Summit in New Delhi the finance minister stated, "Contract farming must be given a thrust, *mandis* must be privatized, APMC Act must be amended. Retail must be opened up especially for food products and FDI allowed."[36]

Yet Metro did not rejoice at Chidambaram's speech. According to the Indian Constitution, agriculture is on the "state list"— that is, the state governments have considerable jurisdiction over it—in contrast to the "central list" of items controlled by the central government and "concurrent list" items over which control is shared. Metro knew all too well that a broad and swift opening up of agribusiness had little political support in India. Too many constituents were involved: the politically well-organized and vibrant small and medium-size retail sector, which continued to stage dramatic protests; large Indian businesses vying for their share of the wholesale and retail markets, which continued to lobby for reform of agribusiness but opposed the entry of foreign direct investment; and finally the Indian press, which ensured that the protests reached the ears of policy makers. Metro had also learned that big speeches and promises made by central government ministers held little significance at the state level. The battle over the APMC Act would have to be fought at the level of each state.

As early as 2003 Metro had begun talks with officials with the state of Karnataka to amend its APMC Act and allow Metro to sell fresh produce in its wholesale markets. Karnataka seemed a plausible candidate for reform because it had been among the first states to grant the National Dairy Development Board, a successful producer-focused national milk cooperative, an exemption from the APMC Act, allowing it to establish its state-of-the-art complex for marketing fruits, vegetables, and flowers in the state. By 2006, however, Metro's talks with Karnataka officials had made scant progress. The Federation of the Karnataka Chambers of Commerce and Industry proclaimed that the *mandis* worked just fine.[37]

Metro continues to do the good work for which it has become respected. In conjunction with a German development funding agency with which Metro had worked in Vietnam and elsewhere, they initiated training programs in four sheep development centers and facilities to promote hygienic handling of fish in several locations in Karnataka. From past experience Metro knows these investments not only help the local population, and thereby build support for Metro's presence, but also pay for themselves by making higher-quality items available to consumers.

Metro wisely decided to temporarily cease trying to unravel the knotty political economy in Bangalore and go elsewhere in India. The company now has aggressive plans to open stores in half a dozen other cities, with one in Hyderabad already up and running. Even the Bangalore store is profitable, despite its shelves being only half full because of the APMC Act regulations. Surely Metro's success in Bangalore is further proof of how much inefficiency still remains in the Indian agricultural system; time will allow its success to grow in Bangalore as well as in other parts of the country.

(Mis)Information about Foreign Direct Investment

"China's cup overflows, India catches the spillage." This fairly typical headline from *The Economist* in March 2005 captures the popular sentiment regarding China's and India's attempts to attract foreign direct investment. China's $55 billion foreign direct investment trumped India's $5 billion, hands down. But what do these numbers really mean?

In China success did not come overnight. It resulted from a series of systematic and organized experiments. FDI was first tested in four Special Economic Zones in Guangdong and Fujian provinces, where the Chinese created conditions that would be conducive to investment. In the first five years after the establishment of the zones, inflows averaged only $360 million annually. In the second phase of the experiment the Chinese opened fourteen more cities across ten provinces to FDI. From 1984 to 1988 FDI inflows averaged just over $2 billion annually. This apple cart was upset when FDI slowed in response to what the Chinese officially call a "political incident" in 1989 and much of rest of the world refers to as the "crackdown" at Tiananmen Square.[38] It took Deng Xiaoping's 1992 "southern tour" (*nanxun*) to once again reinvigorate FDI.[39] Deng's speeches throughout the tour focused on recommitting China to economic reform and railing against opponents. FDI inflows surged the next year from $4 billion to $11 billion. Ups and downs followed, although FDI reached a peak of $44 billion in 1997 before slowing again. In 2001 China concluded its decade-long negotiations to enter the World Trade Organization (WTO). By 2005 FDI was back at record levels.

On the other hand independent India did not welcome foreign investment, suspicious as it was of the outside world. While Deng was opening China to the world, India had just finished booting out Coca-Cola and IBM. Coca-Cola left when it was ordered by the incoming government in 1977 to reduce its equity stake to 40 percent and to transfer intellectual property— namely, the formula for the Coca-Cola concentrate—to its Indian partners. Despite dramatic declines in new equity investments, some multinationals stayed in India. For example, British-owned Imperial Computers Limited (ICL) overcame its initial reluctance and combined its two companies in a transaction that allowed it to dilute its share to the required 40 percent.[40] Firms that stayed did so because between 1960 and 1981 they reported profits that were higher than those attained by minority foreign-owned joint ventures and Indian private enterprise.[41]

A year before Deng's Southern Tour, Finance Minister Manmohan Singh opened the country to FDI in response to numerous payment crises. The International Monetary Fund was brought in, and India's paltry $100 million FDI, a symptom of the economic malaise, came under the international spotlight. But even after reforms were instituted, investors generally took a wait-and-watch approach to India.

Unlike China, India did not experiment and did not try to learn from its own errors or from China. In China Deng established an overarching framework and then gave local governments strong incentives to pursue FDI. Local party officials were rewarded for attracting foreign investment. In India the central government made a half-hearted acknowledgment of the need for FDI but gave locals no incentives to help attract foreign investors. India struggled to rid foreign investors of the perception that its democratic checks and balances were liabilities; these were the same foreign investors who were accustomed to China's red carpet treatment.

The numbers from China and India are not entirely comparable, however. Guy Pfeffermann of the International Finance Corporation has opined that India understates its FDI inflows because of unusual accounting methods.[42] For example, India excludes from FDI all "reinvested earnings"—that is, money that entities already operating in the country have earned by reinvesting in their Indian operations. India also excludes any money that companies raise in stock markets outside India but earmark for investment in India.[43] The government's accounting processes are very conservative, because these cumulative reinvestments in the country can add up. One scholar suggests that hundreds of millions of dollars from companies such as Citibank, Coke, and Pepsi were poured into India but not counted as FDI.[44]

On the other hand China is generally acknowledged to be inflating its numbers by what has come to be known as "round tripping." Domestic investment leaves China and then reenters in the guise of foreign money, because foreign private investors are treated more favorably than domestic private investors. Think of an entrepreneur in Guangdong sponsoring a relative in Hong Kong to invest on his behalf in a factory in Guangdong so that he can be welcomed as a Hong Kong investor. Pfeffermann alleges that FDI inflows into China during 1999 and 2000 would have been cut in half—from $40 billion to $20 billion annually—if round tripping were excluded. In the same two years an appropriate accounting of India's FDI would have reported inflows closer to $8 billion annually rather than $3 billion. Others suggest that further adjustments on a per capita basis would narrow the differences between China's and India's annual FDI even more.

Interestingly India, the laggard of the FDI world, is quick to seize on such a calculation and opines that it has nothing to worry about. The Indian media ceases to emphasize that, even if such adjustments were fully accepted, a gap of $12 billion between the two FDIs is still massive.[45]

Another question is what do the FDI numbers mean? Clearly they indicate that multinationals find investing in China attractive. But my co-author Yasheng Huang has argued that China's FDI is as much an indication of the country's weak microeconomy as of any underlying strength. He argues that China is forced to rely on FDI because it does not have the means to effectively channel domestic savings into productive investments. The state-owned and state-directed banks are largely defunct and used primarily to prop up state-owned enterprises that to a large extent continue to burn money. Thus the nature of the foreign investors and their investments are anomalous compared with FDI in most other developing countries. For example, much investment in the 1990s was from small and medium-size enterprises from Hong Kong, Macao, and Taiwan, not from distant countries or typically larger Western multinationals. Their money was often used in industries not normally the beneficiaries of FDI largesse, like ivory and jade carving and sculpting. Additionally, much of the money coming into China is not being used to finance productive investment in ways that most countries use FDI; rather it is being used to repurchase assets previously owned by state-owned enterprises.[46]

It is worth recalling that India, unlike China, has a viable stock market that is more welcoming of foreign investment and provides numerous asset categories in which foreigners can choose to invest part of their portfolios. For example, the foreigner might opt to buy stock in a factory-owning company listed on an Indian exchange, but might be forced to use FDI to open a factory in China. Thus a comparison of FDI numbers would disadvantage India inappropriately precisely because India has the better financial infrastructure.

The question posed at the opening of this chapter—'Can I *really* make money in China and India?"—is harder to answer than it might seem. Opinions and analyses vary greatly. In 1998, for example, a report issued by China's Ministry of Foreign Trade and Cooperation announced that most FDI in China made "considerable profits."[47] Yet in 1999, the year in which China experienced its first major dip in FDI, an article in *The Economist* titled "Infatuation's End" eulogized the demise of good intent. "[O]ne way or another most came, many with stars in their eyes . . . They still come, but China's numerology has lost its power to enthrall. Too many companies have lost millions, and wasted years of management time dealing with Chinese bureaucracy and the Chinese partners that had been imposed on them. What had seemed to many investors like a market of infinite possibility now looks instead more like a black hole of infinite dimensions."[48] Tim Clissold, in his *schadenfreude*-eliciting autobiography, *Mr. China*, describes how he ran through half a billion dollars of investment with nary a return in the early 1990s. Infatuation with China's possibilities came face-to-face with a business environment that was confusing to Westerners.

Truth lies somewhere between glory and disaster. In 2001 the *China Economic Quarterly* pointed out that the direct and indirect profits of American companies in China were just shy of $3 billion and that this was less than U.S. companies earned in Mexico, a country with less than a tenth of the population.[49] More recent assessments point to measured optimism. A 2004 white paper by the American Chamber of Commerce in China estimated that three-quarters of U.S. companies in China were profitable. Further, the companies that had been in China the longest were the most profitable.[50] Perhaps this is not surprising. It is hard to imagine that long-term investors would stick around if they were continually bleeding. But the information is useful, nonetheless, because it invalidates the notion that investing in China is a quick dip into a full money bag.

The most recent numbers for profitability of FDI in India are quitesimilar to China's. Assessments provided by the American Chamber of Commerce in India and by local organizations representing private enterprise indicate that roughly three-quarters of foreign investors are making money, a few more are breaking even, and only 15 percent are experiencing losses.[51]

Creating My Own Statistics

In 2003 and 2004 I took a firsthand look at thirty Asian multinational subsidiaries operating in China and India.[52] I had several reasons for undertaking this exercise. At that time most studies focused either on individual companies—such as my own descriptions of Microsoft and Metro—or on "large sample" analyses of the few publicly available statistics on individual companies. In the latter the researcher typically subjected the data to a regression analysis to identify which of a medley of factors appeared most related to the metric being studied (profitability, sales growth, or employee turnover, for example). No study zeroed in on multinationals to understand how they were implementing their businesses in China and India, what challenges their people had encountered, and what their perceptions were about their experiences. My fieldwork sought to fill that hole in the research.

I decided to focus on large corporations from Asia, rather than U.S. or European companies, because the Asians are less scrutinized. With the help of Harvard Business School's research centers in Hong Kong and Tokyo, I persuaded a range of companies to participate.[53] In fact, none of the approached companies declined my request. We had companies like Asahi Glass, Hitachi, Honda, Mitsui, and Toshiba from Japan; Samsung, Hyundai, and LG from Korea; Singapore Telecom and DBS Bank from Singapore; and Grace Semiconductor from Taiwan. Many of the companies in my study had operations in both China and India; others focused on one country—usually, though not always, China. As part of the conditions under which several of these companies kindly shared internal information, I committed not to reveal any individual company's data but to form insights based on the aggregate data.

Over several months I subjected experts at each company to a barrage of questions on a range of topics: the history of the operation and key milestones, a description of current and past organization structure, performance aspirations and reality, aspects of the competitive battles in which they found themselves immersed, their thinking regarding their multinational peers as well as local competitors, the effect they thought their presence was having on the business environment, and finally—asked in ways direct and indirect—their relationship with the local and central governments and bureaucracies.

My most stunning finding was the extent to which these established companies needed to adapt their business models to function effectively in a foreign locale. Companies needed to make one set of adaptations for operating in China, one set for operating in India, and one set for operating between each foreign destination and the home country. It was not always clear which set of adaptations was most crucial. The companies were often faced with a common conundrum: how to decide which parts of their business models were sacrosanct and which were subject to change.

As an illustration, consider Dell Corporation's operations in China.[54] (I'm obliged to use an example outside my Asian sample to protect their confidentiality.) At home in the United States Dell ships its computers directly to buyers, thereby avoiding having to build machines to stock; additionally, the company receives many of its orders over the Web, thereby saving both the carrying costs and the obsolescence costs associated with having to update machines. In China, however, Dell could not operate with the same efficiency and economy. The Chinese were unaccustomed to ordering on the Web, not primarily because the technical infrastructure was inadequate but because of the high cost of purchasing a computer. Thus conducting business in China was a paper-based activity. The resulting inefficiencies in logistical infrastructure meant that allowing Chinese consumers unlimited ordering flexibility would require either compromising on the zero-inventory policy or on the speed of delivery. Dell could not have it all, all the time, at least in the medium term. Accordingly, Dell's orders came much less through the Web, only a small handful of preconfigured machines were available to choose from, and Dell relied on distributors rather than going directly to the consumer for much of its sales.

Among the companies in my Asian sample, such adaptation was commonplace and extensive. Indigenous suppliers were used more frequently in India than in China because of the larger number of local companies in India. With an average of thirty-nine years in business, subsidiaries in India had more time to develop local supplier bases than did Chinese subsidiaries with eighteen years in business on average. Many companies left China following the communist takeover, much more than had left India in response to the overt hostility that began in the 1970s. But even for one of the Southeast Asian corporations that entered both China and India in the last five years, reliance on local suppliers—in a setting where there was no government mandate to use them—was 60 percent in India and 10 percent in China.

More interaction with indigenous companies led to a greater effect on the overall economic environment from multinationals in India. For example, compared with Chinese counterparts, management practices diffused more readily among Indian companies, and the multinational-derived impetus to tighten financial controls was more apparent. Multinational subsidiaries in India tended to use local management far more easily than those in China, reflecting the greater availability of local management familiar with global norms. Multinationals in China relied heavily on expatriates and could draw on a large community of expatriate managers, many of whom had acquired the iconic status of de facto locals after having cycled from one multinational to another. It was harder to see this phenomenon in India.

An important aspect of adaptation to the environment concerned transparency. About half of the subsidiaries in India appeared to disclose meaningful financial and market share information to the public, one-quarter disclosed to key stakeholders but not to the public, and the remainder had scant disclosure. These numbers were significantly lower in China, where less than one-quarter had meaningful local disclosure. As discussed in my earlier chapter on financial markets, subsidiaries in India operate in an environment where much more transparency and more disclosure is expected by local customers and markets than is the case in China.

All these observations are consistent with the indigenous private sector's relatively larger presence in India than in China. But it is important to compare the deeper roots that multinationals have in India with the greater aggregate presence of multinationals in China. Several years ago a senior executive at Motorola recounted to me the story of the company's great success in China and of India's irrelevance to its operations. Motorola was a Western pioneer in China. When its chairman, Christopher B. Galvin, first met with Jiang Zemin in Shanghai in 1986, Jiang was a little-known local Party leader, far from the presidential perch he held between 1993 and 2005.[55] Buildup of its groundbreaking manufacturing plant in Tianjin began in July 1992, and until 2003 the company invested $3.4 billion in manufacturing and research and development facilities, more than any other Western company. Motorola thus endeared itself to the senior echelons of the CCP,[56] and as the China operations became more important, a hotline of sorts was established between Beijing and the company's headquarters in Schaumburg, Illinois. Meanwhile the miniscule Motorola operations in India had to first report to Singapore and then navigate a long bureaucratic trail before reaching Schaumburg. It is easy to see why the company's familiarity with India developed more slowly and ultimately was far less than its familiarity with China, where the company was assured direct support from CCP elites. Investing in building up operations was always progressively easier in China than in India.

A similar story in the reverse direction is true for Unilever. Its deep roots in India have resulted in a pipeline of senior management talent from Bombay to London and Rotterdam. Unilever is the first Western multinational to have an Indian manager from the Indian subsidiary appointed to the global corporation's board of directors. Unilever had great trouble gaining traction in China, while its global rival, Procter & Gamble, had success in China earlier than in India.

The Asian companies I studied reported similar organizational realities. Their Chinese and Indian subsidiaries developed independently of each other, relatively idiosyncratically, and typically reported to different people up the organizational hierarchy. The Chinese and Indian operations rarely learned from one another. I view this as a failing of the organization structure. In my concluding chapter I argue that the American firm General Electric is one of the few multinationals that has understood the value of getting its Chinese and Indian operations tightly aligned, with each other and with the rest of the global corporation.

On the surface the subsidiaries I studied seemed to do better in India than in China, though not by an enormous margin. This was true of both objective accounting measures of performance and self-reported expectations of future performance. But as any good social scientist would point out, my sample was not random—the kind you need to have good statistical inference. Rather I chose to focus on large companies because they were more likely to have histories in China and India.[57] Further, the potential drivers of performance are numerous. A closer look showed that, after accounting for other influences on performance—including longevity of operations in the country, extent to which local suppliers were used, extent of disclosure, and extent of local management talent—the performances of subsidiaries in China and India were the same. That is, although the subsidiaries in India did slightly better overall, the difference can be explained by easily measured factors.

How does this finding reconcile with the FDI euphoria that is far greater in China than in India? Is it that the Chinese provide a more attractive package to potential investors than do the Indians? Perhaps, but the Chinese also siphon off, through clever negotiations and hardball much of the value of that package. In other words a multinational in China creates a lot of value—either by providing goods and services Chinese consumers wish to buy or by making things more cheaply for the multinational's customers outside China—but in return China demands a heavy price from the multinational for the privilege of letting it do so.

This payment might take many forms and is unlikely to be direct—if anything, the Chinese provincial governments often go out of their way to offer numerous concessions to attract potential customers. Technology transfer demands are a form of payment, as General Electric discovered when it attempted to stay ahead of Chinese demands for technology for its advanced turbines. Looking the other way when local companies imitate the intellectual property of multinationals is another form of payment. These payments allow the technology to diffuse to Chinese firms, where it spurs competition for the multinational, which ultimately cuts into the multinational's profit margins. Of course the widespread availability of technology to many Chinese firms may cause dramatic price falls, and consumers, including those in the West, become the primary beneficiaries.[58]

Surely savvy multinationals foresee this intense bargaining by the Chinese and stay away as a result. But hope appears to spring eternal, and perception plays a big role in encouraging foreign investment. Even managers of the Asian companies I visited were sure that their Indian operations outperformed their Chinese operations but were convinced that the Chinese operations mattered more to headquarters. Because much of the hype about doing business in China is not grounded in facts and figures, many senior executive meetings will continue to start with the well-meaning but uninformed assertion, "We simply *must* be in China."

Insiders and Outsiders: Vested Interests and Investors

The yawning gap between China's and India's FDI figures has sparked an industry of people trying to ascertain why it exists. The favorite explanation centers on infrastructure. Undoubtedly the absence of roads, bridges, and electricity in India plays a role, but at best that is only a partial explanation. The lack of infrastructure might deter some investors, but it should attract others. After all, one of Metro's primary value propositions was to facilitate the provision of infrastructure—the cold-chain facilities needed to link village farmers to city businesses.

China's spanking new highways attract some foreign investors, but even a cursory glance at the statistics suggests that the surge of FDI into China predates the construction of hard infrastructure. The boom in railroad and highway construction did not begin until the mid-1990s, after many foreign companies had invested in China. In 1997, for example, China had three thousand miles of expressways, just 14 percent of the twenty-one thousand miles it had in 2004.[59]

Corruption levels might offer another explanation for the different levels of FDI in the two countries. One study found that a one-standard-deviation increase in corruption reduced inward FDI by 28 percent, and other researchers report that a rise in corruption from that prevailing in Singapore to that prevailing in Russia would reduce FDI by 65 percent.[60] But China and India have comparably high levels of bureaucratic corruption—as indicated by multilateral organizations in the business of estimating corruption levels—so this can't really account for the significant difference in FDI.[61]

Yet another commonly heard explanation centers on government red tape and foreign-ownership restrictions. Although these too are undoubtedly deterrents to FDI, again they are not the complete answer. In mobile telephony, for example, the government places no ownership barriers on foreigners operating mobile phone services in India, yet indigenous competitors hold the dominant market share. The biggest player is Bharti Telecom, which has single-handedly redefined telecommunications in India, backed by minority investments from the venture capital firm Warburg Pincus and investment from Singapore Telecom. Bharti Telecom claims today to be the lowest-cost operator in the world, bar none. Given that firm's dominance and the subsequent credible entry of two of India's leading business houses, Tata and Reliance, any foreign operator will have its work cut out for it.

The Bharti Telecom example suggests a factor not often considered: the presence of indigenous private-sector competition that can deter FDI. This deterrent is far less evident in China. To provide a range of services and exploit its cheap labor market, China relied primarily on FDI, not indigenous private enterprise. India's situation was the reverse. China's Great Leap Forward and Cultural Revolution virtually wiped out indigenous enterprise. India went through nothing analogous. Even before the emergence of world-class entrepreneurs like Bharti Telecom, India had indigenous private companies. Sheltered by a protectionist state, they had not cut their teeth in market battles and were not as high caliber as today's companies. Nonetheless India's private sector was always a force that foreign investors had to reckon with.

Through the 1950s in India, while individual industrialists eagerly collaborated with foreign technology firms, collectively they lobbied for restrictions on their collaborators.[62] The Federation of Indian Chambers of Commerce and Industry (FICCI) led this charge, insisting that effective control remain with Indians.[63] In 1953 the Swadeshi League—the term *swadeshi* means "self-reliance"—was formed by a consortium of Indian business leaders to fight the monopoly of Lever Brothers (Hindustan Lever in 1956) in the soap industry. The antiforeign rhetoric soon spread, and in its annual meeting FICCI adopted its Swadeshi Resolution. In the late 1960s and 1970s the official rhetoric against foreign investment stepped up. The Monopolies and Restrictive Trade Practices Act of 1969 and the Foreign Exchange Regulation Act of 1973 curtailed expansion plans of multinationals and restricted repatriation of profits, respectively.

Some of this knee-jerk protectionist mind-set persists. The charmingly named Press Note 18 is a case in point. It emerged in 1998, a full seven years after serious reforms had allegedly been initiated, and required a foreign company that already had a partnership in India to seek its partner's "no objection certificate" if the former wished to invest in a new independent venture in India. The foreign investor had to convince the Foreign Investment Promotion Board that the new proposal would not jeopardize the interests of the existing joint venture partner or other indigenous stakeholder. Several new investments were torpedoed by this rule. The KK Modi Group, for example, by dint of its separate joint ventures with Walt Disney and Phillip

Morris, blocked one proposal to set up the Disney Channel in India and another to invest in a major export-based tobacco leaf processing plant.[64]

Any attempt by the government to retire this rule in 2005 was resisted by the leftist parties, part of the ruling coalition, and by their supporting labor unions. In a nod to an age-old bogeyman, the resistance charged that the government was simply succumbing to pressure from multinationals.[65] Thus the government made provisions to dilute it. One Calcutta-based newspaper editorial summed up the ruling's latest incarnation: "[E]xisting and alive joint ventures will still confront Press Note 18, which should keep protectionist elements in the Federation of Indian Chambers of Commerce and Industry happy . . . But there is no denying the positive signal imparted. Effectively, the government has adopted a grandfathering option, retaining the Press Note for several existing joint ventures that are alive, but scrapping it for future ones. That seems to be a sensible way of handling the political economy of resistance in other reform areas as well."[66]

The saga surrounding Press Note 18 also confirms the slow pace of change in attitudes toward foreign capital. The compromise in 2005 was reached eight years after controversy erupted in 1997. In China, things can change drastically—recall the multinationals' exit in the early 1950s and blazing reentry in the early 1980s.

Whether dealing with efficient Bharti-like mobile phone companies or inefficient but protected indigenous competitors, multinationals in India continue to have to contend with the local interests, as did Metro. Sometimes deterring a foreign investment is not a problem for society—for instance, when an efficient local firm exists—but at other times, when protectionism merely serves the interest of the entrenched indigenous company, FDI deterrence becomes a problem.

Chapter Eight

Diaspora Dividends

Paragons and Pariahs from the Overseas
Chinese and Indians

On January 9, 1915, a serious young Indian lawyer arrived in Bombay on a ship from South Africa. He was given a hero's welcome. His *satyagraha* (Sanskrit for "truth and firmness") movement in South Africa had attracted several thousand followers and brought him fame in India. This nonresident Indian (NRI) had fought successfully for the civil rights of South Africa's Indian minority; among other concessions, the Union of South Africa had abolished specific taxes levied on Indians and recognized Indian marriages. Mohandas Karamchand Gandhi, the *Mahatma* (Great Soul), would go on to lead the fight for India's freedom and dominate the next thirty years of Indian politics by sheer moral suasion.

Eighty-seven years later, on January 9, 2002, India held its first annual *Pravasi Bharatiya Diwas* (Overseas Indians' Day). The symbolic date, honoring its most prominent NRI and accompanied by a public relations blitz intended to reach out to contemporary NRIs, was meant to usher in a long-overdue appreciation in India for its diaspora. Unlike China, which has benefited tremendously from its diaspora's wealth and talent, India has historically dismissed and ignored its own. Until recently, as hard as it was for an Indian within India to conduct business, purchase property, or even volunteer time or expertise to any cause, it was even harder for NRIs. Not until 2002, a decade after India launched its economic reforms, did the government create a Persons of Indian Origin policy, which extended benefits and concessions to ethnic Indians worldwide.[1] Although some of these overseas Indians have dutifully sent remittances home, transforming the lives of their immediate families, large-scale investment from this group has been wanting.

I participated in the second Pravasi Bharatiya Diwas and was privileged to share the stage in New Delhi's grand conference center, Vigyan Bhavan, with two stalwarts of modern India: Mukesh Ambani, head of one of India's premier business groups; and Lal Kishan Advani, deputy prime minister of India, strong man of the Bharatiya Janata Party (BJP), and the leader of the ruling coalition government in India at the time. I should mention that although I am an NRI, because I have returned to India three or four times a year, I remain more connected than most Indians living overseas and thus have not felt cut off, shunned, or dismissed.

Ambani spoke first, reminding the audience that his father's businesses began with a diasporic connection in the Red Sea port of Aden. Dhirubhai Ambani, whose life saga is India's most celebrated rags-to-riches story, worked as a gas station attendant in Mumbai before immigrating to Aden, where he started a small-time trading business in the busy Yemen port. Over the next few decades he built one of the world's leading petrochemical and refining groups, famed for its ability to handle large-scale construction projects with ruthless efficiency. Reliance Group was India's only entrant into the world's Fortune 500 list. Dhirubhai's other major contribution to Indian business was to court the retail financial investor. In 1977, desperate for capital, he bypassed India's sultans of high finance and successfully raised large sums from numerous small shareholders, becoming responsible for an important change in Indian capital markets. Last but not least, Dhirubhai had politicians at his beck and call.

Because of this legacy, when Mukesh Ambani called on corporate India to develop the rest of the country and lauded India's diaspora as potential agents of change, his words carried weight. Ambani reminded the audience that wealthy Indian diaspora had come of age in the West and had won worldwide acclaim for its entrepreneurial and academic successes since the 1990s. This welcomed development offers the possibility that India, like China, will benefit from its diaspora's wealth and talent. The potential is great. Today the diaspora's annual income is about $160 billion, a third of India's GDP, with a sizable proportion of the affluence originating in Silicon Valley, home to some three hundred thousand Indians.[2] Whether this potential will be realized depends on whether the Indian government will match recent rhetoric with tangible policy that reaches out to the Indian diaspora.

I spoke after Ambani, focusing on the need to specify a channel through which the diaspora could play a role in India. I argued that specific involvements would breed commitment and familiarity, rather than just rhetoric. Many successful diaspora members, particularly in the United States, are highly educated. Thirty-seven percent of India-born U.S. residents, for example, have master's or doctoral degrees, compared with 8 percent of U.S.-born residents and 18 percent of Israel-born U.S. residents, Israel being another bastion of high-tech prowess. Eighty percent of working-age India-born Americans have tertiary degrees compared with 54 percent of American citizens born in China. I argued that the world increasingly valued knowledge capital, and India's diaspora was synonymous with advanced know-how in software, biotechnology, and the like.

I suggested that diaspora Indians could help shape the world-renowned Indian Institutes of Technology (IITs) and Indian Institutes of Management (IIMs), where many had been educated. At that time, the government's human resource development minister had proposed subjecting the IITs to more government control and oversight, virtually eliminating the decentralized system that had spawned excellence in them. A higher percentage of the seats in the IITs were to be reserved for members of India's most disadvantaged populations, and faculty appointments were to be centralized. The IITs had vigorously protested the proposal. The excellence of the institutions was in no small part due to a grueling examination that selected the best talent and did so from a very level playing field. Reservations would compromise this, and centralized appointments were a recipe for political interference and therefore mediocrity. Government interference in higher education would be a move in the opposite direction from that taken by the country's private sector in the prior decade—dismantling centralization, expanding choice, and fostering competition. Unsurprisingly, a vituperative battle had played out in the media.

I echoed Prime Minister Vajpayee's exhortation that the diaspora could provide a wealth of ideas that would be followed by economic wealth. The surest way to motivate successful diaspora members to reconnect with their universities was to emulate U.S. institutions by assuring alumni their input into the community would be respected and their time well spent. From this assurance and confidence ideas and money would flow. I argued that the government's proposed interference in the IITs and IIMs would cut off the diaspora from constructive engagement with these universities.

Last to speak was the septuagenarian Advani, long a fixture on the Indian political scene. His was the speech of a maestro. He responded to Ambani and me by pronouncing that the time had come for a *jugalbandi*—"a duet" in Hindi—between Indians and their diaspora. This was during the time that Advani's party, the BJP, had articulated the "India Shining" campaign as their election slogan, and was prior to their surprise defeat in the polls a few scant months later. Apparently India had not quite shone for the rural residents who voted them out of office.

At the time of the second *Pravasi Diwas*, Advani was in his element, alleging that democratic norms stitched together Indians and the diaspora. The duet had to occur within democratic norms. Neither Advani nor his government nor the bureaucracy could forge a link. It was up to decentralized action to make it happen. Individual initiative would be the engine of connection.

Since that Pravasi Bharatiya Diwas, I have become more convinced that India could learn a lesson from China about diaspora management—economic incentives coupled with patriotic rhetoric—for the country's economic advantage. By consistently welcoming its diaspora, China has catapulted its economy forward, while India's ambivalence, even patronizing distaste, have held it back.

The difference is that over the last century, with the exception of Mao's time, the Chinese state has viewed the diaspora as part of the national fabric, a resource to be galvanized to aid the country's modernization and economic development. Since the ascent of Deng Xiaoping, successive Chinese leaders have smartly fashioned both policy and rhetoric to lure this group's wealth and investment.[3] Collectively referred to as *huaqiao huaren* (*huaqiao* means "citizens living overseas," and *huaren* refers to foreign nationals of Chinese origin and their descendants) this group has yielded China handsome dividends. No indicator evidences this unique Chinese situation as well as the percentage of the massive foreign direct investment pouring into China—as much as 80 percent in the early years of reform—coming from Chinese living overseas. This involvement is one of the most distinguishing characteristics of China's economic rise.[4] In 1997 the Canadian magazine *MacLean's* encapsulated this unique phenomenon: "[T]he world's 57 million overseas Chinese . . . rule the world's third most powerful economy."[5]

This diaspora-state relationship has been mutually beneficial. China has consistently offered special treatment to overseas Chinese. Thus have the wallets of the *hai gui* or sea turtles—so called humorously because the Chinese word for "return" rhymes with that for "turtle"—been lined, giving them a leg up in the greatest growth story of modern times.

From China to Chinatown: Diaspora Entrepreneurs

Who are the 57 million overseas Chinese? As early as the 1840s Chinese immigrants began to make their way to the West Coast of the United States. In 1848, with the discovery of gold in the California hills, immigration increased dramatically. While a few of them were independent merchants, most were rural peasants—indentured laborers—brought in by mining and railroad companies to work in the mines and build the railroads. By 1860 China had lost two wars to the British and other Western colonial powers; the Opium Wars radically changed China's political and economic landscape. From war-ravaged provinces, particularly Guangdong, huge numbers of emigrants left for the United States. In many parts of China, natural calamities like famine and floods added to the prevailing poverty and deprivation. Roughly 34,000 Chinese were in the United States in 1860.

By the end of that decade, as the Gold Rush abated and railroad construction neared completion, thousands of Chinese suddenly had to seek alternative employment. They soon branched out into service businesses like laundries and restaurants. Before long, however, a slowing American economy and accompanying unemployment gave rise to anti-Chinese sentiments on the West Coast. Slogans like "Yellow Peril" and "The Chinese Must Go" began circulating, and violence against ethnic Chinese individuals and businesses was rising. In response Chinese immigrants clustered in what came to be the Chinatowns, and also began to move to bigger cities, especially in the East. Thus were laid the nuclei of present-day Chinatowns in San Francisco and Los Angeles on the West Coast and in New York and Boston on the East Coast.[7]

Reasons to leave China remained strong. During the second half of the nineteenth century, when economic growth remained elusive and poverty and famine were never far away, emigration remained a coping strategy. However, the profile of the Chinese immigrant changed. Uneducated laborers were replaced by scholars and craftspeople who sought work and business opportunities in the West. By no means, however, was it a homogenous group. Based on generation of immigration, place of origin and socioeconomic and education levels, Chinese immigrants carved out various niches in most countries of Southeast Asia, North America, and Australia.

Boston's Chinatown is in the heart of the city, sandwiched between its financial and theater districts. Not long ago I walked through its *paifang*, the Chinese name for the traditional archway that marks the entrance to every Chinatown around the world. Each archway was donated to a particular city as a gift from the Republic of China, and local contributors financed their construction.[8] Just a few minutes' walk away from Boston's *paifang* is the office of the Fung Wah Bus Company, where I had an appointment with its entrepreneurial founder Liang Peilin. Liang's success is emblematic of the general success of the diaspora worldwide and the material wealth into which mainland China has successfully tapped. I was curious about the Fung Wah Bus Company because of its near-cult following; travelers on the Boston–New York City corridor claim the bus ride is comfortable, easy, and costs a fraction of the price of its American competitors.

I climbed a narrow dimly lit staircase to Mr. Liang's office for a 9 AM appointment. The empty ballroom-like hall contrasted sharply with the crowded Chinatown exterior. Traditional Chinese musical instruments adorned a wall. A middle-aged woman stared at two computer terminals, and without looking up, informed me: "Mr. Liang is at lunch."

With no further explanation forthcoming as to why Mr. Liang's dietary schedule included "lunch" at nine in the morning, I settled down to wait. Founded in 1997, Fung Wah—"magnificent wind" in Cantonese—today operates more than twenty buses with hourly service linking Boston and New York. The company originally provided transportation between Brooklyn and Chinatown for Chinese immigrants in New York, but gradually extended its line to Boston and became the dominant low-cost provider. At $20 per round trip, Fung Wah charges less than half what mainstream competitors like Greyhound and Peter Pan charge.

The boss arrived a half hour late. A short man with high cheekbones and relatively dark skin, he looked about forty. He told me he was Cantonese, from Zhuhai city in Guangdong province. As we talked I learned that he followed his parents to the United States in 1988 at the age of twenty-six. His parents, who were white-collar employees of state-owned enterprises in China and managed to get sponsored by some relatives in the United States, took jobs in clothing factories near Manhattan. Liang took two part-time driving jobs: van driver and noodle deliveryman. At that time the van company Liang worked for served Chinese immigrant workers living in Brooklyn. He explained, "For security, Chinese workers preferred to commute to work in vans run by Chinese rather than taking the dangerous public transport; and so this van business became more and more profitable, especially after 1992 or 1993, when more and more Chinese arrived in New York. Most of them were illegal immigrants from Fujian Province who arrived daily by boat."

After seven years Liang decided he had accumulated enough experience to set up his own company. He secured a license from the New York Taxi and Limousine Commission to operate a bus along 8th Avenue in Manhattan in 1995. One year later, his company, named Fung Wah Vans Incorporated, came into operation. Liang was both driver and boss.

Liang began to see an unmet need within the Chinese transportation market. Chinese parents living in New York regularly visited their children attending Boston's universities. He applied for a permit to transport passengers between the two cities and launched his new service in June 1998. At first no customers signed up, but just before Thanksgiving—typically the busiest travel day in the United States—word of Liang's service spread among Chinese students returning home for the holiday. Within months

Fung Wah had become an urban legend. In 2001, acting on advice from his young customer base, Liang introduced an online ticket-selling system that became hugely popular. "Fung Wah's passengers used to consist of 60 percent Chinese and 40 percent other ethnic people," Liang recalled, "while now 80 or 90 percent are non-Chinese customers. Sixty percent of all the tickets are sold online."

I found it interesting that Liang found a way to profit from the diaspora's needs. In a sense the diaspora is responsible for his success, a success that ultimately feeds back into the mainland. But Liang corrected me: "In my judgment success must translate into making money and in that sense I am not successful at all. When my competitors fail to attract customers, they just cut the ticket price, and I have to follow. I don't make anything." Fung Wah has three main competitors, all of which have been set up by Chinese immigrants from Canton—Liang's province. Although the *New York Times* reported Fung Wah could earn $340 for every round trip driven in 2004, the situation is now different. "The oil price has doubled," Liang explained. "You can see how much profit margin is left, maybe $240 or maybe $140 for a round trip if the bus is full."

This Cantonese domination does not extend to other businesses. Indeed, the diaspora dividend from Boston's Chinatown originates from many of the major communities— Hakka, Teochiu, Fujianese, and Shanghainese— originating from different parts of the mainland.[5] Many of their investments are channeled back to their home provinces.[10] These communities often do not assimilate with each other or with their host communities. Experiences across Southeast Asia also vary. The Chinese diaspora is well integrated in the Thai and Filipino economies.[11] In Malaysia and Indonesia the community is economically successful but politically and socially marginalized. Chinese immigrants in Burma were forced to move north across the border in the 1950s when the Burmese government issued them foreign registration cards barring them from seeking the same opportunities available to locals.[12]

Liang's story of assimilation is telling of most first-generation immigrants. None of his three children are interested in learning Chinese. "The teaching in the local Chinese schools is not suitable to kids. The content is too profound and boring for kids. If they teach how to write Chinese characters through textbooks like the *Analects of Confucius*, how could the kids generate interest in Chinese?" To compensate, Liang insists his children speak Chinese at home. He gives three reasons for his position. First, he believes that they should never forget that they are Chinese. Second, Liang believes that China will be a great power in the world within the next fifty years, and knowledge of at least colloquial Chinese will open doors for his children. He adds, "Things change so fast that no one knows what will happen next. When we were in school in China, we were devoted to the slogan, 'Down with U.S. imperialism.' I never imagined that I would run a business in the U.S."

As we talked that day I learned how Liang's family was largely shaped by the vicissitudes of twentieth-century immigration. His grandfather was part of the massive 1920 exodus from China, when it was wracked by the civil war between the communist and nationalist armies and the war against Japanese aggression. Some two to three million people left China, fleeing either political persecution or economic hardship. Liang's grandfather chose the Philippines. After a few years Liang's grandfather returned to Canton to marry a local girl and brought her back to the Philippines. When Mao imposed strict restrictions on emigration in 1949, Liang's grandfather feared persecution and never returned to China. Liang's father, who was in China, could not leave the country, and the family did not reunite until his grandfather's death.

Liang rationalized, "Perhaps it was because every family in Canton had some overseas relatives, the government could not discriminate; even officials themselves had overseas relatives." But having an overseas relative was costly in other ways: it could impact one's chances of going to college or joining the party. Liang was denied a chance to attend university in China because of his emmigrant great-uncle. After graduation from high school he began to learn Yue Opera—a traditional Chinese opera—from a private teacher.

In November 1985, however, the Emigration and Immigration Law was adopted, for the first time guaranteeing Chinese citizens the right to travel outside China for private reasons. "The overseas Chinese also gradually began to return to visit their family members at home," Liang said. "The fantasies, fresh goods, and money brought back by overseas Chinese sparked the locals' desire to go abroad. I knew I needed practical skills to work in America. Everyone in the U.S. drove, so I gave up opera and became a truck driver in China."

My final questions to Liang were about his current links with relatives in China. His answers reflected the success of the new China that Deng Xiaoping had built. He concluded, "There are great changes! I even could not find the way back to where I used to live. The previous rice field became highways. If China was like this when I left in 1988, I might have dismissed the idea of emmigration."

From Heathrow International Airport to Glassy Junction Pub: The Making of Mini-Indias

London's Heathrow Airport is the world's busiest. Serving as an important destination for ninety airlines traveling to 180 countries, covering three thousand acres, and employing tens of thousands of people, the airport is a veritable city in itself. On arriving in Heathrow, a traveler cannot help but notice the ubiquity of ethnic Indians. Third-, fourth-, and fifth-generation British Indians are visible everywhere as shop owners, cargo handlers, and janitors, as well as, ironically, immigration officers. Effortlessly slipping in and out of Punjabi, the language of India's northern state of Punjab, and the local Cockney, they discuss British football and gossip about the Royal family while translating for a first-time elderly Punjabi tourist to London. A Sikh friend of mine, born, bred, and living in Singapore, told me that the United Kingdom is the only country in the world—including his hometown of Singapore—where he feels at home, even though he has never lived there. He has Heathrow to thank for that sentiment.

Heathrow is just one community in which British Indians cluster and work. London's suburbs have become mini-Indias over the past few decades. Southall, the setting popularized by the global hit film, *Bend It Like Beckham*, is a quintessential example of a contemporary Indian community. The movie features Jess, a British Sikh teenager whose dreams of becoming an accomplished footballer put her in conflict with her traditional Indian immigrant parents. Among Jess's friends, Punjabi Sikhs mingle with Indians from Kenya and Uganda, but it's clear that in Southall the British Indian Sikh community has replicated the chaos and color of the Punjab. Walking down Southall's Broadway, I have observed that these immigrants—whom India has put "out of sight, out of mind"—have certainly kept India in their minds. Sikh *gurudwaras* (temples) and Hindu *mandirs* (temples) are scattered everywhere. The spice bazaars and street vendors are reminiscent of Punjab in earlier decades, as is the Glassy Junction Pub. Apparently the first of many British pubs to accept payment in Indian currency, Glassy Junction displays a sign boldly proclaiming, "Rupees welcome here."[13] Also taped to the wall is a large map of Punjab. A Sikh bartender serves up a range of Indian lagers, and the waiters wear *dhotis*. Baisakhi, a festival, has long been celebrated on Southall's streets, and now is celebrated in the heart of London's Trafalgar Square. Surprised, I asked if people actually attended—and I was snubbed—"some 25,000 were there *ji*."[14]

Indian popular culture has seeped into the life of the mainstream Briton. Indian restaurants, mostly owned by people of Bangladeshi origin, are hugely popular. Chicken tikka masala, ranging in price from £2.99 a portion from the neighborhood grocer's frozen food section to £50 at London's most exclusive Indian restaurants, has outranked fish and chips as Britons' favorite dish. Popular television shows feature British Indian actors and families. In central London, the flagship retailer Marks Spencer sells *samosas* (Indian pastries stuffed with potatoes or mince meat) with cigars. Other retailers like Selfridges showcase *pashmina* shawls and Mughal *itar* (perfume). Central London is also home to the high-end *desi*, British Indians whose wealth and fame has won them a spot among the British elite. The most famous of these is Lakshmi Mittal, the steel tycoon. The *desis* are patrons of the Victoria Albert Museum, members of exclusive clubs and casinos, holders of private booths to watch cricket at Lords, and frequenters of England's famous Ascot race course.

The rise to prominence of the Indian community in London and its environs is ironic because London was the capital of the empire that once subjugated Indians. In the nineteenth century mercantile Britain, having lost its American colonies and bolstered by the productivity gains of the Industrial Revolution, looked to Asia and Africa to relaunch its expansion. The empire's commercial ventures—the creation of railways, plantations, and labor-intensive industries—fueled a demand for labor, and the first wave of Indian immigrants were in fact indentured servants.[15] Typically, newly arrived immigrants were assigned to plantations or other organizations to which they were bound for five or more years. Once their contracts were completed, many stayed on the plantations while others joined nearby rural communities, often combining subsistence farming and wage labor to make a living and staying on even after indentured labor was abolished in 1917.[16]

Mini-Indias also dot the urban landscapes of East Africa, Southeast Asia, and the Caribbean, all of which have British colonial connections. From 1852 to 1937, 1.5 million Indians went to Ceylon and 2 million to Malaya.[17] Until the first half of the twentieth century Indians immigrating to East Africa, Natal, Mauritius, Fiji, and Burma were mostly traders, skilled artisans, bankers, contractors, clerks, professionals, and entrepreneurs who had left their homeland voluntarily. It is true that the earliest immigrants to East Africa were indentured laborers working on the Mombassa railway, but subsequent immigrants to Kenya, Uganda, and Tanzania were driven by the commercial opportunities spawned by the railways. In East Africa, as in Great Britain, the descendants of many indentured laborers became very successful economically, often attaining standards of living exceeding what their families had enjoyed in India. Yet the stereotype of immigrants as indentured laborers remained ingrained in the minds of Indians in India— another reason for India's historical shunning of its diaspora.

World War II and decolonization initiated another wave of Indian immigration. Postwar reconstruction demanded labor, and in response Indian immigrants were on the move again. These were the great-grandparents of today's Heathrow immigration officials.[18] For example, the Anglo-Indian community, descendants of British colonial and military personnel posted in India, was a source of labor for railway projects. Some from this community had sided with the British during India's freedom movement and had struggled to win social acceptance in independent India Many of them left to pursue economic opportunities in the United Kingdom. Britain also recruited medical personnel from India—especially English-speaking doctors from the Punjab's accredited medical colleges—to staff the newly created National Health Service. Although the Commonwealth Immigrants Act of 1962 and the Immigration Act of 1971 restricted further primary immigration, family members of already-settled migrants were allowed entry. The diaspora continued to expand.

In the 1970s a grimmer reason brought another wave of Indians to Britain and America. Refugees were fleeing African oppressors, notably in Kenya and Uganda, after their families had made their homes there for three or more generations.[19] As the so-called economically dominant Jews of Africa, they bore the brunt of resentment when the African nationalist movements gained momentum. Such expropriation of Indians overseas was also experienced closer to India's borders. In response to economic opportunity—the fertile rice fields of the Irrawaddy Delta, for example—Indians sought riches in Burma. Second- and third-generation Burmese Indians carved out comfortable lives, but over time nationalist sentiments forced them out or diminished their stature.

Also in the 1970s the Gulf countries, flush with cash from the oil boom, frantically recruited labor from India. It was as if Arab sheikhs and "Gulf Recruitment" companies now replaced the white colonial administrator who rounded up *coolies* and transported them to colonial hinterlands. More than half of the 3 million Indians who came to the Gulf hailed from the southern Indian state of Kerala. Roughly 70 percent of them were employed as clerks, schoolteachers, stenographers, and construction workers. White-collar doctors, engineers, architects, and chartered accountants made up the remainder. Thus Indian hands built the colonial empire and the Arab sheikdoms of Bahrain, Doha, Dubai, and Saudi Arabia.[20]

In the late 1970s, 1980s, and 1990s, while Indian labor continued building the oil-rich Arab countries, another group of Indians left for a new destination, North America. Unlike the indentured laborers of the colonial era and the semiskilled workers of the Gulf era, these immigrants were mostly doctors, engineers, academics, and entrepreneurs. These highly skilled professionals achieved such visibility and prominence in North American host countries that even reluctant India was forced to recognize them.

A group of engineers and entrepreneurs based in California's Silicon Valley—the hub of information technology in the United States—brought the Indian diaspora to everyone's attention. AnnaLee Saxenian of the University of California at Berkeley points out that Indians run more than 750 technology companies in Silicon Valley, including approximately 10 percent of those started since 1995. Significantly, the valley also allows Indians to circumvent their traditional regional and linguistic divisions. "Groups like SIPA (Silicon Valley Indian Professionals Association) and TiE (The Indus Entrepreneur) create common identities among an otherwise fragmented nationality," Saxenian explains. "Indians historically are deeply divided and typically segregate themselves by regional and linguistic differences . . . [T]he Bengalis, Punjabis, Tamil, and Gujaratis tend to stick together. But in Silicon Valley it seems that the Indian identity has become more powerful than these regional distinctions."[21] Some remarkable success stories emerged. Sabeer Bhatia, founder of Hotmail, sold his company in 1997 to Microsoft for $400 million. Similarly, Gururaj Deshpande is an Indian who has sold and founded several network technology companies. He ranks among the world's richest people, with a net worth in the range of $4 billion to $6 billion.[22]

China's Art of Diaspora Management

By 1949 the Chinese diaspora numbered 10.7 million,[23] and Mao faced the task of developing a policy toward this dispersed and increasingly wealthy group. Would the People's Republic of China shun the entrepreneurial diaspora as capitalists or establish ties with them as had previous regimes?

As precedent, the Qing Dynasty (1609–1911), China's last imperial dynasty, had hoped that the diaspora would aid in China's modernization, and had set up an array of institutions and policies to attract diaspora investments. These policies included setting up chambers of commerce in countries with large ethnic Chinese populations, offering ranks and titles to merchants who made large investments in China, sending out special missions to Southeast Asia to raise funds for large-scale projects, and improving China's business environment by curbing corruption.[24] Perhaps most significantly, in 1909 the Qing adopted a nationality law that made every ethnic Chinese a Qing subject regardless of place of birth or residence. During the nineteenth century the *jus sanguinis* principle, originating in the notion that parents had the right to transfer citizenship to their children wherever born, was adopted throughout Europe and then transplanted to its colonies. The alternative was principle of *jus soli*, Latin for "right of soil," which mandated that the place of birth dictated citizenship. In adopting *jus sanguinis* the Qing were casting a wide net by reaching out not only to overseas Chinese who had been born in China but to *all* ethnic Chinese.

Mao started out by acknowledging the diaspora's importance. He established the Overseas Chinese Affairs Commission and even set up special retail stores for overseas Chinese to access otherwise scarce items. But soon contradictions had emerged. For example, while Mao was keenly aware that hard currency and remittances were of great importance in a closed economy, offering "special incentives" to overseas Chinese was against socialism, where all citizens were equal.[25]

By the time the Cultural Revolution was launched, Mao had increasingly distanced himself from the diaspora, viewing them with suspicion as a potentially destabilizing force. Overseas Chinese investment corporations were closed down, the special retail stores were locked up, and Chinese citizens with overseas connections were verbally abused and physically beaten. Thus the Cultural Revolution unraveled the structure of diaspora management that had been created over the Qing, Guomindang, and early PRC years.

Deng Xiaoping undid the damage that the Cultural Revolution wrought on connections to the diaspora. In 1977 he convened an all-nation overseas conference in Beijing as a first step toward soliciting investments from the diaspora.[26] Additionally, an editorial in the *People's Daily* set the scene for this new policy by proclaiming that good relations with the Chinese overseas were imperative for China's Four Modernizations: modernization of industry, agriculture, science and technology, and the military.[27]

Beginning in 1978 every province, autonomous region, and municipality in China established an Overseas Chinese Affairs Office with the goals of systematically building relationships with the diaspora. Between 1978 and 1990 China passed fifty laws and regulations seeking "equal treatment without discrimination" for all Chinese living overseas, considerations according to the particularities (*yi shi tong ren, bu de qi shi; gen ju te dian, shi dang zhao gu*).[28]

Legislation passed in 1983 and 1985 by the State Council granted special status to overseas Chinese who invested in the Special Economic Zones established along the southern and eastern seaboards of the country. These policies were targeted at the phenomenally wealthy among the 20 million Southeast Asian Chinese, who held assets estimated at $200 billion. *Qiaoxiang*, a Chinese term referring to an area from where a sizable number had emigrated, received special attention. By the mid-1980s, the Chinese had created a large organizational and policy structure dedicated to managing its diaspora. The diaspora dividend became evident when China received 5.5 billion RMB ($727 million) in remittances in the first decade of reform.

In almost all its official statements the CCP refers to the diaspora as a part of China. Party leaders court overseas Chinese, and a series of national conferences are regularly held to encourage the diaspora to invest in provinces with which they have family ties. The Eighteenth World Hakka Conference was held in the Henan province city of Zhengzhou in October 2003. The word *Hakka*, which means "guest," refers to the Hakka people's decades-long emigration from central China first to southern China and then overseas. Dancing and singing during the opening ceremonies focused on the theme of reunion of the Hakkas and was backed up with three hours of fireworks. The conference attracted about three thousand delegates from overseas and China, with the government providing free accommodations to prominent business leaders. Political and business leaders spoke, including Governor Li Chengyu, who emphasized the "emotional relationship" between the Hakka and the province of Henan. The bonhomie prevailing at the conference was expected to lead to investment.

India's Art of Diaspora Mismanagement

The British Raj established no special policies or incentives to lure the wealth and talent of the Indian diaspora. Britons in India were too preoccupied with sourcing cheap labor for their colonies. Less comprehensible is why independent India neglected its diaspora.

Nehru's foreign policy principles and his domestic socialist development agenda offer an explanation. During the height of the cold war Nehru, along with Tito of Yugoslavia and Nasser of Egypt, embraced the policy of non-alignment. The nonaligned countries opted to remain away from any political or economic bloc built on ideology. Specifically they sought to remain outside the influence of both the United States and the Soviet Union. Those principles also led Nehru to advise Indians settled abroad to adopt citizenship of their host countries. Meddling by India on their behalf would be inconsistent with India's attempt to keep the blocs at a distance and could only hurt the overseas Indians.

India's disengagement with the diaspora also reflected its inward-looking economic development policy of import substitution and self-reliance, as well as its penchant for favoring local capital over foreign capital. While China's Qing Dynasty had sought overseas Chinese capital as a substitute for foreign capital, India's anti-imperialism was directed against all foreigners, including overseas Indians. Foreign capital was not seen as contributing to India's economic development.

Under Indira Gandhi, the nation's policies became even more introspective. Populism peaked. Mrs. Gandhi ushered in nationalization, and India's License Raj made the country even more inhospitable for private enterprise, especially unfamiliar foreigners. Ironically, not only did this business environment deter foreign investors, it also led some of India's biggest industrialists to invest and expand outside India. Aditya Birla's investments in Southeast Asia were an early example.

By the 1970s the profile of the Indian immigrant had changed. A large number of professional elite were leaving their homeland for countries like the United States, the United Kingdom, and Australia. The popular press in India labeled this the "brain drain." Emigrants were accused of using India's excellent urban secondary education and medical and engineering schools to advance their own personal careers without giving anything back.

Sarcastic epithets, plays on NRI like "Never Returning Indian" and "Not Required Indian," were often heard. Thus, through the 1980s, when China was busy setting up organization after organization to cater to the needs of overseas Chinese, India shut out its diaspora. Adopting the principle of *jus soli* and deeming only resident Indians worthy of contributing to India must rank as among the most egregious cases of mismanagement of a national resource in recent times. A successful, emotionally connected group of individuals willing to give back to India was repeatedly shunned. It is as though the anachronistic message of some of the Hindu *shastras* (scriptures), forbidding overseas travel, continues to exercise a hold on Indian policy makers. Historically Indians leaving the country were chastised as having crossed *kaala paani*, or black water, and were therefore impure. *Kaala Pani* then became the name given to a penal colony constructed in British India, in the Andaman Islands in the Bay of Bengal, to house a collection of India's freedom fighters. Over time, the term became synonymous with banishment, just as Indians crossing the seas had been banished from the national mindset.[29] Ironically, the Indian Ocean was once symbolic of India's global trade reach and maritime expeditions.[30]

Despite this hostile environment some stalwarts of the Indian diaspora have managed to contribute. Sam Pitroda, born Satyanarayan Gangaram Pitroda Titlagarh in the state of Orissa, pursued a physics and electronics education in his home state, earned an electrical engineering degree at the University of Chicago, and then for two decades led a successful career in several U.S. companies. In India Pitroda is best known for having founded the Center for Development of Telematics in 1984, an attempt to bring telephones to rural India. As Gurcharan Das describes in his book *India Unbound*, Pitroda "decided to start at the top, with Mrs. Gandhi. After waiting five months to get an appointment, he met her and impressed her. He also met with her son, Rajiv Gandhi, with whom he struck a chord. He told them he could bring telephones to villages, improve customer service, change to digital switching and do this all for very little. To everyone's surprise, the government bought his dream."[31]

In three years Pitroda and his group of young scientists had made enormous progress. Rajiv Gandhi appointed Pitroda to head India's Telecom Commission. The work of the nonresident Indian had an enormous impact. In the 1970s it was uncommon for even an upper-middle-class urban Indian to have a telephone. I remember having to walk to a neighbor's house to make a phone call, or being summoned by the corner storekeeper to receive a call. Residents of rural India had to walk for miles to access a functioning telephone line, and in Mumbai the waiting time to purchase a telephone was several years. By 1990, however, thanks to émigré Sam Pitroda, five million Indians had new telephones, and millions of new phones have been installed annually ever since.[32]

Reinventing Nonresident Indians

Jaitirth "Jerry" Rao is another NRI who returned to India and started a successful enterprise. His software business, Mphasis, which he founded in 1998, is one of the India's ten largest.[33] Born in Bangalore and educated in Chennai and the University of Chicago, Rao spent twenty-five years climbing the corporate hierarchy at Citibank. He caught the entrepreneurial itch when everybody and his brother were starting companies. "I used to give business to many of these startups because I had such a large technology budget for various experimental things that they were doing," he explained. "So I said to myself, 'What am I doing? Why don't I do this?'" But he always longed for home and felt he could succeed there. In a poem he wrote several years before starting Mphasis, he said,

> *Exile is a condition of the skin*
> *Boils, bruises, scabs,*
> *Fevers lick the surface*
> *arousing the collagen within,*
> *Cool water is no remedy*
> *for it leaves behind sediments*
> *of salt,*
> *serenades*
> *salt that burns, lacerates*
> *and on lonely September night;*
> *faces ancestral longings.*[34]

Stories like Rao's are becoming quite common. To determine how important the diaspora was to India's software industry, Ramana Nanda, a PhD student at MIT, and I surveyed software entrepreneurs running businesses in India. Of the 208 entrepreneurs participating in the Web-based survey, 58 percent had lived outside India and then returned as NRIs. Further, 88 percent of the survey participants had used the diaspora network to help start their businesses, primarily to obtain contacts in the United States that could help them secure initial contracts for their firms' services. The diaspora was an important source of entrepreneurs for the software industry, and even entrepreneurs who were not diaspora members often sought out the diaspora to help start their businesses. Our analysis also showed that the diaspora was disproportionately important for entrepreneurs located outside the main Indian software centers.[35] In a hub city like Bangalore, an entrepreneur could easily hire talent, seek financing, and find representatives from U.S.-based companies with potential customer bases. For someone trying to establish a business in a so-called tier-2 city like Jaipur or Pune, startup is more difficult and access to the diaspora even more useful.[36] Perhaps in an intuitive recognition of this phenomenon, the Confederation Indian Industry (CII) recently announced the formation of a CII-Indian-American council, chaired by Sam Pitroda, to connect diaspora members seeking to make a difference in their hometowns.[37]

In the past few years gatherings of diaspora members have become more frequent, inside and outside India. In 2005 I was invited to speak at the World IIT Alumni Conference, appropriately held on Democracy Boulevard in Bethesda, Maryland. My role was to moderate a discussion of investment opportunities along with K. V. Kamath, the CEO of India's ICICI bank, and Victor Menezes, the former chief operating officer of Citigroup. Deputy Prime Minister Advani would probably have called this another *jugalbandi*, a duet, between the diaspora and India residents. The presence of high-profile American guest panelists like Thomas Friedman, columnist and writer at the *New York Times*, and Jack Welch, the former CEO of General Electric, was evidence that the Indian diaspora had come of age.

What prompted India to begin moving away from its "not required Indian" syndrome? The answer lies in the country's responses to a crisis and in private-sector initiative.

In 1991 the India was forced to rethink its attitude when a balance-of-payments crisis prompted the government to turn to the diaspora for capital.[38] For several decades remittances from expatriate workers, mostly from the Gulf region, had been an important but unpublicized pillar of financial inflows into India. During the 1973 and 1979 oil crises these remittances had cushioned India from external economic shock.[39] In 1991 the Gulf War had caused these remittances to dry up. Panic-stricken foreign investors pulled out their money, worsening the situation. At its nadir India had only two weeks of foreign exchange reserves left.

India knew it could approach the diaspora for help. NRIs, by their increasing prominence especially in the United States, had acquired mind share in India by then. Silicon Valley entrepreneurs were among the first contacted. Their humble backgrounds, IIT educations, and success stories had become the stuff of lore. Numerically, the Indian population in the United States had tripled between 1980 and 1997, making Indian Americans the third-largest Asian American population in the country, after the Chinese and Filipinos.[40] Further, the per capita income of Indian Americans exceeded that of every other group in the country (including white Americans) except Japanese Americans.[41]

India's dismissive rhetoric about the diaspora thus began to change out of necessity. But a diaspora management infrastructure of the magnitude and efficiency seen in China did not immediately spring up. The government's first concrete action to attract NRI investment was to float the Resurgent India Bonds in July 1998 by India's largest bank, the government-owned State Bank of India. But this action too was prompted by crisis.

In May 1998 India tested a nuclear bomb. International condemnation and economic sanctions followed. The bonds anticipated the erosion of foreign currency reserves and prompted an overwhelming response from investors. The government had to prematurely close the issue because it rapidly exceeded its $2 billion objective by 100 percent. Even taking the bonds' attractive terms into consideration, the unexpected amount of money they raised showed how willing diaspora investors were to assist their homeland.

But perhaps the most "visual" acknowledgment of overseas Indians was the Vajpayee government's appointment of a committee on the diaspora. Coming almost ten years after the reform process was well under way, the committee acknowledged that it was the government's first such effort. To its credit the committee made a number of important policy proposals to engage the Indian diaspora, including the suggestion that the Indian government set up a "single window" organization to manage the affairs of overseas Indians. The committee also acknowledged India's need to learn from other countries' experiences regarding their diasporas, including China's.[42]

The Indian government also widened the definition of the diaspora. While the government had already official recognized the Non-Resident Indian (NRI) and started to give some concessions (for example, the ability to buy property as well as employment and tourists visa waivers), in 2002, the Indian government also issued the Persons of Indian Origin (PIO) cards to several generations of ethnic Indians residing abroad. This action was specially aimed at reconnecting with the parts of the diaspora that resulted from the colonial era. Creating the PIO category was the Indian government's attempt to come closer to the principle of *jus sangunis*. PIO cardholders had the same privileges as NRIs, except the ability to acquire agricultural or plantation properties.[43]

As much as the government did, the private sector did more. ICICI, India's leading private-sector bank, aggressively pursued international expansion beginning in 2001.[44] It realized that as much as 10 percent of its global remittance transfers were made by overseas Indians wiring money to India and typically paying exorbitant fees to Western Union or other wire transfer services. ICICI leveraged its technological infrastructure and relationships with banks in the Middle East—where the big Indian worker population in the Gulf countries could be targeted—to create a low-cost way of sending money home.

Cheaper and better remittance products were also a way to encourage customers to keep their deposits in the bank. Retail deposits were attractive to banks for many reasons. First, they provided a relatively cheap source of funds. The interest rates paid on deposits were about 0.5 percent to 0.75 percent less than the rates banks needed to pay for money borrowed through other channels. Second, retail deposits gave banks the opportunity to cross-sell higher-value products such as mutual funds and other India-based investment services to NRIs and to link those products with a full range of local banking services for NRIs in their country of residence. Finally, in addition to the basic India-linked products such as deposits and remittances, retail deposits enabled banks to tap into other opportunities. For example, many of the migrants from the Middle East who returned to India for a few weeks at a stretch said they were looking to buy or construct homes but found it difficult to locate reputable brokers or builders in the short time they were in India. These opportunities were much easier to capitalize on if banks already had these individuals as customers.

Lalita Gupte, managing director of ICICI, told me that several indicators pointed to the success of its expansion plan. They were signing up lots of new customers in Canada, and an increasing number of their customers were non-Indians. That is, the idea of using the diaspora as a beachhead to enter a new market had proven viable. Gupte said, "I knew we had traction when the immigration officer in Vancouver recognized my ICICI logo from the Internet ads that we had begun to do in Canada with ING Direct, the Internet arm of the global Dutch bank."

Jewel in the Crown of Cobra Beer

Just as ICICI represents the Indian private sector proactively capitalizing on the diaspora, the diaspora has also begun to pay active attention to India. As a result of these duets, at some point the "not required Indian" was transformed into a coveted nonresident Indian. The story of Karan Bilimoria and his firm, Cobra Beer, illustrates this transformation.

Bilimoria was part of the wave of white-collar Indian immigrants that came to the United Kingdom in the 1970s and early 1980s. He studied chartered accountancy and law. "In my case," he told me, "I knew from my high school days that I would have to go abroad to further myself. That's how you got ahead in India. My grandfather was commissioned at Sandhurst, both my mother and father had studied in the U.K., so it was assumed that I would wind up in London."[45]

While living in London, Bilimoria noticed that whenever he ordered beer to go with his spicy Indian food, the restaurant's available lager brands or house beers caused gastric discomfort. The alternative to lager was real ale, but that was an equally poor accompaniment to Indian food. What could Bilimoria do to offer a better choice to consumers of Indian food in Britain? Ale—which is made with a top-fermenting yeast, is usually described as "hearty, robust, and fruity." Lager, which is made with a bottom-fermenting yeast, is characteristically "smooth, elegant, crisp, and clean." Bilimoria wanted to develop a hybrid beer—a lager that was smooth enough to accompany Indian food but that also appealed to drinkers of English ale. The idea was to sell this product to Indian restaurants in the United Kingdom, whose numbers had burgeoned from 3,000 in 1980 to 8,500 in 2001.[46]

Serendipity led Bilimoria to India's leading brew master, the Prague-educated Dr. Cariappa, who worked for Mysore Breweries. Bilimoria and Dr. Cariappa collaborated to create a first-rate Indian beer and to make it accessible anywhere in the world. This collaboration began in 1990, the year before the onset of India's latest reform phase. But local bureaucratic obstacles were manifold. For example, the beer market in India is heavily regulated. More than 50 percent of the retail price is accounted for by excise taxation, and inefficient government-owned distributors often control the distribution of liquor. Moreover, as an item on the so-called state list, liquor is subject to state rather than national regulations, and idiosyncratic rules at the state level often preclude beer sales elsewhere. In Karnataka, the southern state where Bilimoria began brewing his Cobra Beer, state regulations decreed that beer had to be stamped "Not for sale in Karnataka" if it was leaving state boundaries. All of Cobra's production was intended for export outside India. Cobra's beer already prominently indicated this intent. A further label prohibiting sale in Karnataka seemed unnecessary. The state regulator, however, followed the letter rather than the spirit of the law and refused to budge regarding the need for multiple stamps. They held off issuing the necessary permits for production to ensue. Bilimoria had to cajole the excise commissioner in Bangalore to gain the opportunity to explain his position and finally secure an exemption from the rule. Small barriers like that made the first five years very difficult for the fledgling beer company.

For several years Cobra Beer was exported out of Bangalore, mostly to the United Kingdom; not a single bottle was sold in India. World of mouth helped the beer gain traction in the United Kingdom, and sales took off in 1996. Then Bilimoria reached a turning point. "I decided to move the brewery from Bangalore to Bedford in the U.K. It was one of the toughest decisions I have ever had to make, but the quality and consistency of the product from Bangalore were not quite good enough. In retrospect the decision was excellent. Customers did not seem to mind that the beer was brewed in the U.K. even though its origins were Indian. The taste was all that they focused on."

Bilimoria continued his story: "I kept a close lock on the Indian market. By 2002 I saw that liberalization had picked up pace again, and I started exporting Cobra again, this time in the reverse direction, from the U.K. to India. So Cobra, born in Bangalore, brewed in Bedford, was back in Bangalore." In 2005 Cobra finally resumed production in India—in addition to its operations in the U.K. and throughout Europe—after teaming up with and retrofitting a brewery near New Delhi. As Bilimoria readily concedes, it was a bet. Beer consumption is growing at the same rate as Indian GDP, although it could easily grow even faster. Bilimoria is hopeful that India's beer market will grow as did China's, fueled by deregulation. China has now surpassed the United States as the world's largest beer market. Most brewers in the world are watching the market explode, prompting Bilimoria to say, "Every major brewery in the world would like to partner with us. India is the jewel in Cobra Beer's crown," drawing symbolic parallel to the value the British Empire put on their India colony.

In 2003 Cobra Beer's sales exceeded $81 million—half of which came from 5,600 Indian restaurants in the United Kingdom.⁴⁷ In 2004 Cobra launched a deal with Virgin Atlantic Airways to sell Cobra Beer on the London–Delhi route, bringing "passengers a true taste of India."⁴⁸ Since then Cobra has spread worldwide. Production is concentrated in five locations—Belgium, the Netherlands, and Poland, in addition to India and the United Kingdom—and beer is exported to almost fifty countries. London, Mumbai, Cape Town, and New York City are home to regional hubs, and retail sales of Cobra are now over £100m.

Cobra Beer has developed an interesting brand loyalty. British army officers with experience in Asia swore that the brand had been around for close to a century, it was so familiar to them somehow, even though it was scarcely fifteen years old. Consumers in India had begun to think of it as a British import but did not shun it as foreign because it was produced by one of their own.

Besides producing a world-class beer, Bilimoria wants to act as a bridge between the United Kingdom and India. His increasing prominence in public life led to his appointment as the U.K. chairman of the Indo British Partnership Network, an organization set up in 1993 when the British government recognized the need for a bilateral economic relationship with India. Bilimoria accompanied Prime Minister Tony Blair and a delegation of the United

Kingdom's top business leaders on a trip to China and India in September 2005. In January of that year I had the opportunity to watch Bilimoria in action at a luncheon in New Delhi organized by the just-appointed Minister of Overseas Indian Affairs Jagdish Tytler. The meeting was held to solicit input from a handful of diaspora members regarding the charter of Tytler's newly formed ministry. Bilimoria was a passionate salesman for both his country of origin and his adopted country, selling each to the other, and pointing out that the British chancellor's budget in 2004 mentioned India for the first time, and not once but twice. In recent decades enthusiasm for economic relationships of this sort has never been higher. It is as though India is open for business and is feeling its way through various agents to its diaspora. The atmosphere is perhaps what it was like in China in the early 1980s with respect to courting capital from the diaspora.

Tytler was not in his ministerial position long before he was booted out for his alleged involvement in communal riots that took place in India during 1984. But his ministry did survive. That the Ministry of Overseas Indian Affairs exists at all is testimony to India's newfound enthusiasm for its diaspora. Meanwhile, Bilimoria was introduced to the House of Lords in July of 2006 and formally became Lord Bilimoria of Chelsea later that year, a mark of his steep ascent in British society and a symbol of British-Indians' coming of age.

Chapter Nine

Village Engineering and Reengineering

In Search of Rural Fortunes

Paramount in Westerners' thoughts of China and India are images of desperate poverty: malnourished children trudging barefoot down a dusty road, emaciated cows in a dry river bed, ragged peasants toiling in a rice field. In India as many as 290 million people live in grinding poverty, a number that rises to 390 million if poverty is measured by the international standard of those existing on less than $1 a day.[1] The situation is a bit better in China. In 2001 the World Bank estimated that 400 million Chinese had been lifted out of poverty over the prior two decades. By then China had also met the foremost of the United Nation's Millennium Development Goals—to reduce the 1990 incidence of poverty by half—and had done so fourteen years ahead of the 2015 target date set for the developing world as a whole.[2]

China's rising incomes among its rural population are a testament to the government's efficiency in planning, leading, and executing change. In India, however, political emancipation and empowerment for people at the bottom of society has not translated into economic and social gains. The government has not yet learned from the private sector and civil society, which are currently easing individual pockets of poverty.

By far the greatest portions of the Chinese and Indian populations live in villages. To understand what China and India are doing to reengineer living conditions in rural villages, I visited Qiu Village in China and the Self-Employed Women's Association (SEWA) in India's western state of Gujarat. Both are places of hope. Amid teeming rural poverty are places where people's lives *are* changing for the better. For the most part these changes are not difficult to duplicate and thus deserve world attention and support. China and India, despite having vastly different systems and historical policies toward their rural populations, share a need for more places of hope.

Under the Umbrella of the Party

The province of Henan—the name means "south of the Yellow River (*Huanghe*)"—is one of China's most populous regions, home to more than a hundred million people. Zhengzhou, the capital, has been one of communist China's most significant industrial centers and is a major railway junction on the Longhai and Jingguang (respectively, east–west and north–south) railway lines.

My first stop in Henan was the county government seat, Chengguan, a town of one hundred thousand people. I stayed in the main hotel, which lacked most amenities associated with major cities but was scrupulously clean—more than can be said for comparable hotels in India. At dawn I set out for my morning run through the nearby streets and found sizeable traffic, indicating a city on the move. Stray dogs and cats roamed the street, very much like an Indian city. Street vendors did a brisk business serving up a fried donutlike substance and a steaming bean soup to the crowds huddled around their hot stoves.

What struck me most were the street sweepers, hard at work in the early morning hours, face masks protecting them from the dust. The street was entirely free of garbage. How different this was from India, where the city government hires unionized street sweepers who can fail to show up and not worry about being fired because prolabor legislation and electoral politics prevent any threat of retaliatory government action from being credible. Even if the city government farmed out the street-cleaning contract to a private entrepreneur, corruption would likely ensure that the contract was awarded to a crony who would not do the work. Any run in even a major Indian city, let alone a smaller one comparable to Chengguan, would be an exhibition of squalor even at dawn.

I drove from Chengguan to Qiu Village and was impressed by the paved roads we traveled, as well constructed as the Massachusetts turnpike I know at home. The roads led right up to cornfields at the edge of the village. Because of unusually heavy rains, miles of corn ears were spread beside the road, neatly tucked away from traffic, and families were raking the corn back and forth to dry it out before it rotted. By contrast, in India sun-drying agricultural produce is a common sight along major roads, part of a farmer's routine rather than a response to an unusually heavy or untimely rainfall and often the cause of traffic disruption.

Qiu Village displayed not exactly prosperity but at least the absence of the desperation of many Indian villages. There was a friendly informality. I learned that the population of roughly a thousand consisted of five broadly related groups, each comprising twenty to thirty families sharing a common name. I spent an evening at the home of Du Yashen, who had kindly invited several others from his extended family to visit with me. The Du home was made of solid brick. For our meeting chairs had been arranged in the court-yard, where cabbage, chilies, and orange trees grew. Although the courtyard was dimly lit, the house had plenty of electricity.

I sat on a makeshift stool, surrounded by at least twenty men, all looking curiously at me. Some smiled politely while others remained expressionless, waiting for our translator. Some in the group represented three generations—grandfather, father, and son. I hoped the translator, an insider whom these men trusted, would make them feel safe enough to speak openly. Otherwise I knew they would only say what was expected. Everyone was dressed in West-ern attire, with jeans and sweaters most common. The women tended to the children. Two toddlers headed straight to the table displaying soy-based snacks, oranges, and nuts and eagerly slurped down bowls of soybean curd. Soy is a staple of the Henan diet; much is grown there, although China im-ports a large proportion of its needs from Brazil. Meanwhile the adults busied themselves with endless cups of tea-leaf-laced hot water, and snacks of roasted pumpkin seeds and fresh peanuts (groundnuts)—the latter are soft and moist when freshly shelled, quite different from the hard, dried peanuts seen in West-ern supermarkets. This brought back for me pleasant childhood memories of consuming shelled melon seeds and similar fresh peanuts in the villages in the north Indian state of Punjab. One difference, however, was that in China the smell of freshly peeled oranges was mixed with smoke. Virtually every man smoked a locally produced cigarette. Local entrepreneurs have monopolized cigarette manufacturing in China, as Philip Morris painfully discovered in re-cent years. Taxing local cigarette consumption is, of course, a major revenue source for the local government.

My hosts appeared to have plenty of time, but the sixty-year-old village doctor arrived breathlessly, apologized for being late, and said he would have to leave very shortly because he had a line of patients waiting to see him. True to his word, he left fifteen minutes later. In the meantime I learned he had parlayed his two years of training in rudimentary Chinese and Western medicine into a thirty-year career as the local health provider He said it had been determined—whether by him or by some other authority was not clear—that his age made further training an unsound investment. I was puzzled that he had no successor in training, but then I reasoned that the modern local infrastructure made one unnecessary. Good roads mean that the trip from the village to the county hospital is less than a half hour, and summoned ambulances arrive as reliably as they do in the United States. Again I was struck by the contrast with Indian villages, where only the most rudimentary medication is available, and ambulances are nonexistent.

Much had changed in the governance of Qiu Village in the past decade. First, the control of the CCP was stronger than ever. The thousand-odd villagers had about thirty Party members, including a Party head appointed directly by the Party. The villagers elected the village head; in Qiu Village he happened to be a Party member, but that is not a requirement. During my courtyard meeting, I noticed one man to whom the others looked for answers; I learned later that he was the Party head. Clearly his views took precedence over those of the village head. Further, the elders pointed out that among the many villagers applying to join the Party, only a very small fraction of the most promising were admitted each year.

I had arrived in the village during an unusual period of accord between villagers and party officials. The central government had abruptly ceased village taxation entirely, following reports of local officials exploiting villagers and inciting unrest. The central government had even replaced its policy of taxation with one of giving money back to the village. The village head was responsible for disbursing the refund among the inhabitants. Home improvements, new televisions, and cell phones were among the benefits derived from this windfall. I asked if the halt in taxation made any lasting impact, thinking perhaps that it signaled a new relationship between local Party officials and the villagers. No, I was told. The effects were only in consumables and simple material goods.

Mao's Chinese Divide and Deng's Orchestrated Capitalism

Li Yining is a stalwart of the CCP, the founding Dean of Peking University's well-regarded Guanghua School of Management, and a man who had a ringside view of early changes in rural China. When China's reforms were inaugurated in 1978, Li was a confidante of their chief architect, Deng Xiaoping, and helped draft a series of policies that ultimately transformed China. As economic incentives were reintroduced and agriculture revitalized, bumper crops became the norm. Villages in China became the source of widespread economic growth.

My goal in talking with Li was to understand how China's postreform landscape differed from Maoist-era conditions and why the reforms focused on the rural sector. We met at his office at Peking University, often described to me as the Harvard of China. I had to be ushered through a maze of assistants before finally reaching his office, a grand and stately, almost cavernous room. Li rose to greet me in a very friendly manner. A heavyset man, he smoked throughout our meeting, which took place entirely in Mandarin, and was translated deferentially for me by a newly minted Stanford economics Ph.D. graduate. Li impressed me throughout as someone incredibly well read and well informed. Li began by remarking, "In urban areas production was controlled by the state; so were people's lives. In rural areas production was planned, but ordinary lives were outside the control of the state. So in the three-year famine 30 million people died, mostly in rural areas where the state had not usually controlled their lives, whereas in urban areas people did not die of starvation but perhaps of nutritional problems."

Li's brief mention of 30 million people starving to death covered a lot of history. The famine of 1958, unintentionally orchestrated by Mao, was the culmination of a number of events and directives. From Mao's earliest days in power, one of his goals was urban industrialization funded by an economic surplus generated by rural China. To do this, however, he had to divide China so that its rural citizenry would be successfully controlled and galvanized to meet the party's economic goals. In 1955 he introduced the *hukou* system under the "Directive Concerning the Establishment of a Permanent System of (Household) Hukou Registration." A *hukou* was a residence permit issued on the on the basis of a person's birthplace. The government's intent in issuing *hukou* cards was to ensure that rural Chinese stayed in rural China and that all the entitlements granted to a permit holder reflected this rural household registration. The most important aspects of life, including where one worked, went to school, and bought food, depended on where one was born. Thus rural residents were prevented from moving to the favored cities. When the cities needed workers, the government relaxed the *hukou* system, and when the cities became filled with too many workers, the government ushered people back to the villages.

In one of the great ironies of the Chinese revolution, Mao redistributed land to landless peasants and soon after asked them to return it to a collective. The re-pooling happened gradually. During the first phase of the gradual collectivization process, from 1949 to 1952, the government set up "mutual aid teams" in the villages.[3] These teams consisted of a dozen or so households that came together voluntarily and occasionally and pooled their labor and capital. At this stage the individual household remained the basic unit of ownership and production, as it had in pre-Mao China. Over the next couple of years, in the second phase of collectivization, "elementary agricultural producer cooperatives" came into being. Members were required to pool their resources and were given limited freedom to opt out. With individual incentives removed, production failed to reach the government's expected output. In the one year of collectivization's third phase, all small farms were turned into "advanced agricultural productive cooperatives."[4] The government forcibly lowered food prices to provide urban workers with cheap food and to keep costs down. Unfortunately lower prices also discouraged agricultural investments, giving rise to the threat of food shortages.

The *hukou* system proved especially useful in rationing scarce food resources. Just two months after the *hukou* system was announced, Mao issued the "Provisional Measures Governing Grain Rationing in Cities and Towns" directive. Individuals registered in each household were classified according to their resident teams, schools, and work units. Once registration was carried out, thousands of name lists and millions of *hukou* cards were sent to the local governments, which verified the authenticity of the *hukou* cards and issued ration and grain supply cards. The detail was incredible. For example, even animal feed locations were specified.[5]

The final demarcation between rural and urban Chinese was established under the "Criteria for the Demarcation Between Urban and Rural Areas," a directive that divided China into three "spatial categories." These were urban areas, including cities and towns; urban residential enclaves located outside urban areas, where residents worked primarily in state-owned industrial or research facilities; and villages. By 1958 rural Chinese had been completely segregated from their brethren in cities.

As part of the government's Second Five-Year Plan (1958–1963), Mao called for acceleration of the industrialization process. State-owned factories were told to ramp up production. Rural communities were galvanized to mass-produce steel. Provinces and municipalities issued construction bonds and hired as much labor as needed to meet Beijing's quotas. In the autumn of 1958 an estimated 38 million people were mobilized to leave their villages. They left, taking with them their tools and animals. Migration to urban areas peaked. Between the years 1957 and 1960 China's urban population increased from 99 million to 130 million. The *hukou* system was completely ignored.

This artificial labor movement exacerbated the food shortages caused by collectivization. Despite a bumper harvest in 1958, large amounts of agricultural produce were left to rot in the fields.[6] Meanwhile the state needed to feed its burgeoning workforce. As signs of famine became apparent, the government did an about-face, ordering urban factories to close down and sending workers, who had been moved to cities just a year or two earlier, back to the villages. In 1959 the plan was to reduce the state workforce by roughly 10 million, thereby reducing the amount of food and fuel needed in the cities. The rationale was based on arithmetical reasoning but paid little attention to incentives; shortages persisted. Five million laid-off workers were sent back to rural areas with little knowledge of what their rural status meant for their futures. In rural areas officials forbade peasants from *tao huang* (escape from hunger of food). Thus the *hukou* system was again strictly enforced to suit Beijing's convenience.

China's rulers failed to acknowledge the famine and to secure foreign food aid for three years. By taking away all means of private food production (in some places even cooking utensils), forcing peasants into mismanaged communes, and continuing food exports to privileged urban residents, the government made a bad situation worse. The Noble Prize–winning economist Amartya Sen has written that famines are as much about different social groups having different means of accessing food as they are about overall food shortages: "The direct penalties of a famine are borne by one group of people and political decisions are taken by another. The rulers never starve. But when a government is accountable to the local populace it too has good reasons to do its best to eradicate famines. Democracy, via electoral politics, passes on the price of famines to the rulers as well."[7]

As Li Yining explained to me, when Deng and his team came to power they faced the gigantic task of undoing Mao's policies, because by the end of Mao's attempt at economic and social reengineering, rural China lay devastated by poverty. "In 1978 we had several options," said Li. "One was to opt for total privatization, which would mean ending socialism. This would be unacceptable. The general public would not accept this and it would come with chaos and social unrest." Li pointed out that any reform had to have a distinctly socialist flavor to avoid social chaos. "The option we eventually chose," he said, "was gradual reform. We chose to start this with rural areas by introducing the Household Responsibility System [HRS] in 1978. HRS was not privatization of land—that would be chaotic. The HRS meant that markets for agricultural production would be developed slowly."

Under the HRS the collective remained the owner of the land and other means of production. However, members of the collective could lease portions of the land for as long as fifty years. During that period the lessee paid government taxes on the land but no rent to the collective. Additionally the lessee could keep any surplus produce generated from the leased land. Thus the HRS restored the work incentives lacking under the collective system, which offered the same benefits to all workers, laggards and laborers, with the result that very little work was done.

In 1978 the impoverished Chinese peasantry seized the opportunity to lease farmland. Opposition was minimal because the benefits of the HRS were becoming apparent. From 1977 to 1984 grain output increased from

283 million to 407 million tons; oil output grew from 4 million to 12 million tons and cotton from 2 million to 6 million tons. Prosperous food markets proliferated across the countryside, and a primary function of the *hukou* system—distribution of scarce rations—became unnecessary. Ration coupons were abolished and food became available even to holders of rural *hukou*. One of the direct outcomes of the agriculture reforms was that the scope of the government-run procurement and distribution was greatly reduced. By 1985 the number of state-controlled items was reduced to thirty-eight, only 30 percent of the 1980 level. In 1992 some local governments decided to fully liberalize local grain marketing. The economic impact was profound. The agricultural boom raised rural incomes, creating a huge rural market for consumer goods that in turn "generated a reservoir of savings that funded investment in rural enterprises."[8]

According to Li, "The success of [the] HRS in turn freed up surplus labor, and Town and Village Enterprises [TVEs] emerged to absorb it. TVEs were not something that had been planned. They were a natural development."

Most TVEs were owned, operated, and regulated by local cadres purely motivated by the central government's admonition to raise local GDP. Furthermore, there was no separation of powers. Local cadres ran, owned, and regulated a large number of TVEs. Foreign firms doing joint ventures with TVEs found that, in times of disputes, their partner was also the effective dispute adjudicator. Despite these shortcomings hybrid TVEs carried their economic weight. At their peak in the mid-1990s, TVEs produced 30 percent of China's GDP, 44 percent of the total value added, according to official estimates of the Ministry of Agriculture. Moreover, TVEs were responsible for one-quarter of China's tax revenue, one-third of total exports, and 28 percent of the total rural labor force (employing 128 million workers).[9]

I recalled my talk with Li when I visited Weihua Group, a private company in Henan Province that makes large industrial cranes. Located close to a village and descended from a TVE, Weihua is controlled by a single family, although it has about a hundred significant shareholders. At the time of my visit the company was experiencing breakneck growth and, with sales of $70 million per year, was very profitable. The owner insisted that I not use the term *TVE*, saying that it was an anachronism. He clarified that the family held a fifty-year lease on the state-owned land on which the factory was built but that otherwise the company had no connection to the state. "These days, we either have state-owned enterprises, in cigarettes and tobacco and electricity, or we have civilian companies. There aren't that many foreign-invested projects, either wholly owned or joint ventures, in the parts of China less open than the coast."

Weihua is a well-run company. It had reinvested its earnings consistently over the past decade. By paying generous wages, even relative to what graduates could earn in Henan's capital, Zhengzhou, they had managed to attract qualified talent and still remain low-cost. The factory floors and yards where the cranes were assembled did not look as spotless as some of the better factories in the West, but they were well organized. I noticed some surplus inventory that seemed abandoned and guessed that the company's low wages allow it to tolerate some of this inefficiency, especially when competing with Western companies through the export market. As a well-run manufacturing facility able to hold its own in world competition, Weihua distinguishes itself from any Indian factory similarly located in a rural area. Infrastructure problems prevent such success in rural India.

I was also surprised to find women operating cranes lifting hundreds of tons of material. Roughly 15 percent of Weihua's professional employees are women, mostly managers and crane operators. This employment of women is largely the result of China's attention to primary education over past decades. Indian women in a comparable small-town setting have access to far less, if any, education. I learned that six years of compulsory education in Henan's villages are followed by three more years in a nearby town, also compulsory. Mao's memorable remark "Women hold up half the sky" is still a popular slogan in rural China. In 2002, 91 percent of the Chinese populace aged fifteen and older could read and write; 87 percent of females and 95 percent of males in that age group were literate. In contrast, the Indian adult literacy rate was just 60 percent in 2002, with only 48 percent of females and 70 percent of males literate.[10]

Li went on with his historical account. "In addition to the HRS and TVE, the important thing we did, was to create the Special Economic Zones [SEZs]." These were run as experiments. The idea was to create relatively small economic areas and shower them with the incentives needed to attract foreign investment. Deng sent officials to visit free-trade zones and export-processing zones worldwide and replicated them on China's southern coast, capitalizing on the established trading and financial centers of Hong Kong, Macao, and Taiwan.

Li had articulated the economic changes in the post-Mao era. TVEs, the HRS, and SEZs were dramatic breaks from the past. Equally dramatic, however, were the parallel political and administrative changes occurring in the countryside.

For example, the People's Commune, the nerve center of Mao's rural economy, collapsed and was replaced by town and village governments, which took charge of administering rural populations. The immediate consequence of this decentralization was a loosening of Beijing's hold on local economies. A nationwide survey conducted by the CCP Central Committee and State Council in early 1985 revealed that increasingly the Party could not recruit new members, organize, collect dues, implement central policies, and provide updates to senior Party members.[11]

Local cadres rose to fill the vacuum. Unfortunately, decentralization was accompanied by corruption and financial mismanagement. Village finances, which were raised and disbursed locally, were grossly mishandled. Studies showed that nearly 70 percent of villages and townships failed to publicize local accounts. Embezzlement of village public funds occurred in 68 percent of surveyed villages, and bribes of various sorts constituted about 160 percent of the regular salaries of rural cadre members.[12]

As a result, local cadres and peasants came into increasing conflict. The cadres arbitrarily imposed various fees. By the mid-1980s, with the monetary burden on the peasants consistently exceeding their net incomes, considerable discontent became evident, even to the higher authorities. In 1985 the state issued a series of directives to curtail the taxes and fees that local governments could levy, restricting the aggregate burden to no more than 10 percent of a peasant's income. Yet these measures were not enforced. The reserves of town and village governments far exceeded what they could legally collect. Peasants were still being forced to help pay for projects like new schools and infrastructure, being penalized for noncompliance with policies like birth control policies, and being overcharged for routine services.[13]

Beijing responded to this administrative chaos by backing so-called villager committees. Collectively the three- to five-member village committees were intended to augment the administrative gaps of the existing village assembly, which because of its broader scope could not meet daily. On paper this meant that villagers had a voice in a range of issues, such as economic development plans, the use of collective resources (land, water, and energy), and birth control. In practice the village Party branch continued to exercise considerable power. In response to the prevailing confusion regarding decision rights, the CCP declared the "Organic Law of Villager Committees" in 1987 to make Party cadres accountable to villagers and to make the committees self-governing organizations with the right to audit village finances. By 1988 the CCP had begun the process of organizing village-level elections across China. In some villages elections were truly contested, but elsewhere local cadres successfully resisted. Interestingly, some scholars point out that "elections are most successful in those counties and villages which have been chosen by the Ministry of Civil Affairs for demonstration."[14]

The paradox of Chinese reform has been that the role of government—central and local—has significantly expanded during the transition to a market economy with, as the Chinese say, "Chinese characteristics." In 1995 alone 1 million new staff members were added to the state's payroll, a figure that does not include new recruits paid through local revenues.[15] A Beijing-dispatched bureaucracy and local cadres compete over all aspects of village administration. Although Beijing has encouraged local cadres to pursue economic development, it has not always been able to check their excesses.

Under the Shade of the Banyan Tree

India's western state of Gujarat, carved out from the state of Bombay in 1960, is bordered by Pakistan to its northwest and by the drought-prone and poorer state of Rajasthan to the north. Gujarat, home to 41 million, is the economic envy of much of India. It is known for its entrepreneurs, industrialists and, most prominently, as the birthplace of Mahatma Gandhi.

Gujarat is also home to a women's organization called SEWA—Self Employed Women's' Association—an acronym that itself is a Hindi word meaning "service." Consistent with Gandhian idealism, SEWA's founder, the social entrepreneur Ela Bhatt, presides over a membership base of seven hundred thousand women, most of whom live in Gujarat and two-thirds of whom are rural residents.

In September 2005 I arranged to meet SEWA *Sangathaks* (organizers) in Ahmedabad, the commercial (and former political) state capital. Ahmedabad had a reputation of being a safe city where one could safely promenade even at 10 P.M., a statement difficult to make regarding any other Indian city of comparable size. A young, simply dressed and businesslike lady, Ami Shelat, SEWA's coordinator for training and education, received me at a makeshift but clean hotel. Ami ben had kindly offered to travel with me to a nearby village to meet the members of a SEWA group. She immediately asked me to call her Ami ben. Ben translates into "sister" in Hindi and Gujarati, which are just two out of the twenty-four regional languages in India, but which also share a host of common words. Within SEWA every woman is addressed by her first name followed by *Ben*. The phrase is as a mark of sisterhood and solidarity. Using the epithet instead of a last name is also a social equalizer—making the caste, position, and regional background of an individual irrelevant. Accompanying Ami ben was Mr. Desai, wearer of many hats. Besides being a full-time consultant to SEWA, he taught accounting at a local management school that he had co-founded.

Finally, there was a chauffeur, referred to as "driver" in India, Suresh bhai ("bhai" translates into "brother" in Hindi and Gujarati). Suresh bhai accompanied us everywhere, which included a delightful roadside restaurant serving local cuisine, where many dishes are laced with a trace of cane sugar. Suresh lunched with us, a refreshing and unusual trace of egalitarianism and entirely in character with SEWA. In most of urban India, where a dramatic hierarchy acts as a barrier between economic haves and have-nots, the driver would have gracefully vanished from the scene of the restaurant, and would miraculously re-appear when summoned via his cellphone.

The drive from Ahmedabad to the village where I was to meet other SEWA members was in some ways similar to the one I took in Henan, but in other ways it was quite different. Although Henan is one of China's poorer provinces, its countryside seemed far more prosperous than that of Gujarat, one of India's richest states. The road from Ahmedabad, like most roads in India, was bumpy, with slow-moving traffic interrupted by wayward trucks, animals of all sorts, and penurious figures trudging precariously alongside.

SEWA was founded in 1972 as an offshoot of the Textile Labor Union, one of India's oldest and largest trade unions. Originally meant to assist women in the informal sector, particularly wives and daughters of mill workers, within several years SEWA was holding classes in sewing, knitting, embroidery, spinning, press composition, typing, and stenography. In 1977 Bhatt was awarded the Ramon Magsaysay Award, possibly the world's most famous social service accolade, bringing international publicity and recognition to SEWA. Even today SEWA workers use the union rhetoric in daily conversation, though they did not fit my image of a confrontational group of workers agitating against a manufacturing entrepreneur. SEWA still continues to be a trade union, but its links with the Textile Labor Association have broken. In its current form SEWA follows a strictly Gandhian ideology, with nonviolence as its core principle.

Ami ben suggested that I think of SEWA as a banyan tree. Indians attach an enormous amount of symbolism to the banyan, the country's national tree. For Hindus the roots of the banyan tree represent Brahma, the creator of all humankind; the bark represents Vishnu, the preserver; and the branches represent Shiva, the destroyer. For Buddhists the banyan is the tree under which the Gautam Buddha attained enlightenment. Some Indians say the thick milk released from the banyan's leaves sustained humankind before the discovery of grain and other produce, and scores of Indian women revere the banyan tree as a symbol of fertility.

Ami ben explained the banyan's relevance to SEWA. "The leaves are SEWA's 700,000 members; the trunk, SEWA the parent organization. The several branches of the tree signify SEWA's sister organizations, which grow as autonomous workers' member organizations and support the tree—the members and the trunk." What distinguishes SEWA from any conventional hierarchy is its self-image as an organization whose branches send roots to the ground, helping the branches become as thick as tree trunks themselves. These interlinked trees then form a resilient network. Ami Ben cited as an example how a group from one village automatically came to the aid of another group in a flood-stricken village. A real ethos of collective leadership rose from the egalitarianism I had observed.[16]

After an hour's drive we reached our destination: a nursery established by a SEWA group of fifteen women in Devpura, a village in Kheda district of Gujarat. Most of these women came from families of landless agricultural laborers. Thus the additional income from the nursery project was precious to them. The women grew seedlings for flowers, fruits, herbs, and vegetables using every available inch of the one-acre plot.

Five years earlier these women had begun pressing the local *panchayat*, the elected village government, to allow them to use the land. At that time the landlords grew tobacco, a cash crop heavily in demand, on the property worked by tenant farmers. The women complained that the landlords cheated the farmers and committed fraud. Family after family had fallen into debt. Illiteracy and lack of bookkeeping skills were to blame, along with the usual bullying of the farmers. After years of agitating and a plethora of excuses, which included the claim that the land was haunted, the reluctant *panchayat* awarded use of an acre of village land to the women. The most vociferous of them, a forty year-old, dark-skinned, painfully thin woman, concluded this portion of the story with a sentence with which she had admonished the *panchayat*, "Bhoot [ghost] or no *bhoot*, we're taking this land, and if we can't make anything of it, we'll become *bhoots* and haunt it ourselves."

At one end of the nursery I came across a new manual water pump. It used to be that getting a broken pump repaired was a major ordeal. Then a group of women, one woman from each of several villages, organized a new self-help group, inspired by SEWA, that agitated for a license to maintain water pumps for the *taluk* (district). The men in the village scoffed at this effort, believing maintenance of heavy and complex machinery to be their preserve. Their skepticism was unwarranted; the women keep the pump humming along smoothly.

The solution to the pump problem typified the can-do attitude of a set of historically disenfranchised women. They organized through SEWA to tap into another smaller number of women who took nursery management and botany courses in the city to acquire needed expertise. Through SEWA they found contacts in the city to sell their seedlings for a sizable profit (compared with what they would earn as tenants of the landlords). They plowed their earnings into various self-improvement projects that ultimately helped the entire village.

After touring the nursery I sat cross-legged under a banyan tree on a floor made of caked dirt with about forty women ranging in age from early twenties to late sixties, some of whom had traveled up to fifty miles to talk with me. The meeting began abruptly; the minute Ami ben and I settled on the floor, the women broke into a Hindi prayer sung to a popular South African tune, *"Hum Honge Kamayaab Ek Din"* (translated as "We will overcome our difficulties, and be successful one day.") It was inspiring to bear witness to this expression of solidarity. These women had overcome considerable odds to fashion existences that gave them self-respect. They had overcome the burden of the onerous gender bias common in rural India and learned to supplement their husbands' incomes while raising children and working backbreaking hours in the fields. SEWA was clearly the catalyst behind a major social transformation.

Under the tree was a large blackboard on which was written the Gujarati alphabet. Each woman carried notebooks in which they had neatly written the letters and their names. These are the tools of the *jeevanshaala*, or "life university." Ami ben described its genesis in rural women's desire, which they had made abundantly clear to their educated SEWA counterparts, to learn practicalities, not abstractions. The *jeevanshaala* curriculum created in response to this need is divided into four categories—economy, environment, social security, and cultural context. In economy classes women learn about their role, as both producers and consumers, in the village economic system. Social security instruction includes long-term insurance, children's health, and personal savings. Since this group had never had to handle money and lived a subsistence existence, the idea of savings is hard to grasp. Some of them dedicate themselves to teaching others how to save, teaching *"bachat"* (Hindi for "savings"). One idea was to get the ladies to put aside 25 paise daily—a quarter of a rupee, or $0.006. This small amount was more manageable than saving Rupees 10 per month. Saving a little grain daily was easier to relate to than saving cash. Small interventions like that go a long way toward helping rural women improve their lives. Rita ben, a SEWA member from the village of Thala in the Surendranagar District, told me, "We are salt workers, and we work on salt pans. We were therefore unable to go to school. Having joined the *jeevanshaala* classes, we learned a lot of new things. We have now learned to read and write. We can go to *jeevanshaala* classes even when we are staying in the desert. There are a number of other women like me. I can now read letters and newspapers."[17]

Perhaps the word that I heard most frequently during the day was *himmat*, Hindi for "courage." The women told me they recognize that change is difficult and that it will be opposed by the social milieu within which they operate, but success has taught them the value of persistence. Their success may have an intergenerational impact as well. Ami ben told me that she could not think of a single woman who had attended *jeevanshaala* and still sent her children to work in the tobacco fields instead of to at least a rudimentary school. It was a simple illustration of the well-known finding in social science that the benefits of educating women spill over onto others in their environment.[18]

A woman sitting beside me carried a pouch of medicines containing aspirin, medications to treat the symptoms of flu, stomach relief medicines, and tablets to disinfect drinking water. As a "mobile doctor," she dispenses these to women in several villages. When I asked if she had received any training, the woman told me that she approached SEWA whenever she needed advice and they then arranged the requisite training. Even this rudimentary medical care is considerably more than what had existed before. The women described their reluctance to admit feeling unwell, even to the men in their families, and felt more comfortable obtaining simple medications from the mobile doctor. Another type of mobile doctor inspects the sanitary conditions of basic utensils in a handful of houses to ensure that they are not repositories of infection, providing a simple disinfectant when needed. SEWA has documented that these mobile doctors are remarkably effective in stopping the spread of malaria during floods.

By teaching women to repair a village water pump, SEWA has helped entire families to escape disease from unclean water. By teaching women to read and write, SEWA has helped them avoid exploitation from fraudulent legal documents. By showing women the value of saving less than one cent a day, SEWA has helped them gain some financial security. These practical lessons can propel women out of poverty and obscurity and into security and self-respect in their villages. Thus SEWA is helping to break the cycle of women being exploited by dominant men, especially moneylenders and landlords, and instilling in women the value of educating their children.

Categorizing Indians

While Mao was busy solidifying the rural–urban divide in China with policies such as the *hukou*, the founding fathers of India faced two gigantic tasks in 1947. The first was to create an economic plan that would lift almost a half billion villagers out of crushing poverty. The second was to create a political framework that would reflect India's heterogeneous society.

Unlike Mao's uncontested economic agendas, India had to accomplish these tasks in a democracy, which required adherence to parliamentary processes and preservation of private freedoms. Three stalwarts of the newly emerging nation clashed repeatedly on these issues: Nehru, India's first prime minister; Bhim Rao Ambedkar, the framer of the Indian Constitution; and Gandhi, the Father of the Nation.

On the question of economic and industrial policy, Gandhi and Nehru held opposing views. Nehru favored Soviet-style central planning and an emphasis on industrialization. Gandhi, who famously said "India lives in her villages," advocated rural and small-scale industrial development, with an emphasis on the nation's half million villages. He pushed for village-level governance, envisioning *gram swaraj* ("village republic") as the edifice of Indian democracy and development.

Ambedkar had no faith in the concept of *gram swaraj* because he believed that village-based governing bodies would fall prey to India's ancient caste system, which had perpetuated systemic social and economic discrimination for centuries. Ambedkar, himself from an underprivileged caste, had reason to be skeptical. The caste system, rooted in sacred Hindu texts dating back 2,500 years, prescribed a strict four-level hierarchy for Indian society. At the top were the Brahmins: the priests, teachers, and philosophers whose primary role was to be the trustees of education and religion, enclaves they guarded fiercely. One rank lower was the Kshatriya or warrior class, which included rajas, kings, and others primarily concerned with governance and defense. Next were the Vaisyas, the traders, responsible for agriculture and commerce. At the bottom were the Sudras, who served the upper three castes by undertaking menial functions. These four *varnas* ("categories") traditionally described the caste system. In reality, however, each *varna* contained thousands of *jatis* ("sects"). For instance, the Vaisyas could be subdivided into bankers, traders, brokers, and merchants. The *jatis* could be identified by language, vocation, or the deity they chose to worship. Outside the four-*varna* hierarchy were the Dalits, or untouchables, a group that included leather workers, poor farmers, and landless laborers.

Perhaps the most notable challenge to the caste system came from Buddhism, which professed that caste was irrelevant because a person's position in life depended on actions and not birth. Despite the fact that Buddhism was a predominant religion in India between the fourth and sixth centuries, the caste system survived. In fact, the caste system permeates Buddhism. As recently as the 1990s, a matrimonial in a daily newspaper invited an alliance with a "Buddhist (*Mahar*) girl." Ironically, the *Mahar* sub-caste had come to augment a girl's Buddhist identity.

Reformists within the British colonial administration also tried to change the social hierarchy by enacting affirmative action policies on the eve of independence in 1947. Nevertheless, the traditional Indian village continued to revolve around the hereditary caste system. In this context Ambedkar chastised Gandhi's vision of *gram swaraj*. In the Constituent Assembly on November 4, 1948, Ambedkar said, "[T]hese village republics have been the ruination of India. I am therefore surprised that those who condemn provincialism and communalism should come forward as champions of the village. What is the village but a sink of localism, a den of ignorance, narrow mindedness and communalism?"[19]

Prime Minister Nehru had to reconcile these realities of rural India with his vision of a sovereign, socialist, democratic India. How could a socialist society, whose very essence was equality, discriminate positively or negatively based on the ancient concept of caste? What role would caste play in modern democratic India? What would be the consequences of legislative affirmative action in a deeply caste-riddled society? Perhaps most importantly, would caste-based political representation translate into benefits for the marginalized sections of society?

Eventually the opposing sides struck a series of compromises regarding political inclusion. Independent India's constitution outlawed untouchability. But Ambedkar, the prime drafter of the constitution, saw to it that quotas were mandated in the Indian Parliament and in state-sector employment. *Panchayats*, the village-level mechanisms for self-government that Gandhi advocated and Ambedkar reviled, found a place in the so-called Directive Principles of the Indian Constitution. These principles are only guidelines and are not legally binding. Each state government attempted to ensure people's participation in governance by enacting statutes supporting the *panchayat raj* (rule by Panchayat). Unfortunately the state efforts only resulted in the emergence of self-styled, caste-based groups forming a parallel governance structure that denied the lower castes any hope of participation.

Like Mao, Nehru instituted an industrialization policy that focused on urban areas and central planning. Agriculture, the means of livelihood for most of the rural population, was neglected. As in China, neglect combined with a growing population to expose the shortcomings of India's economic plan. In the mid-1960s India came dangerously close to famine. The Malthusian threat—when population exceeds food production—seemed a real possibility in many villages facing food shortages.

The government's frantic attempts at food self-sufficiency culminated in the Green Revolution. From 1967 through 1978 the widespread use of imported high-yielding strains of wheat and rice, along with better irrigation and farm area expansion, resulted in massive improvements in agricultural productivity.[20] Economically the Green Revolution was a success. The northern Indian states of Punjab and Haryana especially benefited with incomes rising along with productivity.

The most significant political trend in this period was the rise of caste-based political parties, particularly in northern India. It was as if Nehru's worst dreams had come true. Caste, rather than being irrelevant in modern India's socialist democracy, was becoming a defining characteristic of its polity. In what was perhaps the greatest irony of Nehru's legacy, his own daughter became a master at "vote bank politics," a phrase used to describe the phenomenon of members of the same caste voting as a bloc for one candidate or party.

As one minister explained to me recently, "[E]veryone is after a special interest. In such an environment you are best off catering to the demands of, say, a 10 percent, an extreme fringe. If you can cater to that 10 percent, well, that will be enough to get you elected. So you don't serve the bulk of folks at all." This marginalization of the polity is exacerbated by caste-based special interests demanding their own quotas and reservations, and was phrased thusly by one of the parties:

"*Vote se lenge PM/CM, arakshan se SP/DM,*" or "*we*'ll take the offices of the Prime Minister and the Chief Minister through votes, we'll take through reservation the offices of the Superintendent of Police and the District Magistrate."[21]

The northern state of Uttar Pradesh (UP), which was home to Nehru and Indira Gandhi's electoral constituency, Amethi, illustrated the rising trend. In 1971 Indira Gandhi called for sudden national elections. She campaigned on a populist platform and her slogan, "*Garibi Hatao,*" or "Out with Poverty," was heard throughout the state. During her campaign she addressed India's poorest and most marginalized. The scheduled (lowest) castes, Muslim women, and the Dalits thus became her vote banks. Mrs. Gandhi won by a landslide that year. Caste politics had paid handsomely.

By 1980 Uttar Pradesh and Bihar, both populous northern states that sent large numbers of members to the Lok Sabha, had become battlegrounds for caste-courting politicians. Every politician asked: Who would get the Muslim vote? Who would win the Dalit vote? What about the Other Backward Classes (OBCs)? Even today anyone resting at a roadside truck stop or traveling by train through the rural parts of northern India is commonly asked, "*Kaun Jat Ho?*" ("What is your caste?") rather than "What is your name?"

In 2004, during the BJP's second term, the government unveiled a new television ad campaign featuring the slogan "India Shining." India's economy had grown about 7 percent over the last six years, and the BJP wanted to highlight its success. When Indians voted in May of that year, however, the results were shocking. The BJP suffered a massive electoral loss. No sooner had the polls closed than political pundits began to analyze the reason for the apparent upset. The ultimate conclusion was that all of rural India was disenchanted.

Although India had been shining for the upper and middle classes in urban and suburban areas, an agrarian crisis had been brewing. In the summer of 2002 rains had failed. With 70 percent of the population still making its living off the land, this spelled disaster. But a drought was not the only thing plaguing Indian agriculture. Years of neglect of agriculture compounded and magnified the problems. Even after the reforms capital formation in the sector had declined as a percentage of total domestic capital, from 6.8 percent in 1993–1994 to 5.5 percent in 1998–1999. But perhaps more importantly, public investment had declined.

The share of agricultural activities in the total outlay of all the five-year plans had declined from 6.1 percent in the Sixth Five-Year Plan to 4.4 percent in the Ninth Five-Year Plan. Further, irrigation and flood control received just 6.5 percent over the recent plan periods compared with 10 percent in earlier plans.[22] As a result, Indian agriculture suffered from a series of paradoxes. While food stocks grew in government storage facilities, millions of Indians continued to be threatened by malnutrition and starvation. Moreover, despite a system of input subsidies for agriculture and minimum support prices offered to farmers, the poorest farmers continued to be plagued by the inefficiencies of government-run agriculture procurement and distribution systems, synonymous with corruption and inefficiencies. Farmers, uninformed about urban business, are exploited by unscrupulous agents in the government *mandis*—the large open markets where farmers sell their goods but rarely receive just compensation or adequate distribution.

At the most basic level a fundamental difference between Chinese and Indian reforms is that the former focused on rural areas and the latter has not. In India's case the situation was even more tragic because the country had figured out a way to produce more grain. Successes like the Green Revolution in India were never accompanied by privatization of the purchase, sale, and marketing of farm produce. In continuing to rely on state-run procurement and distribution systems, grain did not get to those who needed it most.

Pinstripes in Indian Villages

SEWA-like self-help groups offer one way to circumvent restrictions imposed by caste. Despite its seven hundred thousand members, however, SEWA touches too few. An even brighter future lies in Indian corporations reaching out to farmers. Like civil society, and unlike politicians, corporate India is immune to the short-term temptations of pandering to caste-based divisions. In fact corporate business models are usually more inclusive. Companies want to get goods and services to as many people as possible rather than select based on caste or social criteria.

Indian Tobacco Company (ITC) is perhaps the most prominent example of corporate India's newfound enthusiasm for the village backwaters. ITC's chairman, Yogi Deveshwar, was recently featured on the cover of *India Today*—India's equivalent to *Time*. Although the photograph showed Deveshwar dressed in a suit and tie, the colorful turban wrapped around his head—the kind that protects millions of farmers from India's merciless noonday sun—and the heavy sickle resting on his shoulders conveyed the image of a man with a mission. The accompanying article outlined his plan, but the cover photo had already made the point: Deveshwar, head of a large private corporation, not a bureaucrat and not a politician, was ready to transform the untransformable—village India.[23]

Yogi, a nickname for Y. C. Deveshwar, is a Sanskrit word meaning one who has realized spiritual nirvana and is "all knowing." While this Yogi makes no such claim, he has experienced an epiphany: India's development is sustainable only if built on the solid economic foundation of stronger villages. Deng realized as much in China in 1978. On the surface, Deveshwar's village-focused development agenda sounds like "old wine in new bottles," similar to the vision Mahatma Gandhi articulated sixty years earlier. But Gandhi wanted the government to carry out his vision. Deveshwar sees no role for the government or politicians in his plan. He wants to use technology and commercial skill to bring rural India into the mainstream. Unlike many visionaries, Deveshwar has a workable prototype. Under his leadership ITC has created e-*choupals* (*choupal* means "meeting place" in Hindi). The idea is to put computers with Internet access in the heart of villages, thereby enabling farmers to exchange information on available produce.

The project unfolds like this. ITC chooses a location to establish its e-*choupal*, usually in a village where it has already been buying produce. Then ITC sets up an Internet-linked computer in an educated farmer's house; he is the *sanchalak*, the host farmer. Linked through telephone lines or satellite, a single e-*choupal* serves an average of six hundred farmers in villages within a three-mile radius. Any farmer can access daily crop prices and other information at no cost. The *sanchalak* is compensated by ITC with a fee on all e-*choupal* transactions. The average farmer is thus in a position to negotiate successfully with dealers and can completely avoid the disorganized, filthy, and often corrupt *mandis*. Farmers can also use e-*choupals* to order agricultural inputs like seeds, fertilizer, and even consumer goods from ITC or its partners, all at prices potentially lower than those available from village traders. During harvest time ITC offers to buy the crop directly from any farmer at the previous day's closing price, a price that the farmer is well aware of. If the deal is struck, the crop is transported to an ITC processing center, where it is weighed electronically and assessed for quality. The farmer is then paid the deal price for the crop and a transport fee. ITC also awards bonus points for crops with quality above the norm, exchangeable for ITC products.

By enabling the farmer to avoid the bureaucratic, cumbersome, and corrupt government procurement process, ITC had thoroughly transformed the lives of many farmers in rural India. By mid-2003 more than 1 million farmers in thousands of villages had used e-*choupals*, and the system was rapidly expanding. ITC then began to use this distribution channel for its other products. Today, Yogi has hired farmers and traditional middlemen in an attempt to touch every part of rural India with an e-*choupal*.

Deveshwar's model is largely immune to the socioeconomic hierarchies of rural India. Allegations that *sanchalaks* are usually members of the upper castes miss the point that the host farmers derive their incomes from administering as many e-*choupal* transactions as they can. They have incentives to include rather than exclude classes of farmers. In that sense Deveshwar's model for rural development has the potential to alter age-old inequities that so far have survived generations of would-be reformers—Gandhi's passion for change and the government's well-intended but poorly planned affirmative action schemes. Caste is simply irrelevant to corporate India, which has increasingly realized that money will be made by including the masses.

A Triumvirate of Government, Civil Society, and the Private Sector

In a sense, civil society and the private sector, rather than the government, have provided health, education, and sanitation to rural India. SEWA's and ITC's innovations are based on a simple but powerful idea, borrowed from the world of technology: the more participants a network has, the more powerful the network becomes. The e-*choupal* succeeds in proportion to the number of farmers using it for transactions and information. SEWA's *Karyakartas* (worker groups) need to be sufficiently large to offer the benefits of specialization and to form a credible lobby for change. This need for numbers means the inclusion of all social classes and castes.

There is a natural marriage of organizations like SEWA and ITC. Even the imagery works—*choupal*, or meeting places, often take place in villages under a large banyan tree. SEWA has partnered with several corporations. Gram Mahila Haat (Village Women's Market), a SEWA affiliate that provides marketing, management, and technical services to a large group of rural producers, was the group to consolidate produce for purchase by ITC. The women's market relied on a vast network of poor and women farmers that spanned fourteen districts and with whom strong social relationships had formed. At the same time ITC had established itself as a credible and clean produce buyer. The partnership gave SEWA members a better price and

ITC-quality produce. Of course, challenges arose. As one SEWA document on the partnership stated, "ITC found SEWA's work iterative and diverse. ITC had to learn to put poor women in the center, not only profits. SEWA had to learn to focus on systems that can sustain rapid growth. New agricultural produce is on the agenda for expansion."

The civil society–private sector symbiosis does not extend as easily to partnerships with the government. How large-scale reform can be accomplished without government involvement and initiative thus remains the unsolved question in development efforts in rural India. Reema Nanavaty, one of the main administrators of SEWA, explained why: "SEWA stands for and maintains its values of secularism, truth. It has a large membership base yet has remained apolitical; it is therefore perceived as a threat." She assured me that "SEWA has always partnered with the Government—State and National—to address the issue of poverty." But the government had not always reciprocated. Nanavaty once wrote to me to express distress at an ongoing dispute with the state government. Per Nanavaty, the government unexpectedly withdrew its earlier financial commitment to a relief effort, leaving SEWA holding the bag with sizeable incurred expenses. Poor women were forced to borrow at high interest rates to get by.

> I have no words to say how terrible I feel that I am returning from Mumbai to Ahmedabad without going to New York for the Clinton Global Initiative. A crisis has forced me to cancel my visit. For the past 6 months 12000 poor earthquake recovering women members of SEWA have not received any wages, which are withheld by our own Government of Gujarat under one reason or the other. Peaceful and constructive negotiations were reaching their end. The matter, very delicate for our members from various religions, has broken out in media tonight. We have no idea what tomorrow morning holds for us. I must join my colleagues in Ahmedabad to face it.[24]

SEWA, despite its good work, likely ran afoul of some vested interests. Of course vested interests are in rural China as well. Most indices of corruption, as produced by multilaterals like Transparency International, rate China and India as both quite corrupt. One significant difference, however, is that government officials in rural China have incentives to increase the size of the economic pie. Their skimming off the top does not detract from the fact that the resulting pie is still larger, for the most part, than it was in the prereform era. In India the skimming occurs without any value added by the Indian government. The private sector and civil society are left to fill the void.

The good news is that not all experiences of cooperation with the Indian government suffer an outcome as disastrous as that experienced by the earthquake victims in Gujarat. One person working successfully to narrow the gap between public and private entities is Vishal Sehgal, a former employee of ICICI's social initiative programs and an alumnus of the Kennedy School of Government, whom I first met when he was a student in my graduate class on emerging markets. I first noticed Sehgal trudging across the bridge that connects the Kennedy School with the Harvard Business School. What caught my attention was his shoulder bag. Rather than the black leather satchels or rugged backpacks in vogue on campus, Sehgal carried his books in a cloth bag I recognized as hand-crafted in India and usually worn as a distinguishing feature of the "uniform" of the socially conscious who work at places like SEWA. Its bright colors stood out in gray Cambridge in the same way as Sehgal's work stands out in India and at Harvard Business School. I couldn't help but think that the bridge he crossed was also a metaphor for the bridges he crosses between corporate Harvard Business School and the world of civil society.

During a class discussion one day, Sehgal brought to my attention the Mumbai-based nongovernmental organization he worked in, Pratham (a Hindi word meaning "first"). He explained it was created to help government spread primary education. One of Pratham's most successful programs is the Balwadi Pre-School Program, which targets children in the three- to five-year-old age group from the lowest-income families in urban cities. All instructors are volunteers, drawn from the community itself. The Balwadi program in Mumbai has been funded so far through corporate donations and funds provided by Indian residents in Houston, New York, and New Jersey. The government of India also provided a grant of Rs. 145 million ($360,000) for the work with children in the higher age group in 1999–2000.[25]

Sehgal explained Pratham's philosophy: "You can't ignore government; they are too big and have too much vested. Our goal is to make them more efficient. We can't create an entirely parallel system of education. The government invests millions of rupees in education, but we can use their money better and make their money go further." He added, "The idea behind Pratham's organization and vision was threefold; one, to work with government; two, to run it with private money and business management skills; and three, to have it be owned by civil society."[26] ICICI has helped expand Pratham's activities to thirteen states in India, raising funds from local governments, local citizens, and businesses. Pratham's network is also used to provide basic health and computer education. In 2000 the Global Development Network Award, sponsored by the World Bank and the government of Japan, was awarded to Pratham, recognizing it as one of the three "most innovative development projects."

As Sehgal put it, "The key is to avoid a turf war with the government, and to create checks and balances to make their work more efficient."

Hukou and Caste Today

Shaadi.com is an online matchmaker for young Indians, the modern ana-logue to Brahmin seers and family matriarchs of yore. The Web site, like others of its type, serves as an electronic clearinghouse for young singles whose profiles are posted by Internet-savvy parents or concerned friends and siblings. Not surprisingly an "advanced search" for a potential partner brings up a section titled "Religious and Social Background," in which caste details are commonly posted.

Shaadi.com is a good reality check on the lingering importance of caste, evidence that it remains part of daily life in India, even in sophisticated urban India. Even though India's recent president, K. R. Narayanan, is a Dalit, an untouchable, caste remains not just symbolically important in village India but a defining factor in economic existence.

In China the importance of the *hukou* is waning, especially for educated persons among the Chinese working population. But the *hukou* is a symbol of the party's authority, an authority that remains largely unchallenged despite being tested by the legacy of economic decentralization and by Beijing's lack of information about rural China.

Unlike India's caste-based special interests, the Chinese government is not beholden to any special interests other than its own. Disillusionment with income inequality has led to simmering protests in rural China, forcing the CCP to align its interests with those outside the eastern seaboard and the southern Pearl River Delta, the focus of most economic growth in past decades. For example, the recently completed railway line to Lhasa, capital of Tibet, will likely bring economic development to the province, presumably an attempt to buy the allegiance of young Tibetans. It is likely that the railway will smother Tibetan culture. But it is also unsurprising. China's state-led physical infrastructure development contrasts with India's ground-up approach.

Chapter Ten

Barefoot Doctors and Medical Tourists

Futile Attempts to Confront the Grim Reaper

Outside the former capital city of Kazakhstan is a region considered the birthplace of the apple. Botanists are currently investigating wild apple trees in the area's remote forests to find varieties highly resistant to disease. In fact the previous name of the old capital, Alma-Ata (now Almaty), translates to "father of the apple."

Botanists are not the only researchers in Alma-Ata. In September 1978 Alma-Ata hosted an international health conference attended by 134 countries and 67 international organizations. Out of that conference came the Declaration of Alma-Ata, which stated, "Governments have a responsibility for the health of their people" to a "level of health that will permit them to lead a socially and economically productive life." Conference participants pledged a commitment to primary health care that was reiterated in the slogan "Health for all by the year 2000."[1]

Nearly thirty years later the goals of the Alma-Ata health conference are still woefully out of reach in China and India. Atul Gawande, a surgeon at Brigham and Women's Hospital in Boston, describes a public hospital in his ancestral town, Nanded, four hundred miles east of Mumbai: "The examining rooms are ovens in the heat of the summer. The paint flakes off the wall in jagged strips. The sinks are stained brown and the faucets don't work. Each room has a metal desk, some chairs, a whirring ceiling fan,

213

torn squares of paper under a stone for writing prescriptions, and a crowd of four, six, sometimes eight patients jockeying for attention. Examinations take place behind a thin rag curtain with gaping holes in it." Doctors laboring in these conditions must care for a couple of hundred people each day, many of whom demand surgical attention, and the wards are packed to capacity.[2]

By Indian standards, public hospitals in China are reasonably well functioning. They are clean, free of crowds, and well run. But as of 2003 some 80 percent of China's rural population—roughly 640 million people—still lack health insurance. In a ranking of 191 member nations on the overall health of their populations, the World Health Organization's 2000 report ranked China 81st and India 134th. In terms of equitable distribution of health, the same report ranked China 101st and India 153rd.[3] Although India has a number of charismatic individuals whose work in private-sector entrepreneurship is heartening, India's public-sector health failure, which is far more prevalent, is absolutely heart-wrenching.

To complicate the picture, India has begun to offer world-class health care to those who can afford it, including foreigners from the West. When Europeans and Americans fly to India for complicated, highly skilled surgeries that cost a fraction of what the procedures would cost at home, they receive not only a mended heart or hip but also a revised image of India. No longer can these Westerners hold onto the stereotype of India as a poverty-stricken, cow-populated country. Medical tourism is changing Westerners' ideas about the meaning of what Kipling termed the "white man's burden."

Mother Teresa's Heart Surgeon

Dr. Devi Shetty cuts a smart figure. His crisply starched shirt, Wall Street–like suspenders, gleaming black shoes, and stately Mercedes seem out of place on the dusty road out of Bangalore. During the drive to his hospital, Narayana Hrudayalaya ("God's compassionate hospital" in Sanskrit), Dr. Shetty spent the entire hour describing to me his vision for improving the health of the world's poor, what he called the "Wal-Martization" of health care. Like the worldwide retail behemoth, Dr. Shetty aims to radically cut the cost of delivering his product, health care, and then plans to offer lower-priced services to hundreds of millions of consumers. Dr. Shetty's idea is to drive down the cost of health care so dramatically that it will become an accessible commodity to all. "Look," he said, pointing in the direction of the neighboring Electronic City and Infosys, one of India's leading software services firm, "they are world class because their quality keeps going up as their costs decrease. Health care is a peculiar beast—in spite of all the new technology, costs keep going up.

That is a strange paradox. We are out to buck that trend. We cannot afford to let the masses be deprived of top-class tertiary care."

As a skeptical academic, I immediately pepper him with questions. How do the success rates of his procedures compare to those of hospitals in the West? How much have per-procedure costs actually fallen at his hospital? Has the hospital managed to attract more surgeons who share his vision? He has all sorts of answers and is armed with fistfuls of paper with data and tables, but also says to me, "Most of the things worth doing in the world were declared impossible before they were done." It is hard not to be taken in by the charismatic heart surgeon's enthusiasm.

When we walked in the front door of the hospital, Dr. Shetty was mobbed by patients and their families, mostly indigent and all grateful not to be turned away from a state-of-the-art hospital they normally could not have afforded. He related to each person with warmth, listening to individual tribulations, making it seem as if he had infinite time. Inside the main entrance I was surprised to find a section of windows devoted to obtaining visas, much like those found in government offices. Seemingly out of place in a hospital in South India, far from any borders, this service is part of patient outreach. Dr. Shetty explained, "We have set up a system so that we are informed immediately if there is a person in Pakistan needing treatment, so that we can expedite the visa-related paperwork to get the patient to us." India and Pakistan have been unfriendly neighbors during the past few decades, complicating the process of obtaining a visa. Dr. Shetty, who treated a young Pakistani girl some years ago free of charge, possibly did more to warm the collective hearts of the dueling nations than a decade of efforts by hardened diplomats.

Dr. Shetty pointed out another feature of the hospital's patient outreach: a circular chapel just outside the main entrance. He described it as divided into four equal and independent quadrants, each a place of prayer and meditation for the four main religious faiths of its patient population: Hindus, Muslims, Christians, and Sikhs. To symbolize the unity of human faith, the four quadrants converge at the center of the chapel.

When we reached the doctor's office, an elderly man, old enough to be Dr. Shetty's father, staggered into the room, supported by his son, and fell, with great difficulty, at the doctor's feet. In India touching a person's feet is a gesture of respect, reserved for very close elderly friends or relations or for exalted leaders. The old man made the gesture partly in recognition of Dr. Shetty's skill as a surgeon but more so in response to the power of the doctor's compassion.

Dr. Shetty began his surgical training at a hospital in the small town of Mangalore and completed it with six years at Guy's Hospital in London.

Then he returned to India, to a hospital in Calcutta, where he cared for Mother Teresa, the Albanian-born nun who won the Nobel Peace Prize and was canonized as a saint by the Catholic Church. "I believe she is singularly responsible for much that I have achieved," Dr. Shetty told me. "Somehow, even though I am a scientist and do not expect to find God, meeting her was almost like an encounter with the divine."

In Calcutta, where Dr. Shetty first heard "the call" to service, he founded a heart hospital and a heart foundation. But few would have imagined he would go on to set up one of the best pediatric cardiac surgery units in the world in Bangalore—on his own and without state assistance—let alone provide full-service cardiac care at a fraction of the prices seen in the West. The prices of conventional surgeries at Narayana Hrudayalaya are significantly lower compared with prices not only in the developed world but also in India's other leading private hospitals. As Dr. Shetty was quick to point out, "Our performance numbers are as good as the best. We have better metrics than the hospitals in the state of New York, and interns from all over the world have started to come to learn from the techniques we are developing."

How is this possible? How can a state-of-the-art hospital in a dusty suburb of Bangalore provide world-class care, operate at a fraction of the cost of similarly equipped hospitals, and charge patients nothing? Over the years, I have spent many hours discussing these questions with Dr. Shetty, usually in his office, where he wears his hospital uniform—green surgical scrubs—and where we are shielded from the din of traffic. In India traffic is very, very noisy. Drivers lean on car horns so excessively that nobody pays attention to the incessant blaring of horns. Inside Dr. Shetty's office, the peace and quiet allows us to think clearly and listen well, an opportunity as rare as the hospital he has built.

Several factors make Dr. Shetty's compassionate care possible. The high rate of congenital heart disease among Indians, combined with a large and chronically underserved population, attracts a steady stream of cardiac surgeons to Narayana Hrudayalaya. Relentless practice in operating on thousands of patients has radically reduced the unit cost of procedures. "The kinds of advanced procedures that I performed a few times a month in the West I often do several times a day here," said Dr. Shetty. His team consists of doctors and surgeons of Indian origin who have experience operating in North America, Europe, or the upscale hospitals of the oil-rich Middle East. Their relatively low salaries are partly compensated for by India's low cost of living and, more importantly, by the comfort of raising their families in the cultural familiarity of their homeland.

A rigorous system at Narayana Hrudayalaya controls finances. Every patient receives the same quality of basic care, although wealthier patients have the option of paying for comforts like private rooms. Those paying higher prices subsidize those who cannot. The cash balances are monitored to ensure that a viable balance is maintained between subsidizers and subsidized. Patients undergo discretionary procedures when they need urgent care and have the resources to pay for that care. The net result of focusing on patient flow is that, for the most part, the poor are not turned away. When they might have been turned away, some background foundations cover the cost. Dr. Shetty's version of charity is business centered, relying on almost no subsidy. The hospital's continual expansion—a floor with the latest equipment is added each year—is financed from internally generated cash. The result is a high-quality specialty hospital, not an organization providing Band-Aid care to a waiting room full of modestly dressed people. The equipment is state-of-the art, often very expensive. "I do not want people to say that the poor are not deserving of high-quality care," Dr. Shetty told me.

Several years ago members of a local milk cooperative asked for his help in getting health care for their families. Dr. Shetty realized that this was an opportunity to assist a large, organized group of middle- to low-income people who had long been unable to access the care they needed. In 2002 he conceived and convinced the Karnataka state government to launch Yeshasvini, a health insurance policy for 1.7 million farmers and their families that became operational in 2003. All farmers who are members of any state cooperative for at least six months are eligible to participate, regardless of their medical histories. For the equivalent of about eleven cents a month, cardholders have access to free treatment at four hundred hospitals in twenty-nine districts of the state for any medical procedure costing up to Rs. 100,000 ($2,200). The government contributes 50 percent of farmers' contributions. Among the range of treatments available is cardiac care at Narayana Hrudayalaya. The beauty of the scheme is that it capitalizes on the glut of hospitals built as a result of past skewed incentives by the state government.

Dr. Shetty insisted I accompany him on his daily visit to Narayana Hrudayalaya's telemedicine facility, where technology is used to provide basic cardiac care to underserved rural populations. He explained, "If a patient with chest pains walks in to see a general practitioner, the only available doctor in the rural area, the doctor usually thinks it is indigestion, so he'll be given an antacid and sent home. Twenty-four hours later the heart fails and it may be too late." Nine coronary care units (CCUs) were set up across India, each equipped with beds, medication, computers, electrocardiogram (ECG) machines, videoconferencing devices, and technical staff trained to operate the equipment. When a patient visits a CCU the doctor on duty first takes an ECG, which is transmitted to a specialist at Narayana Hrudayalaya or at the hospital in Calcutta that Dr. Shetty founded. A software program allows

ECG images to be scanned and transmitted via an Internet connection. With the patient and doctor on the screen, the heart specialist diagnoses the condition and advises the doctor on the appropriate treatment, including arranging for a potential transfer to a major hospital. In very remote areas without videoconferencing facilities, a network of about a hundred family physicians can still use the software to transmit ECG images for diagnoses at Narayana Hrudayalaya.

Dr. Shetty observed, "Whenever it is the man in the household with the cardiac problem, I always find that it is better to talk to the woman who accompanies him. The women run the show when it comes to health issues. The man cannot process the gravity of the problem and will either deny it or fall apart in despair." It's just this sort of sensitivity to the social fabric that is key to the doctor's success. By comparison, it is fair to say that most of corporate India does not recognize the woman's prominent role in supporting the Indian family.

Before our visit came to an end, Dr. Shetty, looking a full decade younger than his fifty years, lay out his outlook for the future. "My vision is to create a new health care economic model, and within a radius of several miles, we want to create a Health City with a capacity of five thousand beds and treatment for everything—oncology, ophthalmology, neurology, nephrology, orthopedics—with Narayana Hrudayalaya serving as the backbone hospital." He smiled, as if to assure me that this grand task was well within his grasp, and offered this rationale: "We have reached a plateau in cost reduction by increasing our volume of surgeries. The yearly increase in procedures is now small, but our resources are still underutilized—our machines, sterilization department, blood bank, et cetera can be used by other hospitals within Health City, and this will drive unit costs even lower."

Just two years later when I returned to visit with Dr. Shetty, development of Health City had already begun, with two specialty units completed—one for ophthalmology and the other for orthopedics—and ground being broken for a few other specialties as well. In 2006 the World Economic Forum recognized Dr. Shetty as its social entrepreneur of the year. The doctor did not travel to the Swiss resort town of Davos to receive his award, however; he was too busy performing surgeries and building hospitals in Bangalore.

Indian Health's Broken Promises, Mismanagement, and Weak Political Will

Private-sector entrepreneurship like Devi Shetty's is an exception amid India's public-sector health failure, where basic care for the rural poor is either nonexistent, unaffordable, substandard, or all three. Tragically, independent

India's health care story is one of broken promises, weak political will, and mismanagement of already meager resources. I spoke about these issues at length with sociologist Ravi Duggal, a coordinator for the health research and advocacy group the Center for Enquiry into Health and Allied Themes (CEHAT). The acronym sounds like the Hindi word for "health."[4]

In 1946, shortly after independence, the government issued a report from the Bhore Committee, which had been established in 1943 to analyze and make recommendations on India's public health system. The report emphasized India's need for preventive medicine and universal health care, lauded mass mobilization, and reaffirmed the government's faith in Primary Health Centers (PHCs) as the cornerstone of rural health care. The report recommended establishing one PHC for each population group of ten thousand to twenty thousand, each with seventy-five beds, six doctors, six public health nurses, and one bed for every 175 people in the population. Influenced by Nehru, who was enamored of Western science, the Bhore Committee did not envision a role for traditional Indian medicine.

Duggal told me, "The Bhore report was a fairly comprehensive and good plan. Basically, Bhore had recommended that some 2 percent of GDP be spent on health, which was about 15 percent of government expenditure. As a percentage of national income, this was not that much. It was also clear that the Bhore report was influenced by the Soviet system but also drew from Britain's National Health System."

The Bhore Committee's vision remained only a vision. Resources and political will did not buttress it. According to Duggal, "There were ominous signs from the beginning. At the first health ministers' conference in 1948, the ministers stated that the states simply did not have the money to implement Bhore's proposals." The Congress Party government implemented a diluted version of the committee's recommendations, spending just 5 percent of government revenues on health as opposed to the recommended 15 percent. Further, rather than creating a comprehensive national policy, the provision of health care was absorbed into Soviet-style five-year plans.[5]

"Other problems emerged through the 1970s," said Duggal. "The central government funded nationwide programs to eradicate particular diseases— TB, malaria, smallpox. But these detracted, rather than complemented, basic health care because there was no comprehensive plan. Today diseases like malaria and TB have returned." Policy makers paid attention to PHCs only when doing so advanced their political agendas.

Duggal continued, "The biggest problem, which surfaced in the 1960s but really gained momentum in the 1970s, was the fact that the Indian state became obsessed with family planning, believing that all society's ills were due to overpopulation. They began implementing family-planning quotas."

He added that this ideological and program shift was most damaging to the PHCs, which were driven away from their initial mandate of providing basic primary health care to achieving family-planning targets. As health officials scrambled to meet population targets, eventually embarking on forced sterilization campaigns, PHCs came to be seen solely as family planning centers. "This policy completely discredited the PHC and ruined its image in the rural areas," commented Duggal. "The first question on a registration slip at the PHC would ask whether or not you were sterilized or whether you were using any other type of contraception."

As a final blow the state governments, not the central government, were delegated the primary responsibility for health care. States and districts with the poorest health status also tended to have the poorest health infrastructures. Moreover, states did not focus on preventive care but were constantly playing catch-up by focusing on curative care.

Not until 1978, at the Alma-Ata health conference, was the inability of the Indian bureaucracy to create a viable health care system finally exposed. India was jolted into action. Duggal noted, "So in 1983, some three decades after independence, Indians prepared their first national health policy."

Duggal refers to the years following the 1978 Alma-Ata "health care for all" pledge as the "golden age of public health in India." When Indira Gandhi was reelected prime minister in 1981, she realized a focus on rural areas was essential. The Minimum Needs Program was revived.

Duggal continued, "In Maharashtra, for instance, there was actually one PHC for a population group of thirty thousand. This was as close as we had ever been to the Bhore ratios, and this soon happened in other states. Furthermore, if one were to analyze health-spending data, one can see that as a percentage of GDP, the numbers peaked through the 1980s. Mortality rates fell, life expectancy increased, rural and urban disparity fell."

The 1983 policy created two additional categories of health care units. Subcenters, with one trained female and one trained male health care worker per five thousand persons, would be supervised by the PHC. Also created were community health centers (CHCs), essentially upgraded PHCs. Each CHC, equipped with thirty beds, was intended to serve 80,000 to 120,000 persons and operate as a referral center for up to four PHCs.

A decade later, however, India was no closer to universal coverage. For example, in Bihar, Orissa, and Punjab the proportion of villages with subcenters was as low as 5 percent; and less than 30 percent of villages had access to primary health care centers or hospitals in Bihar, Gujarat, and Madhya Pradesh.[6]

Studies have shown that most PHCs, which were still meant to be a first line of defense against illness among rural Indians, continued to lack essential medical equipment. This was especially true in the poorer states.

Fewer than 20 percent of PHCs had the equipment required to medically terminate a pregnancy. Most lacked essential drugs: only 15 percent had stocks of iron and folic acid tablets, 56 percent had contraceptives, and 61 percent had vaccines.[7]

In 2000, the year in which health care for all was supposed to have been established, expenditures on health in India, both public and private, totaled 4.9 percent of GDP. Only 1 percent was government money; the rest came from private pockets. Thus the government was spending $4 annually on health care for each Indian. The infant mortality rate was 68 per 1,000 live births, and the maternal mortality rate of 407 Indian women per 100,000 live births was one of the highest in the world, higher than many sub-Saharan African countries.[8]

By 2000 it had also become clear that the failure of India's health care system was attributed not only to an absolute lack of monetary investment in health infrastructure but also to bad governance and nonaccountability. As evidence, a World Bank study titled "Missing in Action: Teacher and Health Worker Absence in Developing Countries" highlighted what rural Indians had been complaining about for years. Health care workers were nowhere to be found. India's absenteeism rate was 40 percent, worse than in eight other developing countries. Villagers traveling miles to a clinic could not count on a clinician being there to care for them.[9]

The rural population was driven to seek help from the private sector. Unlike in China, private health services in India had continued to coexist with public health care from the outset, and over time they became the predominant health care sector. By the mid-1980s more than 80 percent of rural Indians used the private sector for outpatient services as a first line of treatment in both urban and rural areas.

The rural private services, unlike their flashy counterparts in urban India, were shockingly inadequate. Unregulated, they allowed a plethora of undertrained doctors and nurses to begin filling the gap. For an Indian living in poverty, the average amount spent on private health care was more than 200 percent of annual per capita consumption expenditure.[10] As a result many households fell into debt, which in turn prevented reinvestment in their livelihoods and in educating their children, perpetuating a cycle of dependence.

In cities, private-sector health care was characterized by waste and erroneous diagnoses. Duggal pointed out that World Health Organization guidelines state that no more than 15 percent of births in a population should be by cesarean section. In one study in Chennai, private hospitals had a cesarean section rate of 50 percent compared with the rate in public hospitals of 10 percent. He further noted, "Private health care has been around forever. The state has subsidized it in at least two ways. The first is by way of the ridiculously cheap medical education provided by the state. In the 1990s the state spent some 2 million rupees [$50,000] per year to train a doctor and the student pays just 6,000 rupees [$150] a year, and most of them go into private practice; there is no social benefit at all. Second, the state subsidizes drugs, but here there was a social benefit because of price controls and some accountability with the state requiring pharmaceutical companies to keep prices low."

These are the kinds of dispiriting and disastrous statistics that make Devi Shetty's practice of first-rate medical care in a sound business model as extraordinary as it is exemplary.

Chinese Health's Clean Beds but Misaligned Price Caps

In 2005 I visited the third-largest hospital in Henan, one of China's poorer provinces with a population exceeding a hundred million. The locals were proud of the comprehensive-care provincial hospital, which appeared well run and far superior to the public hospitals I had seen in India. The entrance was sparkling clean and was not overrun by people. I was intrigued by a rather imposing electronic bulletin board. Continually scrolling were descriptions of an array of detailed medical procedures—from the very mundane to the fairly complex—with the price for each procedure clearly indicated.

Close to the hospital entrance were color photographs of all the physicians in the hospital, with their names, ranks, and specialties clearly specified. I was told that a routine consultation cost less than two yuan (roughly twenty-five cents), but at that price the sick person could not choose a physician. For a few more yuan a person could choose to wait for a particular physician. The stars, the doctors who held the rank of professor, were the most expensive. The information available in the hospital lobby made it quite clear what a visit with each health provider would cost and that the doctor would keep 40 percent of the consultation fee. Given this level of transparency—more than what one might see in even the best Boston hospitals—I surmised that using bribery to gain access to a popular physician was difficult.

Near one of the hospital's side entrances were several clearly marked counters where blood work and other laboratory tests were performed. A nurse sat at one counter offering to take blood pressure and temperature readings for free. At a series of windows people could pay for treatments using various payment options, and at another window families could get information about patients.

I peered into as many rooms in the hospital as my hosts allowed me to without being overly intrusive. The rooms were clean, sometimes a bit rundown, but not dingy. Beds were made up with sheets that looked old and gray but not soiled. Most rooms contained three beds. A person could pay more to get a private room if one was available, though priority was often given to patients with the most serious conditions. I noticed quite a few patients resting on beds in the hallways, presumably as a result of overcrowding—a situation I was told was quite normal. Finally, there was a sunshine room in the corner where patients could play cards or watch television.

A corner of the first floor housed two pharmacies; one dispensed Western medicines and the other traditional Chinese medicines. The latter contained dozens of dark-red wood shelves, each containing a single kind of herb; pharmacy assistants used Chinese balances to mix the herbs in the prescribed proportions and wrapped them in coarse, yellow straw paper. Both pharmacies were equally busy. Although private pharmacies operating outside the hospital system do exist, the ones in the hospital enjoy substantial business, and most reputable pharmacists stay within the hospital system.

Traditional Chinese medicine (TCM) still plays a very important role in China. The dual pharmacy structure is common in hospitals. Most Chinese traditional medicines are herbs, although some mineral and animal products are prescribed. The basics of TCM diagnostics are to observe (*wang*), hear and smell (*wen*), ask about background (*wèn*), and read the pulse (*qie*). I accompanied my Chinese colleague to a TCM clinic. The doctor felt his wrist for his pulse, observed the color of his tongue, and then prescribed an herb for him to take home and steep in water in a special ceramic pot. The cooking time depended on the formula but generally would be about a half hour. He would then filter the liquid before drinking it and follow it with a lump of sugar to counteract its bitterness.

I also visited a local hospital in the vicinity, much smaller than the provincial hospital. There were dirty mops lying around in the corridors, and some unused wards were in disarray. The bathrooms were filthy, similar to those in Indian public hospitals. Nevertheless, the organization of the local hospital appeared similar to that of the provincial hospital. Photographs of the doctors were clearly displayed with their qualifications and fees, the windows and counters were appropriately staffed, and the pharmacies did brisk business.

That night I had dinner with a handful of local medical doctors. When I told them that the health care system I observed in China seemed to provide services superior to those available in India's public-sector hospitals, my Chinese hosts replied that public health care in China currently is far inferior to what it once was. Mostly the physicians regretted that more than half their income was based on the procedures they recommended and on kickbacks they received from the prescriptions they directed to the hospital pharmacy. Although they acknowledged that the compensation scheme compromised medical care, attempting to change it was beyond their control. They knew that the resulting price inflation meant that they had to turn patients away, but it also helped them line their pockets.

Another result of this system is that patients feel disconnected from and distrustful of their doctors. My student at Harvard, Noah Friedman, a Mandarin-speaking Sinophile, who spent the summer of 2005 in China researching Chinese hospital practices for a medical device company reported to me, "It is alarming to see that patients in China simply do not trust their doctors. At the crux of this disconnect are misaligned incentives. Doctors get paid on the basis of number of procedures performed and medicines dispensed, and patients want to limit interaction." Friedman added, "In the twenty-five hospitals that I visited, most doctors reported disputes with patients and in several, I actually witnessed protests by patients against their doctors' conduct."[11] A term *yi nao* (litarally "medical fuss") is used in connection with such disputes. Professional protestors hired by aggrieved families, even police stationed for staff protection, are now part of some hospital settings.

Government-set price caps on routine exams, surgeries, and basic prescriptions have led many physicians to favor procedures on which prices are not capped—notably, new technologies and drugs. For example, the rate of births by cesarean section in 1978, before China unleashed its health care reforms, was 10 percent. After reforms an average of 50 percent of babies born in Chinese hospitals were delivered by cesarean section, and in some hospitals the figure was as high as 70 percent. The reason was simple: the billable rate for cesarean births was much higher than that for natural births.[12]

Yet once upon a time China provided accessible and free health care for almost all rural Chinese, and the urban population enjoyed health benefits that were directly linked to their employment status at their *danwei* (work unit). At the 1978 Alma-Ata international conference, China's health care system was celebrated as a model for the developing world.[13] But the central government's "marketization," reforms introduced after 1978, eventually made health care inaccessible to the average Chinese. By 2003 about 80 percent of China's rural population—some 640 million people—lacked health insurance. A report published in 2005 by China's Development Research Center of the State Council stated that the "business- and market-orientation" of the Chinese health system was "absolutely wrong" and conflicted with the proper goal of public health.[14]

Barefoot but Healthy

Mao did not inherit a healthy China. For his revolution to succeed, however, it was imperative that the peasant and worker be healthy. Health was also a natural extension of the services that Mao's regime had taken upon itself to provide—employment, food, education, and other social services.

At the First National Health Congress, held in 1950 in Beijing, Mao declared four basic guidelines that were to form the basis of the health care system: medicine should serve the workers, peasants and soldiers; preventive medicine should take precedence over therapeutic medicine; traditional Chinese medicine should be integrated with Western scientific medicine; and health work should be combined with mass movements.[15] These guidelines established health as an inseparable part of the communist rhetoric.

Two structures were established to provide medical services, one rural and the other urban. There were three layers of medical services for the rural population. The first tier was made up of Mao's "barefoot doctors," a term that originated in 1965 at the Chiangchen People's Commune on the outskirts of Shanghai. There a team of urban medical workers began providing medical services in rural areas and training young peasants to function as barefoot doctors (chijiao yisheng). Part-peasant, part-doctor, these individuals trained for three to six months, studying both Western and traditional Chinese medicine. Women barefoot doctors learned midwifery, maternal care, child care, and family planning. The slogan of this crucial first tier of medical services was "Prevention first." Above the barefoot doctors were the township health centers, which served primarily as outpatient clinics, each serving between ten thousand and thirty thousand people. Assistant doctors who were chosen from the medical staff but did not hold formal medical degrees, manned the clinics. Finally, only the most seriously ill patients were referred to the third and final tier, which were the county hospitals that served two hundred thousand to six hundred thousand people each and were staffed by senior doctors who held degrees from five-year medical schools.

Urban health care had a similar three-tier system consisting of hospitals at the street (subdistrict), district, and municipal levels. Two government-sponsored health insurance schemes covered almost all urban Chinese: the Government Insurance Scheme (GIS) covered government employees, retirees, disabled veterans, and university teachers, staff, and students; and the Labor Insurance Scheme (LIS) covered state enterprise employees, retirees, and their dependents. The GIS was financed by government budgets, and LIS coverage was financed by funds from state enterprises. In addition, the government subsidized about 50 percent to 60 percent of public hospital's recurrent costs, based on what was required to pay the salaries of health care personnel. The remaining revenue came from fee-for-service activities under a government-controlled price schedule.[16]

Each urban danwei issued an insurance card to its workers that was usually good at one hospital for free service and free prescription drugs. In addition, all hospital emergency rooms were open to everyone on a fee-for-service basis. Finally, in addition to the three-tiered hospitals, neighborhood health stations were set up under each neighborhood committee and manned by trained health workers.

Thus, between the urban and rural three-tiered systems, Mao covered almost the entire population by the early 1950s. By the mid-1960s, the groundwork for the Cultural Revolution had begun, and one area on which Mao focused his new agenda was health. In imperial style Mao stated his directive on training the health workers China so desperately needed:

Medical education should be reformed. There's no need to read so many books . . . In medical education there is no need to accept only higher middle school graduates or lower middle school graduates. It will be enough to give three years to graduate from higher primary schools. They would then study and raise their standards mainly through practice. If this kind of doctor is sent down to the countryside, even if they haven't much talent, they would be better than quacks and witch doctors and the villages could better afford to keep them. The more books one reads the more stupid one gets . . . In medical and health work put the emphasis on the countryside.[17]

This belief resulted in a steady transfer of authority from the Ministry of Health—the urban-biased and Western-educated Weishengbu—to the Nine-Man Sub-Committee, an organization originally set up to carry out the mass health promotions. Health directives were now issued directly by Mao or Zhou Enlai, a member of Mao's inner circle at the time. No new students were admitted to medical schools between 1966 and 1970. Instead, Mao emphasized training part-time health workers, like the barefoot doctors in the countryside as well as the "Red medical workers" (*hongyi*) in the urban neighborhoods.

Eventually, when the medical schools reopened in 1970, standard entrance examinations were abolished, and the curriculum was reduced to three years in all medical universities, with training emphasizing practice rather than theory.[18] As part of a larger *xiafang*—the movement to send intellectuals to rural areas—urban and Western-trained doctors were sent to live and work in the countryside to train the barefoot doctors. To a large extent, Mao's universal health care regime succeeded. The so-called Cooperative Medical System (CMS) at its peak covered 90 percent of China's rural population.[19] By the time of Mao's death, the life expectancy in China had reached 65 years.[20]

The economic reforms, which began in 1978, destroyed Mao's health care system. The CMS, anchored in the commune, also collapsed. Barefoot doctors suddenly became private providers, asking for fees in the unregulated new economy. Nothing stopped them from providing services for which they were completely unqualified. Further, in September 1980 the State Council approved the Health Ministry's request to permit private practice, which had been phased out during the Cultural Revolution (1966–1976). Private clinics flourished in the countryside and by 1985 replaced collectively run health stations as the dominant health institutions at the village level. Even township health centers and country hospitals were forced to embrace fee-based services. Eventually the cost of an average hospitalization exceeded the average annual income of 50 percent of the rural population (480 million people).[21] Because hospitals remained mostly state owned, these changes did not lead to privatization but were referred to as marketization

As early as 1992 the State Council began an attempt to reintroduce the CMS. In 1994, in conjunction with the World Health Organization, the council started rural health insurance pilots in fourteen counties, aiming to tap into local collective risk sharing. Most of these efforts, and the even more aggressive ones made later, failed despite strong central government ideological support.[22] In 1993 less than 10 percent of the rural population had any health insurance.[23]

By 2000, the year in which signatories at Alma-Ata had promised health care for all, China and India faced health crises. In both countries most of the population lacked access to affordable health care.

The New Challenge: The Specter of HIV and AIDS

In 2005 over 5 million Indians were infected with HIV, more than in any other nation other than South Africa. In China the rate of infection is much less clear. Recent estimates range upward from 650,000, but many experts believe the real number is much higher.[24] Because AIDS often snatches people at the peak of their productive years, leaving behind destitute families who enter a cycle of poverty and high-risk behavior, the disease has the potential to derail national growth. New Delhi's National Council of Applied Economic Research (NCAER) warned in 2006 that HIV and AIDS could knock a percentage point off India's average annual rate of population growth. The RAND Institute in California similarly suggested that the disease could cost China between 1.8 and 2.2 percentage points of growth.[25]

Until recently, when it came to HIV and AIDS, China and India behaved like the proverbial ostriches sticking their heads in the sand. Although this attitude has been officially replaced by an energized central government in Beijing, famously symbolized by Premier Wen Jiabao's public clasp of an infected patient's hands in 2005, the change in attitude has not yet been matched by enthusiasm at the local government level. In India the government's efforts are too little, too late, and civil society is trying in vain to fill the gap.

Gang Song, a young thirty-something, worked on an AIDS education project in the Liangshan Yi Autonomous Prefecture of the southwestern province of Sichuan. When I met him he had completed a stint with Médecin Sans Frontières (MSF; Doctors Without Borders) and subsequently worked for the United Nations Development Program in Beijing. The MSF project Gang worked on primarily involved AIDS-related education and advocacy. Despite obtaining permission from the prefecture government, however, Gang and his colleagues found it very hard to get cooperation at the local level. Local officials denied the existence of a problem. Admitting to widespread illness and the resulting social breakdown would not endear them to their provincial and central superiors.

Opposition manifested itself in many ways. First the local authorities refused to grant the MSF team the permits they needed to start working in the targeted towns. Through sheer persistence the MSF workers eventually overcame this refusal. They targeted karaoke bars, detoxification centers, and custody houses. Sex workers, mostly women from the mountain villages, desperately poor and struggling to make a living, populated the karaoke bars. The detoxification centers were bustling with activity in this drug-prone area. The custody houses were detention centers for those who had been unsuccessful in their search for jobs in other locations and had been deported home. Gang described all these places as being unsavory locations and way stations in the migration of HIV virus. In all these locations, the MSF workers role-played how needle sharing resulted in the transmission of the virus and demonstrated the proper use of condoms. Before MSF started working in the area, public security officials imprisoned women found walking the streets carrying condoms. MSF had to work with the officials to change public decency norms and laws.

Initially the local Public Security Bureau was particularly active in impeding MSF's work, not because it ran afoul of provincial health ministry guidelines—the Provincial Department of Health was supportive of MSF efforts in local areas—but because the local Department of Culture and Propaganda thought that admitting the existence of AIDS in the region would sully its image and prevent investment inflows. When I asked Gang how his project team overcame this resistance, he said they knew that bribes would not work. Rather, MSF went out of its way to invite the public security officials to their regular informational meetings and diligently kept concerned officials and departments apprised of their activities.

In two years infection rates went down dramatically. When the *New York Times* reported on the successful efforts of the local officials,[26] MSF arranged for the locals to be recognized in Beijing. Gang said that it was difficult to persuade the locals to go to Beijing because they were wary that their achievement was a double-edged sword. The mere admission of the problem could adversely affect their careers. An agency funded by the British government worked on spreading the project to many other prefectures, and the pharmaceutical giant Merck donated $30 million to scale up the programs.[27]

Nonetheless, Gang was sanguine about these apparent signs of progress: "I would be cautious about concluding that HIV infection rates have really fallen. HIV transmission has just become very diversified in China, such as through contaminated blood, heterosexual and homosexual sexual relations, mother to child, and intravenous drug use. Infection rate of one transmission route may decline due to partially effective interventions, but even this could be counteracted by rapid rising infection rate of other transmission routes."[28]

The MSF experience in Liangshan is not typical. The central government, spurred by international outrage at the extent of the problem, is keen to make progress, but the levels of cooperation among local officials vary widely. While Gang Song's team chipped away at local resistance, Henan Province, the AIDS capital of China, still resists offers of outside help. AIDS in Henan is a residue of a blood-selling scandal in the 1990s, when penurious inhabitants were persuaded by slogans like "It is glorious to sell your blood." Many people supplemented their incomes by making frequent donations under unsanitary conditions, each donation fetching the equivalent of roughly $5. Because the rural health care system was in shambles, both patients and doctors in the countryside needed new means of financing.[29] "Blood heads," the locals in charge of fostering this mini-industry, worked closely with other local government officials.

A French journalist recently referred to Henan as China's "ground zero of AIDS." His experience underscores the tremendous shame inherent in China's denial. "When I travelled to the 'AIDS villages' last year," he wrote, "I had to arrive at midnight and leave before daybreak to avoid the militias formed to stop journalists and non-government organizations, both Chinese and foreign, from visiting AIDS patients."[30] During my own visit to Henan in 2005, local well-wishers cautioned me forthrightly about traveling to AIDS-stricken regions, where I was sure to be harassed by local authorities. With China's large migrant population, the AIDS-heavy regions like Henan and Guangxi contribute to the spread of the disease. Seventy-one percent of migrants are between fifteen and thirty-four years old and sexually active.

It took a full decade after the first reported case of HIV for the State Council to publish its "Medium- and Long-Term Plan for AIDS Prevention and Control." Even as late as 2000 China had allocated just one-seventh of the funds that Thailand had used to successfully check the spread of HIV and AIDS. This low investment has meant shortages of infrastructure and trained people to contain the diseases. In the late 1990s, for example, only one lab was capable of testing for HIV for every 300 million people. By 2003 officials became more serious. Premier Wen Jiabao and Vice Premier Wu Yi announced the policy of "Four Frees and One Care." This policy includes free anti-HIV drugs to rural and urban AIDS patients with financial difficulties, free voluntary counseling and testing, free drugs to HIV-infected pregnant women to prevent mother-to-child transmission, HIV testing of newborn babies, free schooling for children orphaned by AIDS, and care and economic assistance to the households of people living with HIV or AIDS.[31] Numerical targets for treatment and counseling are now more common. However, open discussion of HIV and AIDS remains sensitive.

The state's control of information and denial of public health dangers are not unique to AIDS. During the 2002 outbreak of sudden acute respiratory syndrome (SARS) in Guangdong, China's southeast coastal province, the central government denied its spread until April 3, 2003, when Health Minister Zhang Wenkang, in a news release, reported that Beijing had seen twelve SARS cases and three deaths from the disease and that 1,190 cases had occurred across China. But Dr. Jiang Yanyong, the former director of the surgery department at the No. 309 Military General Hospital and a fifty-year loyal member of the Communist Party, called the government's bluff. He angrily proclaimed a government cover-up in a statement picked up by the *New York Times*. Jiang disclosed that the No. 309 Hospital alone had sixty SARS patients and that seven patients had died from the disease by April 3.[32] Dr. Jiang alleged a cover-up. While Congress was in session, the Ministry of Health mandated silence on the part of the hospital officials regarding SARS in Beijing.

Its hand revealed, the Chinese government suddenly reversed its position on the SARS outbreak and began active cooperation with the World Health Organization. On April 19, Premier Wen Jiabao warned that local officials attempting a cover-up would be punished. Health Minister Zhang was dismissed shortly thereafter, as was Meng Xuenong, the Party secretary of Beijing.

In Henan Province I learned more details of the cover-up from government insiders. Although government-controlled news reports gave the impression that SARS was a common communicable disease, not much more serious than the flu and under control, in fact local governments were worried about the rural migrant workers returning home from SARS-ravaged areas. In the Zhengzhou railway station in Henan, all passengers from Beijing were strictly examined. Anyone with a fever, whether resulting from SARS or not, was condemned to a special quarantine zone. People released from quarantine were ordered not to leave their homes for fourteen days, and during that time they had to report any physical discomforts to local health bureaus.

The measures in rural areas were even stricter. Officials and police at county, town, and village levels set up checkpoints. Vehicles had to be disinfected before entering. Returning rural laborers had to live in quarantined areas outside their villages, in fields or empty classrooms, for a period of observation often lasting two weeks before being allowed to head home. Local officials who failed to keep track of returned migrants were summarily dismissed. These extreme measures were generally effective. Even the populous Henan Province, with its poor health care, had no known SARS-related deaths. In Beijing almost all employees at the Foreign Ministry were allowed to stay at home instead of reporting to work. Two-thirds stayed home. The last time that level of absence had occurred was during the Tiananmen Square incident in 1989.

Some of the factors contributing to the prevalence of AIDS in China are the same in India: lack of education, lack of sanitation, and the mobility of high-risk individuals—for example, truck drivers who engage in unprotected sexual activity with many partners in remote truck stops along the length and breadth of the country. A meager allocation of public resources to health care perpetuates the problem.

India launched its National AIDS Control Program in 1987, but its implementation has been haphazard. Program officials have focused primarily on arguing that outsiders are overestimating AIDS in India.[33] A surveillance system put in place by the government is inadequately funded. The social stigma attached to AIDS remains unabated; even health care staff at the program shun AIDS patients. In an address to Parliament in 2001, Prime Minister Vajpayee referred to the spread of HIV and AIDS as the country's most serious health challenge in 2001, but India's elite—the people with the money and influence needed to meet the challenge—refused to acknowledge it.

It is ironic that India, a major producer of cheap antiretroviral drugs, has failed to provide the same drugs to its own people. Joanne Csete, director of the HIV/AIDS program at Human Rights Watch, said, "But for millions of Indians, access to these medicines is a distant dream."[34] A government program in 2003 intended to provide free antiretroviral drugs through the largest generic drug companies in the country has not been well run. The head of Cipla, one of the generic drug manufacturers, said, "If the government wants to buy, they must let us know for how many, when, and do they have the money?"[35] This plan has been further compromised by the rising costs of the drugs following India's accession to a World Trade Organization treaty on intellectual property rights.[36] The result was that by the end of April 2005, of an estimated 770,000 patients who needed the antiretroviral drugs, only 35,000 were receiving them, and most of those were served by the private sector.[37]

Civil society is stepping in. The Bill and Melinda Gates Foundation has been leading the charge since April 2003. Ashok Alexander, a former consultant at McKinsey and Company, is responsible for running the foundation's

$200 million, five-year initiative called Avahan, Sanskrit for "call to action." Alexander has pointed out how much harder it is to control AIDS in India than in Botswana, the African country that has successfully contained the spread of the infection. "By 2008, we want to halt the spread of the virus that leads to AIDS. It's a huge and very complicated epidemic. There are 600 districts in India, each with a population roughly the size of Botswana's, so in effect we have 600 Botswanas."[38]

Inadequate AIDS education is only part of the problem. For example, in the "red light" district of Mumbai, 94 percent of sex workers are aware of the disease, as tested by eight AIDS-awareness questions suggested by the World Health Organization. The real problem is social despair; infected sex workers are forced into their high-risk occupation by depressed social circumstances stemming from a lack of education. Avahan is also focused on India's truck drivers. Alexander has broken down the seemingly insurmountable problem of reaching all truckers along a massive and remote highway system into a manageable assault on the key parts of the network that are most responsible for nurturing and spreading the disease.

The spread of HIV and AIDS exposes all the fault lines in the health care systems of China and India. China continues to try to cover up the extent of its affliction, while the Indian state seems incapable of responding effectively to the epidemic and is relying on civil society to ease the nightmare.

The Solution: Public-Private Cooperation[39]

The Chinese and Indian health care malaise must be arrested, if only because inexorable demographic forces are raising the stakes. China's working-age population grew by only 2.1 percent annually from 1975 to 2000, and that growth rate will drop to 0.5 percent in the next quarter century. Meanwhile steady growth in the nation's dependent population means that China will not be rich when hundreds of millions have grown old and are afflicted with poor health. India's demographic projections appear more optimistic. Growth in its working-age population has shrunk from 2.3 percent to 1.6 percent annually, but more importantly the annual growth in its dependents has fallen from 1.5 percent to 0.5 percent. India now expects to benefit from a demographic dividend of the sort that China did at the onset of the latter's reforms.

However, complacency in India is unwarranted. An unhealthy working-age population, no matter how young, cannot spur economic growth. Once-eradicated diseases have resurfaced, malnutrition is still widespread, and AIDS could yet become an epidemic. Both countries need a solution. China has acknowledged this. Health Minister Gao Qiang, in a speech in October 2005 at the Harvard School of Public Health, recognized widespread public dissatisfaction with health care in China. By contrast India remains disturbingly nonchalant, official rhetoric notwithstanding.

In India civil society is trying to compensate. One example is Dr. Bindeshwar Pathak's organization, Sulabh International, founded in 1970.[40] Sulabh created a low-cost toilet technology that not only helped maintain sanitation but also restored the dignity of millions of "scavengers," the cleaners of human excreta who are traditionally untouchables.[41] The West's toilet technology, composed of sewage and septic tanks, was unaffordable for India's teeming millions. Pathak's technology relies on two simple pits and sealed covers. While one pit is in use, the other is left to decompose, forming a fertilizer that can be used in agricultural fields. Equally important, human waste no longer requires manual cleansing.

Today Sulabh operates more than 5,500 community complexes in 1,075 towns across India. These complexes have electricity and twenty-four-hour water supplies. The complexes, with separate enclosures for men and women, charge each user a nominal fee. Some of the Sulabh complexes have bathing and shower facilities, cloakrooms, telephones, and primary health care providers. A pay-and-use system ensures self-sustainability without putting any burden on the public exchequer. The Sulabh sanitation movement boasts fifty thousand volunteers.

But Sulabh has barely scratched the surface of India's needs. For example, even in urban areas only 28 percent of the population has access to flush toilets connected to a sewage system, and just 21 percent use toilets connected to septic tanks or leach pits. In rural areas a mere 20 percent of the population has access to sanitary toilets. Almost three-quarters of a billion people still defecate in the open or use unsanitary bucket latrines. Sadly, India remains far from reaching the goal Nehru articulated in his comment, "The day every one of us gets a toilet to use, I shall know that our country has reached the pinnacle of progress."[42]

Meanwhile a growing number of uninsured sick or injured people from the developed world are flying to India. A North Carolina carpenter, one of 43 million Americans without health insurance, had his heart valve replaced at a leading facility in India for a total expense of $10,000, including round-trip airfare and a side trip to the Taj Mahal.[43] Compare this with the unaffordable cost of surgery for the uninsured in the United States: $200,000, with a required initial deposit of $50,000. Why would aging Britons not want to have their hips replaced in India, and enjoy luxurious convalescences in the process, rather than endure the typical six-month waiting periods required by their country's national health system, which groans under its own resource constraints?

Dr. Pratap Reddy, founder of Apollo Hospitals, India's leading hospital and medical services group, is aggressively pioneering medical tourism. He has built a chain of world-class hospitals throughout India and has expanded globally, competing successfully with Western hospital groups to run facilities in Colombo, Dubai, Kuala Lumpur, and elsewhere. South and Southeast Asians and Middle Easterners flock to his hospitals for affordable, high-quality care. Reddy told me, "I want to bring Apollo health care to a large cross-section of the Indian population—and to the world. My vision is to develop the large pool of talent in India. Health care could be the single biggest employer in the country and a resource to the world. Patients will come from everywhere to India for advanced health care. We enjoy a huge cost advantage. But more importantly, our culture is very compassionate. India is now in a position to give patients the best of the East and the West—compassion and advanced medical technology."[44]

Some members of the Indian media have objected to medical tourism, suggesting that it diverts India's scarce talent away from the nation's more pressing needs. I find this criticism misguided. Regulations that seek to ban medical tourism will probably not persuade private entrepreneurs to finance medical care for the poor. If the latter were a commercially viable enterprise, they would invest in that in addition to medical tourism. The problem is not a scarcity of doctors.

The real problem is that building a viable business model to cater to hundreds of millions of poor people is a tremendous challenge. At its best India's vibrant private-sector health care system can serve only a few tens of millions, a drop in the bucket compared with what is needed. A person with means can easily access superb tertiary health care, far more cheaply than in the West. In any major Indian metropolis a specialist can be coaxed into making a house call, even in the dead of night. The same cannot be said for Boston, for all its cutting-edge medical research. But a stroll down the main streets of the Indian metropolis will make it clear that for most people, even the simplest Band-Aid is unavailable.

Nor will companies, in the normal course of their own activities, likely attend to the health of their workers, even those facing devastating illnesses. Consider piecemeal corporate efforts to contain the spread of AIDS. The large South African mining company Anglo American Corporation felt its direct interests threatened enough by HIV and AIDS to act privately. Put simply, miner mortality was too high—as much as 25 percent of its workforce was infected at one point—so it paid the costs of providing education, treatment, and care.[45] Usually, however, companies find it more expedient to ignore the ambient threat. In a survey administered by the World Economic Forum, only 10 percent of companies report having written HIV/AIDS policies, 17 percent have informal policies, and 64 percent have none.[46]

Why these dismal numbers? First, firms that invest in HIV/AIDS programs will strengthen the health of people in their communities, thereby helping firms that have not expended similar resources. This free-rider problem weakens the spending firm's competitiveness relative to the nonspending firm, creating an incentive to do nothing and let others take the strain. Further, for most businesses the effect on customers is slight because HIV and AIDS are predominantly diseases of the poor, who are not major consumers. Many firms, moreover, sell to other firms or to foreign markets rather than directly to consumers, so the effect is spread thinly. As morbid as it seems, even in a country with a high prevalence of HIV, a large surplus labor pool makes replacing lost workers easy.[47] Because infected individuals can live with the virus many years, future employers may reap a firm's investment in today's employees. Therefore firms might consider it financially sensible to let society pay for sick workers' treatment by laying them off and replacing them with healthy workers.

That is why the public sector has a vital role. China had this figured out before initiating its economic reforms in 1978. Its experience was the opposite of India's. Privately delivered care was scarce, but public delivery of health services was well governed. Unfortunately, when China abandoned its focus on primary care, like that provided by barefoot doctors, its public health system deteriorated rapidly. So-called public-sector medical services began catering to those who could afford to pay and turning away the poor. The resurgence of barefoot doctors today—in southwest Guizhou Province they deliver babies for $4[48]—is testimony to China's belated realization of its missteps.

Civil society also has a role to play. India is host to a range of such efforts. Avahan and Sulabh are only two examples. Even China, suspicious of civil society, has begun to change its rhetoric. Just as China is more tolerant of foreign private firms than it is of its homegrown entrepreneurs, so also international nongovernmental organizations (NGOs) have had more traction than local groups. For example, several international NGOs have for years worked to check the spread of HIV in China, among them the Ford Foundation, Save the Children–United Kingdom, Australian Red Cross, Marie Stopes International, MSF, Salvation Army, and Oxfam–Hong Kong.[49] The focus of these groups has evolved from education and information to intervention among high-risk groups.[50] But the state remains deeply ambivalent. According to Human Rights Watch, activists and NGO staff continue to report constant state surveillance, a web of bureaucratic obstacles, and even open harassment in the course of doing their daily work.[51]

Yet given the problem's enormity, the efforts of the public or private sector alone are not sufficient. The way ahead may lie in public-private partnerships.

Devi Shetty's cardiac care hospital is a case in point. In his telemedicine and health insurance schemes, the state appropriately acts as part-financier, not service provider. States are well placed to provide financial incentives to firms and to assist in the design of programs according to social goals. Private firms, on the other hand, run programs effectively. In Punjab, for example, the Department of Health and Family Welfare invited private health care providers to participate in the operation and maintenance of selected government hospitals. In Orissa, experiments with handing over the operation of Primary Health Centers to NGOs have had some success. The same ideas will likely work well if applied to caring for patients with HIV or AIDS. Contracting projects out to businesses and rewarding them when the programs reduce HIV prevalence; strengthening AIDS-related knowledge, attitudes, and practices; and extending treatment for AIDS are ways of enlisting significant business support.[52] Avahan is a nonprofit, but its advocacy toward AIDS reduction among rural truck drivers is accelerated by a partnership with the Indian Oil Company, whose numerous "petrol pumps" across India dispense gas and also double as truck stops.

When it comes to promoting public-private partnerships, once again private enterprise and civil society have taken the lead. The best outcomes appear to result when the public sector allows itself to be steered by private enterprise and civil society. One can only hope that the private sector, with its good governance and operations, will have an impact on the governance of the public sector. If so, then the meager resources dedicated to health care in India will go much further. That's at least a start.

In China the way forward centers on the state. Partnerships between the state and private entities will be halting, held hostage to the suspicions of the state. Awareness of the fiasco wrought by the past quarter century is becoming acute. However, most important for Chinese health care is the government's finding its lost script, the one that put primary health care in the starring role.

PART III

FUTURE

Chapter Eleven

Old and New Roads
to Mandalay

Hard Power in Burma and Beyond

In February 2007, when President Hu Jintao visited Africa, I happened to be in both Nanjing and Johannesburg in the same week. While in Nanjing I saw how the Chinese media lauded the president's African tour as part of China's "peaceful rise" on the world stage. The official message was that China was bringing jobs and prosperity to a neglected continent.

Bame Pule, whom I met in Johannesburg a few airports and days later, gave me a more nuanced view of the Chinese investments in Africa. Bame is a Botswanan and a recent graduate of Harvard Business School. He works for a Pan-African venture capital fund in Johannesburg. Having lived and worked in Boston, Los Angeles, and Lagos before coming to Johannesburg, Pule has a unique worldview.

Almost as soon as we sat down to dinner he exclaimed, "I can't believe I'm paying $6,500 a year to learn Mandarin. That's an extraordinary amount of money for language classes in Africa!"[1] But as a good MBA student, he had presumably done the math and figured out that he had a decent chance of a good return on his investment. "Trade between China and Africa will be so prevalent in the coming decades that it will be worth it. I feel I can probably do something entrepreneurial related to China or China–Africa. The growth and market size are so immense that I have to get involved."

Will the Chinese be the new colonialists in Africa? Will they add value to the continent or just exploit Africa's riches? Although Pule expressed concern about China's human rights abuses, he was generally pragmatic about the economic threats and opportunities that China brings to Africa. Although his fund is "always mindful of the actual or potential competition from Chinese companies," because "China makes such a wide variety of products affordably, we usually consider Chinese companies as potential sources of supplies and raw materials."

Overall Bame was enthusiastic about China's interest in Africa, saying that it has "encouraged African governments to build and improve infrastructure by using Chinese construction companies, Chinese labor, and Chinese financing." On a personal level he appreciated that increased exports from China have decreased the price of clothing and shoes and that he can now get Chinese food just about anywhere in Africa.

China's ascent in Africa and elsewhere has been largely achieved through what political scientists call hard power, the ability of a country to coerce and get its way through military power and economic weight. Joseph Nye, a member of the Clinton administration and a former dean of the Kennedy School of Government, coined the contrasting term *soft power* as "the ability to get what you want through attraction rather than coercion or payments. It arises from the attractiveness of a country's culture, political ideals and policies."[2] In recent times China's hard-power global expansion has been the result of premeditated and orchestrated state policy, while India's influence in the world has largely been achieved through soft power. In British India the allure of the "road to Mandalay" was celebrated by Kipling. Today a new road to Mandalay is being laid by China, as it builds both literal and metaphorical "roads" to oil and gas.

Yet most of the projects Chinese oil companies have invested in are located in countries with serious social and ethnic problems, such as Sudan, Nigeria, Angola, Kazakhstan, and Venezuela. More money is flowing into parts of Africa from China than from South Africa, the more logical source. Regarding human rights, China stepped up its investment precisely when the civil war in Sudan was raging and the situation in Darfur had become a crisis. In 1999 China National Petroleum Corporation was a major force in drilling in Sudan. The company, which at that time held a 40 percent stake in the Great Nile Petroleum and Oil Corporation, sent a Chinese-made pipeline a thousand miles from southern Sudan to a port in the Red Sea and stepped up operations when the leader of the Sudan Population Liberation Army (SPLA) announced that the oil company workers would be regarded as legitimate military targets. The SPLA threat came after hundreds of people had already been killed and more than six hundred thousand were forced to flee their homes.[3]

Despite criticisms of its human rights violations, over the last five decades China's presence has gradually and convincingly eclipsed India's in Southeast Asia, the region comprising modern Brunei, Cambodia, Indonesia, Laos, Malaysia, Burma (Myanmar),[4] the Philippines, Singapore, Thailand, and Vietnam. This ascent to economic dominance is especially dramatic because India's influence in the region was at one point unrivaled. Currently, between 30 million and 40 million ethnic Chinese reside in Southeast Asia. In Singapore 2 million ethnic Chinese make up approximately 80 percent of its population.

More than any other country, Burma starkly reflects the power hand-off to China from India. In Burma the Chinese community numbers more than 2 million. Culturally, this change in influence is especially apparent in the city of Mandalay, which is equidistant from both China and India. Chinese consumer goods and immigration are so ubiquitous in Mandalay that a visitor might mistake it for a Chinese city. Reminders of the Indian presence—the mansions built by rich Indian merchants and the Sikh *gurudwaras* ("places of worship")—have been entirely erased. As in other Southeast Asian countries, the Chinese presence in Burma resulted not only from migration but also from a premeditated, state-sponsored effort to secure cost-efficient and reliable oil and gas pathways. China's hunger for resources and its fear of continuing to rely on maritime pathways that might close makes it eager to invest in Southeast Asia.

Burma: A Nineteenth-Century Silicon Valley

Jaspal Kaur Singh, a nonresident Indian with shoulder-length black hair and graceful ways, is a Professor of English at Western Michigan University. Singh is also a third-generation Burmese-Indian. Her family originates from Punjab, India's predominantly Sikh northern state, and her family's century-long odyssey parallels the shift in Burma from Indian to Chinese influence.

Singh's two grandfathers arrived in Burma at the turn of the nineteenth century, soon after the British conquered Burma in 1886. As Singh told me, "Stories that Burma was the place where money could be made had somehow reached India, and with farming getting tougher in British India, I suppose they arrived in search of a better life."[5]

Nineteenth-century Burma was the Silicon Valley of its day. For British soldiers, settlers, and administrators, the possibilities seemed endless: several dozen oil fields; ruby, sapphire, and jade mines; superb Burmese teak; and most of all, the fertile Irrawaddy Delta. As conquerors the British moved the capital from Mandalay to Rangoon, establishing that city as a substation of the British Empire in India.

Mandalay, however, is important to the predominantly Buddhist Burmese people. The Burmese believe that Siddhartha Gautama, the founder of Buddhism, climbed Mandalay hill on one of his four legendary travels to Burma and prophesied that on the 2,400th jubilee of Buddhism, a great city would be founded on its foothills. In 1857 King Mindon, a devout Buddhist, issued a royal order that laid the foundation of Mandalay city and had his palace built based on Brahmin Buddhist cosmology to represent the center of the world, with the palace's four walls facing the four cardinal directions.

Unlike most immigrants, Singh's grandparents settled not in a large city like Mandalay or Rangoon but in the remote northern city of Taunggyi, capital of the Shan States. Her "Dada" (paternal grandfather in Hindi) became a cloth trader and her "Nana" (maternal grandfather in Hindi) became a tailor. "It put them at the middle level," Singh told me. "They were not like the rich Indian merchants with homes in Rangoon, and neither were they the lowest level of the unskilled labor, but somewhere in the middle of Burmese classes."

By the time Singh's father was born in the 1920s, several thousand Indians had made their way to Burma. By then Burma was firmly ensconced as part of British India. But there was a longer historical connection between Burma and India. Burmese schoolchildren will tell you that Burma began when an Indian prince from ancient times established a kingdom at Taguang, north of Mandalay, several thousand years ago, even before Buddhism came into being. The British had exiled Burmese King Thibaw to India and the last Mughal Emperor of India, Bahadur Shah Zafar, to Burma.[6] In the 1920s cosmopolitan Rangoon had more immigrants than did New York: 53 percent of Rangoon's population was Indian; 32 percent Burmese; 8 percent Chinese; and the rest were Arabs, Jews, and Europeans.[7]

One of the most prominent of the Indian groups was the Nattukottai Chettiars, a merchant community originating from the Chettinad tract of what is now the southern Indian state of Tamil Nadu. The Chettiars, originally salt traders, first sensed an arbitrage opportunity in financing businesses in Ceylon (modern Sri Lanka) and then began to follow British financial institutions into Malaya and the Straits Settlements, reaching Burma as troops and laborers arrived in Tenasserim with the British. The Chettiars were major financiers of the transformation of the fertile Irrawaddy Delta. As agricultural development expanded to encompass trade and commerce in rubber, tea, and opium, the Chettiars embraced the increased demand for credit and gradually moved away from their businesses in southern India to entrench themselves in the Asian colonies, with Burma most dramatically accounting for two-thirds of Chettiar financing worldwide.[8] Sean Turnell, a scholar studying Chettiar commerce in Burma writes, "[B]y 1930 Chettiar moneylenders collectively had 750 million rupees of capital employed in

Burma in the form of loans outstanding and other investments . . . This was a figure equivalent to all British investments in Burma combined."⁹ The Indian Chettiars thus emerged as Burma's financial backbone and acted as intermediaries between Western banks and Burmese cultivators.

India's golden age of trade, from the early nineteenth to the early twentieth centuries, included more than Burma. Marwari traders from the state of Rajasthan traded jute and commodities in Europe after World War I. The historian Claude Markovitz, in his book *The Global World of the Indian Merchant, 1750 to 1947*, points out that trade between Europe and India was monopolized by big British trading houses but that trade with Asia and Africa was primarily in the hands of Indians. Asian trade included first opium and then cotton from China. Markovitz calculates that in 1830 the Indian merchant diaspora of the Indian Ocean, Persian Gulf, and Red Sea numbered a few thousand. A century later Indian traders and commercial employees outside India numbered 1 million, 60 percent of whom were in Burma, Ceylon, and Malaya.¹⁰

But India's dominance in Burma was virtually erased in just a decade. Paddy prices nearly collapsed with the onset of the Great Depression. Rice cultivators foreclosed, and the Chettiars seized collateral—land. Because they were the only people with money, the Chettiars had been accumulating land as part of their normal business practices. At their peak they controlled a fourth of the prime land in the Irrawaddy Delta. Unsurprisingly, the Chettiars were then vilified in the Burmese public arena as heartless, parasitic landgrabbers. The tensions finally resulted in the Indo-Burmese riots of 1930.

Around that time, during the Sino-Japanese war of 1937, the Japanese were expanding into northern China with the intention of heading south. As a defense against the Japanese invasion, the British constructed the Dian Myanmar Road, linking Lashio in eastern Burma with Kunming in southern China's Yunnan Province. This 717-mile road became the main supply route for the Allies carrying war materiel to inner China. But Rangoon fell easily to Japan's imperial army, and in its wake the Indian mercantile community exited Burma en masse.

World War II came to Burma in the form of an advancing Japanese army and U.S. troops. The Japanese attacked Pearl Harbor in 1941. The so-called CBI theater—China, Burma, and India—became important, on the theory that Burma's collapse would inevitably render China vulnerable. In the wake of the atrocities that gripped the Buddhist kingdom and Rangoon's fall to the Japanese in 1942, four hundred thousand Indians left Burma, most of them taking a treacherous overland route to India. Eighty thousand or so perished in the process. By the end of 1942 all of Burma was under Japanese control.

Singh's family did not escape the wrath of the war. Her father, pregnant mother, and grandparents took refuge from bombs in the jungles of northern Burma. According to her parents' stories, the bombs fell indiscriminately on all sides. " 'What allies?' my parents used to say angrily. 'They were bombing everyone, not just the Japanese.' " Scavenging for food and hoarding salt to trade, the family finally left for Calcutta on a train from Rangoon. From Calcutta it was a long journey to their hometown of Rawalpindi (in modern Pakistan), about twelve hundred miles away. But it seemed that the Singh family's fate was irreversibly tied to Burma. After having made the arduous journey from Rangoon to Calcutta to Rawalpindi, and after being received with much fanfare by "Hindu and Muslim friends alike" in his hometown, Singh's grandfather returned to Burma just two years later. This time the catalyst was the partition of India, which took place simultaneously with its Independence in 1947.

Meher Singh, Singh's grandfather, wanted to stay in India, but was eventually convinced by her father that it was time to go. "They made it over to India" Singh said. "Unlike many others, their train was not attacked by mobs. The irony was that by now India was a strange land to them and Burma familiar—so back to Burma they went."

Nehru's Charismatic Shadow

On January 4, 1948, U Nu, a devout Buddhist and prominent Nationalist, was sworn in as the prime minister of independent Burma. Burmese astrologers had declared the date auspicious. Euphoria heralded the lowering of the Union Jack and U Nu's ascent. But U Nu's first year was wracked by nine separatist insurrections that were waged by various minority communities—for example, by the Karen, a Christian community—which stemmed from the economic distress wrought by the agrarian crisis of the 1930s. U Nu's response to the insurrections was to embark on a massive program of nationalization at the expense primarily of land-owning Chettiars. This proved to be a hugely popular move among the Burmese, who had long resented the wealthy group of Indians.

Paradoxically Singh's family prospered despite the nationalist storm. Unlike the rich and prominent Chettiars, they did not attract attention. Her father, who was by now the head of the family, had established a successful shop in Taunggyi. Singh described the shop as selling "every imaginable feminine product as well as beautiful fabrics from Manchester and other parts of Europe." She added, "The food was plenty, and I remember my father bought a new car. My father heard about properties being seized in Rangoon from the Chettiars but he was not very concerned about us. The northern Shan

States of Burma, with their minorities, had always been protected by the British from the majority Burmese." Singh was referring to the view that the British deliberately created fissures between the Hindus and Muslim communities in their Indian colony to make it easier to administer.

The British had permitted the country's several minorities to exercise limited autonomy by dividing Burma into two regions. Burma proper (including Arakan and Tenasserim) was administered by direct British rule, but in areas where the Burmese were the minority—the northern hill areas that included the Shan States; the Karen States; and the tribal groups in the Kachin, Chin, and Naga hills—the traditional leadership had been allowed to remain, albeit under British supervision. Singh added, "There were a number of Sikhs from Punjab in this region. We had our own *gurudwara* and our own procession. We had a good life."

Nehru, a personal friend of U Nu, cemented India's goodwill toward Burma with specific acts. He overlooked Burma's debt to India—namely, capital assets left by the government when India separated from Burma in 1937. Nehru also chose not to intervene on behalf of disenfranchised Chettiars and other Indian business interests in Burma, stating that "there is not going to be a policy of claiming any special privileges for Indians, particularly Indians with vested interest . . . In the past a great deal of injury has been done to India's relations with Burma by the insistence of Indian business and other interest for privileged treatment."[11] From Nehru's point of view, this was consistent with his policy of nonalignment. To establish a position equidistant from the great powers—the United States and the Soviet Union—India could not become especially close, or especially far, from anyone else's internal affairs. A latter-day by-product of nonalignment then became India's propensity to perpetuate distance from its diaspora.

U Nu, already intellectually aligned with Nehru's beliefs in socialism and nonalignment, appreciated the Indian prime minister's decision not to interfere in the affairs of Burmese Indians. Nehru continued to champion actions in independent Burma's interest. For example, in spite of his hesitations, he assisted Rangoon against the communist insurgency A grateful U Nu was prompted to say, "From the middle of 1949, when Mr. Nehru's rifles began arriving, the enemy's threat was first contained then eliminated."[12] India extended aid into the 1950s.

For Burmese Indians, India's influence was apparent not only in the Buddhist connection or Chettiar commerce, both examples of soft power, but also in Indian popular culture, especially the extremely popular Hindi movies. Singh reminisced: "Nehru and Gandhi were of course larger than life for us. Our parents were full of praise for them and for the cause of Indian independence. In fact when Subhash Chandra Bose [Indian leader organizing armed resistance against British] visited Rangoon before the war, my grand uncles even joined his Indian National Army.[13] But we were young, and for us India was the beautiful landscapes of Kashmir—the ones we saw in movies. I particularly remember [matinee idol] Raj Kapoor movies, a big hit in the 1950s, and of course the Bengali star Joy Mukherjee."

In China's Embrace

Nehru's finest hour was perhaps at the Bandung Conference held in Indonesia, in 1955. The conference was intended to establish solidarity and camaraderie among twenty-nine Asian and African states, most of which were newly independent. Uncertain how to set policy against colonialism and wary of the West, the other states looked to Nehru for vision. Biographer Shashi Tharoor writes, "Jawaharlal Nehru at forty six was the glamorous face of Indian nationalism just as Gandhi was otherworldly deity . . . [A]bout him was a presence that went beyond mere charisma."[14] In Joseph Nye's words, it seemed that India's soft power had established "observable but intangible attraction."[15]

Nehru, however, did not steal the show in Bandung. That distinction went to Zhou Enlai, Mao's emissary and foreign minister. Zhou repeatedly reassured the delegates at Bandung of China's peaceful intent, even in the face of the conference's open critique of communism and its advocacy of nonalignment. Zhou's off-the-cuff speeches at the conference, and the fact that he had brought along his Chinese chef to entertain dinner guests made him a hit. According to Amitav Acharya, a historian at the National University of Singapore and a chronicler of Bandung, Nehru did not feel that the "show had been stolen from him." but declared that "it was not India's purpose . . . to seek the limelight. Some newspapers, especially in India, naturally played up India's role. We felt, however, that it was better for us to work quietly. The fact, however, remained that the two most important countries present at the Bandung Conference were China and India."[16]

Of course Zhou would not have upstaged Nehru if Nehru had not allowed it. Nehru had insisted that Bandung without China would have been pointless and had arranged for Air India' s Kashmir Princess to bring several Chinese diplomats to Bandung. (The plane was blown up midair, allegedly by Taiwanese saboteurs.)[17]

The irony of Bandung was that it was preceded and followed by events in which China upstaged India. China, in an attempt to secure its borders and to spread the gospel of communism, had moved into Tibet by then. In 1950 Mao's People's Liberation Army entered the western Kham (Khams) and Ü-Tsang (Dbu-gtsang) regions of Tibet, which like Burma shared borders with India. Offering almost no resistance, Tibet was occupied by China in 1951. In May that year representatives of the Dalai Lama and communist China signed the Seventeen-Point Agreement on Measures for the Peaceful Liberation of Tibet. For the first time in its two-thousand-year history, Tibet was part of China.

The takeover of Tibet by the Chinese caught the world by surprise. Not knowing how to respond, the world watched to see India's reaction. *The Economist* assessed the situation: "Having maintained complete independence of China since 1912, Tibet has a strong claim to be regarded as an independent state. But India must lead in this matter. If India decides to support independence of Tibet as a buffer state between itself and China, Britain and U.S.A. will do well to extend formal diplomatic recognition to it."[18]

Nehru rejected appeals from his home minister, Sardar Vallabhai Patel, who was wary of Chinese expansionism. Nehru pointed out that neither the United Kingdom nor the United States had any interest in embarrassing China by recognizing Tibet and stated, "We cannot save Tibet, as we should have liked to do, and our very attempt to save it might well bring greater trouble to it. It would be unfair to Tibet for us to bring this trouble upon her without having the capacity to help her effectively. We may be able to help Tibet to retain a large measure of her autonomy."[19] Thus Zhou's protestations of peace in Bandung came after the Tibet imbroglio. Nehru, by visiting Beijing in October 1954, ensured that Tibet was nowhere on Bandung's agenda. The Panchsheel agreement that Nehru signed at the Bandung Conference pledged "peaceful coexistence" with China.

The further irony of Bandung is that it was followed by the military drubbing that India received from China in a border skirmish in 1962. The so-called Sino-Indian War resulted in more than four decades of frosty relations between China and India and dramatically attenuated Nehru's prestige, ultimately leaving him a broken man and his country bereft of its postindependence swagger. For India especially, 1962 marked a blow and a turning point in its relations with China, one from which it is still recovering.

When I was in school Indian textbooks cast the Sino-Indian War as an example of Chinese duplicity. On India's northern border, an Indian reconnaissance party discovered that the Chinese had completed a road running through the Asksai Chin region of the Landhak District of Jammu and Kashmir, India's northernmost state bordering China. Soon skirmishes began to take place, and in January 1959 Zhou wrote to Nehru rejecting Nehru's suggestion that the border, known as the 1914 MacMahon Line, was legal and denying that any Chinese government had ever accepted its legality as a border. Unable to agree on disputed territory along the two-thousand-mile Himalayan border, the Chinese attacked India on October 20, 1962.

Two decades later I stumbled onto the Chinese version of the story. A casual conversation with an eminent Chinese scholar of Indian relations in Beijing evolved into an icy dialogue when the man took offense at my rendition of events. He pointed out that Nehru had been obtuse in rebuffing Zhou's 1959 suggestion that both countries cool off by withdrawing their guards twelve miles from the line of actual control to avoid clashes. China unilaterally withdrew its guards anyway, and Zhou went to Delhi to patch things up in 1960. Nehru reiterated that the MacMahon Line was "firm and definite and not open to discussion," a phrase that several Sinologists in Southeast Asia have since pointed out to me was offensive in how it closed off dialogue. When Indian maps continued to show the disputed territory as part of India, China preemptively attacked.

Neville Maxwell's book *India's China War* endorses this view and offers a scathing critique of India's ineptitude. Not only were military mistakes committed, but also New Delhi interfered with the generals on the ground. When the Indians surrendered, the political establishment presented the loss as one stemming from the Chinese army's sheer size and the treacherous Himalayan terrain. No one asked why the war had been fought in the first place.[20] In the war's aftermath the Indian government commissioned an investigation of the causes of the war and the reasons for defeat, but the relevant documents are still classified by government order.

For India the 1962 war was a humiliating national tragedy. For China it was merely a border dispute. One of my Chinese students at Harvard pointed out that "in our textbooks, there was just a paragraph or two about the 1962 war with India. Whereas there are pages and pages about the war with Japan and museums dedicated to troops who died in the Japanese conflict." The Indian press retreated into a reflective and humiliating slumber, always asking how Nehru could have gotten it so wrong and what value intangible goodwill—a source of soft power—held in the face of aggression.

Meanwhile China's posture toward Tibet and its "solution" of the Indian border problem clearly signaled its intentions, no matter how much it might have endorsed peace at Bandung. In 1950 units of the People's Liberation Army, calling themselves the Chinese People's Volunteers, crossed the Yalujiang River into North Korea. They were acting in response to a threat to northeast China they perceived as coming from United Nations forces (led by the United States) in the Democratic People's Republic of Korea. This paralleled the People's Liberation Army's assertion of Chinese sovereignty over Tibet, a region that had essentially been independent of Chinese rule since the fall of the Qing Dynasty in 1911. Clearly China would not give up territory.

China's exercise of hard power was meant to compensate for its "century of humiliation" to foreigners since the Qing Dynasty's Opium Wars. Since then, China had ceded much territory in one-sided treaties. Hong Kong was lost to Britain, Taiwan to Japan, and much of the north to Russia. Meanwhile all of China's possessions soon evaporated, with Vietnam, Laos, and Cambodia falling to the French, Burma to the British, and Korea to Japan. Mao and his comrades believed that communist China would surely revive the strength and prosperity of ancient China.

In 1962 China also flexed its muscle in Burma. By that time U Nu's government was unraveling. Rampant instability prompted U Nu to make the unusual move of inviting his army chief of staff, General Ne Win, to take over the country. The general first stabilized the country and then, after U Nu briefly returned to power, mounted a successful coup. Burma was declared a socialist state run by the Revolutionary Council composed of senior military officers. The ascent of the generals hastened a rapprochement with China. While U Nu had consistently made clear his dislike for China for supporting the communist insurgencies in Burma, China's relations with Ne Win were dramatically better. A French ambassador to Rangoon at that time made a prescient observation: "[The Burmese government] seems anxious to promote the opening and development of rail traffic between Western China and the outside world using the Rangoon line . . . They do not seem worried by the eventual implications regarding Burmese sovereignty."[21]

Once in power, Ne Win's Revolutionary Council fully nationalized the industrial and commercial sectors of the economy and imposed a policy of international isolation on Burma. Indians' days in Burma were numbered. The bamboo curtain was drawn on Burma, and the livelihoods of Indians evaporated. Those who chose to leave could take nothing with them. Between 1964 and 1968 about 150,000 Indians left Burma.[22] A few years after General Ne Win took power, his Revolutionary Council nationalized all property, roughly 60 percent of which was owned by Indians.

Until then, Ne Win's political misgivings had not affected Jaspal Singh's family, who enjoyed a relatively comfortable life. Singh recalled that in the early 1960s, although in cities like Rangoon Ne Win had virtually taken away all property owned by Indians and the drastic devaluation of the kyat was "stripping Indians of their wealth," her father was convinced that those calamities would not be repeated in Taunggyi. Her father believed "they are only concerned with the big capitalists, not us. Ne Win told us that there will not be any more closing of shops." Despite her father's views, Singh recognized ominous signs that the political climate was changing in her hometown. She remembered being told by some Burmese that "Indians smell kaala" (kaala is a Hindi term meaning "black" and has been used by the Burmese to denigrate Persians, Arabs, and Europeans).[23] Her teacher, who had always been perfectly nice to her, became rude and condescending, and her brothers were beaten and bullied for wearing traditional Sikh turbans.

In 1965 the Singh family's worst fears came true. "One day trucks rolled in, put the shutter down on my father's shop, and all that we owned was gone. Just like that. I still remember he came home looking shaken and broken and said to my mother, 'They took it all.' My mother's response was, 'We'll build again.' "

Despite the previously warm relations between Ne Win and China, the Burmese levied discrimination and violence against resident Chinese as well as Indians. In 1967 tensions culminated in rioting. Singh told me about one particularly gruesome memory: "My sister was a student at the Rangoon medical college and witnessed the 1967 riots. According to her the mob was actually coming for the Indians but somehow, no one quite knows how, got deflected towards the Chinese. Later the body of one of her closest Chinese friends was brought in as a cadaver at the medical school. My sister was shattered." In response to this violence China withdrew aid that had come with the nonaggression pact signed with Burma during the "Sino-Burmese honeymoon" of the early 1960s. The Chinese continued to support communist insurgencies against Burma.

As hopeful as Singh's mother's response to the confiscation of the family property had been, and as much as they had wanted to rebuild in Burma, that was not to happen. Two years after the Ne Win government closed her father's shop, the family left for India.

By the early 1970s India's regional and international stature had significantly weakened. Nehru's politics of peace had not yielded dividends of influence. China's influence and stature had grown as it exported its communist ideology. This did not always have a positive outcome. In many countries ethnic Chinese populations bore the brunt of racism and nationalism. Nevertheless, exporting communist ideology was a form of soft power, and it was backed by hard power in the form of military aid and money. Mao used both effectively. In contrast India's era of influence resulted primarily from exporting soft power.

Baja Yunnan

"My father was one of the biggest smugglers in Taunggyi," Singh declared matter-of-factly, remembering her family's last two years in Burma, before they were forced to finally leave. "It was the only thing left for him to do. After all, he had a family to feed. He specialized in buying and selling the watches that were making their way over the border from Thailand and China. My brother started helping my father out. He would take a few watches in a bag on his bicycle and sell them whenever he got a chance. But one day, just when my father was going to make a trade, the police arrived. My Chacha [father's brother] grabbed the watches from him and took the blame. He was sentenced to six months in a maximum security prison. This was the last straw for us. When my Dadi [grandmother] insisted we leave for India, my father—hesitant but humiliated—agreed."

The process by which the Indian community was driven to the economic underground formed Baja Yunnan, a term I use to refer to the northern part of Burma. The area fell increasingly under the influence of the southern Chinese province of Yunnan, its immediate northern neighbor. Baja Yunnan is to Yunnan as Baja California, the northern Mexican state, is to America's El Dorado, California, "baja" meaning south.

Singh described the smugglers' setting,

> As the sun set, suddenly out of nowhere, it would be like a mela (Hindi for "carnival" or "fair") and a large makeshift flea market would spring up. You could buy everything you wanted. The chaps with the money to buy all of this were the people in the Burmese army. Who else had money at that time? But the word that my father was engaging in contraband had gotten out and officially they were keeping a close eye on him.

Singh's father's experience and her own memories of the smuggling and illegal trade in contraband in the late 1960s were merely the tip of the iceberg. The most important side effect of Sino-Burmese relations was the establishment of a vibrant illegal trade along its porous borders from the early 1970s through the 1980s. Burmese insurgents, communist guerillas, and Burmese and Chinese soldiers transformed from enemies on either side of a daytime border skirmish to collaborative illegal traders at night. Suddenly, one could exchange Chinese consumer goods—ranging from household utensils to bicycles—for Burmese rubies and timber. By some estimates, in the mid-1980s illegal trade in Burma was three times the official trade; the total illegal trade (excluding drugs) made up about 40 percent of GNP, or about $3 billion annually. For near-bankrupt Burma, smuggling provided sustenance. For India the territorial and ideological battleground that was Burma had morphed into an economic battleground with China.

In September 1988 a large prodemocracy movement was violently crushed by the military junta. India condemned these actions, and the Indian embassy in Rangoon became a makeshift hospital for students injured in the crackdown. Since then India has not given military support to Burmese activists and, while declaring ideological support for the prodemocracy movement, has followed a policy of disengagement in relation to the Burmese government. China, however, supported the antidemocratic junta. When the United States imposed economic and arms sanctions against the Burmese junta, China thumbed its nose at the international community and cemented its ties with Burma, exchanging recognition and hard cash in return for timber, raw materials, and access to sea lanes. Cozying up to the generals represented a departure from the Maoist policies of supporting communist insurgencies in Burma. As part of a broader trend, Chinese financial support to communist movements worldwide dropped from 4.5 percent of the total fiscal expenditure in the late 1960s to 0.8 percent until 1979.[24]

Other signs indicated that China no longer emphasized spreading the communist gospel. Unlike Mao's ideology-led nation, China had a new kind of engagement powered by domestic economic success. In 1982 the political report of the Twelfth National CCP Conference stated, "We Marxists and Leninists believe that communism will definitely be realized worldwide in the future, but revolution cannot be imported and should be chosen by the people in different countries themselves."[25] Thus Beijing began leveraging its economic clout to support its political preferences.

Over the next decade military and economic cooperation between Burma and China overshadowed any previous relations between the two countries and the cooperation that Burma had with any third country. Moral outrage from democracies worldwide was ignored. Burma was flooded by Chinese aid, arms, and consumer goods. By the mid-1990s the Burmese junta had acquired tanks, aircraft, artillery, and other arms from China with an estimated value of $1.2 billion.[26] By 1995 the value of trade between China and Burma amounted to an unprecedented $767 million. But given the trade in contraband, it was clear that official trade statistics grossly underestimated the level of trade between the two countries. During the mid- to late 1990s it appeared that George Orwell's *Burma Days* and Amitav Ghosh's *Glass Palace* novels, which told tales of British colonialism and Indian commercial dominance, were quaintly anachronistic. Even a staunchly nationalist Burma, the very Burma that had thrown out the Indians and targeted Burmese Chinese in riots during the 1960s, had come under the Chinese spell. Burma had become Baja Yunnan.

In 1996 Jaspal Singh revisited her hometown of Taunggyi after thirty years. "Three things struck me," Singh said. "Food, people, and shops were all Chinese. I bet that 99.9 percent of the goods for sale were from across that border. I was shocked. Instead of the Buddhist pagodas that were such a prominent part of the landscape, all I could see were these new Chinese pagodas, which were far gaudier. I asked my friends, 'How did so many of them come here? How can they live here, they are not allowed to buy property?'" Singh's friend whispered back, "The Chinese in Burma call themselves the 'Wa' and claim that they are a Burmese tribe, and are even listed in the Taunggyi museum."

Indeed, what Singh witnessed was the ongoing "Yunnanization" of northern Burma. Illegal immigration was widespread. Soon, a million Chinese had crossed into Lashio, north of Mandalay. To accommodate a population that was half Chinese, Lashio ordered its primary schools to teach primarily in Chinese.[27] The population of Mandalay, the soul of Burma's Buddhist religion and culture, was one-fifth Yunnanese. Economically Mandalay was viewed as a Chinese city. One analyst pointed out. "The Chinese can move down to Mandalay; they are not supposed to go there but they do. They can buy land by buying Burmese residency permits; they purchase registration cards from people who die and so on."[28]

Indian inaction is visible in the status of the Kunming Initiative, an agreement that in principle boosts China's trade with South Asia. The initiative was signed between China, India, and Burma in 1999 when the countries' representatives met in the Yunnanese capital, Kunming. One of the issues discussed was the revitalization of Stillwell Road—also called Ledo Road—stretching for about eleven hundred miles from Kunming to Ledo, a rail depot in India's northeastern state of Assam.[29] U.S. Army General Joseph Stillwell, regional commander during World War II and Chiang Kai-shek's chief of staff, had built the road as a supply route to counterattack the advancing Japanese forces that had dealt him a severe blow in Burma. About 35 miles of the road ran through India, 650 miles were in Burma, and 400 miles were in China.

Not surprisingly, the Indian part of the road is in disrepair but China has developed its part into a six-lane highway from Kunming to the Burma border. In keeping with their ability to build cities overnight at home, the Chinese have invested their money and expertise—in the form of surveyors—into reducing the Burmese portion of the road by half through a series of shortcuts. Also in keeping with India's chaotic and unproductive policies, an Indian official in China admitted that he had no idea what the time frame was for India to change its stance, a statement that came soon after an Indian ambassador had asked the Kunming delegations to be patient.[30]

But the Indians have a tough task ahead. The territory is very rough, and security concerns are paramount. An important part of the problem is that even though trade between northeastern Indian states and the bordering Chinese provinces has faltered, northeastern India is itself wracked with tension and isolated economically from the rest of India. Intercommunity and secessionist violence in Assam and other states are both a cause and a result of this failure to develop.[31] Thus the direct land trade route cannot be used. Goods have to travel in a roundabout fashion from Kunming to Zhanjiang in Guangdong Province and then on ships to India through the Strait of Malacca, traversing more than thirty-seven hundred miles.[32]

While Indians have relied on the soft power of goodwill and immigrant commercial ties to exercise influence in Burma, the Chinese have exerted their influence with all their resources—military, economic, *and* cultural. The Chinese have engulfed Burma with a little bit of everything. This approach was visible elsewhere in Southeast Asia, where Chinese trade has also increased dramatically. At the same time India's influence has declined.

In the early 1990s India's foreign policy took a U-turn. Nehruvian idealism was replaced by economic realism and the once-denounced junta generals were wooed. Nevertheless, India appears wracked by uncertainty and indecision—witness the standstill regarding the Kunming Initiative—and remains far behind China in its ability to win over Burma. Nowhere is this more apparent than in the energy field.

New Roads to Mandalay: Oil and Gas

Burma, once a battleground for rubies and teak, is now a strategic player in the battle for another natural resource—oil—and for access to waterways to transport oil. By 2020, 70 percent of China's oil needs will be imported.[33] Most of its oil comes from the Middle East and Africa through the Strait of Malacca, a sea route that can be blocked by the United States, Japan, and potentially India. Burma, accessible by land and sea, is the safest alternative route and one that China is pursuing aggressively. In July 2004 Premier Wen Jiabao and the Burmese prime minister Khin Nyunt discussed building a pipeline from Burma's western deep-water port of Sittwe to southwest China, a route shorter than the Strait of Malacca by 1,820 sea miles.[34]

Virtually every Chinese energy company is active in Burma. China National Petroleum Corporation (CNPC) began producing natural gas a decade ago. China's third-largest offshore oil and gas producer, China National Offshore Oil Corporation (CNOOC), began to cooperate with state-owned Myanmar Oil and Gas Enterprise and two other foreign companies to explore an onshore block in Burma's western area in 2004. China Petrochemical Corporation (SinoPec), the largest state-owned refiner, also signed production-sharing contracts in 2005 to explore oil and gas in the north of Rangoon.

China has not hesitated to deal with states that the West labels pariahs. Its continued relations with Burma are a textbook example. Indeed, after the arrest of the democracy activist and Nobel Peace Prize winner Aung San Suu Kyi by the military junta in 2000, the United States strengthened sanctions on Burma, and Secretary of State Condoleezza Rice named Burma an "outpost of tyranny." The irony is that the billion-dollar Burma–China bilateral trade significantly offsets the economic losses caused by sanctions, estimated at roughly $200 million annually.[35] In 2003 Beijing announced a $200 million loan to Burma for improving electricity generation capacity at almost the same time that the Bush administration signed into law the most recent round of economic sanctions preventing Burma from exporting textiles the United States.

Arguably sanctions suit Chinese oil giants, because sanctions ensure that the playing field is clear of Western oil giants in places like Burma, Iran, Sudan, and Venezuela. China also uses its position and influence in international organizations, such as the United Nations, to lobby for the interests of what are otherwise pariah states. In addition many states selling oil to China—Iraq, Iran, Sudan, Angola, and Nigeria—are buying Chinese weapons. Beijing views selling arms to these countries as a way not only to build close ties but also to decrease its energy import bill.[35]

India too is short of oil. But the Chinese trio of CNPC, CNOOC, and SinoPec outmaneuvers India. For example, Angola's state-owned oil company Sonangoal blocked India's state-owned Oil and Natural Gas Commission (ONGC) from buying Shell's 50 percent stake in Sonangoal. The deal would have yielded about 5 million tons of crude oil daily for India from 2008. Angolan authorities did not appreciate Shell's direct deals with the Indian company. India, after all, offered only $200 million for developing railways, whereas the Chinese were willing to ante up ten times as much for several projects in Angola. Not surprisingly China won the deal. "Aid for oil" has emerged as part of a multidimensional Chinese approach toward energy-rich states. Chinese leaders have been all over Africa in recent times. In Zimbabwe, dealing with Robert Mugabe's unsavory regime, China has invested in minerals, roads, and farming and supplied the dictator with jets and other weaponry.[37] No conditionality is attached to these deals, especially in terms of political reforms.

T. N. R. Rao, a former petroleum secretary—the chief bureaucrat in India's energy ministry—summarized why the Indian companies are handicapped in such competition: "In issues of energy security, along with commercial considerations, it is equally important to factor in non-commercial and geopolitical considerations and any comparison with values purely arrived at on a textbook basis makes no sense," said Rao. "When China bids, for instance, it [regards] issues [in terms of] national interest whereas in India, where post-mortem of any large financial transaction is the rule, it is always necessary to have some benchmarks that can stand scrutiny."[38]

Regulatory red tape compounds Indian companies' inability to compete. Before he was deposed, Subir Raha, acting as the CEO of ONGC with three decades of oil industry experience, appeared to spend as much time trying to outmaneuver the Chinese—unsuccessfully—as he did fighting regulators and politicians who were allegedly on his team. Government policy appears to be as coordinated in China as it is disorienting and uncoordinated in India. The unseemly fracas between Raha and India's minister for energy ostensibly dealt with the latter's attempt to appoint a bureaucrat to ONGC's board of directors. Raha objected on the grounds that the appointment amounted to government meddling. "Public-sector companies cannot be treated as government departments," he said, adding, "Companies are expected to make profits, departments are not." The minister felt obliged to intervene to ensure that he received sufficient information from Raha's team and that Raha did not treat ONGC as his own fiefdom. The net result compromised operational efficiency.[39] Of course dissent between regulators and operators is not rare—witness Russia's Gazprom or Brazil's Petrobras—but it severely limits the ability of Indian firms to compete with Chinese firms. To complicate matters further, after Raha stepped down from his post at ONGC, no one was named to take his place. Instead political factions argued over who should be appointed as the firm's CEO.

The Indians appear to agree with the Chinese that searching for equity oil—that is, securing equity positions in oil fields worldwide—is the only way to guard against scarcity. An early exponent of this approach was post–World War II France. Starved of its own natural resources, the only well on native soil at Péchelbronn in Alsace, discovered in 1745 in the time of Louis XV, France exposed its energy vulnerability in the war years by relying solely on American oil companies. Subsequently the French government financed Total Petroleum's forays overseas,[40] and when it realized that was insufficient to insulate it against OPEC's maneuvers in the 1973 oil crisis, France embarked on a program to encourage the use of nuclear energy. Today France relies on nuclear plants for 80 percent of its energy.

Vijay Kelkar, a former Indian petroleum secretary, told me that both China and India were simply mimicking this precedent.[41] If they had France's technological wherewithal—France benefited from a long tradition of research in nuclear sciences—they might have pursued the nuclear option. But Kelkar believes that China and India should not feel an urgency to nail down equity oil but rely instead on the market mechanism for acquiring oil. In Kelkar's opinion either you pay for oil as and when you need it, or you pay for it up front when you acquire the equity position in an oil field. He suggested that India, situated among some of the world's largest natural gas reserves, will move toward a reliance on natural gas, making a furious surge for oil unnecessary. The economics of natural gas might leave the buyer less vulnerable to scarcity than buyers of oil. A gas seller is wedded to a particular buyer by virtue of a physical pipeline fixed in the immediate term, and cannot easily deploy its wares elsewhere. Oil, in contrast, can be shipped by tankers anywhere, thus obliging buyers everywhere to bid against one another for access to scarce oil.

But the race for equity oil continues. China's ability to use its wealth and its willingness to deploy it in places where the Western world's oil companies are constrained has made it the leading influence in Burma and elsewhere. China's patronage is well understood on the streets of Burma. "As long as China remains friendly nothing will change. China can provide everything the country needs from a needle to a nuclear bomb."[42] Meanwhile India's oil policy, which has evolved from condemning the "generals" to accommodating them, thereby taking a page out of China's book, continues to lack the sure-footedness that the Chinese have perfected.

From Poems to Planes

Beginning in the Han Dynasty (206 B.C.E.–220 C.E.) and peaking during the Tang Dynasty (618–907), China-Burma relations were characterized primarily by cultural exchange. The prince of what was then called the Pyu Country led thirty-five artists to China for a goodwill visit, and the renowned poets Bai Juyi and Yuan Zhen eulogized "the music of Pyu."[43] In the Ming (1368–1644) and Qing (1616–1911) dynasties the court set up a translation organization and invited scholars to teach and translate the Burmese language. Burma was one of the first nonsocialist countries to recognize the People's Republic of China and, along with China and India, advocated the Five Principles of Peaceful Coexistence. The late Chinese marshal Chen Yi composed more than a dozen poems describing his visits to Burma. "To Burma Friends," for example, intones, "At the top of a river lies the home of me / At the other end, that of thee / Infinite feeling we harbor for each other / As from the same river we fetch drinking water."[44] Poems like this are still widely recited by the peoples of the two countries.

But long ago sharing poetry yielded to financing communist insurgencies, then to economic inducements backed by military might, and finally to the Chinese emigration from Yunnan into northern Burma. The emergent Chinese approach to Burma reflects its bulging muscles in the region. Even the United States has found itself being edged out by the Chinese-orchestrated Shanghai Cooperation Council, which embraces oil-producing central Asian republics today.

Whether by engaging in diplomatic niceties, exchanging Chinese weapons for oil and gas from pariah states, or investing in cobalt and copper in civil war–torn Central Africa, China leads with its wallet, unrestrained by politically correct norms of international relations. Chinese rhetoric today, which privileges its "peaceful rise" and "harmonious society" while continuing to operate with abandon in war-torn Africa, echoes China's behavior in 1955 when it took aggressive action in Tibet and Korea while charming delegates at the Bandung conference with its talk of peaceful engagement.

Chapter Twelve

Film Stars and Gurus

Soft Power in Bollywood and Beyond

Late one night I was strolling around Beijing's Forbidden City with a Chinese colleague, and we ran into a thin, wiry man who politely offered us his services as rickshaw driver and local guide. I immediately took to him; a Westerner might have been concerned at his ability to pull a rickshaw, but I am accustomed to seeing far more emaciated men do the job in India and Africa. Mr. Ji from Anhui Province pulled us along effortlessly for more than an hour and seemed grateful for the 50 percent tip we offered. He explained that he and his wife, who sold tea-boiled eggs and noodles in one of the ubiquitous roadside stands, had come from Anhui Province and became part of Beijing's "floating" population—the illegal or in some cases semilegal migrants who come to the city from the provinces to make a living. My colleague and I calculated that his monthly income, equivalent to about 3,000–5,000 RMB ($400 to $650), was commendable given the cutthroat competition among rickshaw pullers in the vicinity of Tiananmen Square. Regrettably, although close to the average starting salary among white-collar workers, it probably did not go very far in Beijing.

I asked Mr. Ji what most readily came to mind when I mentioned India. He spontaneously burst into song, humming the Hindi words of "Awaara Hoon," the title song of a famous Hindi movie from 1951, *Awaara* (Hindi for "vagabond"). My colleague confirmed that most Chinese adults would recognize the song. In the movie Raj Kapoor—a major star in Indian films of the early 1950s—plays a vagabond estranged from his father, a renowned judge. In the opening scene the vagabond is on trial and is being defended by a beautiful young lawyer—who just happens to be the ward of the judge—with whom the vagabond ultimately falls in love. As their love story and the courtroom drama unfold, the film explores the eternal nature-versus-nurture debate, exploring how social and economic class affects upbringing.

Awaara gripped China's imagination. The film's anticlass theme particularly resonated with Chairman Mao, who declared it to be one of his favorite movies. His admiration was echoed by audiences worldwide, especially all over the Middle East and Russia. A reporter commented, "This film of the fifties broke office records (as the phrase goes) in a hundred places, places that ancient Indian colonialism hadn't reached."[1]

My colleague and I continued our walk and close to midnight met more *Awaara* fans. We walked past beautiful willow trees by an old, stately house adorned with the traditional red trappings considered auspicious in China. Unexpectedly, a flashlight shone in our direction and polite but firm voices inquired after our purpose. Two women emerged from behind the beam. We assumed they were the homeowners, but they turned out to be directors of the local Resident Committee, the smallest administrative unit in China's system of governance. Part of their job was to ensure that nothing was amiss on the streets. These fifty-year-old women had been educated until high school then sent off to the front lines during the Cultural Revolution. When they returned they became self-educated. In the period following the Cultural Revolution, they could—like others sufficiently motivated—read and educate themselves, hire teachers to help them through tests, and earn a diploma. My query of India again brought the prompt reaction of movies. One of the women tried unsuccessfully to hum *Awaara Hoon*, but it was recognizable enough. The other woman waved her hands around her face, in a gesture indicative of beauty, later translated by my colleague. She thought of movies first, but not about a particular one, just the color of the traditional Indian *saree*—a long cloth typically draped around the waist by Indian women and part of the costume and set in any movie—and of the melody and myriad song sequences. Intriguingly, or perhaps this was the reason for the response, her clothing was incredibly drab.

Awaara of course is only one of the thousands of Indian movies seen by cinemagoers worldwide. India's film industry—Bollywood—is the principle means by which India exports its soft power. The scale of Bollywood has eclipsed that of Hollywood; in 2003, 3.6 billion people attended eleven hundred Bollywood movies compared with the 2.6 billion moviegoers who attended six hundred Hollywood films.[2] Film star Amitabh Bachchan outpolled Chaplin, Olivier, and Brando in a BBC online vote as the "greatest star of stage or screen."[3] By some accounts Bollywood has produced twenty-seven thousand feature films and several thousand documentaries in fifty-two languages.[4] These numbers attest to the success of the industry's entrepreneurship, unaided and relatively unregulated by the state.

A common street scene in movie-mad Bombay—on Juhu Beach in the suburbs or in the sylvan surroundings of suburban Aarey Milk Colony—consisted of actors or actresses going through multiple takes of a particular scene surrounded by film crews that were made up of camaramen, equipment, and film directors. A large portion of this milling humanity included aspirants from smaller towns and villages who believed they were headed for the glamour of Bollywood.

An early boyhood memory is of an actress, Kamini Kaushal, who was our neighbor in the early 1970s in Bombay's ritzy Malabar Hill, home to several other film stars as well. I remember Kamini Kaushal most fondly because she hosted a Sunday kids television program on which I was once invited to participate with other children my age. I knew that being on national television with a film actress was something special, but I have no recollection of the event. My parents now assure me that my own participation was entirely unmemorable, consisting of noisily eating a snack at an inopportune moment.

According to the political scientist Joseph Nye, "Much of American soft power has been produced by Hollywood, Harvard, Microsoft and Michael Jordan."[5] What are India's channels of exporting soft power other than film? India has never produced aspiring athletes such as Jordan, so that channel is easily dismissed. The most obvious candidate is the software industry—the major reason India has reemerged on the world economic map. On a recent trip through half a dozen cities in central and eastern China, I conducted an informal survey to test the legitimacy of that candidate. Over a couple of weeks I asked some forty individuals—among them doctors and academics, Party officials and city functionaries patrolling streets, shopkeepers and rickshaw drivers—what images were conjured by the word *India*. A resounding 80 percent pointed to the film industry, and this was in 2005, at least fifteen years after Indian films stopped being the only available fare for Chinese moviegoers. A distant second was Buddhism, and the software industry ranked third.

Another viable contender among India's primary soft-power exports is the nation's intellectual tradition. The last two hundred years have witnessed many examples of what the nineteenth-century diplomat Sir Charles Eliot called "the spread of Indian thought."[6] One of the most significant was Swami Vivekananda, the orange-robed monk who took the Chicago Conference on World Religions by storm in 1893. Vivekananda characterized himself as a "compact India," a cultural and spiritual ambassador of his country's philosophy. His influence survives in the dozens of missions that continue his teachings in the United States over a hundred years later. A more modern cultural ambassador is Deepak Chopra, the Indian immigrant and doctor who is America's resident self-healer. Over the past two decades Chopra has emerged from the mainstream of American medicine to propagate inner healing and to spread the gospel of yoga.

China has no comparable cultural ambassadors. Why the discrepancy? One reason lies in the role of government in culture of the two countries. Many Indians would consider a seat at the Oscars—Hollywood's premiere award ceremony—as valuable as a seat on the Security Council and participation in an art auction at Christie's—New York's famed auctioneer—as significant as a place at the table of a White House state dinner. That mind-set would be highly unusual in China. Filmmakers and artists in China are on the government payrolls, serving as mouthpieces of official propaganda rather than ambassadors of culture. Indian artists are nothing if not loudly critical; indeed, that is the source of their legitimacy. Bollywood, responding to India's appalling record on human development, focuses its cameras on Indian society's underbelly, be it caste, communal violence, or its favorite theme, government corruption. The messages these ambassadors send are not always cohesive and reveal no overarching national algorithm to reach superpower status. The contrast with China's disciplined approach to attaining power—and to my mind, there is much to commend about the discipline—whereby it declares quantifiable goals (like having five of the world's leading universities and twenty Fortune 500 firms), is palpable. India's soft power cannot follow a disciplined plan because its decentralized message emanates from its diversity, its entrepreneurial spirit, and more recently its international ambition.

On China's side the baton is passed from premiers to generals to party cadres. Team India passes it from internationally acclaimed film director Mira Nair to spiritual strongman Deepak Chopra to academic conscience Amartya Sen to software czar Azim Premji.

Making Cinema Indian

On December 28, 1895, Auguste and Louis Lumière showcased ten short films lasting a total of just twenty minutes in the basement lounge of the Grand Café on Paris's Boulevard des Capucines.[7] The most sensational of these showed a train pulling into the station. Reportedly many people in the audience got up from their seats and ran for safety as the train pulled in. Yet that day is remembered in film history not because of the content of the Lumières' films but because it was the first demonstration of the cinematograph, a device that effectively functioned as a camera, projector, and printer and changed the world of film.

Just six months later the Lumière brothers held another demonstration of their revolutionary technique in Bombay's Watson Hotel. Within a year films were being shown regularly in major cities throughout colonial India, most notably Bombay, Calcutta, and Madras. In Bombay, Clifton and Co. announced daily screenings at their Meadows Street Photography Studio. In 1889, two Italians, Colorello and Cornaglia, organized film shows in tents at the Azad Maidan, Bombay's equivalent of New York's Central Park or London's Regent's Park.[8] Despite a rich indigenous culture of dance and theater, Indians embraced the medium of film. Dozens of entrepreneurs saw great opportunities in filmmaking. They began not only to screen imported films but also to buy equipment from England and produce films with varying degrees of ambition. By the 1910s film was making inroads into rural India. Around that time the man who would come to be known as the Father of Indian Cinema, Dundhiraj Phalke, witnessed the screening of *The Life of Christ* at the American-Indian Cinema in Bombay. Over the next few months Phalke—who had previously worked as a photographic assistant, portrait photographer, stage makeup artist, and illusionist's assistant—saw every film he could and studied all the available literature on film technique. He was convinced that the only way an indigenous film industry would be established would be by tackling Indian themes. "Like The Life of Christ we shall make pictures on Rama and Krishna," he said, referring to heroes of Hindu epics.[5]

In 1912, financed by a personal loan, Phalke sailed to London to learn the tricks of the trade from British filmmakers. In a few months he returned to India armed with a Williamson camera, a perforating machine, developing and printing equipment, and some raw film stock. He immediately confronted two obstacles to making his Indian epic. The first concerned financing. His longtime friend Yeshwant Nadkarni, a Bombay dealer of photographic equipment, had expressed interest in funding Phalke's film. To convince Nadkarni that his project was a sound investment, Phalke filmed an astonishingly simple subject: a pea plant sprouting in an earthenware pot. When his short film, appropriately titled *Growth of a Pea Plant*, was showcased in a small theater, audiences were astonished to see the plant grow in just a few minutes.[10] Phalke won Nadkarni's backing.

The second problem Phalke confronted was finding female talent. Although for centuries theater and performing arts had been held in high esteem, no respectable Indian woman was willing to act in Phalke's film. Even a prostitute turned down his proposal to make her his female lead. Eventually Phalke resorted to casting an effeminate male cook to play the heroine. Phalke then launched *Raja Harishchandra,* a silent four-reel film with subtitles in Hindi and English. The film told the story of a righteous king who sacrificed his kingdom and family for the sake of his principles. The gods, impressed with his honesty, restored him to his former glory.

The subject was not surprising given Phalke's upbringing in an orthodox Brahmin family and his desire to Indianize cinema. The movie opened to a large audience on May 17, 1913, at the Coronation Theater in Bombay. Phalke played the lead role of the king, with the cook as lead female and Phalke's son playing the king's son.[11] The movie was entirely a product of private enterprise; Phalke directed, wrote, photographed, and distributed the film under the name Phalke Film Company. The government was completely disinterested and uninvolved. Perhaps that was one reason for its resounding critical and financial success.

Soon after, Phalke moved his company to Nasik, a small town that today is a four-hour drive from Mumbai. Phalke Film Company has been likened to the Indian "joint family system," in which several generations live together and engage in a family business overseen by the patriarch. Phalke was responsible for all aspects of pre- and post-production. The film cast lived at the family compound, which served as studio, set, and home. Perhaps most importantly Phalke drew on this group of family and friends to fund his movies.[12]

By 1918, when the joint family system could no longer sustain the company's growth, Phalke launched Hindustan Films Company and turned to the market to raise funds. Financiers were convinced that World War I would have a strong negative impact on the business of movies. After all, material required for filmmaking was primarily imported from Germany. Nevertheless, Phalke turned to Bombay's commercial classes, who had made their fortunes from the cotton boom and wielded both economic and political power.[13]

Another pioneer from this era was Jamsetji Framji Madan. Following a career as an actor, Madan bought the theater company in which he had worked.[14] By 1905 he had turned to producing and backed a film depicting a protest rally against the partition of Bengal.[15] Like many other Indian filmmakers, Madan realized the power of showing real images to a wide audience, be they the glories of British colonial rule, *durbars* (Hindi for "court scenes"), or raucous protests. Two years later Madan started building the first theater chain, the Elephantine Picture Palaces. In addition to showing imported movies and filmed stage plays in his theaters, he began making his own movies. By 1918 grand sets had become the norm for Madan productions, and he claimed ownership of some three hundred cinemas in India. His exclusive contracts with British and American companies ensured a steady supply of films to screen at his theaters, something other Indian cinema owners could only dream of. Madan's Elephantine Picture Palaces became India's largest production-distribution and exhibition company and expanded to neighboring Sri Lanka and Burma.

Thus, within only a decade of the Lumière brothers' arrival in Bombay, extraordinary events had occurred in the world of Indian film. Entrepreneurs often imported talent, technology, and equipment from overseas; such collaborations were not disdained. But the films' themes were strictly Indian. The Indian directors of the time understood the significance of religion and mythology to their audiences. Phalke and Madan drew extensively on major Indian classics like the *Mahabharata* and *Ramayana*, two epics at the heart of Hindu religion. If a film's plot was not a strict telling of one of those two sagas, viewers could rest assured that some aspect of the tales would be invoked. For example, a righteous woman would evoke the memory of King Rama's devoted but suffering wife, Sita, of King Rama. An evil family member would remind one of an evil uncle of Krishna, in the *Mahabharata*.

Films also mirrored popular culture. As Satyajit Ray, one of India's most acclaimed film directors, noted dryly, "[T]he ingredients of the average Hindi film are well known; color (Eastman preferred); songs (six or seven?) in voices one knows and trusts; dance—solo and ensemble—the more frenzied the better; bad girl, good girl, bad guy, good guy, romance (but no kisses); tears, guffaws, fights, chases, melodrama; characters who exist in a social vacuum; dwellings which do not exist outside the studio floor; locations in Kulu, Manali, Ooty, Kashmir, London, Paris, Hong Kong, Tokyo . . . See any three Hindi films, and two will have all the ingredients listed above."[16] Ray believed that the songs and dances so prevalent in Hindi films are producers' attempts at simplifying their fare for a largely uneducated audience brought up on the simple traditions of the *jatra*, a form of rural drama.

To Ray's generalizations, I will add two, one conspicuous by its absence, the other by its presence.

Absent is any hint of political intervention or government interference. In India politics remained aloof from film. Despite film's obvious influence on people, neither the British Raj nor the independence movement tried to use the medium for propaganda purposes. Political leaders did not appear to consider film a vital part of the national infrastructure, denying it the stature given to "nation building" industries like steel. Perhaps the mythological themes of Indian film caused them to look away disinterestedly. Of course films portraying anticolonial sentiments were being made. One example is *Bhakta Vidur*, which was banned in Hyderabad (Sind province in modern Pakistan) because its protagonist bore a strong resemblance to Mahatma Gandhi. The film was "banned in Madras and Sind, becom[ing] Indian cinema's first censorship controversy."[17] Some filmmakers chose to comment on delicate social issues; for example, the unsavory aspects of caste were depicted in *Achoot Kanya* (*Untouchable Girl*), a 1936 film that famously depicted a love affair between a high-caste Brahmin boy and a low-caste untouchable girl.

Present, in contrast, is the very special experience of attending a movie. What makes cinema Indian is the movie going experience. In Bombay, when I was a boy it began with the ordeal of standing in line for hours on end; an affluent moviegoer would send an office peon as a stand-in. Inside, the second part of the Indian experience began: the sound and noise of the theater, and I do not mean just the movie's musical numbers. From the stalls—the cheap seats in the house—cheers and catcalls punctuated the dialogue and served as "thumbs up" or "thumbs down" reviews of the film's songs and dances. As a boy, I listened as much to the audience as to the dialogue— unless, of course, we were watching cartoons.

The Devil's Second-Class Opera

The filmmaking innovation of the Lumière brothers came to China on August 11, 1896, the first recorded date of a motion picture screening in Shanghai. But Western film was seen as a lesser entertainment than Chinese opera—a popular art that had been performed in huge theaters since the twelfth century. Film was relegated to second-class status and was perceived to have originated from Chinese shadow puppetry, in which figures made of paper or animal skin were manipulated against a backlit translucent screen. Thus the Chinese referred to the new type of entertainment *Dianguang Yingxi* as "electric shadow play" and did not see moving pictures as a dramatic break from what they had already mastered. As one Chinese author said, "The entertainment centers offered a somewhat lowbrow alternative to Chinese opera." Screenings were "often located in rooms on the top levels of department stores;, they featured story tellers, jugglers, acrobats who might otherwise be plying their trade on the streets."[18] By contrast, the first cinemas in India were located in high-profile urban centers and on British cantonments.

A decade after the Lumières' Shanghai showing, the film industry in China was moribund. A review of *Shadow Magic* (in Chinese, *Xiyang Jing*), Ann Hu's 2000 film that reconstructs the political context around China's nascent film industry tells why that was so:

> With . . . *Shadow Magic* . . . we are transported back to the . . . days of 1902 Beijing, where moving pictures were not only considered a devilish "foreign trick," but, according to Hu's vision, a fearsome technology that threatened to single-handedly destroy Chinese culture.... *Shadow Magic's* story begins two

years after the Boxer Rebellion was brutally crushed by western expeditionary forces and a weak-willed Qing court that reneged on its support of the anti-foreigner Boxers . . . In the wake of staggering remunerations and the humiliation of China's government—including the insult of having GI Joes squatting in the Forbidden City for an entire year—Beijingers weren't exactly eager to hear the West's latest bright new idea.[19]

Unlike in India, it was foreigners who ushered film into China. James Ricalton, an American, began screening films in teahouses. The first Chinese film was made in 1905 by Ren Jingfeng at his photography shop in Beijing. The film, titled *Dingjun Mountain*, was a recording of one act from a Beijing opera. Ren, who had studied photography in Japan, bought a manual camera and fourteen sets of films from a German merchant and proceeded to churn out opera recordings.[20] Opera house owners naturally saw this as theft of their property. Mysteriously, Ren's photography shop burned down in 1909.[21] But by then motion pictures had acquired notoriety among the Chinese. Upper-class Chinese society still enjoyed opera, but film drew its followers from a cross section of society.

An American, Benjamin Brodsky, capitalized on China's new acceptance of film by founding the Asia Film Company in 1910. Brodsky had a virtual "monopoly of the business [controlling] eighty moving picture theatres scattered from Peking to Kong-Tchang, and from Canton to Tyng-Choo."[22] Nevertheless, the business was not as profitable as Brodsky had hoped. A couple of years into this venture he sold the business to an American insurance executive named Yashell. Wanting to give the studio a distinctly Chinese look and feel, Yashell hired Zhang Shichuan, a trader with no specific background in the arts but with connections in Chinese theater, and Zheng Zhengui, a leading figure in Shanghai theater. With Yashell behind the scenes, Zhang and Zheng produced China's first fictional feature. Titled *The Difficult Couple*, it was released in 1913, the same year Phalke's *Raja Harishchandra* started playing in Indian cinemas. In contrast with the mythological theme of *Raja Harishchandra*, the story of *The Difficult Couple* was a comic look at the wedding rituals traditional in Zheng's hometown in Guangdong Province. Other Chinese films, made in Hong Kong and produced with American money, like *Zhuangzi Tests His Wife* (1913), likewise were based on everyday Chinese traditions and ways of life rather than religious or mythological themes.[23]

Reels of Propaganda

China's *minzu dianying* (national cinema), after being buffeted by antiforeign sentiment, had to contend with civil war between the Communists and the

Nationalists first, and then the Japanese invasion and brutality. The normal development of the film industry finally began in the late 1920s, with different production houses, including some all-Chinese ones, focusing on different genres—like the social problems genre and the martial arts genre. But political intervention soon put an end to such normalcy.[24]

By 1927 Chiang Kai-shek's nationalist army had achieved success against the Communists and had settled in Hankou, Shanghai, and Nanjing. The nationalists established the National Film Censorship Committee in 1931 to impose strict controls on film content. Interestingly, while a nationalist government was in power, foreigners continued to dominate film exhibition in China. Major theaters, including those managed by the Chinese, showed first-run Hollywood films acquired through agreements signed with American film companies beginning in 1932. Behind the facade of mutually beneficial alliances, however, were tensions between Hollywood and China regarding film content. Soon the Chinese were protesting against cultural imperialism and their negative portrayal in Hollywood productions.

One particular movie, *Shanghai Kuaiche* (*Shanghai Express*), illustrated the strain between U.S. filmmakers and Chinese audiences. Produced in the United States by Paramount Pictures in 1932, *Shanghai Express* was an adventure-thriller depicting prostitution, train robberies, and civil war—not activities considered palatable by a "modern China." The movie was banned by the Guomindang censorship committee. Executives at Paramount responded by agreeing not to show the film in China, but they did not destroy their prints as the censorship committee had ordered. When the censors reacted by declining permits to other Paramount films, the U.S. film giant ignored the ban. That behavior sparked complaints from the censors, which led Paramount to threaten not to submit any other films for review. Ultimately Paramount was sheltered by the extraterritorial protections offered to ventures in the International Settlement. Hollywood coercion tended to work when it commanded technological superiority and economic power, especially in the treaty ports where Chinese laws did not apply.

Hollywood was challenged in China by the nationalism of a substantial number of Chinese artists who routinely denounced the hub of U.S. filmmaking as culturally imperialist.[25] In the early 1930s three major studios (Lianhua, Mingxing, and Tianyi) and two smaller ones (Xinhua and Yihua) dominated Chinese cinema. Each studio had clear political alignments. Lianhua's overly moralistic themes, which supported the Guomindang's mission to root out "base culture," allowed that studio a privileged position. In turn Lianhua produced some of the most notable films of the period. Tianyi studio was forced by the Guomindang into making propaganda films in the aftermath of the Japanese invasion of Manchuria. However, almost all the major studios, including Lianhua, had Communist Party supporters within their midst. In fact, the Communists had secretly organized the League of Leftist Performing Artists. When one studio—Yihua—crossed the line with its progressive leftist tones, the Guomindang initiated a riot that destroyed most of the studio. The responsibility for the act was taken by the Anti-Communist Squad of the Shanghai Film Industry.[26] Despite such coercion, some Chinese directors managed to make films that depicted the disillusionment of ordinary people under the Guomindang.

As far as the studios were concerned, they had barely taken sides between the Guomindang and the Communists before the Japanese invaded. Both sides were aware of the importance of film in disseminating propaganda. Later, when Mao took full control of Chinese cinema, he perfected the earlier attempts of the Guomindang and the Japanese. Even before the formal establishment of the People's Republic of China in 1949, Mao had set up the Central Film Bureau (CFB). China's three largest studios fell completely under the control of the new system. Altogether the CFB oversaw more than three-quarters of China's film output. As one scholar put it, during four decades under the Communists, Chinese cinema "often seemed one long reel of propaganda."[27] In the seventeen years before the Cultural Revolution was launched, 603 feature films and 8,342 reels of documentary and newsreels were produced—all sponsored by the CCP. The party dispatched Chinese filmmakers to Moscow to learn the art of filmmaking. Later on the Central Film Bureau, through the Beijing Film Academy, continued to specify targets for films on agriculture, worker productivity, and the like.

On one rare occasion in 1947, a movie not only pleased the Chinese Communists, but amazingly the Indian Congress and the British colonial forces. It helped that it exemplified genuine Sino-Indian friendship developing at the time. Directed by the renowned V. Shantaram, *Dr. Kotnis ki Amar Kahaani* (*Dr. Kotnis's Immortal Story*) is the true story of Dr. Dwarkanath Kotnis. In 1937, after the Japanese invaded China, the communist general Zhu De asked Nehru to send Indian doctors to China to help in the war effort. Nehru felt it was his obligation to help a neighbor fighting for freedom from Western oppression, just as India was doing. After Nehru visited China in 1938, he dispatched a team of five Indian doctors, including Dr. Kotnis. Kotnis spent five years treating wounded Chinese soldiers in mobile clinics. In 1939 Kotnis joined the Eight Route Army led by Mao Zedong at the Jin-Cha-Ji border in the Wutai Mountain era, near the midwest of modern Hebei Province. In the movie, Kotnis married a Chinese girl, Ching Lan, and eventually died in battle. Ching Lan immigrated to India with their infant son. The movie, replete with nationalist rhetoric, ends unrealistically with

Kotnis making an emotion-ridden speech from the grave asking when his wife will return "home."

A brief period of respite for Chinese film came in the summer of 1956. The CCP decided to experiment with dissent. In a speech given in July, Zhou Enlai pointed out the need for introspection and intellectual insight. "We are not afraid of exposure, even if the criticism is not completely correct. . . . We should allow people to challenge us with opposing views." Zhou continued, "We should have the courage to face facts and acknowledge our shortcomings. When we have made mistakes, we should be strong enough to admit them and correct them, instead of being afraid to have them exposed."[28]

Mao, the Party chairman at the time, supported Zhou's idea and in a speech titled "On the Correct Handling of the Contradictions Among the People" said, ". . . it is only by employing methods of discussion, criticism, and reasoning that we can really foster correct ideas, overcome wrong ideas, and really settle issues."[29] Earlier the party had launched the Hundred Flowers Campaign to promote the acceptance of diverse points of view, including those critical of the CCP. During the campaign some famous movies, in particular Xie Jin's *The Red Detachment of Women* (in Chinese, *Hongse Niangzi Jun*), won acclaim. Xie's film, which depicted the liberation of a peasant girl from her cruel landlord and her subsequent enrollment in the CCP, won the Best Feature Film prize at the First Hundred Flowers Awards in 1962.

However, the invited criticism soon became unwelcome. As a plethora of letters by intellectuals criticizing the CCP arrived at Mao's doorstep—some intellectuals audaciously suggested that the CCP give up power—Mao called off the Hundred Flowers Campaign. In 1966, when Mao launched the Cultural Revolution to systematically eliminate any ideological dissent, the film industry virtually vanished. Almost all pre–Cultural Revolution films were banned; one exception was a watered-down remake of *The Red Detachment of Women*, which included blunt pro-CCP propaganda. Film activities were banned, except adaptations of the Peking Opera, which were the favorite entertainment of Jiang Qing, Mao's wife at the time.

Even after the 1978 opening up of China, the "Growth first, freedom later" slogan was applied most cruelly to the film industry. Content had to reflect the values of the "social spiritualist society," values that dominated artistic or commercial considerations. Several films continued to be financed by the state and produced at the state-owned studios in Beijing, Shanghai, Xi'an, and Guangxi.

A parallel process began in 1982 when a new generation of about a hundred Chinese filmmakers graduated from the Beijing Film Academy, an institution that had been formed in 1956 but was shut down during the Cultural Revolution. These young filmmakers came to be known as the Fifth Generation. Zhang Yimou, who has won international acclaim and is slated to codirect the opening ceremonies at the 2008 Beijing Olympics, is one of the leading Fifth Generation filmmakers. Born in 1951, Zhang grew up in a China dominated by class struggles. His father was a former member of the nationalist army and his mother was a doctor—both politically undesirable occupations at the time. Zhang was in secondary school when Mao launched his Cultural Revolution. Like many teenagers, Zhang was dispatched to work on a farm in Shanxi Province. Remarkably, Zhang developed his artistic talents by drawing portraits of Mao. After graduating from the Beijing Film Academy, Zhang was posted to the regional film studio in Guangxi, founded in 1974.

As a relatively new studio, Guangxi was ready to experiment. In 1983 it accepted a student suggestion to set up a Youth Production Unit. "The film students did not want to learn the established rules of traditional Chinese Social Realistic Art, as the generations before them had done."[30] Young directors in the program soon embarked on their first film, *One and the Eight* (*Yige He Bage*, 1984) and Zhang worked as a photographer on the film, which was based on a narrative poem penned during the Japanese war. Almost immediately the censors demanded that the film's plot and characters be amended before its release.

In 1987 Zhang made his directorial debut with *Hong Gaoliang* (*Red Sorghum*), a film that also sparked controversy. The movie depicted the life of a young woman of the 1920s whose family sells her into a marriage with a wealthy winemaker. At first a loveless union, the relationship blossoms into one of strong friendship and mutual respect. Initially officials condemned the film as an example of "spiritual pollution" and banned it from release in the provinces. To placate the censors, Zhang added scenes depicting the main characters fighting against invading foreigners, the Japanese. By making this artistic compromise Zhang ensured that *Red Sorghum* would be seen by a Chinese audience.[31] Viewed on film screens worldwide, it went on to win the 1988 Golden Bear Award at the Thirty-eighth Berlin Film Festival and was a massive success in China.

Censorship was reinvigorated after the Tiananmen Square incident. *Farewell My Concubine*, the work of another Fifth Generation director, was internationally acclaimed but shown clandestinely in China. Zhang co-produced and financed a film titled *To Live* that was shown at Cannes, again without the authorities' permission, and presold before it could be censored.

As reform accelerated, the CCP continued to confront the same dilemma. How could it continue to open up economically without allowing for some of that "spiritual pollution" that threatened to unravel its "socialist spiritualist society"? Sources of pollution were intensifying. By 1994 the number of cabarets in China had increased from one to several hundred, there were at least two hundred thousand karaoke bars and sixty thousand video viewing rooms, and video piracy was unrestrained.[32] Moreover, the low quality of government-censored and approved films did not exactly inspire viewers to stay away from these alternatives.

Like other state-owned enterprises around China, the state-run studio system began to show signs of disintegration, prompting private film companies to spring up, some in collaboration with financiers from Taiwan and Hong Kong. The state studios responded weakly by producing films that reflected the patriotic principles long espoused by the state. In 1998 the Xi'an studio produced only five films.[33]

Brand India

India's economic reforms, which received a massive impetus with deregulation in 1991, affected the film industry in a particularly extreme fashion. Until that time foreign films, largely because of the bureaucratic approval process of the National Film Development Corporation, accounted for less than 5 percent of the market. Deregulation made Hollywood blockbusters legally available in India within months of release in the United States and spurred a renaissance in theaters—everything from the quality of seating to the freshness of popcorn improved. From 1999 to 2000 India's revenues from Hollywood films saw a tenfold increase as attendance soared from 8 million to 50 million.[34]

In China Harrison Ford's *Fugitive* was released with great fanfare, only to be withdrawn within a week. *China Business Times* reported that the official reason for pulling the film was the fear that it would allow foreign distributors to "invade" China's movie industry. Other media sources claimed that the real reason was a tussle between the Beijing Film Distribution Company and the China Film and Export Cooperation over the rights to the proceeds of the film.[35] China Film had booked the movie directly with Beijing theaters, bypassing the local distributor. The enraged local Beijing distributor had taken the matter to the city's Cultural Bureau and to the Central Propaganda Department, with allegations that the film violated Chinese political values. The controversy further sparked a national debate in the press about the impact of allowing only ten Hollywood films to enter China annually. *The Fugitive* reopened eventually, but the episode illustrated continued official uneasiness. Even in the wake of changes to meet World Trade Organization commitments, creative control remains strong.

In 2006, revenues of the Chinese film market were approximately $737 million, out of which the box office accounted for about $337 million.[36] However, Chinese as well as Indian markets are poised for unprecedented future growth—about 30 percent for both countries.[37] The key question remains whether China will be able to use its film industry as a branding and cultural ambassador for the country (something the Indian film industry has shown it can do) given the Chinese government's consistent effort to censor films critical of the regime. In other words, can Chinese films create "Brand China" when they are constrained from portraying important realities of life in China? As one scholar stated, "Over the last 10 years, many Chinese movies are winning at international festivals but aren't doing well in China. It makes people ask if they are real reflections of Chinese life, or if they were made to appeal to western tastes."[38]

The Indian film market is twice as large as that of China. India produces more than eight hundred Hindi-language movies a year, and its film industry has an estimated annual turnover of nearly $1.3 billion, employing 6 million people.[39] I can walk into any of the numerous Indian stores in the Boston suburbs of Cambridge, Brookline, or Newton and find stacks of Hindi movies—most undoubtedly pirated, most of dubious quality. They are an incredible revenue source, not just for Indians but also for immigrants of every hue and country of origin. Why do these films succeed? Satyajit Ray posited, "[I]t is possible for a film to work . . . whenever it leaves its regional moorings and rises to a plane of universal gestures and universal emotions . . . In fact, this is exactly what the vast majority of Hindi films do . . . they present a synthetic, non-existent society, and one can speak of credibility only within the norms of this make-believe world."[40]

Gurus of Yesterday and Tomorrow

"Sisters and Brothers of America. It fills my heart with joy unspeakable to rise in response to the warm and cordial welcome which you have given us. I thank you in the name of the most ancient order of monks in the world; I thank you in the name of the mother of religions; and I thank you in the name of the millions and millions of Hindu people of all classes and sects."[41]

Thus intoned orange-robed Swami Vivekananda at the Parliament of Religions in Chicago in 1893. The conference, held in connection with the World's Fair, took place on the site where the Chicago Art Institute now stands. No one expected a monk from India to steal the show. The American poet Harriet Monroe saw and heard many of the "brilliant group of strangely costumed dignitaries from afar" and remarked, "[I]t was the last of these, Swami Vivekananda, the magnificent, who stole the whole show and captured the town . . . The handsome monk in the orange robe gave us in perfect English a masterpiece. His personality, dominant, magnetic; his voice, rich as a bronze bell; the controlled fever of his feeling; the beauty of his message to the Western world he was facing for the first time—these combined to give us a rare and perfect moment of supreme emotion."[42]

Vivekananda was a precursor to Bollywood as a representative of India's soft power. He was an exporter of ideas, credited as the first to introduce Hinduism, yoga, and Vedanta to the West. He lectured throughout the United States introducing the topics and wrote the first Western-published books on yoga. He later taught hundreds of students privately in free classes held in his New York apartment beginning in 1895. Inculcating a spirit of respect and goodwill for exchanges between the East and the West, he took American disciples to India to be initiated as swamis and brought Indian swamis to America to become teachers. Gandhi is said to have been influenced by Vivekananda's philosophy. The Ramakrishna missions, which he founded in 1897, have 106 centers in India, 12 in the United States, and a smattering in fourteen other countries.

Christened Narendranath Dutta on his birth in 1863, Vivekananda was the son of a well-known Calcutta lawyer who often included the boy in scholarly discussions and encouraged him to point out flaws in the arguments. After completing his college education the restless Vivekananda undertook a quest for answers to questions of religion and philosophy. After toying with movements that sought to reform Hinduism, he found his spiritual home with a Bengali man named Ramakrishna Paramhansa, who preached that all religions have the same goal and spiritualism is superior to blind adherence to ritual. Paramhansa based his teaching on *Advaita* ("not two"), emphasizing what Hindu philosophers call the indivisibility of the Self (*Atman*) from the Whole (*Brahman*).

More recently Deepak Chopra has become an exporter of Indian soft power. He has been called "America's head cleric of the soul" and a "one-man diversified conglomerate on a mission to reveal a spiritually-infused vision of the good life."[43] Educated at the All India Institute of Medical Sciences, India's premier medical school, and a successful endocrinologist in Massachusetts, Chopra grew disenchanted with modern medicine. After years in a high-powered career that left him addicted to coffee and cigarettes, he made a dramatic transformation in 1980 when he learned transcendental meditation. He declared, "It changed my whole life, my diet, my work, my relationship with my patients and with others. I became ten times more efficient."[44, 45]

Fame followed this life-changing event. Chopra soon became famous as the wonder doctor practicing transcendental meditation and promoting Ayurveda, the five-thousand-year-old Vedic system of health care that focuses on health, not disease, and takes into account the patient's entire personality—body, mind, and spirit. Chopra's best-selling books offered Ayurvedic solutions to a gamut of ordinary afflictions. An American population arose that was more familiar with yoga and the Vedas—classical Hindu texts—than many

Indians, and eventually Chopra's influence touched his homeland as well. The testimony of Vinati Dev, my Delhi-born, U.S.-educated research assistant, is telling: "While my grandfather would often—but only in passing—refer to yoga techniques for stress relief and health benefits, it was not something that youngsters during the 1980s and 1990s imbibed. It was too complicated—too slow and hard to understand. But recently there has been a resurgence of interest in yogic meditations. . . . [S]uddenly all everyone talks about is yoga and how we must return to the Vedas. I think it has a lot to do with people like Chopra who have raised the profile of this ancient exercise form and in part to the arrival of cable TV in India—which now has several channels dedicated to yoga masters and other religious discourses."[45]

Both Vivekananda and Chopra creatively blended Hindu philosophy with contemporary needs to reach an audience that could not be convinced by traditional diplomatic missions or government propaganda. Like Vivekananda's teachings, Chopra's are also grounded in the Vedas. Furthermore, both Vivekananda and Chopra have been able to creatively blend Hindu philosophy with contemporary needs. Just as the Ramakrishna missions provide fingerprints of Vivekananda's influence in this country a century after his visit, "Chopra Centers for Well Being" are spreading from California to Vancouver. Chopra is as media savvy as Oprah Winfrey, who incidentally is one of his clients. Of course, he has been far more commercially successful than Vivekananda. Chopra sports a La Jolla residence; Vivekananda barely survived his two-month trip to the United States.

While traditional Chinese medicine and martial arts have plenty of followers in the West, no single ambassador has achieved the fame and influence of Vivekananda in his time, or Chopra today. The paucity of such Chinese ambassadors surely has something to do with the attitude of the CCP to cultural activity over the past decades. Censors' intervention in the world of film is just one example. Remember that this stifling attitude was superimposed on a society where creativity, freedom of thought, and intellectual activity had been comprehensively wiped out during the Cultural Revolution.

For example, the ancient Chinese martial art of tai chi chuan ("great spirit fist") was forbidden during the Cultural Revolution because it was "old" and "traditional." Tai chi is based on the concepts of the yin-yang relationship, the idea of opposing but complementary forces. "Yin is the darker element, and considered passive, dark, feminine, downward-seeking, and corresponds to the night; yang, the brighter element, is active, light, masculine, upward-seeking and corresponds to the day."[47] The relationships also underlie much of Chinese medicine, which sees the organs of the body as interrelated.

Dakun Zhao, my colleague hailing from Henan Province, embraced tai chi for a fairly typical reason as a teenager in China: exam-related stress.

Dakun's experiences with the art at home and in the United States are quite revealing. In the mid-1990s he was introduced to a tai chi master who taught the class on a sidewalk in Dakun's hometown of Jiaozuo at a time when formal tai chi programs did not exist. A retired military officer had created tai chi in Jiaozuo 350 years earlier. Located between the Tai Hang Mountain in the north and the Yellow River in the south, Jiaozuo is a relatively small city in central China with less than two hundred thousand inhabitants and more tranquil than other cities around. For as long as Dakun could recall, the martial art had always been taught in wide-open places. He recalled his teacher assuring him that though they were now practicing on a sidewalk, things had been much worse. Authorities used to punish anyone practicing the art. His own master had practiced tai chi clandestinely "at night in the wild areas alongside the Yellow River, where it was safe to do so."

When Dakun became a student of international relations at Brandeis University, he made a cultural presentation of tai chi to his fellow students, a class of some eighty-five students from about forty-six countries. The students greatly appreciated the presentation, but it also sparked a curious realization for Dakun. Several of the students had heard of tai chi but had never seen it performed. Those that had seen it commented that Dakun's version was very different from what they had seen. They identified tai chi mostly with its aggressive aspects—the Bruce Lee version of martial arts that Hong Kong films had popularized by the 1980s. Dakun recalled that his own initial attraction had been similar: "As a young man I became very interested in practicing the fighting skills in tai chi and did not care about internal energy flow. I moved fast and hit my fist with full strength . . . Even so, my health improved. After some time, through reading some classical tai chi guidance books, I gradually realized the real essence of tai chi, its much greater help for internal energy flow than fighting, and the importance of gentle flowing movements."

But outside China few professional teachers truly understood the art form well enough to simplify its complex philosophy for students and followers. Dakun resolved to do his small part to spread the message of tai chi. He organized short tutorials but soon realized how difficult it was to communicate something that even he, with the benefit of expert guidance and the background of growing up in China, could not easily articulate or communicate. He also asked his fellow students about yoga, trying to figure out if there were lessons he could adopt that would be relevant to the teaching of tai chi. "I asked a Turkish student how many students there were in her yoga class, and she told me only about twenty because the participants had to pay some tuition . . . but at that moment another participant in my session added that at Brandeis tai chi was free but only three students [were] in class."

A quick stroll through Newton Center, a Boston suburb, reveals several thriving yoga centers. Several yoga centers are thriving in Newton Center. Yoga aficionados are keenly aware of the subtle differences between the types of yoga. Market segmentation has run amuck, with prenatal yoga being one of the most popular types. A recent survey further confirms the greater penetration of yoga than of tai chi, perhaps corroborating Dakun's experience with the difficulty of communicating the essence of tai chi.[48] Eight percent of Americans report having tried yoga in some form, whereas only 3 percent have tried tai chi. Signs of yoga's continued rapid adoption abound—the bookseller Barnes & Noble and the high-end grocery store Whole Foods report that *Yoga Journal* is the best-selling title in their fitness categories. In an attempt to popularize tai chi, one enterprising instructor reports choreographing tai chi movements with yoga postures.[49]

Daily reminders of India's soft power extend beyond movies and yoga. Not long ago I was at the local YMCA where my children are on swim teams. I noticed that their coach, Brian Connor, sported an *om* tattoo on his upper left shoulder. I was curious how this sign that looks like a 3 with a long tail and that begins every Hindu prayer got on Connor's back. One day I finally summoned up the courage to ask.

"Oh, a friend of my sister had a tattoo like this because she thought it looked cool," he replied. "Then I found out it's the word and symbol for 'sound,' and beyond that it means 'calm and peace.' I'm into music and played in bands while growing up. So what it stood for appealed to me. Tattoo artists always tell you to think about it for a year. Well, I procrastinated, and after two years, decided to get it inked." The All-American Connor, with no obvious connection to or even interest in Asia, chose an ancient Indian symbol to be prominently displayed on his torso. He said, "I often have people coming up to me and sharing their experiences about the *om* sign with me."

India's Continuing Tune

In recent years China has called attention to an emissary of its soft power, Zheng He, the admiral who helped China rule the seas from 1451. He famously made seven spectacular voyages past the South Asian seas as far as East Africa in fleets of three hundred vessels and thirty thousand men. Historians tell us these voyages would have put to shame the ships of Columbus and Vasco de Gama, roughly his contemporaries, and certainly that of southern India's Chola Empire, whose influence had spread eastward to Southeast Asia a few centuries before.[50] Zheng He was a native of present-day Yunnan Province and belonged to the Semur minority, adherents of Islam originally from central Asia.[51] As a child he worked for Duke Yan and then accompanied the duke when he usurped the throne and ruled China from 1403 to 1424 as the third Ming emperor Yong Le. There is some controversy about the purpose of Zheng He's voyages. Joseph Needham has pointed out that his ships "were fully armed, but never attempted to conquer other nations, build forts or pose any military threat."[52] In any event the ships spread China's influence far and wide until Zheng He reportedly died in the southern Indian port city of Calicut. Soon after, China ceased its maritime interactions with the outside world, thereby precluding the principle means by which it could have exported its influence. Its reasons for the isolationist move still preoccupy experts, but surely one is the Mongol threat from the north, which caused the Ming state's resources to be redirected toward fortifying itself behind the Great Wall.

But Zheng He lived six centuries ago. It is harder to find more contemporary ambassadors of soft power from China. Confucianism did have some impact on East Asia but that should be compared to Buddhism, which is covered in the next chapter. There is no Chinese equivalent to the orange-robed monk Vivekananda or the prolific author Chopra.

Examples of contemporary soft-power exchanges between China and India hark back to the movie industry. In 2004, in an attempt to continue the cultural interchange begun by the movie *Dr. Kotnis ki Amar Kahaani*, China and India agreed to increase the content of each country's programming on the other's state-run channels. As a result, a family melodrama produced in India plays on Chinese TV.[53] While waiting for a meal at a restaurant in the port city of Ningbo, I heard playing in the background a popular song from a contemporary Indian movie—*Muhabatten (Loves of My Life)*—and observed a waiter swaying to the tune though apparently oblivious to the words. Later I ran into a shopkeeper on the street corner who could readily hum the tunes of songs from old Indian movies when prompted by just a few opening bars. During a subsequent trip to Shanghai, standing in the lobby of the newly opened Royal Meridien hotel, I was again surprised to hear music from an Indian movie of the 1960s playing in the background. I searched out several staff members as to why that particular music was being played, only to receive blank stares. The music was recognizable from the streets of Ningbo to the swankiest parts of Shanghai, yet its provenance was, to the Chinese, unknown.

And Hong Kong filmmakers are importing Indian film music into their latest productions. The movie *Perhaps Love*, a musical directed by Peter He-Sun Chan, features dances choreographed by Farah Khan of Bollywood fame; the film was Hong Kong's entry for Best Foreign Film at the Oscars in 2005. Another Chinese film, *The Myth*, directed by Stanley Tong Kwai-Lai and starring Jackie Chan, also features Bollywood actress Mallika Sherawat.

Bollywood's soft power continues.

Chapter Thirteen

Buddha and Software

Old Links and New

And now the wheel of fate has turned full circle and again, India and China look towards each other and past memories crowd in their minds; again pilgrims of a new kind cross or fly over the mountains that separate them, bringing their messages of cheer and goodwill and creating bonds of friendship that will endure.

—Jawaharlal Nehru[1]

Nehru posited the idea of a natural camaraderie between China and India and referred to them as "two great countries and two great civilizations."[2] In his book *Discovery of India* Nehru diligently presented evidence of ancient religious and scholarly exchanges—centered in large part around Buddhism traveling from India to China—and suggested that these millennium-old links presented untapped opportunities to learn from each other and cooperate.

The times demanded that Nehru envision a future for Asia in which his India and Mao's China would cooperate, despite India's declaration of secular democracy and China's embrace of what Mao called a "democratic dictatorship." Nehru orchestrated China's presence at Bandung in 1955 accordingly. But his hopes were subsequently dashed by the Sino-Indian War in 1962. Following India's defeat, relations remained chilly for four decades.

Today the stakes are once again high. Asia's future is inextricably linked to the 2.4 billion people living in China and India. Recently China's commerce minister, Bo Xilai, and his Indian counterpart, Kamal Nath, raised the target of bilateral trade to at least $50 billion by 2010.[3] An official statement by Nath reads, "The India-China two-way trade is now US$1 billion a month, compared to US$1 billion a year a decade ago. This twelve-fold increase in the last decade only goes to prove that though we are competitors in many respects, we are also complementary and supplementary to each other."[4]

Symbolism—particularly Buddhist symbolism—has also been revived. References to the ancient ties centered on Buddhism as well as ancient trade and commercial connections now form the backdrop against which present-day official business is conducted. For example, many Indian leaders, including Prime Minister P. V. Narasimha Rao in 1993 and Prime Minister Atal Behari Vajpayee in 2003, have made treks to the Baima Si (White Horse) Temple in China's Henan Province. The Baima Si Temple is the monument that marks Buddhism's arrival in China from India in the first century. According to legend, the temple was built to commemorate two Buddhist monks, She Moteng and Zhu Falan, who came from India with the scriptures of their religion borne on the back of a white horse.

The Chinese are becoming adept at marrying Buddhism and business. My colleague Dakun Zhao, who was part of the Chinese reception committee welcoming Vajpayee to Baima Si, told me, "There were two topics discussed between the governor of Henan Province and His Excellency [Vajpayee]. The first was Buddhism and the second was software. The governor showed great interest in India's software. His Excellency suggested the governor explore the industry in India."[5]

Renewal of commercial links between China and India offers possibilities of learning from each other. Just six months after Vajpayee's visit, Zhao was en route from China to Hyderabad, which is in the Indian state of Andhra Pradesh. Zhao's delegation was to meet Chandrababu Naidu, India's technology-savvy chief minister. It was Naidu who first dubbed Hyderabad "Cyberabad," recognizing the city as a major player in India's ongoing software success story. As one of the many Chinese government–sponsored delegations to India, Zhao's team was intent on exploring many aspects of the Indian software industry and taking that knowledge back to China, which was struggling with building software enterprises. That mission echoed Chinese efforts made millennia earlier to absorb India's Buddhist thinking.

Unfortunately the Indian government has been unable to create a framework within which it can take lessons from China. Any urgency to learn from the Chinese or benefit from Chinese markets manifests itself in individual initiatives of the aggressive Indian corporate private sector.

Buddhist Residue

The Buddha, born Siddhartha Gautama in what is now Nepal, preached that attachment to worldly material realities is the cause of mental and physical suffering. This truth is revealed to all who follow the Middle Path—intuitive principles of good living that proscribe both overindulgence and unnecessary asceticism while prescribing quiet contemplation and meditation. The Buddha named no successor; rather he held that anyone can become a Buddha— an enlightened one. "You must each be a lamp unto yourselves," were his dying words.[c] Buddhism attempts to instill peace in each individual living in a world suffused with suffering and turmoil. In this sense, its lessons remain relevant today.

In the United States the novel *Siddhartha*, widely read in the 1960s, created a surge in popularity for Buddhism. Written by the Nobel Prize– winning German author Herman Hesse, the novel follows the spiritual jour- ney of an Indian man named Siddhartha who lives during the time of the Buddha. Many of its themes—suspicion of doctrine, finding one's own path to enlightenment, and the struggle between acquiring material possessions and attaining spiritual enlightenment—resonated strongly with the "youth movement" of that decade.

The Buddha's teachings are part of any good high school education in India. Building on that familiarity, I have acquired likenesses of the Buddha from a range of countries over the years, a collection started by a rosewood statue from southern India, a gift from my parents when I first arrived in the United States as an eighteen-year-old college freshman. My home is now a repository of Buddha statues or images acquired not just from China, but also from Nepal, parts of Southeast Asia, and even Australia. The localiza- tion of the images tells the curious tale of the spread of Buddhism. The images are both the residue of past commercial and political interactions and symptoms of a latent camaraderie that might yet lubricate future inter- actions. Unsurprisingly, therefore, I found myself meandering away from my usual commercial haunts to some of the most important modern mani- festations of Buddhism in China, the remnants of centuries of sustained interaction between China and India.

My wanderings led me to the Baima Si in Lucyang City, located in the west- ern part of Henan Province at the mouth of the Silk Road. Actually a network of interconnecting roads and caravan tracks spanning five thousand miles, the Silk Road served as the major highway for goods and knowledge between Europe, the Near East, China, and India for two centuries from 200 B.C.E.

The legend of Baima Si begins in 60 C.E., when Emperor Ming of the eastern Han Dynasty dreamed of a "golden man" with a halo hovering over his head. The dream so affected the emperor that he asked his advisers for an interpretation. One replied, "In the West there is a god called Buddha. His body is sixteen chi high [12 feet] and is the color of true gold."[7] Curious, Emperor Ming dispatched a diplomatic mission to India to learn about Buddhism and bring back its sacred texts, the Sutras. The mission returned in 67 C.E. with two eminent Indian Buddhist monks, She Moteng and Zhu Falan,[8] and one white horse transporting the Sutras and a figure of Buddha. The legend concludes with the construction of Baima Si to commemorate this introduction of Indian Buddhism into China.

Today the temple complex is more of a tourist site than a place of meditation. Scores of sophisticated street-side hawkers sell glazed-pottery horses and camels, ochres, and incense sticks. During my visit incense vendors pursued me diligently, intoning "One per Buddha," meaning I should buy one stick for every Buddha image to which I intended to make an offering. The growing commercialism of Baima Si is also reflected in its entry fee of 35 yuan, equivalent to about $4.50. An old-timer commented that Indians used to be admitted free, perhaps in recognition of the origins of Buddhism. Given the number of Indians wandering around China these days, the temple undoubtedly decided it could not afford to forego the revenue.

Walking from the entrance to the temple proper, I was treated to a panoramic view. The temple itself is reddish brown, blending harmoniously with the natural environment, and monks move about in a flurry of orange as they perform monastic chores, their silhouettes visible long before their visages. On the temple's immediate periphery, a stylized replica of a white horse, weighed down by manuscripts, symbolizes the temple's defining moment.

Today's 430,000-square-foot complex was constructed during the Ming Dynasty (1368–1644), with a roofed arch at the entrance providing three doorways onto a south-facing rectangular courtyard. The original Baima Si, built of wood, could not survive the ravages of either wars or time. Japanese records suggest that it stood in the center of the present-day temple complex. Indian Buddhist temples typically have a pagoda at the center, surrounded by halls and towers. The centrality of the pagoda (the word is of uncertain etymology; some believe it to be derived from the Sanskrit word *bhagavat*, or holy, as in the Hindu holy book, Bhagavat Gita) appears symbolic of Hinduism's influence on Buddhism in China, conveying the belief that the temple is the center of the world.

The inner complex is a dense collection of shrines, each separated by small courtyards. The pall of incense smoke hovers overhead, occasionally limiting visibility. Ancestor worship, as symbolized by thick clouds of fragrant incense, is an important ritual. In any of the small courtyards, dedicated individuals can light thick bunches of incense and bow to all sides of the temple to secure "merit" for themselves and for their ancestors before placing the lit incense sticks in crowded burners. Monks efficiently remove spent sticks and clean the ashes to make room for new offerings.

In a thickening incense haze I struck a conversation with a monk who appeared to be in his early forties. He was sweeping one of Baima Si's small courtyards as he chanted to himself. He talked energetically with me for about twenty minutes before becoming either uncomfortable or impatient to get on with his task. I noticed that while we were talking, another monk hovered nearby, moving incense sticks and presumably incredibly curious.

From the monk, I learned that, as in most organized religions, upper-level appointments to positions in the monastic hierarchy are subject to intense jockeying. The difference in China is that for all five of the nation's major religions—Christianity, Confucianism, Daoism, and Islam in addition to Buddhism—senior appointments, such as the abbot of Baima Si, are made by the CCP rather than by any religious authority. Not surprisingly this policy has led to controversy. For example, in 2000 Beijing and the Vatican sparred over the appointment of Catholic bishops on the mainland by the party and over the pope's canonization of 120 Chinese martyrs without seeking Party approval.[9]

The monk told me that being admitted into the service of the Buddha is a tough task, one embraced by teenagers and fifty-year-olds alike. Young aspirants must have their parents' permission to enter into temple service. It takes many years of study and an internship of sorts before ordination. After being ordained monks are free to move to any monastery in China at any time, though of course the higher they get in the monastic hierarchy, the more the Party intervenes to determine their assignments.

Monks and Merchants: The Indianization of China

Although legends are alluring, truth lies in scholarship. I spoke at length with Tansen Sen, a New York–based Sinologist of Indian origin who disputes the Baima Si legend. "The earliest transmitters of Buddhism to China were probably merchants rather than monks,"[10] Sen told me, referring to the voyage of Zhang Qian (died 114 B.C.E.), who was sent from the Han court to find an alternate trading route to central Asia. In fact ample evidence exists to support the theory that commerce and trade among central Asia, China, and India preceded the arrival of Buddhism.

However, the period during which Baima Si was built remains important because it was around that time that Buddhism began to receive generous patronage from China's new political elite. Other political conditions within China also created the opportunity for a foreign religion to prosper. Northern

China had fallen under the control of non-Han people who did not practice either Daoism or Confucianism, the two major religions in China at the time. Similarly Chinese rulers who had become increasingly dissatisfied with Confucianism's tenets occupied southern China. Buddhism offered a radical alternative. By the fourth century roughly 90 percent of the people in northwest China were Buddhist. In 477 an estimated 6,478 Buddhist temples and 77,258 monks and nuns occupied the north of China, and 2,846 temples and 82,700 clerics were in the south.[11]

"There were two distinguishing features of this era," noted Sen. "Trade and translation were both sustained by Buddhism." Translation was necessary because Buddhist texts were originally written in Sanskrit and housed in India. The Chinese knew that translation of tenets was a precondition for preaching to larger audiences and for establishing a monastic institution. Sen continued, "The mechanics of translation were not easy, in that the Chinese did not speak Sanskrit, and so translation often involved up to four people: one reciting the Sanskrit texts, one translating, one scribe, and then the fourth proofreading. It was very ritualistic, involving big entourages of monks that were housed in monasteries, and survived on patronage, both from merchants and monarchs."

Court-sponsored translation projects brought several Indian Buddhist monks and their Chinese counterparts together during the Sui and Tang periods. Jinagupta, an Indian monk who arrived in China in the second half of the sixth century, translated thirty-seven original texts into Chinese, thus winning the favor of the Tang emperor.[12] Most of the Buddhist translations during that period were concentrated in three renowned court-sponsored temples. These were the Da Xing Shan, founded by the Sui emperor Wen in 582; the Da Cien Si, established in 646 and famous for its acquisition of the works of Xuanzang, a famous monk, scholar, traveler, and translator; and Ximing Si, founded in 657 by Emperor Gaozong. In Luoyang, home of the Baima Si, translation activities continued, and after the Sui emperor Yang moved his capital from Daxing to Luoyang, he ordered the formation of a "translation bureau" (fan jing yuan), which included foreign and Chinese experts.[13] Within that bureau Dharmagupta, a monk whom Nehru called "Indian master," translated numerous Buddhist texts from Sanskrit into Chinese.

By the fourth century scholars and monks were among the Chinese venturing to India. One such traveler was Faxian, who left the ancient capital of Chang'an (present-day Xi'an in Shaanxi Province) in 399, went overland to central Asia, visited Buddhist sites in India, and then took a maritime route home that took fourteen years. In his travel journals Faxian refers to India as Madhyadesa, which in Sanskrit and Hindi means "Middle Kingdom," the same term the Chinese used to describe China (Zhongguo). Faxian's contemporaries were sufficiently enamored of India as the site of Buddhist relics that they referred to China as the borderland.

Perhaps the most prominent Chinese monk to visit India was Xuanzang, celebrated in Indian history as the Chinese monk hosted by Harshavardhan, ruler of much of what is now Northern India. He traveled across India in the seventh century and spent several years at Nalanda University, the center of Buddhist learning at that time and one of the world's oldest universities.[14] Xuanzang referred to India as Yindu, a term still used in China.

Sun Shuyun, who retraced Xuanzang's travels along the Silk Road from central Asia to India and back, chronicled her journey in *Ten Thousand Miles Without a Cloud*. "Xuanzang knew he had finally found the intellectual and spiritual home he had been searching for," she writes. "He tells us admission to Nalanda was competitive: a few questions by the monks at the gate sent most aspirants home; those who got a foot inside the door were grilled by masters, who would reject four out of five. The 10,000 monks who were finally admitted were the crème de la crème. In them he found a true match for his curiosity and appetite for learning."[15] To give a modern reader some sense of the splendor of this ancient university, Sun adds, "The majestic ruins of Nalanda are . . . spread over fourteen acres with block after block of monks' cells, five temples and eleven monasteries . . . You would have some idea of the magnificence of the place today if you imagined four or five of the largest Oxford colleges placed side by side, and then destroyed as if by an earthquake."

As the popularity of Buddhism grew among the upper echelons of Chinese society, so did the demand for ritual items, most notably Buddhist relics. Entrepreneurial Indian and central Asian merchants responded by exporting relics and ritual items to China. As Sen told me, "There was a comfortable nexus of merchants and monks. Monasteries served as hotels and clinics for traveling merchants. They were places to stay, and if someone got sick the monks tended to them. Often merchant ships gave rides to Buddhist pilgrims. The sense that this patronage would bless them definitely existed and contributed to their alliance. In fact it was these very merchants who were some of the biggest patrons of these Buddhist monasteries and temples."

In the 1930s Hu Shih, a professor of philosophy at Beijing University, gave an address at Harvard University's tercentenary celebrations in which he made the startling claim that during the sixth century the Buddhist influence in China led to its "Indianization." According to Hu, it was a case of cultural borrowing as massive as the Christianization of Europe. Given the ocean of difference between then-dominant Confucianism (which emphasized posterity and ancestor worship) and Buddhism (which preached negation of life, meditation, and attainment of nirvana), Hu argued that the establishment of Buddhism as the official religion for several Chinese dynasties was remarkable.[16]

By the eighth century, however, some monasteries—each a small, self-contained city—acquired notoriety by switching from religious pursuits and monastic endeavors to farming, trading, and money lending. With this transformation came corruption and the perception that monks were exploiting the local citizenry. Emperor Wuzong, who ruled from 841 to 847, responded by ordering the general destruction of all Buddhist establishments, corrupt or otherwise.

Nevertheless, Sen informed me, Buddhism in its new form continued to thrive in China under the Song Dynasty (960–1279) as well as in eastern India. "By the end of the tenth century," he explained, "Buddhism in India and China had taken two very different paths. While Indian Buddhism developed its own philosophical and ritualistic (esoteric) traditions, the Chinese clergy formulated and propagated their own indigenous teachings. This divergence ended the millennium-long epoch of a vigorous Sino-Indian intercourse stimulated by the transmission of Buddhist doctrines and pilgrimage activity."

In India the onslaught of Turkish Muslim invasions, which stretched from the ninth through the twelfth centuries, rang the death knell of Buddhism. The invaders destroyed several monastic universities in northern India and killed several well-known monks. In 1193 the Muslims attacked and conquered Magadha, which had been the heartland of Buddhism in India. Buddhist monasteries at Nalanda were completely wiped out. Only excavated ruins remain—a mere 10 percent of what Xuanzang recorded as existing at Nalanda's peak—as well as a modern center for Buddhist studies, which was founded in 1951.

Buddhism eventually died out in India, but commercial links between China and India remained. The only difference was that Buddhist merchants were replaced by Muslim and Hindu merchants. During the Tang (618–907) and Song (960–1279) dynasties China's trade with the southern Indian kingdom of the Cholas flourished. The power of the ancient Chola Dynasty began to peak in the middle of the ninth century, and it eventually became the largest empire southern India had ever seen. Records from the Tang Dynasty report that Arab traders often stopped at ports in India and along the Strait of Malacca on their way to southern China. That Muslim diasporas dominated trade on all sides of the Indian Ocean has been confirmed by the writings of Abu Abdullah Muhammad Ibn Battuta, the celebrated fourteenth-century Arab traveler who served the Sultan of Delhi as his ambassador to China. Ibn Battuta surmised that this new commercial resurgence was responsible for bringing Islam into Southeast Asia.[17]

According to Sen, "In the twelfth century . . . Chinese merchants began to travel to Southern Asia . . . . Consequently, for the first time in the history of India-China relations, court officials, traders, and ships from China made recurrent trips to the coastal regions of India, contributing to the surge in maritime commerce and official exchange between the two regions." China, then under the reign of the Ming Dynasty, rose to become one of the great maritime powers. This was the era during which the fifteenth-century explorer Zheng He led seven spectacular naval expeditions along the Indian Ocean between 1404 and 1433, the first of which saw his "treasure fleet" heading to Calicut, southern India's major trading center.[13]

The arrival of European powers in the sixteenth century, most notably the Portuguese, again redefined the China–India connection, this time around opium. The first records of opium cultivation in India are from the fifteenth century and refer to the state of Malwa as a "great" center of production.[19] The finest opium was derived from the poppies grown in the fertile alluvial plains of the Ganges, India's holiest river. Initially Arab and Indian merchants were the opium traders, but by 1637 opium had become the main commodity of British trade with China. Indian opium was traded for Chinese tea. Once Britain took political control of India in 1776, the ruling Mughals conceded their rights to the opium trade to the British government and independent merchants.

India thus went from exporting religion to exporting opium. When the Chinese authorities attempted to suppress the use and import of opium, to which a large part of China's population had become addicted, China faced the wrath of the British and other colonial powers. Two Opium Wars were subsequently fought. China lost both. One of the direct consequences of China's defeat was that it was forced to open up its ports and grant trading privileges to foreign merchants. Lubricating this commerce were private merchants who served as middlemen for the imperial powers. Notable among these were Parsi merchants from India who had built extensive trading networks out of Canton and Hong Kong in the first half of the nineteenth century. The Parsis, along with the Jews and Eohrah Muslims (who also came from India), had established extensive trading networks out of cities like Canton in China and Bombay and Calcutta in India even before the Opium Wars. Following the wars the Parsis simply leveraged their experience and helped facilitate commerce between the two countries.[20] Throughout all this Mohandas Gandhi condemned the opium trade as immoral and chastised Indian merchants for contributing to the addiction of China.

As the trade in opium waned, cotton trading became more vibrant. Until 1870 Manchester, England, had filled virtually all of China's cotton needs, but as the monopoly of the East India Company came to an end, Indian merchants took the lead. Bombay soon became the nerve center of cotton export to China, just as it had been for opium.[21]

From Buddha to Software: Possibilities of Cooperation Between China and India

Cooperation is just like two pagodas—one hardware and one software. Combined, we [China and India] can take the leadership position in the world. When the particular day comes, it will signify the coming of the Asian century of the IT [information technology] Industry.

—Premier Wen Jiabao, speaking in Bangalore, India[22]

Hangzhou, a two-hour drive from Shanghai, is a city known both for its Buddhist temples and for being the center of China's growing software industry. Like Baima Si, the Lingyin Si temple embodies ancient Sino-Indian connections. It is said that Lingyin was built in 326 by an Indian monk named Huili, who arrived in China from western India. Although the temple, like other Buddhist sites in China, has succumbed to aggressive tour guides and street vendors hawking memorabilia, it still evokes a tremendous sense of history and faith.

During a visit to Lingyin Sin, I was staring at the pure limestone peak towering seven hundred feet above the temple compound when my guide told me, "The monk Huili told the people of Hangzhou that while the limestone peak did not fit in with the rest of landscape in Hangzhou, there were similar hills in Magadha," the center of Buddhism in India located in the region that is now the state of Bihar. Huili proclaimed that this was a *fei lai feng*, or a "peak that flew from afar." The people believed him and so named the peak Tianzhushan (Indian Hill). On one of the inner walls of the temple, I spotted another piece of evidence of ancient Chinese and Indian exchange. I recognized a rock inscription of the symbol for *om*, the word uttered at the beginning of almost all Hindu prayers. The latest evidence of Sino-Indian ties that I find at this temple, however, is neither historical, nor does it have to do with Buddhism and its accompanying legends. The presence of Indian people in the city told the newer story of collaboration.

It is a story of how the Chinese government, in an effort to create a software industry, has provided incentives for Indian software companies to invest in China. Consequently, Indians are living and working among Chinese in Hanghzhou. Just as Indian monks made court-sponsored journeys to translate Buddhist texts in ancient China, Indian software experts are being lured by the Chinese state to convert their software prowess into a form that can benefit the Chinese.

Before the 1980s the concept of a Chinese software industry was an oxymoron. At the time no significant software product had come from any of China's state-owned research labs. State-controlled resources—money and talent—had primarily been directed toward key hardware projects for civil and military use. Then the Chinese government declared that a modern IT industry had to be built to upgrade and modernize China's economy. Specifically, the government argued that IT projects would focus on key sectors of the Chinese economy. The government's Golden Card project encouraged the adoption of IT in banking, the Golden Bridge project focused on national telecommunications networks, and the Golden Custom project encouraged computer networking for foreign trade. Despite these national efforts, however, a vibrant software sector did not emerge. By the end of the 1990s the Chinese software industry still comprised small, fragmented firms that lacked management skills, had little experience with large-scale projects, and had virtually no international clients. No high-quality domestic product was created. Analysts argued that it was unlikely that a software industry would take hold in a country where intellectual property rights were not protected.[23]

Around that time India's software industry began to make international news. Indian companies had taken the world software market by surprise. Interestingly, the rise of the Indian software industry was as much a product of chance and timing as it was of India's huge repository of highly qualified English-speaking computer engineers and entrepreneurs. Because the Indian government had been so preoccupied with regulating the hardware market, the software industry grew almost without recognition. As one pair of scholars put it, the success of India's software industry " for the most part, has been a combination of resource endowments, a mixture of benign neglect and active encouragement from a normally intrusive government, and good timing."[24]

At the beginning of the new millennium, the contrast between the Chinese and Indian software industries was stark. The Chinese industry had many small firms. For example, the top seventy firms accounted for a total of less than $3.2 billion in sales, or half the total output; in India the top twenty-five firms accounted for more than two-thirds of the industry's total revenue. The top software firms in China had revenues far below those in India and far fewer employees. The largest software companies in China such as China's National Software and Service Company and Neusoft, had forty-two hundred and eight thousand employees on their payrolls, respectively, compared with the largest Indian companies, which employed more than ten thousand employees each. Perhaps most important, the work of Chinese software companies added little to the world industry compared with that of their

Indian counterparts, and less than 6 percent of China's software industry output was exported compared with 70 percent of India's.[25]

Within China the gap between its IT development and India's became increasingly obvious. An editorial in the *People's Liberation Army Daily* in 2000 had already warned against "information colonialism" and argued that China must develop its own software because "without information security there is no national security in economics, politics, or military affairs."[26] In response the Chinese government issued two policy briefs meant to rejuvenate the domestic software industry.

The first one, issued in 2000, was titled, quite literally, "No. 18: Some Policy to Encourage the Development of Software and IC Industry," and the second, issued in 2002, was "No. 47: Action Plan to Rejuvenate Software Industry." Both listed myriad tax incentives for China's software industry as well as training and education subsidies. The government also created a series of Special Economic Zones dedicated to developing the technology industry. That is, having failed to develop world-class software firms on their own, the Chinese were giving leading foreign software firms the opportunity to operate in China, enabling the Chinese to watch and learn.

Hangzhou Hi-Tech Industry Development Zone is a product of that effort. As one of China's eleven software industry bases, it covers an area of thirty-three square miles and is host to fifteen hundred enterprises. A zone commission handles all issues concerning establishment of companies or projects, their registration, application for land transfers, tax payments, applications for patents, personnel transfers, and other administrative matters. Further, the Chinese trademark—preferential treatment to foreign direct investment—is extended to firms wanting to locate in Hanghzhou.[27]

Indian entrepreneurs have availed themselves of these opportunities. In 2002 Tata Consultancy Services (TCS), a subsidiary of one of India's oldest business groups, the House of Tata, set up a global development center in Hangzhou that provides end-to-end services for TCS in the Asia-Pacific region. The center collaborates with some of the leading universities in China, including Zhejiang University in Hangzhou. Joint research and development made it TCS's first engineering solutions center outside India. By 2003 the firm's CEO, Subramaniam Ramadorai, had been named honorary IT adviser to Shandong Province and the city of Hangzhou.[28] Infosys Technologies swiftly followed TCS to Hangzhou, tapping into the local talent in China.

In 2007 I met entrepreneur Brian Yang in Nanjing, another town within China's emerging Shanghai-Hangzhou-Nanjing software complex. Yang, formerly a senior official in one of China's largest, and therefore state-owned, apparel companies, described why he started a business process outsourcing

(BPO) company called Unitedinfo that specialized in customer relationship management—a key task in any up-to-date company's marketing function:

> I met an Indian classmate at Harvard Business School in 2005 whose company had been very successful in providing offshore business process outsourcing services for large western companies. He described how he was using his call-centre and other state-of-the-art information technologies to serve the needs of global clients far away from India. Today the company has grown up to a 25,000 people giant. The business model, and what he had gone through, was relevant to me. After I returned from HBS, I started to explore the possibility of providing the same service in China and I firmly believe that I have at least one advantage that my Indian classmates won't have a chance to compete with me: China's fast-growing economy has created a huge domestic demand from both local and localized foreign firms.
>
> I realized that [the] Chinese could learn a lot from the Indians in this space. To convince a customer to give us their key data so we can help them manage their marketing needs requires incredible process discipline. We have to reassure them that their data are safe and not misused. This is something that Chinese software companies don't have yet. But we are getting there.[29]

I asked him about the Indian BPO companies operating in China. Yang was not sanguine about these. "They will find it difficult to operate in an environment where *ren mai* is important and the letter of an agreement is often not the only thing in business. They are too used to the international environment of contracts to find operating in China easy."

"What if they hired good Chinese talent?" I countered.

Yang found this mildly amusing. "Maybe in the long run—very long run—they will find this feasible. But for a Chinese to go to work for a GE [General Electric] is okay. Such large American companies are not competing with the Chinese, they are too far ahead. But to work for an Indian company is like working for a competitor. If the Indians can do it, so should we."

Could it be that India's BPO giants and Chinese startups like Unitedinfo were focusing on different segments? Yang said, "My target is companies in the RMB 50-500 million [$7 million to $70 million] sales range. Right now 90 percent of my sales are to the Chinese subsidiaries of Western multinationals, whose size is mostly in this range. In the longer term I hope that more local Chinese companies will embrace our product. But this is an education process. Remember it took the Indians a decade to convince Westerners to use their software, and they never convinced Indian companies. It is going to take us some time."

Indian companies confirm that they are after the same segments. After all, firms like TCS and Infosys first came to China to serve the needs of multinational clients that were more comfortable with them than with the indigenous Chinese offerings available at the time. Certainly launching a domestic Chinese business is difficult, for the same reasons that Yang mentioned. However, although Indians have to learn to hire and motivate Chinese talent and survive in the murky world of Chinese relationships, ultimately the Chinese have to learn modern private-sector discipline and process skills.

Brian concluded with a mirror image of the comment he made about the need for Indians to learn how to attract the Chinese."If I [could] figure out how to absorb senior Indian talent into my firm, I would love to do so. With their facility in global business, their connections worldwide, and their process discipline, we would be unbeatable." The success of firms like Anand Mahindra's Mumbai-based tractor company in combining Chinese and Indian talent indicates that it can be done.

As Yang's story and innumerable state-level initiatives suggest, the Chinese are attempting to learn. Are the Indians doing nearly as much? In sharp contrast to China's state-led and state-executed plan to invest in creating an environment that fosters learning from the best in the software business, and in contrast to Indian entrepreneurs' eagerness to become part of that environment, stands the inability of the Indian state to plan or execute similar investments in areas where India lags behind the Chinese.

India could, for example, learn from China's success in the hardware sector, among the most efficient in the world today. Over the last twenty years the world's technology giants have taken advantage of the low labor costs and incentives offered by the Chinese to set up factories on the mainland. By 2003 a fifth of total exports—and more than a third of the growth in China's exports—came from such factories.[30]

Kiran Karnik, head of India's NASSCOM (the software industry lobby group in Delhi), told me that the Chinese sent delegation after delegation to Bangalore and Hyderabad to study and learn from India's software success. The Indian government has failed to create even the semblance of a framework within which Indian firms can learn from Chinese prowess. Although Indian firms like Infosys, TCS, and NIIT (one of India's most successful IT education and training companies) are all invited to educate Chinese graduates in the best practices of India's software industry, India does not attempt to learn from China.

The major Chinese telecom vendor Huawei Technologies was one of the few technology-intensive companies that invested in efforts to tap into India's talent. That investment opened up a prime opportunity for Indians to learn from the Chinese, especially from a firm that was challenging the supremacy even of Cisco. Unfortunately, any chance for mutualism was quashed, not only by the claim that Huawei was in a sector that would endanger India's national security but also by traditional suspicions of outsiders.

In the 1950s Nehru commented on India's historical unwillingness and inability to learn from China: "During these thousand years . . . each country learned something from each other, not only in regions of thought and philosophy, but also in the arts and science of life. Probably China was more influenced by India, than India by China, which is a pity, for India could well have received, with profit to herself, some of the sound common sense of the Chinese, and with its aid checked her own extravagant fancies . . . China took much from India but she was always strong and self confident to take it in her own way and fit it somewhere in her own texture of life. Even Buddhism and its intricate philosophy could not change or suppress the love of live and gaiety of the Chinese."[31]

Nalanda Revisited: Learning and Scholarship in China and India

Centuries ago ancient Buddhist universities like Nalanda facilitated secular exchange between the Chinese and the Indians in areas as diverse as mathematics, astronomy, literature, linguistics, music, fine arts, medicine, and public health.[31] Even during the nineteenth century, although the opium trade had soured relations between British India and China, the potential for intellectual exchange had remained foremost in the minds of several prominent Chinese and Indians.

For example, Rabindranath Tagore, the Indian novelist, poet, educator, and Nobel Prize winner, had a profound knowledge of historical Sino-Indian cultural interchange. Possibly attempting to re-create Nalanda, Tagore set up the Cheena Bhavana, the department of Sino-Indian studies, in 1937 at Visva-Bharati University, the school he had founded thirty-six years earlier in the West Bengal city of Shantiniketan. At the ceremony marking the opening of Cheena Bhavana, Tagore announced, "This is, indeed, a great day for me . . . when I should be able to redeem . . . the pledge to maintain the intercourse of culture and friendship between our people and the pledge of China (. . . .)." He continued, "(On a visit) to China several years ago I felt a touch of the great stream of life that sprang from the heart of India and over flowed across mountain and desert into that distant land, fertilizing the heart of its people (. . . .). My friends, I have came to ask you to re-open the channel of communication which I hope is still there (. . . .). The hole which is to be opened today will serve both as the nucleus and as a symbol of that larger understanding that is to grow with time."[33]

Tagore found a collaborator in the Chinese scholar Tan Yun-Shan, whom Tagore first met in Singapore in 1927 and subsequently invited to teach at Shantiniketan. Tan helped Tagore raise funds and procure a hundred thousand books for the Cheena Bhavana from China through the Sino-Indian Cultural Society, which Tan established in Nanjing in 1933.

When Tagore appointed Tan as the director of Cheena Bhavana, the Chinese scholar refused a salary because of the school's financial situation. The Chinese government stepped in to provide an honorarium. Tan had become a kind of special envoy between the Chinese and Indian governments. In fact it was through Tan that Nehru, Tagore, and others sent messages of India's support for China against the Japanese, many of which Tan delivered in person to Chiang Kai-shek. The Tan connection culminated in Generalisimo Chiang Kai-shek and his wife visiting India. The duo was pleased with the work of the Cheena Bhavana, and China announced a further donation of Rs. 50,000 ($18,000) at the time.

After India won its independence in 1947, Tan was given the additional title of cultural representative. Prime Minister Nehru congratulated Tan: "I hope that with your assistance and advice we shall develop further cultural contacts with China."[34] The birth of the People's Republic of China under Mao created only a temporary hiatus in terms of cultural exchange, and its renewal came with a special donation of Rs. 500,000 ($152,000) for a new central library at Visva-Bharati.

In 1954 Nehru signed the Panchsheel Agreement with the Chinese.[35] The Panchsheel—in Hindi, Panch is five and Sheel refers to modes of conduct—was seen as a guarantee against war between China and India. Indians responded with the euphoric cry "Hindi-Chini Bhai Bhai" (literally, "Indians and Chinese are brothers"), and at Tan's urging Premier Zhou Enlai was invited to receive an honorary degree at Shantiniketan. In the spirit of the times, Gandhi told Tan, "I long for the real friendship between China and India based not on economics or politics but on irresistible attraction. Then will follow real brotherhood of man."[36]

Zhou Enlai's trip to Shantiniketan was to be the last sign of "real friendship," however. By 1960 border tensions between China and India were beginning, and diplomacy was rapidly fading. When the Indian parliament questioned Tan's activities, Nehru apparently snubbed the legislators, asserting that Tan had been a friend to India for thirty-five years. But at the 1962 convocation ceremonies of Visva-Bharati, a "broken Nehru" stated that, despite the Sino-Indian War, Indians and Chinese should remain friends. Tan wept openly in the audience. His life's work had come to a sudden end. Cheena Bhavana was transformed from a great cultural and intellectual think tank to a mere Chinese-language institute.

However, Tan remained fixated on his goal of promoting Sino-Indian ties. On retirement from Shantiniketan in 1971, Tan had a vision that propelled him to work for the establishment of the World Buddhist Academy, to be located in Bodh Gaya. The chief minister of the Indian state of Bihar granted Tan the necessary land next to the Chinese temple that Tan helped build many years ago. Once again, the money poured in from Hong Kong and Singapore in response to Tan's fund-raising. In 1979 Visva-Bharati conferred an honorary degree on Tan. He died in Bodh Gaya four years later.

No leading Chinese or Indian university today presents the possibility of re-creating the excellence of a Nalanda as does Visva-Bharati University. Leading Chinese universities like Tsinghua look toward Western models of business schools, a reasonable perspective given the worldwide success of the American MBA model. On the other hand, tracking down Chinese faculty interested in Sino-Indian business issues is akin to searching for a needle in a haystack.

The paucity of scholarly interest and collaboration is duplicated in India. The illustrious Indian Institutes of Management, producers of India's top business talent, are aggressively linking themselves to Western schools. The Indian School of Business in Hyderabad, which is an attempt to craft a business school entirely on American lines and is staffed primarily by U.S.-trained faculty, claims to be dedicated to augmenting management talent not just in India but in all of Asia. But little is done to foster learning about China. This is true of other subjects as well. Although New Delhi houses the Institute of Chinese Studies, growing out of an informal group of Indian scholars interested in the social sciences in China, and Beijing does have political scientists and sociologists focused on South Asia, those commendable efforts are miniscule relative to the information and understanding gap that exists today between the two Asian giants.

Looking at recent history, however, is not indicative of what will come in the near future. The communication gap between China and India is already being overcome. Every day Chinese passengers ride public buses to work in Gurgaon, the New Delhi suburb that is home to a sizable share of foreign investment in India, and Indians flock to Indian restaurants in Hangzhou.

Narayan Sen is, like his son Tansen Sen, a well-known China scholar. He recalls the warm reception he received when he arrived as a student in Beijing in the winter of 1955, the recipient of a cultural exchange program catalyzed by Zhou Enlai's visit to India. He described his odyssey from Calcutta, one indicative of the era: "The ship reached Hong Kong after nineteen days, and I boarded a train for Shenzen on February 5. In those days foreigners going to China by train from Hong Kong were first to go to

Shenzhen, then cross a bridge on foot, and again board a train to go to Guangzhou, and from there to Hankou, cross the Yangzi River by a ferry boat and take a Peking-bound train." In Narayan's day transportation was an impediment that was later compounded by political tensions.

Distance no longer hampers scholarly, intellectual, and commercial cooperation. The first direct flight from Beijing to Delhi began in March 2002, and direct flights are being planned from secondary cities in China to secondary cities in India. The future looks brighter already.

Chapter Fourteen

Corporate Bridges

Linking China, India, and the West

Throughout history individuals have tried to construct bridges between China and India. Indian monks took the Buddha's teachings to China. The Indian doctor Dwarkanath Kotnis joined Mao's army to treat Chinese soldiers wounded in the Sino-Japanese War of 1937. Nehru reached out to China, only to have his affection rebuffed with hostility and misunderstanding. History is also replete with people who have tried to interpret China and India to the West. The China historian Jonathan Spence has written eloquently about the attempts of outsiders—physicians, missionaries and scholars—to change China over the centuries.[1] While many of the would-be change agents have succeeded in integrating themselves into Chinese society, often spectacularly so, they have not managed to change China. China has changed them.

Corporations far outdo the well-intentioned efforts of individuals, even though a story of corporate success appears less inspirational than individuals defying Herculean odds. Corporations effect social change in developing countries like China and India by helping citizens engage more fully in the world economy. This is much more useful than corporate social responsibility, a term sometimes used to describe stopgap measures like monetary aid or corporate giveaways that fail to provide a profitable and therefore long-term platform on which hundreds of individuals can bridge divides, including those between countries.

My favorite example of a company that has changed both China and India for the better is General Electric (GE). It has taken GE more than a decade of effort in each country, preceded by a less substantive commercial presence lasting nearly a century, to figure out how to profit from being in China and India and to contribute substantially to both countries. It has taken even longer for its operations in China and India to learn to work together, making the proverbial whole greater than the sum of its parts. Of course GE's achievement is a work in progress—with the usual share of embarrassments and failures—but it shows more progress than most other comparable corporate works under way in either country.

The story of GE begins when then-CEO Jack Welch first traveled to India in September 1989. He was looking for populous developing countries that were about to break out of poverty. His visit to India convinced him that "their research labs were filled with scientists equal to or better than those in the United States—and in a lot more disciplines than software."[2] In response to a report from one of his managers that a team of GE scientists in India "aren't doing nearly the quality of work in India you think," Welch responded, "The engineers and scientists in India were on *his* payroll, yet he was making a distinction between his people 'here' in the United States, where he was located, and 'there' in India." As Welch has said, "I always knew we had a problem getting the whole organization's mindset around the idea of global intellect, tapping every great mind in the world no matter where it was located."[3]

Welch made many substantive and symbolic moves to signal the importance of globalization to GE. In 1999 he decreed that 40 percent of sourcing should come from countries like China and India. At that time any GE employee in the top 10 percent of a talent cohort and hoping to be promoted first had to do a stint in China or India. Symbolically, back in 1991 Jim McNerney, ultimately CEO of GE Aircraft Engines and GE Lighting and one of the finalists in the race to succeed Welch, was appointed CEO of GE Asia. Although McNerney had no direct business unit responsibility, appointing someone of his accomplishments to Asia meant that GE was serious about globalization.

Acquiring Chinese Corporate Citizenship

Chih Chen, CEO of GE Healthcare China, is the mirror image of my Harvard student, Andy Klump, whom I featured in my introduction to the book. Klump was brought up in America and embraced China. Chen was brought up in Taiwan, matured in his career in the U.S., and became part of the *hai gui*—returned Chinese—in China. Chen, like Andy, has a deep understanding of both the Chinese and Indian societies. As individuals, their efforts, which occur in corporate contexts, are magnified by well-honed corporate processes. Chen, for example, has created a platform on which a Fortune 500 company can help integrate tens of thousands of Chinese into the world economy. I am convinced that the Chens of the world, and the people they inspire in the course of their self-interested pursuits, are critical to the West's learning to live with and profit from the rise of China and India.

I met Chen in 2005, when he was working out of a factory in Wuxi, near Beijing. GE Healthcare China was then the leading provider of medical diagnostics equipment. It had not been so when Chen arrived there in 1997. Speaking about that time, Chen compared his efforts to "working in the jungle"—a phrase I later realized was a metaphor for both the jungle of corporate China and the jungle of the fierce competition within GE. In 2005 Chen had an impressive record of revitalizing GE's previously staid medical diagnostics business in China. But even more amazing was how invaluable GE Healthcare had become to the medical community in China.

The key to Chen's success was corporate largesse, not in the sense of giving away money but in the corporation having found ways to allow people in Chinese society to productively participate in its business ventures. For a corporation to reach the stage where it can act with this kind of largesse takes persistence and experimentation.

Chen received a PhD in mechanical engineering from Lehigh University in Pennsylvania and gained experience with GE in California, Singapore, and Taipei before joining GE Medical—GE Healthcare's predecessor organization—in China. Although GE had been in China since the early 1900s, exporting and trading through agents and representatives, not until the early 1990s did China came into focus. Jack Welch said then that China "is so vast and complicated and so hard to figure out. I don't know the answer . . . that's probably why I am retiring. Somebody else is going to have to figure it out."[4] Even so, Welch's initial foray into China in 1993 paved the way for GE Medical and GE Plastics, the two businesses that emerged as the company's most successful ventures in China.

When Chen took charge at GE Medical, all was not well. Its China operation was a jungle of vested interests. How had that happened? Initially GE established separate joint ventures for its various product lines as a means of working with the many Chinese regulatory authorities, like the Ministry of Health and the State Drug Administration, the approximate equivalents of the U.S. Food and Drug Administration. GE's joint ventures were necessary to get the buy-in of all the separate regulatory authorities, each of which had its own affiliated companies and therefore interests to protect. Chen described the challenges of these ventures: "In one joint venture, the partner firm would receive orders for equipment, and then service the orders from its separately wholly-owned factory, thus cutting us out. We couldn't stop this practice. So we had to renegotiate."[5] By 2002 GE had acquired 100 percent ownership of two of the ventures and 90 percent of the third.

Chen explained, "When I arrived, we were losing money. Management was in chaos. Our strategy was right, we manufactured well, and distribution was in good shape. But management did not have the right GE values. Chinese people know how to please the boss and survive, though they may behave very differently in the background." The GE principles of allowing employees to take the initiative and holding them accountable for results was thus in direct opposition to the belief held by Chinese management that their jobs were to please. Chen continued, "Most expatriate managers stay above the clouds, including the overseas Chinese. They rely on locals to deliver results. Most of the staff at GE were expats at the time, often from Singapore, Hong Kong, and Taiwan, and they didn't get their hands dirty."

Chen also realized that, contrary to expectations, China had no amorphous and large talent pool just waiting to be tapped. The situation was more complicated. He explained that "there was no 'the best talent'; there had to be 'my best talent.' I had to build talent and corporate culture, not just rely on acquired skills." Chen used discipline and incentives to shape that talent. "I had to shake up the organization, taking out people who had wrong values. My salespeople protested, some resigned—as many as thirty to forty out of the two hundred people who were there when I arrived. The discontented salespeople started spreading rumors that the big ship was sinking. They sent messages back to headquarters. But headquarters had confidence in me. I told those who resisted me, 'You'll get fired before I get fired.' "

But firing unsuitable employees comes naturally to many corporations, especially to companies emerging from rough-and-tumble corporate America. Simply firing part of a workforce rarely suffices, especially when suitable talent is scarce and when it is difficult for talent to find equivalent opportunities. For all the talk in China of abundant talent pools, the labor market does not yet work as smoothly as it does in the West. Recruiting and nurturing a skilled workforce remains a major challenge. Unskilled workers abound, and less than a tenth of each year's college graduates are deemed employable by multinationals.[6]

Next Chen met various workers on their own terms, tailoring his message to their particular circumstances.

> *The mind-set of those growing up in China is quite different from those coming from the outside. In the planned economy, if you were an electrical engineer, that's what you remained all your life, and you figured out how to manage upward in the electrical engineering professional line. You have these vertical*

skills. But I think in the market economy you need to be able to collaborate with other skill sets, you need one deep skill set and then shallow lateral skills. I worked hard to develop a training program that borrowed from the West and from China to communicate this. So now we hire one person with double the pay but expect that person to do the work of three. But this empowering is done after the person is molded. Without the molding you create chaos.

To motivate the older members of his staff, Chen matched GE corporate language to Chinese revolutionary rhetoric. To motivate the younger workers, he relied on conventional business school language. He compared GE management style to the leadership of Chinese political reformers like Deng Xiaoping. For example, he quoted Thomas Edison, the inventor and founder of General Electric, who said, "My inventions are from practice, not because of genius." Chen pointed out to his employees that Deng had intoned, "Practice is the sole criterion for testing truth." Thus, Chen's ability to translate GE Medical's values into language that seasoned Chinese veterans could relate to and understand, and his creativity in drawing out parallels between GE and Party culture, made GE that much less of an outsider.

The problem with most Western companies and many expatriates is that they don't realize that the life experiences of so many people in China are different from both what they've seen, and different from each other. The current twenty-somethings in China are spoiled; they are the one-child-at-home generation, the result of a one-child policy. They take everything for granted. To shape them, I need different tricks. Graduates from the elite Western universities come with different challenges; they are snobbish and won't dirty their hands. But we have created a good environment for talent. We've gone from two hundred people in the mid-1990s to fifteen hundred in our main facility in Wuxi and another twelve hundred around China. The expats are not necessarily the most senior people in GE Healthcare China today.

Chen built support from inside the organization. The second thing Chen did when he took the helm was to get the sales force to direct its efforts to more than just major urban areas and to recognize opportunities in huge swathes of China that had been neglected. At the time, Beijing accounted for the bulk of GE Medical's sales. If nothing else, catering to suburban and rural areas would earn Chen and GE an enormous amount of goodwill. Chen recalls that "I said at the time, 'Let the Beijing market go down. I will focus on 90 percent of the Chinese market outside Beijing.' This is because the salespeople who controlled access to Beijing customers were not supportive of my efforts, as it upset their existing system. So I simply developed good salespeople from outside Beijing. They had been neglected before and worked with me. I gradually began transferring my salespeople into Beijing and promoting those who did well."

Chen reminded me that his tactic to ultimately approach urban China from a position of strength in the nonurban areas had a historical parallel. In fact Mao Zedong had relied on the peasantry to launch his communist revolution. "You have to understand, I come from Taiwan. Chiang Kai-shek, who was forced into Taiwan by Mao, had made the mistake of using only people from Jiangsu Province, while Mao got people from all over the countryside. I was going to use all the tools at my disposal. I still grew business by 15 percent, although I got no growth in Beijing." Mao's approach is, of course, a well-known and admired maneuver in China. Ren Zhengfei, founder of the telecommunications firm Huawei Technologies, also attributed his company's rise to such an approach, targeting rural provinces that multinationals like Ericsson and Alcatel had ignored.[7] Chen, the GE veteran but consummate local, was thus able to take a page out of the local playbook.

With motivated and nurtured talent Chen could compete, not just with the less technically advanced competitors in China at the time but with seasoned internal GE teams from other parts of the world. "We decided we did not want to continue to be a screwdriver operation in China," Chen explained. "Korea and India, and a newly acquired unit in Japan, all wanted the same position as GE's worldwide center of excellence for producing low-cost medical diagnostic equipment that was used all over the world. Within GE, there is extensive competition for the right to be the center. GE set up a 'tiger team'—the term used to indicate a team focused on this project—that went around every three months examining competing bids. We won after a year and a half of inspections of competing GE factories worldwide."

Once they were plugged into world demand, Chen's operation could move far from its historically reactive business model. It no longer simply responded to the occasional order received in GE Medical's Hong Kong regional administrative center or Milwaukee headquarters.

What did Chen's internal credibility, his willingness to work with Chinese talent, and his focus on underserved parts of China buy him? A lot, it turns out.

Chen bought himself the credibility to work within the system as a collaborator, rather than in a lecturing or hectoring capacity. GE became an important voice in the very vocal health care debate in China. Favorable health indicators, developed under Mao's stewardship, had given way to falling indices of quality and access. China had recognized the failure of its attempt after 1978 to move the health care system from using purely publicly funded providers to offering market-based incentives to local health care providers. In that climate collaboration from the world's technical leader in medical diagnostic equipment, especially one willing to work with the Chinese, was greatly appreciated.

For example, GE worked hard to convince the Chinese regulators that permitting a market for used diagnostic equipment was in their interest. Properly regulated, it was not an indication of substandard care. Keith Morgan, a senior legal counsel with GE in Milwaukee, pointed out, 'Some years ago, brokers purchased used medical equipment from the West and dumped it in China. The Chinese government deemed this insulting and banned the sale of used equipment. We spent a lot of time suggesting that the problem was not with the equipment but with the lack of rules governing its use. Without such equipment, rural hospitals would be denied functionality. Even the U.S. allows a regulated used equipment market."[8] GE also became part of the medical education community. As in other developing countries, they attempted to familiarize medical students, researchers, and doctors with their equipment. A simple, proresearcher policy won GE much support. Researchers who used GE equipment were financed to travel to conferences to present their work.

The ability to harness and motivate talent that Chen has demonstrated will be of increasing value to GE. GE headquarters have realized that China is not just a place for low-cost manufacturing but also a repository of talent that can participate in the best research teams worldwide.

This emphasis on talent is part of CEO Jeffrey Immelt's focus on innovation, trying to leave GE different from the company he inherited from his predecessor and legend Jack Welch. Welch's GE had already cut costs to the bone. Immelt's GE returns to the roots of founder and inventor Thomas Edison of 1878. GE's long-familiar tagline "We bring good things to life" has been replaced by the newer "Imagination at work." Multipage inserts in the Wall Street Journal show a beaming baby, symbolizing imagination, and precise diagnostics applied to a beating heart, signifying innovation. The House of Magic, a research laboratory in Schenectady, New York, established in 1900, is back in business. The lab flourished through the 1940s but withered thereafter because later CEOs veered GE toward "scientific management" rather than "basic science."[9]

With a focus on science GE consciously recognized that the United States and the West did not have a monopoly on scientific talent. As one GE Healthcare executive commented, "The cure for cancer might well come from China."[10] The comment is not just idle speculation. In fact the U.S. monopoly on research that once existed has been diminished by regulation and litigation. For example, the United Kingdom has been leading the move to a more personalized model of health care in which patients are not given generic treatments but are assured of treatment regimens tailor-made to their genetic makeups. Societal consensus regarding privacy concerns associated with storing and using genetic data has proved less elusive in the United Kingdom than in the United States. U.K. Biobank links DNA and tissue samples to individuals' medical information in an effort to create databases that track half a million people over thirty years.[11] Medical experimentation has also received greater public support in countries outside the United States. The rapidly aging Japanese population has been especially keen to promote new diagnostic technology, and China has been willing to invest heavily in a state-of-the-art health care delivery system for underserved rural areas.

As part of GE's renewed embrace of science, Immelt orchestrated an audacious $10 billion acquisition of U.K.-based Amersham corporation in April 2004. While GE Medical used its engineering expertise to build medical diagnostic equipment, Amersham created the biological contrast agents that help sharpen image quality from within the human body. Amersham had the life sciences expertise that GE sorely needed. Knowledge of the underlying biology was as useful to doctors in China and India as it was to those in New York and London.

Because much of the relevant life sciences research was occurring in London, Seoul, and Singapore, the best scientists would not easily come to the United States. GE solved this problem by deciding to go to the leading researchers, wherever they were, and stitch them into a worldwide innovation web complemented by new laboratories in China, Germany, and India. Omar Ishrak, a Bangladeshi with GE Healthcare, commented, "Some of our centers have been opportunistically set up because we've acquired companies that have done pioneering technical work in specific areas—for example, in Norway, for cardiac ultrasound, which is now a worldwide cardiac ultrasound center. We've built a dedicated sales force for them in the U.S., their main market. People don't want to move away from their hometown. So we respect that. It's people dependent. Not just one person."[12]

GE's actions toward talent outside China brought it credibility on the mainland. So did public statements by influential GE spokesmen. GE's vice chairman, Sir William Castell, and I were on a panel in London early in 2005, discussing the effects of the rise of China and India on the Western world. Castell began his comments with a dramatic admonition to the audience regarding the need to recognize that the West had no monopoly on talent. To drive his point home, he described Dresden's rise and fall: "We have no God-given right to remain on top. I went to Dresden in the former East Germany recently. In the 1700s, at some point, Dresden acquired ceramics and porcelain know-how from the Chinese. By the 1900s, it was a leading commercial center in the world. Today it is a dead city with 22 percent unemployment and more than 10 million square feet of unoccupied office space."[13]

Castell's presence at the apex of GE, answering only to CEO Immelt, made a credible statement about GE's commitment to global operations.

Castell had been CEO of Amersham. The subsequent move of GE Healthcare's headquarters from Wisconsin to the United Kingdom reaffirmed the importance to GE, now a $350 billion market capitalization corporation, of being an active world player rather than another American corporation with a world presence. In the same way that GE moved its laboratories to wherever it found key talent, GE Healthcare moved its headquarters to London, partly to accommodate Amersham's scientists.

Thus GE Healthcare was able to bring to China its advances in the life sciences. Castell never tired of telling anyone who would listen about the triumvirate of "biology, bytes, and broadband" that he saw as the future of health care. He believes that an understanding of the life sciences, aided by the collection of data (the bytes) and the ability to communicate that data wherever it is needed (through the broadband), will determine how patients are treated and cured.

Life sciences are of enormous interest to the Chinese state. As early as 1986, during the Seventh Five-Year Plan, a comprehensive National Biotechnology Development Policy Outline was issued.[14] Moreover, China, the only developing country to participate in the International Human Genome project, has sequenced 1 percent of the human genome. More than twenty biotechnology parks have been set up in Beijing, Shanghai, Guangzhou, and Shenzhen, where the enterprises are offered preferential policies on taxation, finance, introduction of talent, imports and exports, and so forth. In classic top-down fiat fashion, the Ministry of Science and Technology committed in 2005 to propel China to the top of life sciences by 2020, when life sciences output is supposed to contribute 7 percent to 8 percent of GDP.[15]

In light of these claims, certainly a corporation committed to life sciences and biotechnology, and willing to invest in related research and development in China, was going to receive the red-carpet treatment. The synchronization of GE's corporate intent with China's appetite for science dovetailed into Chen's efforts to become a credible corporate citizen in China.

Much remains to be done, particularly with regard to harmonizing what GE does in China with its global standards. That is, as much as GE shows good citizenship and an ability to adapt to local conditions, some adaptations it simply will not do. For example, the importance of relationships (*guanxi*) as a determinant of business transactions is difficult to mesh with a corporate culture that tolerates strictly commercial supplier relationships—no bribery, no nepotism, even at the cost of losing businesses.

Chen's success with GE Healthcare is greater than that of many of his peers in other GE units. But to their credit, all the units in China have weathered substantial experimentation as they learned to come to terms with an unfamiliar environment. They have learned that success in China involves contributing to social development. In some instances that lesson has been hard to learn. For example, GE Energy, formerly GE Power Systems, had to deal with the Chinese state's increased self-confidence. Rather than just buy turbines at the lowest possible price as it used to, the state makes GE Energy compete aggressively with companies such as Siemens and Mitsubishi. Companies have to think carefully about the amount of technology they are willing to share, what the Chinese call "technology for market [access]."[16]

Other units within GE have benefited from GE Healthcare's success. For example, China's rudimentary financial markets compromised the traditional strategy of GE Capital. It had to scale back its foray into consumer finance—the business of lending money to consumers for purchasing cars, white goods, even homes. Ultimately GE Capital was able to secure business in China from other business units, financing aircraft purchases and leases for GE and financing used equipment for GE Healthcare.

India's Corporate Ambassador to the World

As GE gave to China it also gave to India. GE put India on the world corporate map by legitimizing the offshoring of business processes—the low-cost performance of routine corporate tasks performed by cheap but skilled labor. By engaging in offshoring for itself, GE India launched one of the country's best-known entrepreneurs, Azim Premji of Wipro Technologies. Wipro became the parent to several other startups and engaged in some of the first major corporate attempts at large-scale, cutting-edge research in India.

Again Castell's comments in London are relevant: "India will plug into our global research and development engine. We have large laboratories in Shanghai and Bangalore. What we're finding is that the research coming out of Bangalore is more affecting GE's global operations in plastics, medical devices, aeronautics, and complex statistical algorithms. GE Healthcare in particular has over two thousand algorithm writers in Bangalore."[17] Castell stressed a key message, "The Indians are very hungry for success. They will stop at nothing."

As in China, GE did not achieve success in India easily. Its India saga also constituted a series of experiments and several decades of low-intensity involvement, culminating in a successful business model. GE entered India in 1902 to install the country's first hydroelectric power plant on the banks of the Cauvery River. However, the power plant, along with a small manufacturing unit in Pune near Bombay, was soon forgotten. Fast forward several decades, and India returned to the spotlight when Jack Welch cast GE Medical as the most globally active business unit that could possibly play a role in India, mostly selling low-cost medical diagnostic equipment.

In 1989 Welch interviewed several candidates before deciding to partner with Azim Premji of Wipro in a joint venture for GE Medical. The goal of the joint venture was to distribute medical equipment in India. Welch believed that India was going to be a huge market and that the obvious infrastructure problems would be handled by the bureaucracy. An entrepreneur like Premji would be free to focus on the business.

At that time Wipro was a shadow of the software powerhouse it is today. Premji had abandoned undergraduate studies at Stanford to take over the family company when his father became ill. He was in the process of changing the company's focus from edible oils to technology. Five years later when I first met Premji in Bombay, he had already begun to speak warmly of the GE relationship.

In keeping with Welch's initial vision of selling in India, GE Medical tried to localize its products to suit India's needs. Failing to do that cost-effectively, the company then decided to make products for the world market, focusing on ultrasound machines that they felt could be sold in other developing countries. As a former GE and Wipro manager described to me, "This program ended in 1995 and was the first time GE had tried to develop products outside the U.S. The first 1993 product was a disaster. It was test-marketed in developing countries but failed reliability tests. The Indian mind-set was never focused on reliability. We shipped fifty units to Brazil, Indonesia, China. Forty-nine came back with problems, and the fiftieth was lost in transit."[18]

Progressive learning over several years, and the borrowed expertise of GE divisions in other countries, notably GE Japan, made the Indian operations ultimately meet GE's exacting standards for manufacturing. By the late 1990s, when GE Medical wished to move a plant out of Belgium to a lower-cost country, the Indian subsidiary outcompeted its better-known Mexican counterpart in an internal competition. It was similar to what had happened under Chen's stewardship in China and reflected GE's willingness and ability to create opportunities for talent in developing countries.

Meanwhile the CEO of GE Medical at the time, John Trani, noted that software work in India, unlike manufacturing, met all GE's reliability standards, even in 1994. In response to a recession in the United States, Trani moved much software work to India. By then GE had raised its stake in the joint venture to 51 percent, thereby retaining all the intellectual property being developed. Premji decided to dilute his stake in return for GE's commitment to provide enterprise software work to Wipro. That agreement propelled Wipro's software business forward, making it one of India's largest companies. Premji became not only the richest Indian but also one of the world's wealthiest men. Welch always spoke admiringly of Premji. "He does business straight, eyeball to eyeball."[19] The close relationship between the two men was apparent as late as 2000, when they both rang the opening bell at the New York Stock Exchange.

When GE boosted Premji and his team as it did, it conferred legitimacy to Wipro and offered a novice team interaction with a globally savvy corporation. In turn Wipro was one of a handful of software companies—Infosys and Tata Consultancy Services was another—that took the world by storm. Wipro itself has both spawned some notable spin-off companies, like Mindtree Consulting, and launched senior talent to positions of influence elsewhere.

GE Medical, which Welch had singled out as being able to flourish in India, had to work hard to become a success. Fortunately the company did so in a way that also nudged India's corporate infrastructure forward. A major problem was the upgrading of local suppliers to world standards. An executive explained, "You just can't go to the local chamber of commerce in India or China and find workable suppliers—it must be a long-term strategy."[20] GE Medical's eight-year relationship with Bharat Electronics Limited (BEL) of India reflects the time and commitment needed to develop a supplier. For several years a twenty-person sourcing team of GE engineers spent 25 percent of its time and a seven-person quality team spent 50 percent of its time working with BEL. GE initially purchased simple, noncritical parts from BEL and over time bought more complex parts. By 2001 BEL was supplying all of GE with parts that were once only made in the United States and Japan, and BEL had attained the coveted six-sigma rating indicating very high reliability.[21]

The investment in world-class suppliers like BEL is akin to investing in indigenous entrepreneurs like Wipro's Premji. Over time those investments have created numerous GE allies in the country. The constituency of support has been vital to GE's success in India.

GE Capital followed GE Medical to India in 1995. Again experimentation was key. A consumer finance business did not work out easily, given the high-interest-rate environment and the difficulty of predicting consumer default risk in an unfamiliar environment. To make its numbers, GE Capital turned to business process outsourcing (BPO), redirecting its voice-based calls to India. GE thus inadvertently sowed the seeds of the BPO industry in India. Simple targets helped. For example, for the software development that preceded BPO, GE had adopted a 70/70/70 mandate—that is, 70 percent of software should be outsourced, 70 percent of the outsourced software should be offshored, and 70 percent of the offshored facilities should be located in India. In late 2004 GE sold 60 percent of its outsourcing arm to venture capital firms for half a billion dollars, having created enormous wealth in the process and helping to put Indian services on the world corporate map.

The BPO revolution has branded India in the eyes of the world. It has employed a population of young people who might otherwise have been unemployed or at least underemployed. They lead independent existences—buying televisions, refrigerators, and cars; buying their own homes rather than living with their parents; and taking out loans and using credit cards. These successful new members of the workforce are big supporters of on-going economic liberalization and therefore of multinationals like GE.

In 2000 GE took the next step of capitalizing on India's talent by setting up its first and largest research and development center outside the United States, naming it in honor of its just-retired CEO. The Jack Welch Technology Center in Bangalore is larger than similar centers in Munich and Shanghai. Research is not limited to software but includes advanced tools for analytics, thin-film testing facilities, furnaces, reactors, a synthesis laboratory, and chromatography for molecular separation and identification. Other than the Bolivian-born German who heads the center, the research staff is entirely Indian.

GE adapted to India, just as it did to China. But the results of the adaptation were different in the two countries, reflecting different local circumstances. For example, in China GE's strategy accounts for the presence of several of the company's major Fortune 500 customers—Dell, Nokia, Samsung, Hewlett-Packard—and for the dependability of manufacturing facilities in China. This is not the case in India. Not only has GE not acquired a critical mass of clients that are multinational companies, but also GE India has yet to achieve excellence in manufacturing. In India GE taps into what Indians do best—software and intellectual capital.

Scott Bayman, head of GE India reflected on GE's evolution in the country: "When we came in the early 1990s, there were a lot of expats, and we all struggled with housing, getting settled into the same hotels. As many multinationals have localized, there are fewer expats coming and going. Those that are here are often nonresident Indians. In any given meeting of the American Chamber of Commerce in New Delhi, as many as 90 percent of those attending are of Indian origin, part of the Indian diaspora." I asked Bayman what the big change was in his role. "In the early 1990s," he replied, "I spent 70 percent of my time interacting with government. Today it is closer to 20 percent."[22]

Corporate Morality and the Bhopal Disaster

To appreciate the example of GE, consider a different extreme.

Just minutes after midnight on December 3, 1984, forty tons of deadly methyl isocyanate gas (a precursor for the pesticide Sevin) escaped from a Union Carbide India Limited (UCIL) pesticide plant in the crowded city of Bhopal, capital of India's central state of Madhya Pradesh. Within hours the deadly gas that leaked from the plant had enveloped the densely populated shantytowns surrounding the factory; dark clouds of smoke loomed. By dawn the carnage was apparent. Scores of human and animal carcasses lay piled in the streets; television crews captured the slaughter and zoomed images across the country. Eyewitness accounts stated that those who fell, coughing and wiping their burning eyes, were not picked up, they just fell and were trampled by others who were running from the ubiquitous fumes. It was clear that this tragedy was one of the biggest industrial disasters of modern times—some termed it India's Hiroshima.

All eyes were on UCIL and the Indian authorities. How would justice be done? Who would be held accountable? Entire families had been decimated. Children were left maimed and orphaned. Union Carbide's reputation and, by implication, the reputation and credibility of foreign multinationals in general were in tatters.

Within days Union Carbide's chairman, Warren Anderson, flew to India on a trip meant to be reconciliatory. But passions were running understandably high, and soon after he got off the plane Indian authorities charged Anderson with homicide and detained him. He was then released on $2,000 bail and promptly flew back to the United States. Since then Indian activists and prosecutors have wanted Anderson extradited to stand trial, but that has not happened. Union Carbide has consistently stated that the chemical explosion was an accident by an unnamed employee, not the result of company negligence.

In 1986 a U.S. district court judge transferred all Bhopal litigation to India, and it took three years for the Indian government and Union Carbide to reach an out-of-court settlement for $470 million. The amount of the compensation was—by developing-nation standards—sizable, but analysts point out that if a similar disaster had occurred, say, in the United States, the compensation would have run into the billions of dollars. In any event the deal was struck, and it was better than Union Carbide's first offer of $50 million and its second of $80 million.

Warren Anderson, cited as chief defendant in a culpable homicide case for tens of thousands of people, remains untouched by the legal process and is spending his eighth decade of life in lavish homes in New York and Florida. Union Carbide was absorbed into Dow Chemical.

The actions of Union Carbide bespeak a moral lassitude that is a far cry from the uprightness of GE. Accidents happen, but when a multinational fails to hold itself morally accountable for the human aftermath, especially in a developing country like India, it shames itself and tarnishes its country of origin.

The Indian government too was negligent in its handling of the Bhopal disaster, waiting until 2003 to formally request Anderson's extradition out of fear, critics say, of a backlash from foreign investors. In June 2004 the United

States rejected India's request because the extradition did not "meet requirements of certain provisions" of the bilateral extradition treaty. Even worse, most of the S470 million paid by Union Carbide remained in a bank account and was not distributed to the families of Bhopal victims until July 2004, two decades after the tragedy.

Largesse and Profits

Yet GE is not an aberration. In fact the company has drawn on the experiences of other enlightened multinationals and taken a long-term view of success in emerging markets. Unilever, for example, began nurturing Indian talent decades before GE. Unilever's global rival Procter & Gamble (P&G) has done likewise in China.

As early as the mid-1930s Unilever began transforming the management of its foreign divisions, appointing nationals to managerial positions in India and elsewhere.[23] The change came slowly but continuously. In 1940 virtually all of Unilever's 150 managers in India were expatriates, but by 1966 only 6 of 360 managers were expatriates.[24] In 1961 Unilever became the first major foreign company to appoint an Indian national as chairman of its Indian subsidiary, Hindustan Lever Limited (HLL), thereby effectively branding Unilever as an Indian citizen. Every subsequent chairman has been Indian. An Indian senior command made negotiating and dealing with the Indian bureaucracy—particularly in a regulatory climate that was quite antiforeign— far more feasible.

HLL's local credibility was enhanced by its activities in rural India. The Etah Project, praised as early as the 1970s, turned around a fledgling rural milk factory by providing farmers with knowledge of animal husbandry and setting up a medical scheme to promote health and hygiene. For the first time a corporation helped implement an integrated scheme around its narrower corporate needs.[25]

Such initiatives are part of HLL's DNA. Chih Chen would see growth for GE in rural China much later on, but very early on perceived its competitive advantage in learning to access rural India's back roads. In 2000 HLL partnered with several self-help women's groups to create Project Shakti (*shakti* is Hindi for "power"). Using self-help groups throughout rural India, Shakti set out to distribute products in a way that generated employment for rural women. The project proved to be a cost-effective distribution channel into village India and created hundreds of "Shakti entrepreneurs." To address the needs of very low-income rural consumers, HLL created small packaging for many of its products and priced them at discounts. By 2004 HLL was selling miniversions of shampoo, hair oil, skin creams, toothpaste, and soap, and twelve thousand women, spread over fifteen states and fifty thousand villages, were helping them do it.[26]

The value of such initiatives should be viewed against the backdrop of India's dismal record on women's issues. The World Economic Forum ranks India fifty-third among the fifty-eight countries surveyed to measure the breadth of the gender gap worldwide in 2005.[27] Discrimination of women begins at birth.[28] As the Nobel laureate Amartya Sen pointed out in his ominously titled essay "More Than 100 Million Women Are Missing," death rates are higher for women than for men until they reach their late thirties, other than immediately following birth.[29] When India launched its economic reforms in 1991, less than 40 percent of the 330 million women aged seven and older were literate; this accounted for more than 200 million illiterate women.[30] A project like Shakti promises to change lives and open new opportunities.

As important as India is to Unilever, so China is to P&G. Only five years after launching its business in China in 1988, P&G was earning sufficient profits to be one of the highest taxpayers to the Chinese government. Like Unilever in India, P&G established a mainstream corporate discourse that was respected for generating scores of well-trained managers. In fact P&G has been nicknamed the Huangpu Military Academy for brand managers in China, equating it to one of China's most famous military academies. A Chinese marketing expert once referred to P&G as a corporate Lei Feng, after a Chinese man who was known for selflessly helping others.

Mutualism: Bridges Between China and India

What distinguishes GE from Unilever and P&G is its achievement of symbiosis between its China and India operations. Unilever succeeds in India and P&G succeeds in China; succeeding in both is what makes GE unique.

The China operations of GE are better off *because* of those in India, and vice versa. Again, this is a story of organizational experimentation and gradual, repeated change. At GE Healthcare, Chinese hardware marries Indian software. The 719 parts of a high-end Proteus radiology system were developed in GE facilities in a dozen countries. Development of software algorithms and the scanner's generator took place in Bangalore, and final assembly was done in Beijing. One executive described the value of having subsidiaries in both China and India: "The ability to set up parallel groups of highly skilled engineering talent in both countries is invaluable. It raises the efficiency of product development and fits in with a competitive culture within GE."[31] GE is redirecting the two countries' competitiveness toward an ultimately collaborative end— producing better medical diagnostic products.

It's tempting to attribute GE's success at least in part to its use of country managers with responsibility to global product groups. Each country manager is charged with leveraging the collective strength of all GE units in the country. Each business in a country generally has a so-called dotted-line responsibility to the country manager and primary responsibility to its global business unit. Country managers provide the glue to link various businesses within a country and to link various country operations. However, most major multinationals have similar matrix structures, so this is surely not the entire story.

GE offers multinationals many lessons. The first lesson is to have the humility to recognize the critical importance of experimentation and adaptability to local conditions. In its trial forays GE business units, especially the medical diagnostics business unit, could not profitably develop products for sale in China and India. Nor could they produce the equipment elsewhere at a cost low enough to cater to the low-income populations of the two countries. Substantial experimentation led GE to begin to develop in China and India parts of what the company needed for use or sale worldwide. These experiments required hiring legions of talent in both countries, even before successfully selling to their citizens. It helps that GE's commitment to nurturing talent is credible. For example, Yoshiaki Fujimori, head of GE Medical Asia, ascended all the way up the corporate ladder to CEO of GE Plastic in 2001.[32]

Such hiring of talent serves an important purpose. Apparently it is easier for a company to convince societies that its presence is in their best interests if the company focuses on providing employment and transferring learning in the process, rather than trying to establish a presence by selling goods. The generated employment is an added value for the economy, while items sold are usually mere substitutes for existing products purveyed by indigenous vendors who will naturally resist what they see as an incursion.

GE's second lesson is largesse. Giving back handsomely to the countries in which it operates reflects GE's desire to make money as well as social conscience. In both countries, suppliers and customers of GE disseminate best practices, and GE alumni populate the best corporate offices in China and India. In a vote of confidence for both countries, GE has opened two of its biggest cutting-edge research and development centers in Shanghai and Bangalore.

Benign Self-Interest as a Bridge

A resilient link between China and India through the centuries has resulted from self-interested and mutually beneficial trade. The recent rejuvenation of trade was not as extraordinary as the cessation of contact between China and India over the preceding few decades. Much of the newly established trade is not between two different merchants but within a single corporation. GE facilitates cross-border trade every time it ships a subassembly of an ultrasound machine between subsidiaries in different countries, or every time algorithms from its Bangalore lab and hardware from its Wuxi facility are assembled in yet a third location. Companies can and are acting as bridges between societies.

Within corporate boundaries, individuals' actions are self-interested. Witness Chih Chen's actions in China and Andy Klump's actions to advance his own career. Both served as individual bridges between societies but also enable their respective corporate infrastructures to play their own, larger self-interested bridging roles. GE's multiple bridges between China and India distinguish it from other stalwart companies whose largesse has extended to one or the other country.

Contrast this benign self-interest with the efforts of well-intentioned individuals who wanted to remake China in their own image, not because it was in their narrow self-interest but because they thought it was their duty to do so. According to the China historian Jonathan Spence, the experiences of these do-gooders over several centuries "speak to us still . . . about the ambiguities of superiority, and about that indefinable realm where altruism and exploitation meet."[33] The missionaries, physicians, and others who went to help China develop did nothing of the sort. Many thought themselves better than the Chinese, and though they became insiders, they failed to change China.

They also sometimes found themselves exploited. "[I]t was the Chinese who had gained from the exchange. They had used the Westerners' skills when it suited them, and paid a fair price, but had offered little else in return. What did not concern them they had shrugged aside."[34] Spence's observation about priests who unsuccessfully sought to convert the Chinese to Christianity could easily apply to modern businesses attempting to exploit China for their own ends. The crucial lesson of companies like General Electric is that enlightened self-interest need not be a zero-sum game. That is the key to resilient bridges between East and West.[35]

NOTES

Chapter 1

1. Richard C. Levin, "Baccalaureate Address: China on My Mind," *Yale Alumni Magazine,* summer 2001, http://www.yalealumnimagazine.com/issues/01_07/baccalaureate.html.

2. "Elihu Yale Profile," BBC Wales Hall of Fame Page, http://www.bbc.co.uk/wales/northeast/guides/halloffame/historical/elihu_yale.shtml.

3. Severe Acute Respiratory Syndrome (SARS), see discussion in Chapter 10 titled, "Barefoot Doctors and Medical Tourists: Futile Attempts to Confront the Grim Reaper."

4. For this approximate analysis I defined a major article as one appearing on the front page. Defining it as one that exceeds 900 words does not change the tenor of what I say in these paragraphs. Ideological biases notwithstanding, using the *Wall Street Journal* as a source for the analysis rather than the *New York Times* also leaves the conclusions unchanged.

5. Far more job turnover occurs due to technological progress and the normal tumult of competition in the U.S. economy than from outsourcing.

6. Harold R. Isaacs, *Scratches on Our Minds: American Views of China and India* (White Plains, NY: M. E. Sharpe, 1980).

7. J. K. Fairbank, *Chinabound: A Fifty-Year Memoir* (New York: Harper and Row, 1982), 190, 192.

8. Yasheng Huang and Tarun Khanna, "Can India Overtake China?" *Foreign Policy,* July-August 2003, 74.

9. "The White Man's Burden," by Rudyard Kipling was first published in 1899 in the magazine *McClure's.*

10. April Fools' Issue, *The Harbus,* April 3, 2006 (Boston: Harvard Business School).

11. Taj Medical Group Home page http://www.tajmedicalgroup.co.uk.

12. Anand Mahindra, interview by author, Mumbai, June 2005.

13. "Silicon Valley, PRC," *The Economist* June 27, 1998, 64.

14. Jack Lu, interview by author, China, December 2005.

15. Bruce Claflin, "Huawei's Core Values," *China Entrepreneur,* special issue, no. 18 (2005).

16. Andronico Luksic, interview by author, New York, November 2006.

17. Angus Maddison, "The World Economy: A Millennia Perspective " on behalf of Development Centre Studies, (OECD Publishing, 2001); see also http://www.ggdc.net/Maddison for further details.

18. Shinya Kasugai, *Indo: Kinkei to enkei* (India: Past and Today) (Kyoto: Dohosha Publishing, 1981), 126.

19. Lawrence E. Harrison, *Underdevelopment Is a State of Mind: The Latin American Case* (Lanham, MD: Center for International Affairs, 1985).

20. Alain Peyrefitte, *The Immobile Empire,* trans. Jon Rothschild (New York: Knopf, 1992).

21. The title is that of Charles Baudelaire's poem of the same name in his celebrated *Les Fleurs du Mal* (The Flowers of Evil), first published in 1857.

22. I would be remiss if I did not acknowledge my long-time scholarly compatriot at Harvard Business School, Krishna Palepu, with whom I do much of my work on businesses in emerging markets in general.

Chapter 2

1. The Indian Parliament consists of these two houses. A bill can become an act only after it is passed by both houses of Parliament and the president assents. The government is formed by the party with the

most seats in the Lok Sabha. Members of the Lok Sabha are elected for five-year terms, and the president can dissolve the Lok Sabha if no party gets a majority.

2. This action was widely reported in the press, including the Indian daily newspapers the *Hindu*, the *Telegraph*, and the *Tribune*.

3. Devesh Kapur and Pratap Bhanu Mehta, "The Indian Parliament as an Institution of Accountability," Democracy, Governance and Human Rights Program Paper 23, United Nations Research Institute for Social Development, January 2006.

4. Lee Kuan Yew, *From Third World to First: The Singapore Story, 1965–2000* (New York: HarperCollins, 2000), 596.

5. The name of the organization subsequently became PRS Legislative Research, in response to the Indian Parliament's contesting the use of the word *parliamentary* in the original name.

6. C.V. Madhukar, interviews by author on several occasions in Washington, D.C. and New Delhi in 2005–2007.

7. Amartya Sen, *The Argumentative Indian*, (Great Britain: Penguin Books Ltd., 2005).

8. *Gadakh Yashwantrao Kankarrao v. E.V. alias Balasaheb Vikhe Patil & Others*, AIR 1994 SC 678, Supreme Court judgment quoted in Handbook for Candidates, section 5.3. Election Commission of India, 1998, http://archive.eci.gov.in/handbook/CandidateHB_EVM_.pdf.

9. Simon Leys' translation of *The Analects of Confucius*, (New York: W.W. Norton, 1997). See especially the introduction.

10. Ibid.

11. Roderick Macfarquhar, and Michael Schoenhals, *Mao's Last Revolution*, (Cambridge, MA: Harvard University Press, 2006).

12. Mao Tse-tung, "The Role of the Chinese Communist Party in the National War," in *Selected Works of Mao Tse-tung*, vol. 2, 203–204, available at http://www.marxists.org/reference/archive/mao/selected-works/volume-2/mswv2_10.htm.

13. "Gong si he ying" is a phrase that suggests that the public and private sectors will manage companies together.

14. J. K. Fairbank, *Chinabound: A Fifty-Year Memoir* (New York: Harper and Row, 1982), 350.

15. MacFarquhar and Schoenhals, *Mao's Last Revolution*.

16. Stephen K. Ma, "Chinese Bureaucracy and Post-Mao Reforms: Negative Adjustment," *Asian Survey* 30, no. 11 (1990): 1038–1052.

17. Edgar Snow, *Red Star over China* (New York: Grove, 1968).

18. Ma, "Chinese Bureaucracy and Post-Mao Reforms."

19. Ibid.

20. World Bank, World Development Indicators. These numbers are adjusted for purchasing power parity in constant dollars (for 2000).

21. Asian Development Bank, *Technical Assistance Report to the People's Republic of China for Nongovernment Organization–Government Partnerships in Village-Level Poverty Alleviation*, (April 2005), 1, http://www.adb.org/Documents/TARs/PRC/tar-prc-38234.pdf. The ANB notes that "this figure refers to the official annual per capita income line of CNY627," or about $80.

22. Heike Holbig, "The Party and Private Entrepreneurs in the PRC," *Copenhagen Journal of Asian Studies* 16 (2002): 30–56.

23. Bruce J. Dickson, *Red Capitalists in China: The Party, Private Entrepreneurs, and Prospects for Political Change* (New York: Cambridge University Press, 2003).

24. "Communist Party of China," http://www.Chinatoday.com/org/cpc/.

25. Minxin Pei, *China's Trapped Transition: The Limits of Developmental Autocracy* (Cambridge, MA: Harvard University Press, 2006), 150.

26. Anonymous interview by author, in person, July 2005.

27. See the introduction to Atul Kohli's edited collection of essays, *The Success of India's Democracy* (New York: Cambridge University Press, 2001).

28. Pranab Bardhan made this point in his Radhakrishna lectures at All Souls College, Oxford, in 1982–1983, later published as *The Political Economy of Development in India* (New York: Basil Blackwell, 1984).

29. Vijay Joshi and, I.M.D. Little, *India's Economic Reforms, 1991–2001*. (New York: Oxford University Press, 1996).

30. Jay Solomon and Joanna Slater, "India's Economy Gets a New Jolt from Mr. Shourie," *Wall Street Journal*, January 9, 2001, http://www.sbeusers.csuhayward.edu/~alima/courses/ArticlesWI04/ws040109IndiaPrivatization.htm.

31. "Privatization of Indian Oil Firms Postponed," *DAWN* (the Internet Edition), September 8, 2002, http://www.dawn.com/2002/09/08/ebr19.htm.

Chapter 3

1. In 2005 India was ranked 92nd among 159 countries See "Transparency International Corruption Perceptions Index 2005," http://www.transparency.org/content/download/1516/7919.

2. Sheikh Dawood Ibrahim Kaskar is a don of an organized crime syndicate in Mumbai, and the ISI is Pakistan's Inter-Services Intelligence; both have been linked to terrorist activity and Osama bin Laden.

3. Tarun Tejpal, interview by research associate Vinati Dev, February 7, 2005.

4. *Caijing* editor, interview by author, March 21, 2005.

5. Ibid.

6. "Chinese Newspaper Axed after Criticizing Parliament," *The Guardian*, June 20, 2003, http://www.guardian.co.uk/china/story/0,,981622,00.html.

7. For details on Internet filtering in China, see "Internet Filtering in China in 2004–2005: A Country Study," OpenNet Initiative, April 14, 2005, http://www.opennetinitiative.net/studies/china/ONI_China_Country_Study.pdf; and "China and the Internet: The Party, the People and the Power of Cyber-Talk," *The Economist*, April 27, 2006.

8. In December 1999 Wang Youcai, founder of the China Democracy Party, was sentenced to eleven years' imprisonment for subversion. Two of the accusations involved sending e-mail to Chinese dissidents abroad and accepting overseas funds to buy a computer. There are many more such cases, as cited in Amnesty International's first major reports on the Internet in China: *People's Republic of China: State Control of the Internet in China*, November 26, 2002, http://web.amnesty.org/library/Index/engasa170072002?OpenDocument&of=COUNTRIES%5CCHIN; and *People's Republic of China: State Control of the Internet in China: Appeal Cases*, November 26, 2002, http://web.amnesty.org/library/index/engasa170462002.

9. Currently the Web site is renting a temporary server only to allow former users to back up their old e-mail.

10. "Internet Fuels Rise in Number of Jailed Journalists," Committee to Protect Journalists, December 7, 2006, http://www.cpj.org/Briefings/2006/imprisoned_06/imprisoned_06.html.

11. Translated excerpts from He Qinglian, "Media Control in China," *China Rights Forum*, no. 1 (2004), http://www.hrichina.org/fs/downlcadables/pdf/downloadable-resources/a1_MediaControl1.2004.pdf?revision_id=8992.

12. Stephen Green, *China's Stock Market: A Guide to Its Progress, Players and Prospects* (London: Profile Books, 2003).

13. This term was first coined by David Baron at Stanford and refers most commonly to actions taken to react to or affect government regulations and work with civil society and excludes the prices and amounts of products and services that a company provides.

14 See its mission statement on China Securities Regulatory Commission's Official Website, http://www.csrc.gov.cn/en/homepage/about_en.jsp.

15 Thomas G. Rawski, "What Is Happening to China's GDP Statistics?" *China Economic Review* 12 (2001): 347–54. A later paper considers several criticisms of his arguments and explains why he stands by his reasoning: "Measuring China's Recent GDP Growth: Where Do We Stand?," University of Pittsburgh, August 29, 2002, http://www.pitt.edu/~tgrawski/papers2002/measuring.pdf.

16. Thomas G. Rawski, "Beijing's Fuzzy Math," *Wall Street Journal* (Eastern Edition), April 22, 2002.

17. This paragraph and the following two draw from Tarun Khanna and Krishna Palepu, "The Evolution of Concentrated Ownership in India: Broad Patterns and a History of the Indian Software Industry," in *The History of Concentrated Ownership around the World*, ed. Randall Morck (Chicago: University of Chicago Press, 2005).

18. Preface to R. K. Hazari, *The Structure of the Corporate Private Sector: A Study of Concentration, Ownership and Control* (Bombay: Asia Publishing House, 1966).

19. D. R. Gadgil (with staff of Gokhale Institute of Politics and Economics, Poona, India), "Notes on the Rise of the Business Communities in India," mimeograph, International Secretariat, Institute of Pacific Relations, New York, April 1951: 29.

20. William P. Alford, *To Steal a Book Is an Elegant Offense: Intellectual Property Law in Chinese Civilization* (Stanford, CA: Stanford University Press, 1955), 23.

21. As cited by Alford, *To Steal a Book is an Elegant Offense*, footnote 30, 13.

22. Alford, *To Steal a Book Is an Elegant Offense*, 7.

23. Ibid., 86.

24. S. Sanandakumer, "Tech Breeds Rich Harvest in Kerala," *Economic Times* (a publication of the Maharashtra Economic Development Council) June 26, 2002, http://economictimesindiatimes.com/articleshow/14096578.cms.

25. The Right to Information Act does not extend to the Indian states of Jammu and Kashmir.

26. Alford, *To Steal a Book Is an Elegant Offense*, 26, quoting Stephen Owen, *Remembrances: The Experience of the Past in Chinese Literature* (Cambridge, MA: Harvard University Press, 1986).

27. Randle Edwards, Louis Henkin, and Andrew Nathan, eds., *Human Rights in Contemporary China* (New York: Columbia University Press, 1986), 90.

28. Lee Kuan Yew, *The Singapore Story: Memoirs of Lee Kuan Yew* (Singapore: Singapore Press Holdings, 1998).

29. Elizabeth Perry is cited in the introduction to Merle Goldman's book *From Comrade to Citizen: The Struggle for Political Rights in China* (Cambridge, MA: Harvard University Press, 2005). See also Andrew Nathan, *Chinese Democracy* (New York: Knopf, 1985).

30. Perry Link, "Turned Back at China's Door: Why Princeton Should Speak Out Against a Blacklist of Scholars," *Princeton Alumni Weekly*, February 9, 2005.

31. Jay Taylor, *The Dragon and the Wild Goose: China and India.* (New York: Praegar, 1991, Chapter 7).

32. Guy Pfeffermann, letter to the editor, *Foreign Policy*, November-December 2003, 6.

Chapter 4

1. "Pudong Development: The Last Opportunity for Developing Shanghai," *New Capital Newspaper*, August 20, 2004.

2. By some estimates, these totaled $1.12 billion in the first five years. Compiled by Richard Holman, "World Wire" column, *Wall Street Journal* (Eastern Edition), March 12, 1992.

3. Trish Saywell, "Pudong Rises to the Task," *Far Eastern Economic Review* 163, no. 44 (2000): 56–58.

4. "Shanghai Announces Plans to Develop Pudong New Area," *East Asian Executive Reports*, May 1990.

5. Salman Rushdie, *Midnight's Children* (New York: Knopf, 1981), 105.

6. Ramnath, interview by research associate Namrata Arora, Machimaar Village, Mumbai, March 2007.

7. Harekrishna Debnath, "Charter of Demands of the Indian National Fishworkers' Forum," Library of the *Turtle*, December 6–19, 2001, http://www.voiceoftheturtle.org/library/nff.php.

8. This would require amending Coastal Regulatory Zones and increasing the controversial Floor Space Index.

9. DLF went public in June 2007 with a market capitalization of $22 billion.

10. The Urban Land (Ceiling and Regulation) Act of 1976 imposed a limit on the agglomeration of vacant land in urban areas, regulates the acquisition of such vacant land, and controls the disposal of vacant land. It was repealed by the Urban Land (Ceiling and Regulation) Repeal Act of 1999.

11. "Premier Zhu Rongji on Three Gorges Project Construction Quality," *People's Daily Online*, June 19, 2000, http://english.people.com.cn/english/200006/19/eng20000619_43308.html.

12. "China's Dam Fills to Target," *BBC News Online*, June 11, 2003, http://news.bbc.co.uk/2/hi/asia-pacific/2977404.stm.

13. International Rivers Network (Yi Ming, primary author), "Human Rights Dammed Off at Three Gorges: An Investigation of Resettlement and Human Rights Problems in the Three Gorges Dam Project." Report published January 2003, http://www.irn.org/pdf/threeg/3gcolor.pdf.

14. Sarvepalli Gopal, *Jawaharlal Nehru: A Biography*, vol. 3 (New Delhi: Oxford University Press, 1984). "Nehru was now more aware than he had been in earlier years of the possible 'disease of gigantism.' He had said to himself while surveying the large Bhakra-Nangal dam in 1956, 'These are the new temples of India where I worship.' "

15. In Indian law any civic-minded person can approach the courts, not just an aggrieved party.

16. Friends of River Narmada, (Medha Patkar, primary author), "Without Considering Basic Issues, Supreme Court Surrenders to the Pressures by Power Holders. Unfettered Dam Construction and Displacement Allowed: Assault on People and Constitution," Narmada Bachao Andolan press release, October 18, 2000, http://www.narmada.org/nba-press-releases/october-2000/sc.judgement.html.

17. Articles 19(1)(f), 19(5), 31, 32, 39(b) and (c), 226 and 265 of the Indian Constitution accord the status of Fundamental Right on matters related to property.

18. Dr. Surat Singh, interview by author, New Delhi, March 2005.

19. The term *surplus* is used when private property is taken over for a public purpose. The meaning of the word implies that this property "is providing a surplus for all members of society including the person whose property is being taken albeit minus the loss of his property for which he should be compensated at least to maintain status quo." See Jaivir Singh, *(Un)Constituting Property: The Deconstruction of*

Right to Property in India (New Delhi: Center for Study of Law and Governance, Jawaharlal Nehru University, 2004).

20. Katherine Wilhelm, interview by research associate Vinati Dev, New York, March 2005. See also K. Wilhelm, "Rethinking Property Rights in Urban China," *UCLA Journal of International Law and Foreign Affairs*, 9, no. 2, (fall/winter 2004: 19).

21. Chengri Ding, "Land Policy Reform in China: Assessment and Prospects," *Land Use Policy* 20 issue 2, (2003): 109–120.

22. Songsu Choi, "A Housing Market in the Making: Zhu Rongji Jumpstarts China's Stalled Housing Reforms," *China Business Review*, November 2, 1998, http://www.chinabusinessreview.com/public/9811/choi.html.

23. Chengri Ding and Gerrit Knaap "Urban Land Policy Reform in China," *Land Lines* 15, no. 2 (April 2003), http://www.lincolninst.edu/pubs/PubDetail.aspx?pubid=793

24. Wilhelm, "Rethinking Property Rights in Urban China."

25. Chengri Ding, "Land Policy Reform in China: Assessment and Prospects," *Land Use Policy* 20, no. 2 (2003): 109–20.

26. Karl Moore and David Lewis, *Foundations of Corporate Empire: Is History Repeating Itself?* (London: Financial Times Prentice Hall, 2000).

27. Ke Fang, "Housing Relocation and Housing Property in Beijing," *China Lawyer* 7, no. 5 (1999): 33–36.

Chapter 5

1. Abhijit Banerjee, Shawn Cole, and Esther Duflo, "Banking Reform in India," working paper, Massachusetts Institute of Technology, Cambridge, MA, June 2004.

2. Ibid.

3. "Bonds Hold Attraction for India's Lazy Bankers," *Economic Times* November 25, 2003, http://economictimes.indiatimes.com/articleshow/301960.cms.

4. According to the Reserve Bank of India's *Report on Trend and Progress of Banking in India, 2005–2006*, gross nonperforming assets of scheduled commercial banks in India were \$11.7 billion, or 3.3 percent of gross advances at the end of fiscal year 2006.

5. Diana Farrell, Susan Lund, and Fabrice Morin, "The Promise and Perils of China's Banking System," *McKinsey Quarterly*, Web Exclusive, July 2006, http://www.mckinseyquarterly.com/The_promise_and_perils_of_Chinas_banking_system_abstract and Diana Farrell, Susan Lund, and Fabrice Morin, "How Financial-System Reform Could Benefit China: Serving the New Chinese Consumer," *McKinsey Quarterly*, Special Edition 2006 92–105.

6. Tarun Khanna and Krishna Palepu, "Emerging Giants: Building World-Class Companies in Developing Countries," *Harvard Business Review* 84, no. 10 (October 2006).

7. Stephen Green, *China's Stock Market: A Guide to Its Progress, Players, and Prospects* (London: The Economist, in Association with Profile Books Limited, 2003).

8. Matthew Rudolph, "The Dragon and the Elephant Enter the Matrix Asset Classes, Financial Positions, and the Politics of Securitization in China and India," (Chapter of PhD diss. for Cornell University, presented at the Annual Conference of the American Political Science Association, 2003).

9. Ibid.

10. K. G. Sahadevan, "From Crisis to Recovery and Transformation: India's Experience with Economic Reforms of 1990," *South Asian Journal of Management* 9, no. 4 (October–December 2002): 12–27, http://ganga.iiml.ac.in/~devan/ecolib-sajm.pdf.

11. Suman Dubey, "Speculation Sends Indian Stock Markets Skyward," *Asian Wall Street Journal*, March 16, 1992.

12. Samir Barua and Jayant Varma, "Securities Scam: Genesis, Mechanics, and Impact," *Journal of the Indian Institute of Management* 18, no. 1 (January–March 1992): 3–12, http://www.iimahd.ernet.in/~jrvarma/papers/vik18-1.pdf. Reproduced with the permission of Vikalpa, *Journal of the Indian Institute of Management*, Ahmedabad, where paper was first published

13. "India Orders Probe into Country's Biggest Stock Market Scam," Agence France-Presse, May 11, 1992.

14. Matthew Rudolph, "Diversity Amid Convergence: State Authority, Economic Governance, and the Politics of Securities Finance in China and India," (PhD diss., Chapter 6, Cornell University, May 2006); and Sumit Sharma, "India's NSE Seen Challenging Bombay Stock Exchange," *Reuters News*, October 26, 1994.

15. India was the first country to use a VSAT-based trading system in the capital market. The NSE's VSAT network remains the largest such facility in the financial markets, linking more than four thousand

terminals across 280 cities. See "NSE Forced the Pace of Market Reforms in India," *Good News India,* March 2002, http://www.goodnewsindia.com/Pages/content/milestones/nse.html.

16. Raju Bist, "India: Moving with the Times: The National Stock Exchange," *Institutional Investor,* 30, no. 12, (December 1995): A8.

17. A *dhoti* is the traditional garment of men's wear in southern India. It is a rectangular piece of unstitched cloth, usually about five yards long, wrapped around the waist and legs and knotted at the waist.

18. Manjeet Kripalani, "India's Battle of the Bourses," *BusinessWeek Online,* August 26, 1996, http://www.businessweek.com/archives/1996/b3490154.arc.htm?campaign_id=search.

19. Mark Nicholson, "High-Tech Exchange Spurs Rivals into Action—India's Newest Bourse Gained from the Reliance Row," *Financial Times,* December 7, 1995, 35.

20. Ajay Shah and Susan Thomas, "The Evolution of Securities Market in India in the 1990s. Indian Council for Research on International Economic Relations," working paper 91, Indian Council for Research on International Economic Relations, New Delhi, 2001, http://www.icrier.org/pdf/wp91.pdf.

21. R.H. Patil, interview by author, February 1999.

22. "Mum in Mumbai," *Asia Money,* October 1996.

23. Ravi Narain, interview by author, December 2004; and R. H. Patil, interview by author, February and April 1999.

24. Green, *China's Stock Market,* 9–10.

25. The Shenzhen Market was not officially approved until mid-1991.

26. Green, *China's Stock Market,* 9–10.

27. In the late 1990s most companies had between 20 percent and 40 percent of their shares traded on the market. This illiquidity was partly tempered by the privatization of smaller state-owned enterprises in recent years and by progressive removal of bans on foreign ownership in several sectors by 2004. But through all this the exchange remains fundamentally unhealthy and private companies scarce.

28. Before 1992 the PBOC had decided on the quota governing all securities. The quota system was formally abolished in 2000.

29. Jinhua Chen, ed., *1997 nian Zhongguo Guomin Jingji he Fazhan Baogao* (China's National Economic and Social Development Report, 1997), 26, http://unpan1.un.org/intradoc/groups/public/documents/APCITY/UNPAN014937.pdf.

30. Dongwei Su, "Chinese Stock Markets Plunged Following 1997 Stock Issue Quota Announcement," *Chinese Finance Association* update 3, no. 33 (May 20, 1997), http://www.china-finance.org/update/volume3/v3n33.html.

31. Yasheng Huang, personal communication with author, several times during 2003 and 2004.

32. Mr. Chen, interview by research associate Jin Chen, July 2005.

33. Randall Morck and Bernard Yeung, "The Puzzle of the Harmonious Stock Prices," *World Economy* 3, no. 3 (July 2002): 1–15.

34. Suchintan Chatterjee, "Banking in India: Banking on Retail," *About.com* (Economics column), http://economics.about.com/cs/finance/a/india_banking.htm.

35. "Safe As Houses," *The Economist,* June 8, 2002, 70.

36. "A Merger with HDFC Bank Is Too Expensive," *Rediff.com,* interview with HDFC chairman Deepak Parekh, December 20, 2004, http://in.rediff.com/money/2004/dec/20inter.htm.

37. K.V. Kamath, personal correspondence with author on multiple occasions in 2005–2007. Last in March 2007.

38. Farrell, Lund, and Morin, "The Promise and Perils of China's Banking System."

39. Bharat N. Anand, Nitin Nohria, and John Pegg, "ICICI (A)," Case 9–701–064, (Boston: Harvard Business School, February 22, 2001).

40. "The Worst Banking System in Asia," *The Economist* May 2, 1998, 65–67.

41. Andrew Yeh, "Chinese Banks Dogged by Scandal," *Financial Times,* February 8, 2005, 23.

42. Ibid.

43. Linsun Cheng, "Banking in Modern China: Entrepreneurs, Professional Managers and the Development of China's Banks, 1897–1937," (Cambridge, UK: Cambridge University Press, 2003), 12.

44. Wu Li, interview by research associate Jin Chen, Cambridge, MA, March 3, 2005.

45. This case was extensively discussed in China and elsewhere. Samples of articles include: Yuan Lu, "Exclusive Interview of Sun Dawu's Lawyer: Why We Are Still Not Satisfied?" *Netease Business News,* November 4 2003, http://www.blogchina.com/new/display/15615.html; "Why Sun Dawu Broke the Law? The 86th Why in 100,000 Whys on China's Stock Market," *China Business Times,* November 4, 2003, http://www.cbt.com.cn/cbtnews/frontend/news.asp?ID=51771.

46. Ibid.

47. Liu Bing, interview by research associate Jin Chen, March 2, 2005.

48. "A \$45 Billion Shot in the Arm: China's Bank Bail-Out," "Global Agenda" column, *The Economist,* January 6, 2004.

49. Franco Modigliani and Shi Larry Cao, "The Chinese Saving Puzzle and the Life-Cycle Hypothesis," *Journal of Economic Literature* 42, issue 1 (March 2004): 145–171.

50. From China Central Television (CCTV), *Daily Economic Half Hour,* December 16, 2004, http://finance.sina.com.cn/g/20041216/23181230907.shtml.

51. Arthur R. Krober, "China Tries the India Thing," *China Economic Quarterly,* 5, issue 1, (2001): 35–40.

52. World Bank, World Development Indicators Database, http://gc.worldbank.org/3JU2HA60D0

53. Yasheng Huang and Tarun Khanna, "Indigenous versus Foreign Business Models," in *Asia's Giants: Comparing China and India,* ed. Edward Friedman and Bruce Gilley (New York: Palgrave Macmillan, 2005).

54. Statistics based on data from the National Bureau of Statistics of China, http://www.stats.gov.cn/was40/reldetail.jsp?docid=402317150.

55. Rawi Abdelal, personal correspondence, Boston, spring 2005.

56. Amar Gill, *Corporate Governance in Emerging Markets* report for CLSA Emerging Markets, Hong Kong, (2001).

57. "Is China's Stock Market a Casino?" *Guangming Daily,* February 20, 2001, http://www.gmw.cn/01gmrb/2001–02/20/GB/02^18698^0^GMB2–209.htm.

Chapter 6

1. Jianfeng Xiong, "SASAC's New Goal: 50 Central Enterprises to Make Global Top 500 List by 2010," *China Business News,* April 24, 2006, http://www.china-cbr.com/s/n/000002/20060424/020000011006.shtml.

2. Saumya Roy, "The Private Sector Is India's True Face—Open, Pragmatic," interview with Fareed Zakaria, *Outlook India,* October 11, 2005 http://yaleglobal.yale.edu/display.article?id=6360.

3. "Davos man" is Harvard government professor Samuel Huntington's tongue-in-cheek term to describe the collection of elites who debate the world's future.

4. The analysis of reasons underlying Infosys's success is informed heavily by a project with Krishna Palepu. See Tarun Khanna and Krishna Palepu, "Globalization and Convergence in Corporate Governance: Evidence from Infosys and the Indian Software Industry," *Journal of International Business Studies* 35, no. 6 (November 2004).

5. Gautam Kumra and Jayant Sinha, "The Next Hurdle for Indian IT," *McKinsey Quarterly,* special edition 2003, Issue 4, 49.

6. K. Dinesh, interview by Katarina Pick, 2001.

7. Kumra and Sinha, "The Next Hurdle for Indian IT," 45.

8. My colleagues Krishna Palepu at Harvard and Suraj Srinivasan at the University of Chicago have shown that, just as providers of financial capital need to be reassured that they are dealing with trustworthy entities, the same applies to providers of human capital (that is, employees) and to customers. See "Disclosure Practices of Foreign Companies Interacting with US. Markets," *Journal of Accounting Research* 42, no. 2 (May 2004).

9. "Saints and Sinners: Who's Got Religion?" research report for Credit Lyonnais Securities Asia, Hong Kong, 2001.

10. Filing of forms 10-Q and 20-F are required (by the SEC) within 45 days of the end of the quarter and 180 days of the end of the year, respectively.

11. Khanna and Palepu, "Globalization and Convergence in Corporate Governance."

12. Kumra and Sinha, "The Next Hurdle for Indian IT."

13. For an excellent review of Indian business history, see Dwijendra Tripathi, *The Oxford History of Indian Business* (Oxford, Oxford University Press, 2004). In this section I have borrowed extensively from Tripathi. For more detailed accounts of ancient Indian merchants, see Claude Markovits, *The Global World of Indian Merchants, 1750–1947: Traders of Sind from Bukhara to Panama* (Cambridge, Cambridge University Press, 2000).

14. The British East India Company was a joint stock company granted a royal charter by Elizabeth I on December 31, 1600, with the intent to favor trade privileges in India. The search for new markets following the Industrial Revolution and the rising tide of a laissez-faire economic ideology in Britain created internal pressure to abolish privileges enjoyed by the company.

15. Tripathi, *The Oxford History of Indian Business,* 115.

16. Nehru quote adapted from Tripathi, *The Oxford History of Indian Business*, 285.

17. Ibid., 287.

18. Rs. 200 crores, or Rs. 2 billion equaled nearly $27 million in 1969.

19. Dennis Encarnation, *Dislodging Multinationals: India's Strategy in Comparative Perspective* (Ithaca, NY: Cornell University Press, 1989).

20. Tarun Khanna and Krishna Palepu, "Is Group Affiliation Profitable in Emerging Markets? An Analysis of Diversified Indian Business Groups," *Journal of Finance* 55, no. 2 (April 2000): 867–91.

21. Tarun Khanna and Krishna Palepu, "Why Focused Strategies May Be Wrong for Emerging Markets," *Harvard Business Review* 75, no. 4 (July–August 1997): 41–51.

22. To put this in context, it is important to note that a large part of the contribution to GDP originated in agriculture, and almost the entire GDP in agriculture originated in the private sector. See *Private Sector Assessment—India*, Crisil Infrastructure Advisory, http://www.adb.org/Documents/CSPs/IND/2003/appendix3_private_sector_assessment.pdf.

23. The sections on TCL draw extensively from Tarun Khanna, Felix Oberholzer-Gee, and David Lane, "TCL Multimedia," Case 9–705–404 (Boston: Harvard Business School, 2005). Background information on the relevant aspects of China's political economy draws from Tarun Khanna and Felix Oberholzer-Gee, "The Political Economy of Firm Size Distributions: Evidence from Post-Reform China," working paper, Harvard Business School, Boston, March 2006.

24. TTK, an audiotape manufacturer, was founded in 1981. Li Dongsheng joined in 1982. In 1985, TTK changed its name to TCL.

25. Managers and staff owned another 25 percent, the public owned 38 percent and the remainder was distributed among business partners.

26. The broad definition of *private sector* includes both self-employed individuals and private enterprises. Official publications in China (for example, *China Statistical Yearbook*) distinguish self-employed individuals (*getihu*) from private enterprises (*siying qiye*). The latter have at least eight employees while the former have fewer than eight.

27. John Shuhe Li, "Determinants of Private Sector Development in Chinese Industry" (paper presented at the International Workshop: International Trade, Industrial Organization, and Asia, Hong Kong, 1999), 7, http://www.cityu.edu.hk/ef/research/paper/137.pdf.

28. Maria M. N. DaCosta and Wayne Carroll, "Township and Village Enterprises: Openness, and Regional Economic Growth in China," *Post-Communist Economies* 13, no. 2 (January 2001): 229–41.

29. Li, "Determinants of Private Sector Development in Chinese Industry."

30. Return on assets is an aggregate measure of the efficiency with which the company's overall assets are being used. It can be broken down into submeasures. One of these is return on equity (ROE). TCL's ROE was very high, but that was less a measure of efficiency than it was an indication of very high debt. The more a company is financed with debt, the fewer of its assets need to be financed by equity, and the return on equity rises as an arithmetic truism.

31. In a purely accounting sense, this means that ROEs were quite high, even though returns on assets were low. That is, high leverage inflates ROE.

32. The latter fashion is usually what is associated with countries' development over time. Recent scholarship addresses these issues in the Chinese setting and shows that political reform continued to worsen fragmentation. See Alwyn Young, "The Razor's Edge: Distortions and Incremental Reform in the People's Republic of China," *Quarterly Journal of Economics* 115, no. 4 (2000): 1; and Alwyn Young, "Gold into Base Metals: Productivity Growth in the People's Republic of China During the Reform Period," *Journal of Political Economy* 111, no. 6 (2003).

33. Ian Dingy and Jin Heehaw, "Public vs. Private Ownership of Firms: Evidence from Rural China," *Quarterly Journal of Economics* 113, no. 3 (August 1998): 773–808.

34. In 2003 hourly manufacturing wages averaged $1.01 in China compared with $8.79 in France, according to Economist Intelligence Unit, *Country Forecast (China)*, January 2005, and Economist Intelligence Unit, *Country Commerce (France)*, 2004.

35. Khanna, Oberholzer-Gee, and Lane, "TCL Multimedia."

36. "Ex-IMP Bank Grants TCL US$722 Million Loan," *Business Daily Update*, March 16, 2005.

37. Dexter Roberts and Louise Lee, "East Meets West," *BusinessWeek*, May 9, 2005.

38. Evart Hanks was CEO of Shell Global Chemicals business from 1998 to 2003; Kenneth Curtis was vice chairman of Goldman Sachs Asia; and Erwin Schurtenberger, former Swiss ambassador to China, lived in Beijing as a senior adviser to the China Training Center for Senior Personnel Management officials. The eight-member board of CNOOC still includes four independent nonexecutive directors, though Schurtenberger and one other director from the time of the deal stepped down from the board

in April 2005. Schurtenberger communicated to me that he subsequently became chairman of the international advisory board of CNOCC.

39. "CNOOC Ltd., CEO Annual and Transition Report," June 22, 2005, http://sec.edgar-online.com/2005/06/22/0000905148-05-003391/Section9.asp.

40. Akin Gump Strauss Hauer and Fled LLP, a law firm headquartered in Washington, D.C., was founded in 1945 and has a prominent public policy and regulatory practice.

41. Dan Spiegel, interviews by author in April 2006 and March 2007.

42. Michael Liedtke and Brad Foss, "Big Oil Profits, Little Choice," Seattle Times, April 29, 2006, http://seattletimes.nwsource.com/html/gasgauge/2002960315_earnsoil29.html.

43. The stock price of Hong Kong–listed CNOOC increased from HK $4.25 per share to HK $5.55 per share, up 30 percent, from the onset of bidding on June 23, 2005, to its closing on August 2, 2005. This represented a bigger rise in share price than that for other Chinese oil companies during the same time period (Syncope rose 16 percent and CNPC rose 19 percent both are listed on the Hong Kong exchange) and for the overall market (the Hang Sang index rose about 10 percent).

44. Translated from Chinese. Original article by Wang Shining and Lang Due, "The Course of CNOOC's Bidding for Uncoil," China Entrepreneur, September 1, 2005. The magazine was launched in 1985 in Beijing by Economic Daily Press (a major state-run newspaper) and is targeted at businesspeople.

45. Richard McGregor and Yu Sun "Challenging Change: Why an Ever Fiercer Battle Hinders China's March to the Market," Financial Times, February 23, 2005, 15.

46. William C. Kirby, "China, Unincorporated: Company Law and Business Enterprise in Twentieth Century China." Journal of Asian Studies 54, no. 1 (February 1995): 43–63.

47. Felix Oberholzer-Gee, Tarun Khanna, and David Lane, "Red Flag Software Co.," Case 9–706–428 (Boston: Harvard Business School, October 2005).

48. J. Dai, "Newly Born Private Enterprise Owners in China," Social Sciences in China 23, Issue 1, (2003): 126–136.

49. In the Financial Times, the number is reported as closer to 10 percent. See Joe Zhang, "China's Private Sector in Shadow of the State," Financial Times, October 4, 2005; and Diana Farrell and Susan Lund, "Putting China's Capital to Work," Far Eastern Economic Review, (May 2006), http://www.feer.com/articles1/2006/0605/free/p005.html.

50. Neil Gregory and Stoyan Tenev, "The Financing of Private Enterprise in China," Finance and Development 38, no. 1 (March 2001), http://www.imf.org/external/pubs/ft/fandd/2001/03/gregory.htm.

51. Fourteen coastal cities were open to overseas investment by this time: Dali an, Qinhuangdao, Tianjin, Yantai, Qingdao, Lianyungang, Nantong, Shanghai, Ningbo Wenzhou, Fuzhou, Guangzhou, Zhanjiang, and Beihai. The coastal provinces were generally subject to substantial deregulation; that is, they could import and export, collaborate with foreign companies, and hire and fire workers in exchange for not expecting state subsidies in times of distress. The Wenzhou and Minsheng examples are discussed in David Daokui Li, Junxin Feng, and Hongping Jiang, "Institutional Entrepreneurs," American Economic Review Papers and Proceedings 96, no. 2 (2005): 358–62.

Chapter 7

1. Allison Linn, "Hu Calls Gates a Friend of China,' " Seattle Times, April 19, 2006, http://seattletimes.nwsource.com/html/businesstechnology/2002938692_webhugates18.html.

2. I have borrowed extensively from my previous works on Microsoft. See Tarun Khanna, "Microsoft in the People's Republic of China—1993," Case 9-795-115 (Boston: Harvard Business School, 1995); "Microsoft in the People's Republic of China: 2005 Update," Case 9–706–429 (Boston: Harvard Business School, 2005); and "Microsoft in the People's Republic of China, 1993 and 2005 Update," Teaching Note 5-796-072 (Boston: Harvard Business School, 1995).

3. These numbers assume that all the software in use would have been bought even if it were not available for free. As economists are quick to point out, demand is not inelastic; that is, less is demanded at higher prices.

4. Adapted from "Gates Pushes Microsoft in China Trip," New York Times, March 23, 1994.

5. Brent Schlender, Warren Buffett, and Bill Gates, "The Bill and Warren Show," Fortune, July 20, 1998, 48 and 50.

6. The information in the next three paragraphs draws partly from Andy Y. Sun, "Beijing Court Dismissed Microsoft for Lack of Evidence: Major Software End User Infringement May Return Later," Asia Pacific Legal Institute 1, no 2 (February 2000).

7. "Celebrity Critic," Far Eastern Economic Review, (October 22, 1998).

8. William P. Alford, *To Steal a Book Is an Elegant Offense: Intellectual Property Law in Chinese Civilization* (Stanford, CA: Stanford University Press, 1995).

9. Craig S. Smith, "China's Leaders Concerned About Possible Microsoft Monopoly," *New York Times*, July 17, 2000.

10. A cursory description of Linux and details on Red Flag can be found in Felix Oberholzer-Gee, Tarun Khanna, and David Lane, "Red Flag Software Co.," Case 9–706–428 (Boston: Harvard Business School, 2005). Linux dominated the market for large servers, having outstripped the Unix operating system; in PCs, however, it lagged Microsoft's Windows.

11. Doc Searls, "Raising the Red Flag," *Linux Journal*, January 30, 2002, http://www.linuxjournal.com/article/5784.

12. "Chinese Firms Could Benefit From Microsoft's Loss in China," Gartner Research, January 3, 2002, http://gartner.com/DisplayDocument?doc_cd=103604.

13. Microsoft Corp. press release, "Visiting Microsoft CEO Steve Ballmer Meets Chinese Premier Zhu Rongji and Announces Further Investment in China," September 18, 2000, http://www.microsoft.com/Presspass/press/2000/sept00/chinapr.mspx

14. Michael Kanellos, "Microsoft Gets Diplomatic in China," *CNET*, June 5, 2002, http://news.com.com/Microsoft+gets+diplomatic+in+China/2100–1001_3–932927.html?tag=item.

15. Karby Leggett, "Microsoft to Invest $750 million in China, a Priority for Company," *Wall Street Journal*, June 28, 2002.

16. Sarah Schafer, "Microsoft's Cultural Revolution," *Newsweek* (International Edition), June 21, 2006, http://www.msnbc.msn.com/id/5197528/site/newsweek.

17. Microsoft Corp. press release, "Microsoft Research: Asia Establishes Advanced Technology Center," November 3, 2003, http://www.microsoft.com/presspass/press/2003/nov03/11–03msrbeijingatcpr.mspx.

18. Bruce Einhorn, "China Learns to Say 'Stop Thief,'" *BusinessWeek Online*, February 10, 2003, http://www.businessweek.com/technology/content/feb2003/tc20030210_2338_tc058.htm.

19. Joseph Khan, "Hu Begins 4-Day U.S. Visit," *International Herald Tribune*, April 19, 2006, http://www.iht.com/articles/2006/04/19/america/web.0419hu.php.

20. Microsoft Corp., *2005 Annual Report* (Redmond, WA: Microsoft Corp., 2005), 5.

21. The Government Procurement Law, effective January 1, 2003, stipulated that governments should purchase "domestic goods" but left *domestic* undefined.

22. Perkins Coie, "China Legal Highlights: Government Procurement of Software," http://www.perkinscoie.com/files/upload/intl_03–11_um_chinalegalhighlights.htm.

23. Ibid. Note, however, it is not clear how the benefits from the research laboratories are accounted for in these statements. Perhaps in time these losses could be offset substantially by revenues generated from worldwide sales of technologies accruing from the laboratories.

24. In the first five-year (1951–1956) plan, the state allocated 31 percent of the budget to the agricultural sector partly for the development of up to 6 million acres of irrigated area.

25. M. N. Chaini, "Reforming Agriculture," *The Economic Times*, December 2005, http://www.medcindia.org/cgi-bin/Dec05/PPAGE1.HTM.

26. Eurostat, the Statistical Office of the European Community, published a formal definition of *cash and carry* in 1993, as cited in the online OECD glossary, http://stats.oecd.org/glossary/detail.asp?ID=6234. A committee of trade experts from the Institute of Trade Research at Cologne University in Germany elaborated this definition in 1995 to emphasize the availability of a wide assortment of foods, semi-luxury goods, and tobacco as well as consumer goods.

27. S. Raghunath and D. Ashok, "Delivering Simultaneous Benefits to the Farm and the Common Man: Time to Unshackle the Agricultural Produce Distribution System," working paper, IIM Bangalore, June 2004, http://www.businessworldindia.com/oct2504/images/bw-iimb-agridistr.ps.pdf.

28. Metro's license, initially issued by the Foreign Investment Promotion Board and then amended in 2002, allowed Metro to sell to businesses registered under the so-called Shops and Establishment Act and the Weights and Measures Act, or those carrying sales tax or excise registrations.

29. "Bangalore Wholesalers Protest Against Metro Cash and Carry," *Hindu Business Line*, October 23, 2003, http://www.blonnet.com/2003/10/23/stories/2003102300791700.htm.

30. "Metro Retail Chain Raises CII Hackles," *Rediff India Abroad*, November 13, 2003, http://www.rediff.com/money/2003/nov/13cii.htm.

31. The Indian Constitution divides subjects into Central, State and Concurrent lists. Both center and state governments share jurisdiction of subjects on the concurrent list.

32. "Probe Charges Against Metro, Centre Told," *The Hindu Online*, February 23, 2004, http://www.hinduonnet.com/2005/02/23/stories/2005022308150500.htm.

33. At a country level, estimates suggest that a 1 percent increase in infrastructure stock is associated with a 1 percent increase in GDP across all countries. A study by Deichmann, for Mexico, showed that a 10 percent increase in market access—which had an inverse relationship with travel time—increased labor productivity by 6 percent. Uwe Deichmann, Marianne Fey Jun Koc, and Somik V. Lall, "Economic structure, productivity, and infrastructure equality in southern Mexico," Policy Research Working Paper Series 2900, The World Bank, (2002), http://ideas.repec.org/p/wbk/wbrwps/2900.html.

34. Raghunath Ashok, "Delivering Simultaneous Benefits to the Farm and the Common Man."

35. Fruits and vegetables, 10 percent; rice and legumes, 25 percent; meat and fish, 13 percent; and general groceries, the remainder.

36. "PC Stress on FDI in agri-trade," The Statesman (India), April 11 2005.

37. "FICCI Opposes Proposal to Amend APMC Act," The Hindu Online, June 5, 2005, http://www.hindu.com/2005/06/05/stories/2005060504380400 htm.

38. The events of 1989 were initially referred to as a "counterrevolutionary riot." See "China: Tiananmen Square—Still on the Agenda," Amnesty International report, June 1, 2001, http://web.amnesty.org/library/Index/ENGASA170192001?cpen&of=ENG-CHN; and Bernard Gwertzman, "Kristof: 15 Years Later, Tiananmen Square Remains 'Elephant' in Chinese Politics," Council on Foreign Relations, May 28, 2004, http://www.cfr.org/publication.php?id=7065.

39. "Main Determinants and Impacts of Foreign Direct Investment on China's Economy," working paper, Organisation for Economic Co-operation and Development, Paris, 2000.

40. Dennis Encarnation, Dislodging Multinationals: India's Strategy in Comparative Perspective (Ithaca, NY: Cornell University Press, 1989), 68, 73.

41. Ibid., 73.

42. Guy Pfeffermann, "Paradoxes: China vs. India" (paper presented at the Private Sector Development Forum, World Bank, Washington, DC, April 23–24, 2002).

43. For details, see Nirupam Bajpai and Nandita Dasgupta, "What Constitutes Foreign Direct Investment: Comparison of India and China," working paper no.1 Center on Globalization and Sustainable Development, Columbia University, New York, January 2004, 12, http://www.earthinstitute.columbia.edu/cgsd/documents/bajpai_fdi_india_china_003.pdf.

44. Ibid.

45. "China's FDI Inflows Almost at Par with India," Asia Pulse, May 28, 2002; "India's the 3rd Hottest Destination for FDI," The Economic Times, October 13, 2004; and "China's FDI Merry-Go-Round," Financial Times, April 2, 2003, http://www.fdimagazine com/news/fullstory.php/aid/215/China%92s_FDI_merry-go-round.html.

46. Yasheng Huang, Selling China (Cambridge, Cambridge University Press, 2004). The asset repurchase could be productive if it forced state-owned enterprises to become more efficient.

47. A. T. Kearney, Global Investment in China: A White Paper on the Quest for Profitability, September 1999.

48. "Infatuation's End," The Economist, September 23, 1999.

49. "Bulls in a China Shop," The Economist, March 18, 2004.

50. American Chamber of Commerce (of the) People's Republic of China, "2004 White Paper-Major Trends," April 18, 2005, http://www.amcham-china.org.cn/amcham. show/content.php?Id=289&menuid=04&submid=01.

51. The American Chamber of Commerce in India commissioned a survey by Gallup in 2004. The numbers here are based on a survey of FDI by the Federation of the Karnataka Chambers of Commerce and Industry, "The Experience of Foreign Direct Investors in India," 2004.

52. Seventeen subsidiaries were from companies originating in Japan, nine of which were in China and eight in India, and thirteen subsidiaries from companies originating in the rest of Asia, eight in China and five in India. None of the approached companies declined my request to participate, so this reduces some possible sample biases.

53. Camille Tang Yeh in Hong Kong and Masako Egawa in Tokyo led this effort. Help from Vibhav Kant Upadhyay, Chairman of the India Center Foundation, Tokyo, is gratefully acknowledged.

54. This example and several others are discussed in Tarun Khanna, Krishna Palepu, and Jayant Sinha, "Strategies That Fit Emerging Markets," Harvard Business Review, June 2005.

55. "Winning in China," BusinessWeek, January 27, 2003, http://www.businessweek.com/magazine/content/03_04/b3817010.htm.

56. Motorola China Tianqing page, http://www.motorola.com.cn/en/about/inchina/tianjing.asp.

57. In fact, direct comparisons suffer from what a statistician would call an ex ante selection problem. That is, suppose certain kinds of companies gravitated to China and others to India and that those that

went to each country would not succeed in the other. It is hard to assign any prescriptive inference to direct comparisons of performance in the China sample of multinational subsidiaries with the India sample. As it turns out, plenty of companies are in both countries, and the industries in which subsidiaries operate in China overlap with those in India, so the extreme caution in comparison is unwarranted.

58. In ongoing research, my colleague Felix Oberholzer-Gee and I found evidence, in data from the World Bank Investment Climate surveys, which suggest that the latter explanation was often true.

59. Data on electrified railroads and expressways are from China Statistical Yearbooks, and data on FDI can be found in the World Development Indicators.

60. Nicholas P. Sullivan, "The Effect of Policy and Legal Reforms on Foreign Direct Investment in India and China," unpublished paper, written for the Money Matters Institute, now a part of the Global Horizon Fund (www.ghfund.com), December 2002.

61. China and India rank comparably poorly on Transparency International's Corruption Index, which has been keeping numbers since 1995. Details at: http://www.transparency.org/policy_research/surveys_indices/cpi.

62. Suma Athreye and Sandeep Kapur, "Private Foreign Investment in India," working paper, August 1999, http://www.ems.bbk.ac.uk/faculty/kapur/personal/fdi.pdf.

63. Institute for Studies in Industrial Development, (primary author, Biswajit Dhar), "State Regulation of Foreign Private Capital in India," http://isid.org.in/pdf/statreg.pdf

64. Indrajit Basu, "India's Thorny FDI Rule Under Scrutiny," *Asia Times Online*, May 28, 2004, http://www.atimes.com/atimes/South_Asia/FE28Df03.html.

65. "Left Decries Move to Scrap Press Note 18," *The Hindu Online*, January 14, 2005, http://www.thehindu.com/2005/01/14/stories/2005011406951100.htm; and "Left Hits Out at Scrapping of Press Note 18," *The Economic Times*, January 14, 2005.

66. "The Signpost," *Telegraph India*, January 18, 2005, http://www.telegraphindia.com/1050118/asp/opinion/story_4264326.asp.

Chapter 8

1. The Indian diaspora today includes both NRIs—Indian citizens residing abroad for an indefinite period, whether for employment or for carrying on any business or other vocation—as well as PIOs—foreign citizens of Indian origin or descent. Excluded are ethnic Indians living in Bangladesh and Pakistan.

2. Batuk Gathani, "People of Indian Origin to Play Larger Role in Development," *Hindu Business Line*, October 8, 2004, http://www.thehindubusinessline.com/2004/10/08/stories/2004100800540900.htm.

3. Elena Barabantseva, "Trans-nationalising Chineseness—Overseas Chinese Policies of the PRC's Central Government," *ASIEN* 96 (July 2005): S7–S28, http://www.asienkunde.de/articles/index.html.

4. Paul J. Bolt, *China and Southeast Asia's Ethnic Chinese: State and Diaspora in Contemporary Asia* (Westport, CT: Praeger, 2000), 3.

5. P. C. Newman, "Tapping into the Bamboo Network," *Maclean's*, July 21, 1997.

6. Guohong Zhu, *Zhongguo Haiwai Yimin: Yixiang Guoji Qianyi de Lishi Yuanyin* (Chinese Emigration: A Historical Study of the International Migration) (Shanghai: Fudan University Press, 1994), 65–66.

7. Amy Freedman, *Political Participation and Ethnic Minorities: Chinese Overseas in Malaysia, Indonesia, and the United States* (New York: Routledge, 2000), 120.

8. The Boston *paifang* was donated by the Guomindang government. In later years the People's Republic of China donated *paifangs* to American Chinatowns, such as the one in Washington, D.C.

9. The Hakka have kept their culture and language alive even after they moved from elsewhere into southeastern China over hundreds of years. They live primarily in the Guangdong and Fujian provinces. The term *Fujianese* refers to the locals of Fujian, excluding the Hakka. The Teochiu also live in Guangdong but have their own dialect.

10. Lyn Pan, *Encyclopedia of the Overseas Chinese* (Cambridge, MA: Harvard University, 1999).

11. G. W. Skinner, *Chinese Society in Thailand: An Analytical History* (Ithaca, NY: Cornell University Press, 1957), quoted in K. B. Chan and T. C. Kiong, "Rethinking Assimilation and Ethnicity: The Chinese in Thailand," in *The Chinese Diaspora, Selected Essays*, Vol. II, edited by Ling-chi Wang and Guangwu Wang (Singapore: Times Academic Press, 1998), 18.

12. Martin Smith and Annie Allsebrook, *Ethnic Groups in Burma* (London: Anti-Slavery International, 1994), 64.

13. Alan Rappeport, "A Real Taste of South Asia? Take the Tube to Southall," *New York Times*, January 29, 2006, http://travel2.nytimes.com/2006/01/29/travel/29cayout.html?n=Top%2FFeatures%2FTravel%2FColumns%2FDay%20Out&pagewanted=print.

14. *Ji* is a term of endearment or respect.

15. N. Jayaram, "The Study of Indian Diaspora: A Multidisciplinary Agenda," occasional paper no. 1, Centre for Study of Indian Diaspora, University of Hyderabad, 1998.

16. K. L. Narayan, "Indian Diaspora: A Demographic Perspective," occasional paper no. 3, Centre for Study of Indian Diaspora, University of Hyderabad, 1998.

17. Chandrashekhar Bhatt, "India and Indian Diaspora, A Policy Issue," occasional paper no. 4, Centre for Study of Indian Diaspora, University of Hyderabad, 1998.

18. Nicholas Van Hear, Frank Pieke, and Steven Vertovec, *The Contribution of UK-Based Diasporas to Development and Poverty Reduction* (Oxford: Centre on Migration, Policy and Society, 2004), 14–16, http://www.compas.ox.ac.uk/publications/papers/DFID%20diaspora%20report.pdf.

19. Ibid.

20. Steve Raymer, "Dubai's Kerala Connection," *YaleGlobal Online*, July 12, 2005, http://yaleglobal.yale.edu/display.article?id=5992.

21. AnnaLee Saxenian, *Silicon Valley's New Immigrant Entrepreneurs* (San Francisco: Public Policy Institute of California, 1999), 29.

22. AnnaLee Saxenian, "Back to India," *Wall Street Journal* (Technology Journal Asia), January 24, 2000.

23. Dudley L. Poston Jr. and Mei-Yu Yu, "The Distribution of the Overseas Chinese in the Contemporary World," *International Migration Review* XXIV, no. 3 (Autumn 1990): 480–508.

24. For example, although Chinese based in Southeast Asia did contribute to big projects—railway lines in Fujian and Guangdong provinces—such cases were the exceptions rather than the rule. See Bolt, *China and Southeast Asia's Ethnic Chinese*, 37–43. Other facts in this paragraph regarding the Chinese in Southeast Asia are also from Bolt.

25. Bolt, *China and Southeast Asia's Ethnic Chinese*, 44.

26. Barabantseva, "Trans-nationalising Chineseness."

27. Bolt, *China and Southeast Asia's Ethnic Chinese*, 53.

28. Barabantseva, "Trans-nationalising Chineseness."

29. Onkar Singh, "Kalapani Jail Is 100 Years Old," *Rediff India Abroad*, March 10, 2006, http://ia.rediff.com/news/2006/mar/10firstlook.htm.

30. Sugata Bose, *The Indian Ocean in the Age of Global Empire* (Cambridge, MA: Harvard University Press, 2006).

31. Gurucharan Das, *India Unbound* (New York: Penguin, 2002), 209.

32. Ibid.

33. Material regarding Jerry Rao is sourced from R. D. Wadhwani, "Jerry Rao: Diaspora and Development in the Global Economy," Case 9–805–017 (Boston: Harvard Business School, 2004).

34. J. Rao and C.P. Surendran, *Gemini II: Selected Poems* (New Delhi: Viking, 1994), cited in Wadhwani, 2004.

35. NASSCOM, the software industry lobbying group, estimates that in 2003 23 percent of its member firms were Bangalore based, 19 percent Mumbai based, another 21 percent located in the greater New Delhi area (Delhi, Noida, Gurgaon), and the rest spread across the country.

36. Ramana Nanda and Tarun Khanna, "Firm Location and Reliance on Cross-Border Ethnic Networks: Evidence from India's Software Industry," working paper, Harvard Business School, Boston, 2006.

37. A. K. Diwanji, "CII Hopes to Create the Swades Effect: CII-Indian-American Council Will Assist NRIs Wanting to Help Their Home Towns," *India Abroad*, December 24, 2004, 25–30.

38. A balance-of-payments crisis occurs when the country is about to run out of foreign exchange reserves. This means that the country cannot pay its dues—be it payment for imports or debt.

39. Michael Debabrata Patra and Muneesh Kapur, "India's Worker Remittances: A User's Lament About BOP Compilations" (paper presented at the Sixteenth Meeting of the IMF Committee on Balance of Payments Statistics, Washington, D.C., December 1–5, 2003), http://www.imf.org/external/pubs/ft/bop/2003/03-20.pdf.

40. R. M. Hathaway, "Unfinished Passage: India, Indian Americans, and the U.S. Congress," *Washington Quarterly* 24, no. 2 (spring 2001): 21–34.

41. Ibid.

42. L. M. Singhvi, *Report of the High Level Committee on the Indian Diaspora* (New Delhi: Ministry of External Affairs Foreign Secretary's Office, Government of India, 2000). http://indiandiaspora.nic.in/contents.htm, and http://indiandiaspora.nic.in/diasporapdf/part1-ord.pdf.

43. The PIO status is not available for people of Indian origin residing in Pakistan or Bangladesh. Singhvi, *Report of the High Level Committee on the Indian Diaspora.*

44. Tarun Khanna and Ramana Nanda, "ICICI's Global Expansion," Case 9-706–426 (Boston: Harvard Business School, 2005).

45. Karan Bilimoria, interview with author, April 2006.

46. Phalgun Raju, "Making the Cobra Dance: Beer Founder Karan Bilimoria Encourages Young Entrepreneurs," *Harbus Online*, September 2, 2004, http://www.harbus.org/media/storage/paper343/news/2004/02/09/News/Making.The.Cobra.Dance-601716.shtml?norewrite200608240003&sourcedomain=www.harbus.org.

47. Emma Clark, "The 'Less Gassy' Rise of Cobra Beer," *BBC Online*, August 21, 2003, http://news.bbc.co.uk/1/hi/business/3052349.stm.

48. Cobra Beer Company press release, "Cobra Beer Takes Off with Virgin Atlantic," January 19, 2004, http://www.cobrabeer.com/press/index.php?option=com_content&task=view&id=16&Itemid=19.

Chapter 9

1. World Bank, "The World Bank in India: Country Brief," July 2005, http://siteresources.worldbank.org/INTINDIA/Resources/India_countrybrief_eng-2005.pdf.

2. Martin Ravallion and Shaohua Chen, "Fighting Poverty: Findings and Lessons from China's Success," World Bank's Development Economics Research Group, 2005, http://econ.worldbank.org/WBSITE/EXTERNAL/EXTDEC/EXTRESEARCH/0,,contentMDK:20634060~pagePK:64165401~piPK:64165026~theSitePK:469382,00.html.

3. Qiucheng Tan, "Decollectivisation and Reconstruction of Ownership in Rural China: Some Differences from Central and Eastern European Countries," working paper 52, Rural Transition Series, Center for Central and Eastern European Studies, School of History, University of Liverpool, 2005, http://www.liv.ac.uk/history/research/cee_pdfs/wp52.pdf.

4. Launched by Mao's speech, "The Question of Agricultural Cooperation," July 1955.

5. This section draws heavily from Tiejun Cheng and Mark Selden, "The Origins and Social Consequences of China's Hukou System," *China Quarterly*, no. 139 (1994): 658.

6. Ibid., 665.

7. Amartya Sen, "Nobody Need Starve," *Granta* 52 (1995): 217; and Vaclav Smil, "China's Great Famine: 40 Years Later," *British Medical Journal* 319 (1999): 1619–21

8. See H. X. Wu, "Reform in China's Agriculture: Trade Implications," briefing paper series 9, Department of Foreign Affairs and Trade, Australia, December 1997, http://www.dfat.gov.au/publications/catalogue/eaaubp9.pdf.

9. Ministry of Agriculture (China), "The Report on the Conditions of the TVEs in Our Country and the Opinions on Their Future Reform and Development," 1997.

10. Data from the CIA World Factbook, https://www.cia.gov/library/publications/the-world-factbook/geos/ch.html (2000 China census figures) and https://www.cia.gov/library/publications/the-world-factbook/geos/in.html (2001 India census figures).

11. Xu Wang, "Mututal Empowerment of State and Peasantry: Grassroots Democracy in Rural China," *World Development* 25, no.9 (1999): 1431–42.

12. Ibid.

13. Ray Yep, "Maintaining Stability in Rural China: Challenges and Responses," working paper, Center for Northeastern Asian Policy Studies, Brookings Institution, Washington, D.C., 2002, http://www.brookings.edu/fp/cnaps/papers/2002_yep.pdf.

14. Wang, "Mutual Empowerment of State and Peasantry."

15. Yep, "Maintaining Stability in Rural China."

16. Ami (Ben) Shalat, interview by author, September 2005.

17. From SEWA overview document sent to author by Reema Nanavaty, Executive Director, SEWA, September 2005.

18. Elizabeth M. King and M. Anne Hill, eds., *Women's Education in Developing Countries: Barriers, Benefits, and Policies* (Baltimore: Johns Hopkins University Press, 1993). See also Maria Floro and Joyce M. Wolf, "The Economic and Social Impacts of Girls' Primary Education in Developing Countries," information analyses, Creative Associates Inc. Washington, D.C., 1990, http://eric.ed.gov/ERICDocs/data/ericdocs2sql/content_storage_01/0000019b/80/13/1c/8b.pdf.

19. Bhim Rao Ambedkar, speech in the Constituent Assembly on November 4, 1948, in *Writing Speeches*, ed. Vasant Moon (Mumbai: Government of Maharashtra, Education Department, 1994), 61.

20. Food and Agriculture Organization of the United Nations, primary authors Rinku Murgai, Mubarik Ali, and Derek Byerlee, *Productivity Growth and Sustainability in Post-Green Revolution Agriculture in the Indian and Pakistan Punjabs*, (1997). ftp://ftp.fao.org/ag/agll/ladadocs/econoprod_murgai.doc and http://edugreen.teri.res.in/explore/bio/green.htm.

21. Pranab Bardhan, "Democracy and Distributive Politics in India," University of California at Berkeley, 2005, http://globetrotter.berkeley.edu/macarthur/inequality/papers/BardhDemoDist.pdf.

22. S. Venkitaramanan, "State of Agriculture," *Financial Daiy*, July 16, 2001, http://www.hinduonnet.com/businessline/2001/07/16/stories/041603ve.htm.

23. Rohit Saran, "Call of the Countryside," *India Today*, December 13, 2004.

24. Reema Nanavaty, interview by author, September 2005.

25. Viral Acharya, "Every Mumbai Child in School," *India Together*, February 2000, http://www.indiatogether.org/stories/pratham.htm.

26. Vishal Sehgal, interview with author, September 9, 2005.

Chapter 10

1. World Health Organization and United Nations Children's Fund, "Primary Health Care: Report of the International Conference on Primary Health Care," Alma-Ata, USSR September 6–12, 1978, 3 and 5, http://whqlibdoc.who.int/publications/9241800011.pdf.

2. Atul Gawande, "Notes of a Surgeon: Dispatch from India," *New England Journal of Medicine* 349, no. 25 (December 18, 2003).

3. World Health Organization, "World Health Report 2000—Health Systems: Improving Performance," http://www.who.int/whr/2000/en/.

4. Ravi Duggal, interview by research associate Vinati Dev New Delhi, February 13, 2006.

5. In Russian, Piatiletkas.

6. Nirupama Bajpai and Sangeeta Goyal, "Primary Health Care in India: Coverage and Quality Issues," working paper no. 15, Center on Globalization and Sustainable Development, The Earth Institute at Columbia University, New York, June 2004, 15, http://www.earthinstitute.columbia.edu/cgsd/documents/bajpai_primaryhealth.pdf.

7. Ibid., 17, 20.

8. Ibid., 3.

9. Nazmul Chaudhury, Jeffrey Hammer, Michael Kremer, Karthik Muralidharan, and F. Halsey Rogers, "Missing in Action: Teacher and Health Worker Absence in Developing Countries," *Journal of Economic Perspectives* 20, no. 1 (2006): 107–9.

10. Bajpai and Goel, "Primary Health Care in India," 21

11. Noah Friedman, personal communication, spring 2007.

12. David Lague, "Healthcare Falls Short, Chinese Tell Leaders," *International Herald Tribune*, August 20, 2005, p. 3.

13. Therese Hesketh and Wei Xing Zhu, "Health in China: From Mao to Market Reform," *British Medical Journal* 314, no. 7093, (May 24, 1997): 1543–45.

14. "Medical Reform 'Basically Unsuccessful,'" *China Daily Online*, July 30, 2005, http://www.chinadaily.com.cn/english/doc/2005-07/30/content_464755.htm.

15. Hesketh and Zhu, "Health in China: From Mao to Market Reform."

16. Winnie Yip and William C. Hsiao, "Economic Transition and Urban Health Care in China: Impacts and Prospects" (paper presented at the conference Financial Sector Reform in China, Boston, September 11–13, 2001).

17. "Directive on Public Health," in *Selected Works of Mao Tse-tung, vol. 9*, transcription from Maoist Documentation Project, http://www.marxists.org/reference/archive/mao/selected-works/volume-9/mswv9_41.htm.

18. Samantha Mei-che Pang, Thomas Kwok-shing Wong, and Jacqueline Shukching Ho, "Changing Economics and Health Worker Training in Modern China," *Yale-China Health Journal* 1 (Autumn 2002): 61–84, http://www.yalechina.org/articles/pdf/2002%20Health%20Journal.pdf.

19. Xingzhu Liu and Huaijie Cao, "China's Cooperative Medical System: Its Historical Transformations and the Trend of Development," *Journal of Public Health Policy* 13, no. 4, (Winter 1992): 501–11.

20. The World Bank, World Development Indicators database.

21. William C. L. Hsiao and Yuanli Liu, "Economic Reform and Health: Lessons from China," *New England Journal of Medicine* 335, no. 6 (August 3, 1996): 430–32.

22. The initial counties were in Beijing, Henan, Jiangsu, Zhejiang, Jiangxi, Hubei, and Ningxia, according to 1997 Zhongguo jingji nianjian (Almanac of China's Economy), (Beijing: Zhongguo nianjian chubanshe, 1997), 409.

23. World Bank, "Rural Health Insurance—Rising to the Challenge," Briefing Note No. 6, May 2005, http://siteresources.worldbank.org/INTEAPREGTOPHEANUT/Resources/502734-1129734318233/B N6-ruralinsurance-final.pdf.

24. In August 2001 China's Ministry of Health announced that six hundred thousand Chinese were HIV positive in 2000. However, only one year later the official estimation was raised to one million. According to the most recent survey jointly conducted by the Ministry of Health, USAIDS, and the World Health Organization, 650,000 (range 540,000 to 760,000) people in China were living with HIV in 2005. See "2005 Update on the HIV/AIDS Epidemic and Response in China," http://www.casy.org/engdocs/2005-China%20HIV-AIDS%20Estimation-English.pdf.

25. Robyn Meredith, "Chinese Miracle Busters," Forbes.com, September 1, 2004, http://www.forbes .com/2004/09/01/cz_rm_0901china_print.html.

26. Elisabeth Rosenthal, "A Poor Ethnic Enclave in China Is Shadowed by Drugs and H.I.V," New York Times, December 21, 2001, http://query.nytimes.com/gst/fullpage.html?sec=health&res= 9C01E4DB113EF932A15751C1A9679C8B63.

27. "Merck and the People's Republic of China Join to Fight the HIV/AIDS Epidemic in China: Largest Comprehensive HIV/AIDS Public-Private Partnership Formed in China," Business Wire, May 11, 2005. http://www.aegis.com/NEWS/BW/2005/BW050504.html.

28. Ravi Duggal, interview by author, March 2007.

29. Nicholas Eberstadt, "The Future of AIDS," Foreign Affairs 81, no. 6 (November–December 2002): 22–45.

30. Pierre Haski, "A Report from the Ground Zero of China's AIDS Crisis," YaleGlobal Online, June 30, 2005, http://yaleglobal.yale.edu/display.article?id=5941.

31. State Council AIDS Working Committee Office and UN Theme Group on HIV/AIDS in China, "A Joint Assessment of HIV/AIDS Prevention, Treatment and Care in China," December 1, 2004, http://www.synergyaids.com/documents/China_2004TreatPrev.pdf.

32. Elisabeth Rosenthal, "A Beijing Doctor Questions Data on Illness," New York Times, April 10, 2003, http://query.nytimes.com/gst/fullpage.html?sec=health&res=9D05E2D71F38F933A25757C0A9659C8B63.

33. Ann Hwang, "Aids Has Arrived in India and China," World Watch 14, no. 1 (January–February 2001): 12–21.

34. "AIDS in India: Money Won't Solve Crisis," Human Rights News, November 13, 2002, http://www.hrw.org/press/2002/11/india111302.htm.

35. Ranjita Biswas, "HIV Care in India—Cost Limits Treatment," Positive Nation (United Kingdom), December 2003/January 2004.

36. Ray Marcelo, "New Delhi Tries to Reach Deal with Drug Groups over Treatment for AIDS Patients," Financial Times, December 3, 2003.

37. AVERT, "AIDS Treatments: Targets and Results," August 17, 2007, http://www.avert.org/aidstar-get.htm.

38. Joydeep Sengupta and Jayant Sinha, "Battling AIDS in India," McKinsey Quarterly 21, January 2005.

39. This section draws on my work with David Bloom. See Tarun Khanna and David M. Bloom, "Health Services for the Poor in Developing Countries: Private vs. Public vs. Private-Public," in Business Solutions for the Global Poor: Creating Social and Economic Value, ed. V. Kasturi Rangan (San Francisco: Jossey-Bass, 2007).

40. Sulabh International Social Service Organization, "Profile, Aims and Objectives," http://www .sulabhinternational.org/pg01.htm.

41. Bindeshwar Pathak, "Sanitation Is the Key to Healthy Cities: A Profile of Sulabh International," Environment and Urbanization 11, no. 11 (April 1999): 221–29.

42. Nehru's quote appears in Nirmal Gram Patrika, April–July 2004, http://ddws.nic.in/nirmal007.htm.

43. John Lancaster, "Surgeries, Side Trips for 'Medical Tourists': Affordable Care at India's Private Hospitals Draws Growing Number of Foreigners," Washington Post, October 21, 2004.

44. Quoted in Felix Oberholzer-Gee, Tarun Khanna, and Carin Knoop, "Apollo Hospitals: First-World Health Care at Third World Prices," Case 9–705–442 (Boston: Harvard Business School, 2005).

45. Anglo American seems to have found that "the cost of keeping someone alive is cheaper than the cost of letting someone die"; see Brad Mears, South African Business Coalition on HIV and AIDS. It is also noteworthy that, despite the extremely high efficacy of the treatment regimen that Anglo American offers for free, adoption rates are very low but typically higher in the better-performing subsets of the company's mining operations; see "AIDS and Business: Face Value," The Economist, December 4, 2004, 76.

46. Ibid., Table 14.

47. David E. Bloom and Jaypee Sevilla, "Profits and People: On the Incentives of Business to Get Involved in the Fight Against AIDS," in *Health and Economic Growth: Findings and Policy Implications*, eds. G. López-Casasnovas, Berta Rivera, and Luis Currais (Cambridge, MA: MIT Press, 2005).

48. Peter Wonacott, "Barefoot Doctors Make a Comeback in Rural China: Trained as a Nurse, Ms. Li Treats Datang Village; Delivering a Baby for $4," *Wall Street Journal*, September 22, 2005, http://www.aegis.com/news/wsj/2005/WJ050904.html.

49. UN Theme Group on HIV/AIDS in China, "HIV/AIDS: China's Titanic Peril; 2001 Update of the AIDS Situation and Needs Assessment Report," June 2002, 38, http://www.youandaids.org/unfiles/chinastitanicperillast.pdf.

50. State Council AIDS Working Committee, "A Joint Assessment of HIV/AIDS Prevention, Treatment and Care in China" (2004).

51. "Restrictions on AIDS Activists in China," *Human Rights Watch* 17, no. 5(C), (June 2005), http://hrw.org/reports/2005/china0605/china0605.pdf.

52. For deeper discussion see Bloom and Sevilla, "Profits and People."

Chapter 11

1. Bame Pule, interview by author, Johannesburg, February 2007.

2. Joseph Nye, *Bound to Lead* (New York: Basic Books, 1990).

3. Student report submitted by Dakun Zhao to the author as part of the master's degree requirements at The Heller School for Social Policy and Management at Brandeis University, Waltham, MA, spring 2006.

4. Although Burma's name was changed in 1989 to the Union of Myanmar, for the sake of clarity it is referred to as Burma throughout the chapter.

5. Jaspal Kaur Singh, interview by research associate Vanati Dev, November 2005. Subsequent correspondence with author and Dev informs the entire chapter

6. Thant Myint-U, *The River of Lost Footsteps: Histories of Burma* (New York: Farrar, Strauss, and Giroux, 2006), 43, 182–87.

7. Jaspal Kaur Singh, *The Indian Diaspora in Burma and Identity Politics* in Amitav Ghosh's *The Glass Palace*; and Mira Kamdar's *Motiba's Tattoos*, 2004 International Burma Studies Conference, DeKalb, IL, October 22–24, 2004.

8. Sean Turnell, "Cooperative Credit in Colonial Burma," working paper, Macquarie University, Sydney, Australia, 2005, http://www.econ.mq.edu.au/research/2005/co-opTurnell.pdf.

9. Ibid.

10. Claude Markovitz, *The Global World of the Indian Merchant, 1750 to 1947* (Cambridge, Cambridge University Press, 2000), 17.

11. Gilles Boquérat, "India's Confrontation with Chinese Interest in Myanmar," in *India and ASEAN: The Politics of India's Look East Policy*, eds. Fréderic Grare and Amitabh Mattoo (New Delhi: Manohar/CSH, 2001), 161–89.

12. Ibid.

13. Subhash Chandra Bose, also known as "Netaji" (Leader), was a well-known and controversial leader of the Indian Independence movement. While Nehru and Gandhi were pursuing a policy of civil disobedience and nonviolence against the British, Bose organized and lead the Indian National Army (INA) against the British. The INA comprised former prisoners of war from India and plantation workers from Singapore and other countries in Southeast Asia, including Burma.

14. Shashi Tharoor, *Nehru: The Invention of India* (New York: Arcade, 2003), 100.

15. Nye, *Bound to Lead*.

16. Claude Apri, "Was Bandung in Vain?", *Rediff.com*, April 22, 2005 http://usrediff.com/news/2005/22claude.htm.

17. Tharoor, *Nehru*, 189.

18. Quoted in Dr. N. S. Rajaram, "Himalayan March of Folly: New Light on the India-Tibet-China Triangle," review of *The Fate of Tibet: When Big Insects Eat Small Insects*, by April Claude, http://www-ece.rice.edu/~sranjan/history/rev-tibet.html.

19. "Avoidance Is No Policy," *The Indian Express*, November 28, 1996, http://www.tibet.ca/en/wtnarchive/1996/11/29_5.html.

20. Neville Maxwell, *India's China War* (New York: Pantheon, 1970).

21. Quoted in Boquérat, "India's Confrontation with Chinese Interest."

22. B. Linter, "Burma and Its Neighbors," in *Indian and Chinese Foreign Policies in Comparative Perspective*, ed. S. Mansigh (New Delhi: Radiant, 1998).

23. Myint-U, *The River of Lost Footsteps*, 195.

24. Zicheng Ye, *Diyuan Zhengzhi Yu Zhongguo Waijiao* (Geopolitics and China's Foreign Affairs) (Beijing: Beijing Publishing House, 1998), 331–32.

25. Hu Yaobang, *Report to the Twelfth National Congress of the CCP*, September 1, 1982. Hu Yaobang was the general secretary of the CCP at that time.

26. "China's Ambitions in Myanmar: India Steps Up Countermoves," *Asia Pacific Media Services Limited*, July 2000, http://www.asiapacificms.com/articles/myanmar_influence.

27. David Steinberg, "China's Role in Southeast Asia," testimony before the U.S.-China Economic and Security Review Commission, December 4, 2003, http://www.uscc.gov/hearings/2003hearings/written_testimonies/031204bios/steinberg.htm.

28. David Steinberg, "Dealing with Burma: The Unpleasant Question, (Part 2)," *Asian Times Online*, September 21, 1999, http://www.atimes.com/se-asia/AI21Ae02.html.

29. Edward Lanfranco, "Road Strategies: China, India and America," *United Press International*, April 12, 2005.

30. Carin I. Fischer, "The Stillwell Road: Straight Ahead?" *Himal Southasian* 18, no. 2 (September–October 2005), http://www.himalmag.com/2005/september/analysis_7.html.

31. Ibid.

32. Lanfranco, "Road Strategies."

33. Travis Tanner, "The Oil that Troubles US-China Waters," *Asia Times Online*, June 18, 2004, http://www.atimes.com/atimes/China/FF18Ad04.html.

34. Phar Kim Beng, "China Mulls Oil Pipelines in Myanmar, Thailand," *Asia Times Online*, September 23, 2004, http://www.atimes.com/atimes/China/FI23Ad09.html.

35. Jane Perlez, "Across Asia, Beijing's Star Is in Ascendance," *New York Times*, August 28, 2004.

36. Sergei Troush, "China's Changing Oil Strategy and Its Foreign Policy Implications," working paper, Center for Northeast Asian Policy Studies, Washington, D.C., 1999, http://www.brook.edu/fp/cnaps/papers/1999_troush.htm.

37. Princeton Lyman, "China's Rising Role in Africa" (paper presented to the U.S.-China Economic and Security Review Commission, Washington, D.C., July 21, 2005), http://www.uscc.gov/hearings/2005hearings/written_testimonies/05_07_21_22wrts/lyman_princeton_wrts.pdf.

38. Indrajit Basu, "India Discreet, China Bold in Oil Hunt," *Asia Times Online*, September 29, 2005, http://atimes.com/atimes/South_Asia/GI29Df01.html.

39. Manash Goswami, "Oil and Natural Gas's Raha Asks Govt, to Stop Meddling," *Bloomberg.com*, October 24, 2005, http://www.bloomberg.com/apps/news?pid=10000080&sid=a4aF5aPv.9yE&refer=asia.

40. Horst Mendershausen, *Coping with the Oil Crisis: French and German Experiences* (Baltimore: Johns Hopkins University Press, 1976), 68–69.

41. Vijay Kelkar, interview with author, January 3, 2006.

42. Jane Perlez, "Across Asia, Beijing's Star Is in Ascendance," *New York Times*, August 28, 2004.

43. "Review on Bilateral Political Relations," Embassy of the People's Republic of China in the Union of Myanmar, http://mm.chineseembassy.org/eng/zmgx/t174785.htm.

44. "Frequent Visits Render Kindred Sino-Myanmar Ties Closer," *People's Daily*, July 17, 2000, http://english.people.com.cn/english/200007/17/eng20000717_45628.html.

Chapter 12

1. Philip Lutgendorf, "Awara (The Vagabond)," philip'sfil-ums Awara Page, http://www.uiowa.edu/~incinema/awara.html.

2. Suketu Mehta, "Welcome to BOLLYWOOD," *National Geographic*, February 2005, Vol. 207, Issue 2.

3. Figures from Bollywood, *National Geographic*, February 2005. The numbers are for 2003.

4. Al Lieberman and Patricia Esgate, *The Entertainment Marketing Revolution: Bringing the Moguls, the Media and the Magic to the World*, (Financial Times: Prentice Hall, 2002), 313.

5. Joseph Nye, *Soft Power: The Means to Success in World Politics* (New York: Public Affairs, 2004), 17.

6. Quote from Sir Charles Eliot, *Hinduism and Buddhism: An Historical Sketch*, vol. 1 (London: E. Arnold, 1921), xii, adapted from Jawaharlal Nehru, *Discovery of India* (Calcutta: Signet Press, 1946).

7. "Movies Milestones," NDTV (New Delhi Television) Movie Milestone Page, http://ndtv.com/ent/milestones.asp.

8. "A Chronology of Indian Cinema (1896–1905)," Upperstall.com, http://www.upperstall.com/hist1896.html.

9. "Dadasaheb Phalke," Upperstall.com, http://www.upperstall.com/people/phalke.html.

10. P. K. Nair, "In the Age of Silence: Beginnings of Cinema in India," Screening the Past, no. 6 (1999), http://www.latrobe.edu.au/screeningthepast/reruns/rr0499/PJdrr6.htm.

11. Ibid.

12. "Dadasaheb Phalke," Upperstall.com.

13. Brian Shoesmith, "From Monopoly to Commodity: The Bombay Studios in the 1930s," in History on/and/in Film, eds. Tom O'Regan and Brian Shoesmith (Perth: History and Film Association of Australia, 1987), 68–75, http://wwwmcc.murdoch.edu.au/ReadingRoom/hfilm/BOMBAY.html.

14. "Jamsetji Framji Madan (1865–1923)," India Heritage Jamsetji Madan Page, http://www.indiaheritage.org/perform/cinema/history/jamsetj.htm.

15. The province of Bengal in India was one of the largest. The British claimed that for "administrative purposes" they needed to divide the province. Indian nationalists were opposed to this partition, seeing it as yet another aspect of the colonial government's attempt at "divide and rule." The partition evoked fierce protests in western Bengal, especially in Calcutta, giving the Indian national movement a boost.

16. Satyajit Ray, Our Films, Their Films, (New York: Hyperion, 1994), 90.

17. Ashish Rajadhyaksha and Paul Willeman, Encyclopedia of Indian Cinema, (New Delhi, Oxford University Press, 1994), 19.

18. Jeff Yang, ed., Once Upon a Time in China: A Guide to Hong Kong, Taiwanese and Mainland Chinese Cinema (New York: Atria, 2003).

19. "The Dark Side of Shadow Magic," Beijing Scene 7, no. 2 (January 2007), http://www.beijingscene.com/v07i002/feature.html.

20. "The Birth of Chinese Film," China Culture, http://www.chinaculture.org/gb/en_artqa/2005–02/23/content_66347.htm.

21. Yang, Once Upon a Time in China, 6.

22. Ibid.

23. Ibid.

24. Cheng Jihua, Li Shaobai, and Xing Zuwen, Zhongguo dian ying fa zhan shi: chu gao, (A History of the Development of Chinese Film, 2 vols), (Beijing: Zhongguo dian ying chu ban she, 1980). This is the first and most complete study of Chinese film history.

25. Zhang Yingjin, "From Cultural Imperialism to Globalization: Reflections on Three Filmmaking Strategies in Hollywood and China" Ex/Change 7 (June 2003): 17–23, http://www.cityu.edu.hk/ccs/Newsletter/newsletter7/fromCultural.htm.

26. This section has drawn extensively from "The Dawn of Chinese Film 1896–1949," in Yang, Once Upon a Time in China.

27. Fabian Ziesing, "Zhang Yimou Essay," http://home.rikocity.de/fab.anweb/test3.html.

28. Zhou Enlai, "Exercise Dictatorship and Broaden Democracy," from Selected Works of Zhou Enlai, Volume II, (Beijing: Foreign Languages Press, 1989), 214.

29. Mao Tse-tung, On the Correct Handling of the Contradictions among the People, (Peking: Foreign Language Press, 1957), 53.

30. Ziesing, "Zhang Yimou Essay."

31. Ibid.

32. Rone Tempest, "How Do You Say Boffo in Chinese? The Fugitive," Los Angeles Times. November 29, 1994.

33. Media Entertainment and Arts Alliance, "Australia-China Free Trade Agreement Feasibility Study," June 2004, 7, http://www.dfat.gov.au/geo/china/fta/submissions/cfta_submission_6se05.pdf.

34. Sharmistha Acharya, "Bollywood and Globalization" (master's thesis, San Francisco State University, 2004). Arya references Indian Express article, "Hollywood To Dub Films in Indian Language," 24.

35. Stanley Rosen, "The Wolf at the Door: Hollywood and the Film Market in China from 1994–2000." in Southern California in the World and the World in Southern California, eds. Eric J. Heikkila and Rafael Pizarro (Westport, CT: Greenwood Publishing Group, 2002), 49–78.

36. Paula M. Miller, "Reeling in China's Movie Fans," The China Business Review 34, no. 2, (March/April 2007), 36.

37. By some estimates the Chinese film market is entering a period of high growth, reaching a CAGR of about 36 percent over the next five years and $1.2 billion by 2007; see "China Media & Entertainment Part III: The Chinese Film Market," China eCapital Corporation, March 18, 2005, http://www.researchandmarkets.com/reportinfo.asp?report_id=295865. The Indian industry experienced growth of more than 30 percent in 2001 with a combined turnover of 130 billion rupees compared with 100 billion rupees in 2000; see http://www.ukfilmcouncil.org.uk/filmindustry/india/.

38. Jehangir S. Pocha, "The Rising "Soft Power" of China and India," *Business World*, June 6, 2005, http://www.businessworldindia.com/Jun0605/coverstory01.asp.

39. "Countries Choose Oscar Contenders," *BBC News*, September 27, 2005, http://news.bbc.co.uk/1/hi/entertainment/film/4286446.stm.

40. Ray, *Our Films, Their Films*, 12.

41. Bansi Pandit, *Hindu Dharma*, (Dharma Publications, Inc., January 2001.)

42. Ibid.

43. Tahl Raz, "Chopra: New-Age Prophet," My Primetime Chopra Page, http://www.myprimetime.com/work/life/content/chopra/index.shtml.htm.

44. Suma Varughese, "A Profile of Deepak Chopra—Successful Doctor, Ayurveda Apostle, Best-Selling Author, TV Host, New Age Guru," *Life Positive*, May 1996, http://www.lifepositive.com/Spirit/new-age-catalysts/deepak-chopra/newage-guru.asp.

45. Transcendental meditation, a movement started by Maharishi Mahesh Yogi, "is a spiritual practice called yoga which is presented to the Western world as a 'scientific' way of reducing stress and finding peace within oneself"; see Walter Martin, *The New Cults* (Santa Ana, CA: Vision House, 1980), 91.

46. Vinati Dev, private conversation with author, May 2006.

47. Mark Allen, "The Origins of Yingyang and the Symbol Deconstructed," Taichido.com YingYang Page, http://www.soton.ac.uk/~maa1/chi/philos/yinyangsymbol.htm.

48. Georg Feuerstein, "Comments on Contemporary Yoga," 2003, http://www.yrec.info/contentid-29.html. Data are from an Internet survey conducted by Intersurvey Inc. in 2000.

49. Dan Oldenburg, "Beyond the Mat: Yoga Stretches Out—'Fusion' Makes the Lotus Position Pass," *Washington Post*, August 29, 2004.

50. Chola Dynasty, 850–1279; Vasco da Gama, 1460–1524; Columbus, 1451–1506; Zheng He's voyages, 1405–1433.

51. "Miracle at Sea: Facts Show," *Beijing Review* 28, (2005), http://www.bjreview.com.cn/En-2005/05-28-e/china-3.htm.

52. Huo Jianying, "Set Cloud-white Sails and Cross the Surging Seas: The 600th Anniversary of Zheng He's Sea Voyages," *China Today*, 2005, http://www.chinatoday.com.cn/English/e2005/e200507/p60.htm.

53. "India, China to Sign Co-production Accord," *The Hindu*, February 8, 2004, http://www.thehindu.com/2004/02/08/stories/2004020810541000.htm.

Chapter 13

1. Jawaharlal Nehru, *Discovery of India* (Calcutta: Signet Press, 1946), 199.

2. Ibid., 204.

3. Anjana Pasricha, "China, India Move to Increase Economic Cooperation," *Voice of America*, March 19, 2006, http://www.voanews.com/english/2006-03-19-voa8.cfm.

4. Ramtanu Maitra, "China and India Aim to Extend Cooperation," *Executive Intelligence Review*, (February 18, 2005), http://www.larouchepub.com/other/2005/3207china_india.html.

5. Dakun Zhao, interview by author, Cambridge, MA, spring 2006.

6. Quoted in Perry Garfinkle, "Buddha Rising," *National Geographic*, December 2005, 98.

7. John E. Hill, "Annotated Translation of the Chapter on the Western Regions According to the *Hou Hanshu* (The Book of Later Han)," 2nd draft ed., September 2003, http://depts.washington.edu/silkroad/texts/hhshu/hou_han_shu.html. *Hou Hanshu* is one of the official Chinese historical works compiled by Fan Ye using several earlier histories and documents as sources. It covers the history of the eastern Han Dynasty.

8. The monks are sometimes referred to by their Indian names, Kasyapa Matanga for She Moteng and Dharmaratna for Zhu Falan.

9. Kate McGeown, "China's Tense Links with the Vatican," *BBC News*, April 8, 2005, http://news.bbc.co.uk/2/hi/asia-pacific/4423845.stm.

10. Tansen Sen is associate professor and deputy chair at the Department of History, Baruch College, City University of New York. He was interviewed by the author by phone and in person in December 2005, January 2006, and March 2007. His quotes throughout are from those interviews. See also his book, *Buddhism, Diplomacy and Trade: The Realignment of Sino-Indian Relations, 600–1400* (Honolulu: University of Hawaii Press, 2003).

11. "Political History," *Travel China Guide*, July 11, 2007, http://www.travelchinaguide.com/intro/history/southern_northern/index.htm.

12. Nehru, *Discovery of India*, 193.

13. Eric-Jan Zürcher, "Perspectives in the Study of Chinese Buddhism," *Journal of the Royal Asiatic Society* 2 (1982): 161–76.

14. China's Nanjing University was founded in 258. Other well known ancient universities came much later, such as Al-Azhar University founded in Egypt in 988 and the University of Bologna and the University of Paris founded in the twelfth century.

15. Sun Shuyun, *Ten Thousand Miles Without a Cloud* (New York: HarperCollins, 2003), 244–45.

16. Hu Shih, "The Indianization of China: A Case Study in Cultural Borrowing," in *Independence, Convergence, and Borrowing in Institutions. Thought, and Art* (Cambridge, MA: Harvard University Press, 1937).

17. Nehru, *Discovery of India*, 198.

18. Tansen Sen, "The Formation of Chinese Maritimes Networks to Southern Asia, 1200–1450," in *Journal of the Economic and Social History of the Orient* 49, no. 4, (2006), 421–453.

19. "Opium Poppy—History," *Plant Cultures,* http://www.plantcultures.org.uk/plants/opium_poppy_history.html.

20. Dwijendra Tripathi, *The Oxford History of Indian Business* (Oxford, UK: Oxford University Press, 2004), 120.

21. Ibid., 115.

22. Premier Wen Jiabao spoke to reporters during a visit to the Tata Consultancy Services facility in Bangalore, April 10, 2005; see "Chinese PM India's Bangalore Calls for Closer IT Cooperation," *India Daily,* April 10, 2005, http://www.indiadaily.com/editorial/2265.asp.

23. China's piracy rates is estimated to remain higher than 90 percent. For further discussion, see chapter 6, "Microsoft and Metro: Views from the World's Corner Offices."

24. Mingzhi Li and Ming Gao, "Strategies for Developing China's Software Industry," *Information Technologies and International Development* 1, no.1 (fall 2003): 61–73.

25. Ted Tschang, " China's Software Industry and Its Implications for India," working paper 205, Research Program on Globalizing Technologies and Domestic Entrepreneurship in Developing Countries, Organisation for Economic Co-operation and Development, Paris February 2003, 15.

26. Craig S. Smith, "Fearing Control by Microsoft, China Backs the Linux System," *New York Times,* July 7, 2000, http://www.nytimes.com/library/tech/00/07/biztech/articles/08soft.html.

27. For more information see the Hangzhou Hi-tech Industry Development Zone Web site, http://www.hhtz.gov.cn/english/index01.asp. Newly established software companies are exempt from income taxes for the first two years after they turn profitable, with some deferred taxation in subsequent years. The Chinese government also offers some tax deductions to defray the costs of the salaries and training of software personnel, and it offers foreign companies incentives to buy equipment from within China.

28. For more information see the TCS's Web site, http://tcs.com/.

29. Brian Yang, interviews by author. February and March 2006.

30. Anna Greenspan, "China's Hardware, India's Software," *Asia Times Online,* February 8, 2006, http://www.atimes.com/atimes/China_Business/HB08Cb05.html.

31. Nehru, *Discovery of India*, 199.

32. Amartya Sen, *The Argumentative Indian: Writings on Indian History, Culture, and Identity* (New York: Farrar, Straus, and Giroux, 2005).

33. Rabrindranath Tagore, "Address at the Opening Ceremony of Visva-Eharati Cheena Bhavana," April 14, 1937.

34. Quote adapted from K. P. S. Menon, "My Tribute to Tan Yun-Shan," in *In the Footsteps of Xuangzang: Tan Yun Shan and India* ed. Tan Chung (New Delhi: Gyan, 1999).

35. A resolution of sorts on the Tibet issue had been achieved by then.

36. Excerpt from Mahatma Gandhi, "Letter to Professor Tan Yun-shan, April 29, 1945," in *Collected Works of Mahatma Gandhi* (New Delhi: Ministry of Information and Broadcasting, Government of India, 1969), 94, 199.

Chapter 14

1. Jonathan D. Spence, *To Change China: Western Advisers in China: 1620–1960* (Boston: Little, Brown, 1969).

2. Jack Welch and John Byrne, *Jack: Straight from the Gut* (New York: Warner Books, 2001), 30.

3. Ibid.

4 "GE Shakes Off Its Reserve," *China Economic Review,* (March 2003): 24–26.

5. Tarun Khanna and Elizabeth A. Raabe, "General Electric Healthcare 2006," Case 9–706–478, (Boston: Harvard Business School. 2006).

6. McKinsey & Co. research cited in "Up to the Job: How India and China Risk Being Stifled by a Skill Squeeze," *Financial Times,* July 20, 2006.

7. "Huawei Technologies Co., Ltd.," Case 305–604–1 (Shanghai: China Europe International Business School, 2005).

8. Khanna and Raabe, "General Electric Heathcare 2006.

9. Jerry Useem, "Another Boss Another Revolution: Jeff Immelt is Following a Time-honored GE Tradition: Abandoning the Most Treasured Ideas of His Predecessor," *Fortune,* April 5, 2005.

10. Laura King, interview cited in Khanna and Raabe, "General Electric Healthcare 2006."

11. "Medicine's New Central Bankers," *The Economist,* December 10, 2005, 28–30; and "Information Leaflet," http://www.ukbiobank.ac.uk/docs/infoleaflet0607.pdf.

12. Omar Ishrak, interview cited in Khanna and Raabe, "General Electric Healthcare 2006."

13. Sir William Castell, on panel with author, HBS Global Leadership Forum, London, June 2005.

14. Jikun Huang and Qinfang Wang, "Agricultural Biotechnology Development and Policy in China," *AgBioForum* 5, no. 4 (2002), http://www.agbioforum.org/v5n4/v5n4a01-huang.htm. Under this outline, a number of high-profile technology programs were launched after the mid-1980s. Among the most significant programs were the 863 High-tech Plan, the 973 Plan, the Natural Science Foundation of China, and the Initiative of National Key Laboratories on Biotechnology.

15. China National Center for Biotechnology Development, "Biotechnology and Bio-economy in China," September 2005, http://www.intec-online.net/uploads/media/Biotechnology_and_Bio-economy_in_China__Government_Document_.pdf.

16. Kathryn Kranhold, "China's Price for Market Entry: Give Us Your Technology, Too," *Wall Street Journal,* February 26, 2004, http://userwww.sfsu.edu/~glee/Spring%204.htm.

17. Castell, London, June 2005.

18. T. T. Kurien, interview with author, January 6, 2004.

19. M. Kripalani and B. Einhorn, "India's Tech King," *BusinessWeek Online,* October 13, 2003, http://www.businessweek.com/magazine/content/03_41/b3853008_mz046.htm.

20. Khanna and Raabe, "General Electric Healhcare 2006."

21. Marc Onetto, interview cited in Tarun Khanna and James Weber, "General Electric Medical Systems 2002," Case 9–702–428 (Boston: Harvard Business School, 2002).

22. Scott Bayman, interview with author, March 2006.

23. Geoffery Jones, *Renewing Unilever: Transformation and Tradition* (London: Oxford University Press, 2005), 8.

24. Ibid., 158.

25. Ibid., 173.

26. V. Kasturi Rangan and Rohit Hari Rajan, "Unilever in India: Hindustan Lever's Project Shakti—Marketing FMGC to Rural Consumers," Case 9–505–056 (Boston: Harvard Business School, 2006).

27. Augusto Lopez-Claros and Saadia Zahidi, *Women's Empowerment: Measuring the Global Gender Gap,* (Geneva: World Economic Forum, 2005), http://news.bbc.co.uk/1/shared/bsp/hi/pdfs/16_05_05_gender_gap.pdf.

28. Ibid.

29. Amartya Sen, "More Than 100 Million Women Are Missing," *New York Review of Books* 37, no. 20 (December 20, 1990).

30. Victoria A. Velkoff, "Women's Education in India," October 1998, http://www.census.gov/ipc/prod/wid-9801.pdf.

31. Ishrak, cited in Khanna and Raabe, "General Electric Healthcare 2006."

32. Welch and Byrne, *Jack,* 310.

33. Spence, *To Change China,* from the Introduction.

34. Ibid., 33.

35. Ibid.

ACKNOWLEDGMENTS

The sheer number of debts to acknowledge for a wide-ranging book like this is sobering.

Acknowledgments of this sort usually end with a personal reflection on family support. I feel obliged to reverse the order, and record my indebtedness to my wife, Ruhi, and my primary school-aged daughter and son, Simran and Rishi, who have had to endure my incessant travel, often at very short notice. Without their emotional support, this project, and much of my professional life, would simply not exist. The kids' questions were innocent and typically most revealing about the kinds of things that needed to be clarified for the broad readership I hope to reach. Almost as important as this support was my parents' and my sister's unstinting belief in me; each of them devotedly read the manuscript and urged me forward.

My primary intellectual debt is to the Harvard community that has nurtured and indulged my meanderings through India for close to fifteen years, and has also sustained my ever-increasing interest in China for just over a decade. Of course, the Harvard Business School takes center stage as primary claimant to whom this debt is due, but the rest of Harvard is no less complicit for its intellectual vitality—the departments of history, in particular, and economics and government, and several individuals at the Kennedy School of Government and the School of Public Health.

My students in the HBS MBA, executive education, and doctoral programs have been my greatest inspiration and my greatest supporters—I am always awestruck by how much they encourage the faculty, and indeed indulge our intellectual experiments. Lacking the petri dishes of the natural sciences, exposing ideas to intelligent audiences is the *modus operandi* of a social scientist.

If the students—on our campus and in our programs worldwide—provided the impetus for the book, the protagonists in the book graciously provided the means to make the book a reality. The entrepreneurs of my title include a wide swathe of humanity—the celebrity entrepreneurs, it is true, occupy a fair share of the book's pages, but equally numerous and important are the grassroots entrepreneurs, laboring away either in earlier days of their respective ventures, or in endeavors that do not normally see the limelight. All of them were supremely gracious in giving their time and in shaping my understanding, reacting to what I wrote—usually with incredible encouragement and sometimes, it must be said, with constructive debate, but never once obstructing my intellectual journey. Talking more than anything else, to these active social workers, political entrepreneurs, students, and CEOs, shaped this book far more than did conversations in the faculty offices in Harvard Business School's Morgan Hall.

These intellectual acknowledgments are important, but they are abstract. Let me turn to individuals. The book, quite simply, would not be real without two seminal contributors, now dear friends and partners (even though they are entirely absolved of responsibility for the content and tone of the book). Vinati Dev, my "India Research Associate," as I came to think of her, helped write much of the voluminous briefing material, and filled out many a chapter outline for virtually every chapter in the text. She proved to be a vibrant intellectual sparring partner and continued to shape the book even after she relocated from Cambridge to New Delhi in 2006.

Around the same time, my "China Research Associate," Dakun Zhao, also relocated, in his case to Shanghai. Without Dakun, whom I first met when he asked me to supervise his work for a master's degree from neighboring Brandeis University, much of my meanderings though China in the last few years would have been significantly less productive. Even though the research for specific chapters was anchored by specific individuals, Dakun anchored the entire China research program for me. Like Vinati, his help was invaluable.

I was also fortunate to be able to draw on a team of friends and colleagues, again from multiple walks of life, in each of China and India. These are individuals who were especially gracious with their time on multiple occasions. The informally conceived China team, as it were, included Camille Tang Yeh, who for many years anchored the HBS Research Office in Hong Kong and remains a close friend; professors Regina Abrami at HBS, Bat Batjargal at Peking University, and Bernard Yeung at New York University; Ambassador Erwin Schurtenberger (former Swiss Ambassador to China); my Mandarin language tutor Boyan Zhang; and several students and researchers in Cambridge—Jin Chen, Li Li, and Weilin Li.

The analogous India team was comprised of Professor Pratap Bhanu Mehta, formerly of the Harvard Government Department and now at the Centre for Policy Research in New Delhi; my London- and New Delhi-based MBA student and now entrepreneur, Kartik Varma; my Kennedy School of Government student and now entrepreneur in New Delhi, Vishal Sehgal; my PhD student from MIT and now HBS faculty colleague, Ramana Nanda; and C V Madhukar, founder of the NGO Parliamentary Research Services, an organization dedicated to keeping India's parliamentarians well informed about legislative issues.

Incredibly busy individuals kindly read through the entire manuscript. My foremost debt is to the superb writer and business historian Richard Tedlow, who alerted me to many relevant historical anecdotes, and commented on the overall tone and nuance of the manuscript. India scholar and historian Sugata Bose; China scholar and economist Dwight Perkins; and political scientist and former Dean of the Kennedy School Joseph Nye; all offered valuable insights on multiple occasions. Professors Sea-Jin Chang of Korea University, Kulwant Singh of the National University of Singapore, and Yishay Yafeh of the Hebrew University of Jerusalem all read through the manuscript, as did Pratap Bhanu Mehta, Vishal Sehgal, Camille Tang Yeh, my parents Ramesh Khanna and Dr. Aruna Khanna, and my sister Latika Laul.

It is risky to try to enumerate others who have contributed for fear of missing some inadvertently. But it would be ungracious not to acknowledge those whose input I can, with appreciation, recall. These include the following Harvard colleagues: Rawi Abdelal, David Bloom, Masako Egawa, Pankaj Ghemawat, Gustavo Herrero, Linda Hill, Li Jin, Geoffrey Jones, Rakesh Khurana, Bill Kirby, Warren McFarlan, Nitin Nohria, Felix Oberholzer-Gee, Krishna Palepu, Liz Perry Anand Raman, Jan Rivkin, Jordan Siegel, Debora Spar, and Lou Wells. Former Dean of HBS Kim Clark was especially encouraging of this work, and current Dean Jay Light has been very supportive of this project from the start of his appointment. From outside Harvard, my kind supporters include Dean of the London Business School and now Berkeley professor Laura Tyson, New York-based historian of Sino-Indian relations Tansen Sen, University of Pittsburgh-based Sinologist Thomas Rawski, Hong Kong-based professor Joseph Fan, Mumbai-based NGO founder Rashid Kidwai, Cambridge-based education specialist Michael Shiner, London-based financier Nandita Parshad, Boston-based financier Jayant Sinha, New Delhi-based economist E. Somanathan, and New Delhi-based management consultants Sri Rajan and Ashish and Renuka Singh. I also had formative conversations over the years with professors John Sutton at the London School of Economics and Dani Rodrik at the Kennedy School of Government.

The arguments refined over the past four years in seminar audiences are too numerous to mention. Many of the chapters in this book have accompanying work directed to a scholarly audience. Thus the work on companies promoted by indigenous entrepreneurs in China and India and that on financial markets is closely related to work with my HBS colleague Krishna Palepu, that on the diaspora is related to work with Ramana Nanda, and that on the chapter on statecraft is related to work with Columbia University economists Ray Fisman and Siddhartha Dastidar. And the original inspiration for the comparative effort came from joint work with my MIT Sloan School colleague Yasheng Huang.

Seminars at the Harvard Economics Department, the London School of Economics, the National University of Singapore, Tsinghua University, Korea University, Universidad Catolica de Chile, the Lowy Institute in Sydney, and the Indian Institute of Management were especially influential in shaping the work. Additionally, I have gone out of my way to expose the work to business audiences of a variety of stripes in several locations—groups of managers put together by the Confederation of Indian Industry in various Indian cities and by the Argentine industry lobby in Mar del Plata and by Venezuelan entrepreneurs in Caracas, The Indus Entrepreneurs (TiE) chapters in the United States, India, and Malaysia, the Abu Dhabi Investment Authority, collections of Latin American entrepreneurs in Miami affiliated with the NGO Endeavor, diplomatic settings in Singapore and Sydney, and several NGOs in South and Southeast Asia. Finally, the World Economic Forum, in its annual meetings in Davos, its newly constituted growth companies' meeting in Dalian, China, and its regional meetings worldwide, has provided valuable input and feedback.

As a professor at Harvard Business School, I have the privilege of constantly working with several companies. They inevitably shape my worldview. I want to acknowledge some with whom I have had a particularly deep relationship during the time I was writing the manuscript—the TVS Group of Companies in South India, a century-old and very reputable automotive-centered group; Bunge, the NYSE-traded global agribusiness giant; Samsung, the Korean *chaebol* with global reach; Metro AG, the Dusseldorf-based global wholesaler; and McKinsey, the consultancy.

Finally, editorial help in a variety of ways has been utterly indispensable. Kirsten Sandberg, my editor, shaped the manuscript and dealt patiently with the frustration of a novice, yet opinionated, author. Karen Propp superbly edited the manuscript to a manageable length and Amy Reese read the copyedited manuscript painstakingly. Chris Allen, Sarah Eriksen, and Kathleen Ryan provided exemplary research assistance from Harvard Business School's Baker Library. My publishers in India, Penguin, were incredibly supportive, especially during a management change in New Delhi.

I wrote this book as much in Harvard Square, Newton Center, and on-site in China, India, and the world's airport lounges, as I did in my Harvard office. I hope it bridges the informal colleges of academics and intellectuals with the world of globe-trotting executives, and that of billions of entrepreneurs on the frontlines of the world economy.

Tarun Khanna
Boston

INDEX

Confederation of Indian Industry (CII), 153
Confucius, 39
Congenital heart disease, in India, 216
Congress Party, 83, 84
Constitution. *See* Directive Principles of the
    Indian Constitution; Indian Constitution
Construction Bank of China scandal, 110, 114
Coolie, 50
Cooperative Medical System (CMS), 226
Coronary care units (CCUs), in India, 217–218
Corporate bridges, 295–312
Corporate governance
    in China, 116–117
    in India, 124
Corporate morality, 307–309
Corporations, effect on social change, 295.
    See also Multinational entries Corruption
    in China, 22, 44
    in Chinese banks, 110–111, 114
    exposing, 54–55
    foreign direct investment and, 164
    in India, 22
    indices of, 210
Cotton trade, 126–127, 285–286
Courtyard houses, Chinese, 89–90
Creative entrepreneurship, 20
Credit, in China, 132. *See also* Banking
Credit Lyonnais Securities Asia (CLSA),
    116–117, 125
Cross-border deals, Indian versus Chinese, 137
Cuffe Parade, 73
    development of, 70
Cultural ambassadors, Indian versus Chinese, 260
Cultural interchange, Sino-Indian, 291–292
Cultural Revolution, 41, 179, 268
Cyberabad, 278
Cyber police, Chinese, 58–59
Dai Qing, 79
Dalai Lama, 245
Dalal, Sucheta, 95
Dalit class, 204
Dams, engineering, 79–82
Danwei, 86–87
Das, Gurcharan, 181
Deception, in China, 62–63
Delhi Development Act, 76
Delhi Development Authority (DDA), 86
Dell Corporation, operations in China, 161
Democracy
    China's steps toward, 65–66
    in India, 32–33, 36–38, 45–46
Deng Xiaoping, 35, 100
    economic reform and, 156–157
    open door policy, 35
    policy toward diaspora, 179
    property rights under, 87
    reform agenda of, 41–43, 192
    role in development, 71

Deshmukh, Vilasrao, 75
Deshpande, Gururaj, 178
Desi, 176
Developing countries, entrepreneurship in, 20
Development finance institution (DFI), 106
Deveshwar, Y. C. "Yogi," 207–209
Devpura village nursery project, 201–203
Dev, Vinati, 273
Dharavi slum, 75
Dharmagupta, 232
Diabetes, service innovations related to, 9
Dianguang Yingxi, 264
Dian Myanmar Road, 241
Diaspora
    attitudes toward, 25
    importance to India's software industry,
        182–183
    Indian versus Chinese, 167–170
    management of, 170
    profit from the needs of, 173
    role in balance of payments crisis, 183
    role in India, 168–169
    widened definition of, 184
Diaspora committee, appointment of, 184
Diaspora entrepreneurs, 170–174
Diaspora management, in China, 170, 178–180
Diaspora members, gatherings of, 183
Difficult Couple, The, 265
Dinesh, K., 124
Dingjun Mountain, 265
Dingzihu, 88
Directive Principles of the Indian Constitution,
    205. *See also* Indian Constitution
Disinvestment, 49, 130
Dissent, toleration of, 66
Diversification, in Indian business, 129
DLF Group, 76–78
Doctors, distrust of, 224
Doctors Without Borders. *See* Médecin Sans
        Frontières (MSF)
Dreze, Jean, 66
Dr. Kotnis ki Amar Kahaani, 267–268
Drugs, antiretroviral, 231
Duggal, Ravi, 219
Dutta, Narendranath, 272. *See also*
        Vivekananda, Swami
Du Yashen, 191
e-*choupals*, 65, 208–209
Economic growth, link to property rights, 90
Economic information, access to, 65
Economic reform, in India, 129–130, 270
Economic statistics, fraud and error in, 62–63
Economic ties, mutually beneficial, 8
Eighteenth World Hakka Conference, 179–180
Elections, Indian, 37, 46
Elephantine Picture Palaces, 262–263
Elumelu, Tony, 109, 110
Emigration and Immigration Law (China), 174

ABOUT THE AUTHOR

TARUN KHANNA is the Jorge Paulo Lemann Professor at Harvard Business School. After receiving a bachelor's degree in engineering and the sciences at Princeton where he wrote a book on artificial intelligence, he detoured briefly through Wall Street. He then earned a PhD in Business Economics at Harvard. Since 1993 he has immersed himself with entrepreneurs, investors, and civil society in China, India, and other emerging markets worldwide. In 2007 he was elected a Young Global Leader (under 40) by the World Economic Forum

Dr. Khanna relishes teaching MBAs and executives at Harvard. Executive teaching, research, advisory work, and investing activities take him regularly to China and India as well as to Brazil, Chile, South Africa, Turkey, and the Middle East and Southeast Asian regions.

His recent enduring memories of China include being a guest in a beautiful village in Henan province, sharing a meal of soybean curd with local children, and of traveling roads far better than the Mass Pike to visit spanking new factories in the remote interior. In India, he currently mentors several start-ups in the automotive, financial services, and agribusiness sectors, primarily with his ex-students from Harvard. He also volunteers his time with NGOs, including Parliamentary Research Services in New Delhi, an organization dedicated to providing India's Members of Parliament nonpartisan research input to enhance democratic discourse.

He lives in Newton, Massachusetts, with his wife and their 7-year-old daughter and 5-year-old son. He is desperately trying to pass on to them his enthusiasm for languages and his amateur tendencies as a collector—of stamps, antiquarian maps, and iconic statues—as ways of learning about the peoples of the world.